The Big Book of Life's Instructions

The Big Book of Life's Instructions

Edited by Sheree Bykofsky
and Paul Fargis

Illustrated by Jessica Wolk-Stanley

A Stonesong Press Book

HarperCollins*Publishers*

THE BIG BOOK OF LIFE'S INSTRUCTIONS Copyright © 1995 by The Stonesong Press, Inc. All rights reserved. Printed in the United States of America. No part of this book may be used or reproduced in any manner whatsoever without written permission except in the case of brief quotations embodied in critical articles and reviews. For information, address HarperCollins Publishers, Inc., 10 East 53rd Street, New York, NY 10022.

HarperCollins books may be purchased for educational, business, or sales promotional use. For information, please write Special Markets Department, HarperCollins Publishers, Inc., 10 East 53rd Street, New York, NY 10022.

Text design and typography by Noble Desktop Publishers

FIRST EDITION

A Stonesong Press Book

All brand names used herein are registered trademarks of the corporations that own them.

Library of Congress Cataloging-in-Publication Data

The big book of life's instructions/edited by Sheree Bykofsky and
    Paul Fargis.—1st ed.
        p.   cm.
      "A Stonesong Press book."
      Includes bibliographical references and index.
      ISBN 0-06-273371-0 (pbk.)
      1. Life skills—Handbooks, manuals, etc. 2. Do-it-yourself work.
    3. Self-help techniques. I. Bykofsky, Sheree II. Fargis, Paul.
    1939–
    HQ2037.B54 1995
    646.7—dc20   95-8648

95   96   97   98   99   /   10   9   8   7   6   5   4   3   2   1

*To Steve and Dawn, who always
seem to know the right steps.*

Editorial Directors
Sheree Bykofsky
Paul Fargis

Managing Editor
Lee Ann Chearney

Production Editors
Kerry Acker
Teresa Mamone

Contributors
Roni Sarig
Diana Ajjan
Wilbur Cross
Natalie Danford
Janet Rosen
Laurie Viera

The editors gratefully acknowledge several others who gave their time, patience, and enthusiasm to bring this project to life: Patty Leasure and Rob Amell of HarperCollins; Anna Chapman, a superior copyeditor; and the wonderful proofreaders/editors of Felice Levy/AEIOU, Inc.

Contents

10. Just for the Fun of It

11. Legal

12. The Mind

13. Money, Math, Finance

20. Writing

1. Business

Prepare and Deliver a Speech

Preparation

Initial Considerations

Make sure your topic fits all the specifications required or desired by the audience or organization you are speaking to. Know what kind of audience you will address. Know whether or not it will be an audience friendly to your ideas; know if it will consist solely of one age, gender, ethnic group, or special interest group—these factors may influence your focus. Be aware of the time limit allowed for your speech, and be certain that you do not try to cover more ideas than can be digested within that given time.

Finally, consider what type of speech you want to give. It may be a persuasive speech, in which you attempt to convince the audience of the need and practicality of a plan, or it may be an informative speech, in which you discuss a fact-based topic from an objective viewpoint. Or, you may have been asked to make an introductory or a commemorative speech, in which you will discuss a person, place, or object central to the event.

Research

Carefully research your topic. Even if your speech deals with a subject you are personally acquainted with, get other perspectives or more in-depth information to add resonance and balance to the viewpoint you present. If you are speaking against a particular point of view, know the opposition's philosophy and research. Facts and statistics can add credibility to your position, but never quote them without acknowledging the source. Offer information that is accurate, challenges the audience's perspective on an issue, and presents new facts or ideas. You don't need to tell people what they already know.

Organization

Frame your ideas in an easy-to-follow fashion. Be as clear and orderly as possible. Most speeches consist of an introduction, a body, and a conclusion.

The introduction grabs the audience's attention, introduces the topic, previews the points you will be making, and establishes your authority as an expert speaker on the subject. A variety of techniques can be used to open your speech; try using an anecdote or a quote, or try posing a question or presenting an interesting fact. Use your first words to make the audience think.

The body of the speech is where points are discussed in detail. Here you develop the heart of your argument and present facts to back up your statements.

The conclusion reinforces the ideas presented in the body and prepares the audience for the end. You may want to return to the technique used in the introduction—use a quote, question, anecdote, or fact to bring your speech full circle. Be sure to leave your audience with something new to ponder afterward.

Writing

If your speech is short and relatively straightforward, it may be a good idea to limit your written guides to a simple outline or notes. If the speech is longer and more formal, it will probably be necessary to write out the entire text. If so, write clearly and vividly in a manner that displays your interest in the subject, and follow the rules of grammar. Don't underestimate the importance of using transitions, summaries, and previews to help the listener follow your argument.

Delivery

While some people may feel uncomfortable in front of a crowd, or may believe they possess fewer verbal communication skills than others, there is no reason why anyone with proper preparation and practice cannot deliver a good speech.

Establish Eye Contact

Don't fix on just one person, but try to meet the eyes of many people in the audience or focus on people in the back of the room.

Control Your Voice

For the audience to understand you, it's important not only to speak loudly and clearly, but also to be dynamic by varying your tone, pace, and accentuation. For the most part, though, keep a slow, even pace and tone for clarity.

Don't Rely Too Heavily on Notes

A long, formal speech will probably require you to write a script, while an informal speech requires only some notes or an outline of key words and arguments. Whatever the case, you never want to give the impression you are merely reading. Keep your head lifted and your eyes on the audience. If you have rehearsed your speech well, you will need to glance down at your notes only occasionally. Use your finger or a pen to mark your place so you don't get lost while looking up at the audience.

Use Nonverbal Communication

Body language is a valuable tool in getting across your meaning and emphasizing points. Hand gestures, body postures, and facial expressions can make what you are saying a lot clearer. Make sure, though, that any body language you use is not so excessive as to distract people from your speech.

Use Visual Aids

Extra materials such as a map, chart, or picture can go a long way in clarifying your point.

Make the Speech Easy to Read

If you must rely on a fully scripted speech, make sure it is as fluid as possible so you don't stumble over your words. Triple space the text, retype the last line of a page on the first line of the next page, memorize key passages such as your opening and closing, and don't staple the pages of your speech together. These techniques will help you create the illusion that you are not reading.

Be Flexible to Allow for Changes

Give yourself some latitude in your speech so you can easily improvise and adapt to changes in time allotment or audience, or bring in any new points.

Allow for Interaction with the Audience

A good question-and-answer session can stimulate the group's creativity and bring added depth to your remarks.

Relax

Above all, keep cool. Your worst enemy in delivering a speech is your own nerves. Remember, your audience is on your side. They want you to succeed, not fail. View the audience as an encouraging, not a critical, body. While a little nervousness is natural, practice and a solid knowledge of your subject will keep "butterflies" at a minimum.

Moderate a Panel

Panel discussions allow a group of experts with varying perspectives to exchange and debate ideas; they commonly occur at seminars and professional conventions. If you are highly knowledgeable or otherwise involved in a particular field, you may someday be called upon to participate in such a gathering. As moderator, you will lead the session and direct audience interaction.

1. Introduction. Thank all participants for attending and explain the purpose of the panel. Introduce the panel members, including yourself, and briefly describe the background and expertise of each panelist. Outline the rules of etiquette for the panel discussion and the protocol for asking and answering questions. Be specific about any time constraints, limits, or requirements.

2. Pose an opening question or point. Set the panel in motion. Ask one or all of the panelists to respond.

3. Keep the discussion focused. Have in mind an outline of topics or viewpoints to cover, and steer the discussion to address them.

4. Keep the discussion calm and courteous. Tensions can sometimes flare on controversial issues. Act as mediator in arguments that grow out of hand. Allow equal time to opposing views, and move on to a new topic if no beneficial progress is made, and table questions or issues of debate for focus groups or other bodies for further discussion later.

5. Keep the discussion moving and evolving. Set a pace for the discussion to flow smoothly through the subject during the time allowed for the panel's meeting.

6. Make sure only one person talks at a time. Make it clear that you will recognize participants and allow them to speak; otherwise, everyone will try to speak at once and no one will be heard. As moderator, you are expected to maintain order.

7. Keep everyone involved. One or two members of the panel will be likely to dominate the discussion. If you notice this happening, call on the other panelists to solicit their opinions.

8. Regulate audience questions. Open a portion of the panel discussion to questions from the audience by calling on audience members one at a time. If possible, leave time for as many people to ask questions as want to.

9. Allow panelists to make final statements. When you are nearly out of time, wrap up the discussion by asking each panelist to make one final comment. Do not restrict content or allow other panelists to break in. For a fair and even forum, however, do enforce strict time limitations for all panelists.

10. Make a closing statement. Sum up the consensus of the panel and add any impressions or additional comments you have about the discussion. If relevant, propose further action for future discussions on the topic—perhaps preparing an outline of questions, actions, or concerns for further attention and/or research. Thank the panelists and the audience for their participation before calling the panel to a close.

See "12 Ways to Improve Listening Skills."

Organize and Maintain Files

If you are drowning in a sea of paper and searching for that crucial misplaced document, here are a few suggestions to help transform chaos into order by creating a personal or office filing system.

1. Assess your desk and office space, as well as the volume of paper you need to keep, before purchasing filing supplies. There are many choices to suit your

The San Diego
Rescue
Mission

Women & Children's Center
Men's Life Ministries

"For I was hungry
and you gave me
food, I was thirsty
and you gave me drink,
I was a stranger and
you welcomed me...
Whatever you did for
he of the least of
you did it

n 25:35-40

2138

individual needs, tastes, and spatial considerations: traditional in-drawer filing cabinets, rolling carts with hanging files, or desktop hanging files. Some people prefer to keep pending or "hot" files in desktop hanging files at their fingertips, with everything else inside a central filing cabinet. Would legal or letter size folders better accommodate your papers? Perhaps you constantly need to refer to an important document or type of document, such as contracts or invoices; choose brightly colored file folders to code documents and help you locate them instantly. File folders with staggered tabs help you visually locate files. File folder tab labels may also be color coded. Documents pertaining to a certain year can be coded with labels attached to the side or top of the folder. Labeled hanging folders stay in place inside the cabinet and keep your central filing system orderly, while inner file folders can be easily retrieved and replaced.

2. Start sorting through the mountain of papers to be organized, and divide them into stacks. Call the first stack "To Do." (You may also wish to refer to this pile as "Pending" or "Follow-up.") These are matters that need attention, either immediately or in the near future. They may be bills to pay, clients to call, or personal correspondence to write. These will be divided into categories and may be put in desktop files, desk drawer files, or a rolling desk-side file cart for maximum accessibility. Leave the filing in one big pile for now.

3. Call the second stack "Current." These will be papers you need only refer to from time to time, and can be placed in a central filing cabinet.

4. Call the third stack "Historical" or "Archives." These are papers that you rarely if ever need to see: papers you shouldn't or can't bear to discard. Birth certificates and tax returns might be appropriate for this category. You may choose to place historical files in properly labeled folders inside a file storage box in a closet, leaving room in your filing cabinet for "Current" files.

5. Call the fourth stack "Trash," and treat it accordingly. Will you ever need to see this paper again? Will there be unpleasant consequences if you can't find it? If the answer is no, trash it.

6. Organize the "To Do" stack into separate file folders by task. Here are some sample "To Do" files: Bills to Pay on the 1st, Bills to Pay on the 15th, Letters to Write, Clients to Call, To File, To Read. If you are working on several projects at once, you may also wish to keep separate project files on your desktop or in your desk drawer "hot" file section. If your "To Do" pile is too big (or your desk is too small), an alternative is to make a list of what needs to be done first, and create a corresponding file folder name for each task. Keep the list on your desk and keep the actual files inside a file cabinet, to be pulled as needed.

7. Organize the "Current" stack. Separate the stack into piles by major category, depending on your type of work or projects. These will be further organized into subcategories. Try not to create individual files for only one or two pieces of paper. It may be more efficient to combine files. Filing is supposed

to simplify your life, not complicate it further. Examples of some major file categories are Household, Paid Bills, Financial, Clients, Organizations, Projects, Freelance Work, Personal, Reference, Forms. Files should be labeled with the major category, followed by the appropriate subcategory, and filed in alphabetical order. Examples of Financial file labels are Financial/Bank Statements, Financial/Business Entertainment Receipts, Financial/Money Market Account. Examples of Clients file labels are Clients/Anderson, Lisa; Clients/John Lewis Company. Note that individuals' names are filed with the last name first, and company names are filed exactly as the company name reads, excluding any articles.

Note: Numbers-oriented folks may prefer a numerical filing system. To do this, assign each file a number, keep an index of what each number represents, and store files in numerical order.

8. Label the outside of file cabinet drawers with a general idea of what's inside. Create a file called "Indexes." Make an index of all current files and store in a folder labeled "Index/Current Files" to make files easier to find and to avoid file duplication.

9. Organize the "Historical" stack. Using the same organizational principles described in step 7, create as many files as you need. You may choose to store them in a separate section or drawer of the filing cabinet or place them in a file storage box. Label the outside of the box with a number or with a title, and make an index of all files archived inside. Keep a copy of the index in your current files in a folder labeled "Index/Historical Files" as well as a copy inside the box itself.

10. Consider any lengthy documents or archival material that it would be better to store and back up on your computer's hard drive or on disk, rather than keep as hard copy. Do, however, keep hard copies of all essential documents as precaution against lost or damaged electronic storage systems.

11. Purge your files occasionally. It may be time to change some of your current files to historical status, or—heaven forbid—to throw them away!

Strategies for Efficiency

No matter what business or profession you are in, whether you work at home or in a large office complex, there are devices and stratagems you can use to make your job easier—especially to manage repetitive chores that are time-consuming and bothersome. Keep a daily list of routine matters you would like to abbreviate or eliminate entirely. Consider each function separately and jot down ways you can:

✓ Lessen the requirements
✓ Condense the time required for completion
✓ Assign the task to someone else
✓ Abolish the operation entirely

Make a priority list of all the duties, assignments, functions, and operations your job comprises, and your day-to-day obligations in particular. You may be surprised to discover that the time and effort devoted to each task is not compatible with the assigned priority. Remedy this situation by putting each task in its proper place.

Review your preferences as frankly as you can to determine how seriously your personal likes and dislikes may influence the time and effort you apply to each of your responsibilities. Make an honest adjustment.

Start each day with a period of reflection, during which, in a relaxed way, you can review mentally what you will have to accomplish during the work day and how you can go about your job. The time you select can be at home, en route to work, or at the office, but make sure it is uninterrupted.

When you schedule your day and decide what you intend to accomplish, assign realistic time blocks for anticipated interruptions, such as routine staff meetings, expected telephone calls, or co-workers who need information or are asking questions. Try to set routine times when you will be accessible to other staff members. Keep personal chat to a minimum—others will follow your lead.

Examine your workspace for its maximum efficiency potential. Do you have easy access to all equipment you need, such as a computer, printer, or fax? Is your workspace too close to the photocopier or coffee bar? Work to make your space as functional and private as possible.

Keep an accurate log of the time you devote to all projects and assignments you are involved in.

Have your telephone calls screened, if possible. If not, install a message machine so you have the option to screen callers before answering—particularly during hours when you do not want to be disturbed.

Shortly before leaving work each day, stop whatever you are doing at a point that is easy to pick up and continue the next morning. Try not to leave while facing an impasse. Don't begin complicated projects an hour before the work day ends.

Establish the next day's priorities at the end of each day. This should not be something to wrestle with when you first arrive at work.

Delegate details to subordinates. If you have no such assistants, sort details out on paper rather than in your head. Allow enough time to determine when and how to tackle each task in turn. Don't try to do everything at once. Set realistic time limits for each job on your list. Don't be afraid to discard minor projects that are not worth the effort.

Know the difference between stubbornness and determination when faced with on-the-job challenges.

Keep a small file of appropriate reading matter in handy places (your briefcase, car, or kitchen), so you can make good use of your time while standing in line, waiting in a doctor's office, caught in a traffic gridlock, or holding the line for a delayed phone call.

Find out about electronic technology—from beepers and cellular phones to notebook computers, modems, and on-line services—that might dramatically increase your personal and office efficiency. Make a presentation to management to recommend attaining such services.

Speed Write

Speed writing, commonly known as *shorthand* in business, is a brief, rapid method of writing that goes back many centuries. The Gregg and Pitman systems, conventional today, use curved lines that resemble script to replace syllables, words, and even groups of words. Stenographs, or keyboard machines, function similarly and are used by trained secretaries, especially courtroom stenographers.

You can take a course in shorthand at almost any secretarial school, but it will not be useful unless you keep in practice and use it frequently. Most people, however, devise their own personal shorthand for those infrequent, but often vital, occasions when it becomes necessary. Use speed writing dictionaries to make up your own list of words and phrases you use often and would like to abbreviate when writing texts, making lists, or taking notes during a lecture. Shorthand is written most effectively by *sound*. Thus, *aim* is written "am" (long sound of "a"), *cat* is written "kat," and *knee* is written "ne."

No matter how you go about it, the following suggestions will be helpful:

1. Practice frequently, using a second hand or stopwatch to improve your speed on selected passages of a measured length. Repetition is the key to effective speed writing.

2. Use a ball-point pen that is well balanced. The ink should flow easily with as little pressure or movement as possible.

3. Keep the nib close to the paper, to avoid lifting or jerking the pen, thus improving speed and efficiency. Think of the motion as *flowing*, rather than writing.

4. Use a spiral-bound steno notebook, which is ruled to keep you on line, is specially designed for flipping from one page to the next, and has paper that takes ink cleanly.

5. Arrange your seating and desk table position so you can write quickly without tiring your fingers, wrists, or arms.

6. Convert your shorthand into longhand or typescript as soon as possible, while the sentences are fresh in memory—especially while you are a beginner.

7. If you take a standard course and learn the system of your choice, make it a habit to read well-written samples of shorthand frequently as well as to practice your own.

8. Purchase a notebook computer and "speed type." The ease of the keyboard should dramatically increase your speed if you are already an efficient typist.

9. Tape record interviews or lectures while practicing until you are confident about your speed writing capability.
10. Concentrate. Focus on key words or groups of words. If appropriate, ask the speaker to repeat or speak more slowly.

Negotiate

Whether you are buying a car, going after a new business account, approaching the landlord about an increase in rent, or choosing a vacation spot with your spouse, negotiating skills will affect the quality of the agreements you make every day. Negotiators are generally hard bargainers, who won't give an inch and look at the negotiating process as a battle to be fought and won, or friendly facilitators, who make concessions too readily to avoid distasteful confrontations. Neither tactic produces the best agreements for both parties in most cases. Use these techniques to become more open-minded about reaching agreements while strengthening and enhancing your personal and professional relationships.

✓ Respect the other party's position whether you agree with it or not. Listen to what others have to say instead of simply waiting for them to stop talking so you can make a point you have already formulated in your mind. Repeat your opponent's point in different words to show that you understand and have processed it.
✓ Look for "win/win" resolutions. Once both parties fully understand each other's goals, a mutually satisfying resolution can be formed as long as the participants understand what each is truly looking for and are flexible enough to work together. Holding too strictly to one set of goals at the expense of your negotiating partner does not necessarily create a winning situation for either.
✓ Get to the real problem. Disentangle the real areas of conflict from any peripheral issues. Set an agenda for resolving issues in a mutually agreed order of priority.
✓ What you see, and hear, is what you get. Pay attention to body language and emotions—both your own and your negotiating partner's. Try to be as objective as possible.
✓ Make allies out of adversaries. One positive outcome of this approach is an enhanced understanding where none existed previously.

Set Up a Ledger

Every small business owner or successful freelancer comes to the moment of truth when it is time to establish formal books of accounting. Record-keeping seems a daunting and meticulous task. But with the proper advance planning, basic accounting procedures are quite simple to set up and follow through. With the expert guidance of a good accountant, determine the needs of your business and decide on the best organization for your financial records. Research the many good computer accounting programs now available for a variety of business types and transactions as well as for at-home use.

Observe these record-keeping basics:

✓ Set up a chart of accounts. Assign an account number to each basic income or expense type and category of your business. For example, the expense category "Overhead" would have account numbers for "phone," "photocopying," and "office supplies"; the income category "Direct Mail" could include account numbers for "individual," "corporate," and "library." Accounts should be discrete units of income and expense that you want to track easily.

✓ Maintain a payroll account. Set up regular payroll tallies and corresponding tax or insurance payments. Keep a calendar file for an instant reminder of due dates, and hold onto all postmarks and receipts to prove the date and amount of payments in case you need to dispute any late penalties or fees.

✓ Set up a database of addresses, social security numbers, and federal ID numbers of freelancers or clients who should receive 1099 forms.

✓ Keep estimated and actual cost worksheets for individual projects to track how closely your real income and expenses meet your predictions.

✓ Set up "Accounts Receivable" and "Accounts Payable" records to accurately track all monies expected to come in or out of your business during any fiscal quarter or year.

✓ Consider setting up an inventory, royalty, invoicing, or purchase order system if any of these functions are relevant to your business. Excellent computer programs now exist that are tailored to specific industries like retailing and shipping.

✓ Once you have a year's worth of organized financial data, analyze it for ways to spend more efficiently or to discover areas where your business can grow. Plan income and expense forecasts for the immediate fiscal year, and also formulate a five-year plan.

✓ Consult your accountant about preparing a formal business plan and investigating grant or loan opportunities available to owners of small businesses. Consider how to attract investments if the business begins to take off.

✓ Keep a copy of all financial records off-site in a safe deposit box in the event of fire or theft at your place of business. Make sure up-to-date records are stored; insurance companies pay benefits based only on the copy of the accounting records they receive.

✓ Keep good files. File paid invoices according to vendor and label folders with both vendor name and fiscal year.

Interview for a Job

Aside from your qualifications, the interview is the most important factor in getting a job. How well you present yourself will inevitably make an impression on an interviewer that will make all the difference when the firm makes a hiring decision. Here are some hints on how to succeed in this anxiety-inducing situation:

1. Know about the company, the industry, and if possible, the person who is interviewing you (at the very least, know the interviewer's name and use it). Do research.

2. Be on time and alert.

3. Dress neatly and professionally. Depending on the job, most offices appreciate conservative dress. Don't let extreme weather conditions tempt you to dress down.

4. Bring any materials you may need, such as an extra resume, references, or samples of your work, even if they are not required. Carry a briefcase or some kind of business carrying case if it is appropriate.

5. Give a firm handshake, and sit only when asked. If you can choose which chair to take, sit in the one directly across from the interviewer or otherwise in the closest chair to her or him.

6. Be friendly, courteous, and respectful. Don't speak to the interviewer as if you can anticipate his or her needs, concerns, and requirements for the position.

7. Ask questions about the duties of the job and display your interest and character. Don't ask only about vacation and benefits. The interview should not be one-sided. Interviewers are impressed with intelligent questions that show thoughtfulness, curiosity, and research.

8. Write a thank-you letter as soon as you get home. This is not only a courtesy but will keep you in the interviewer's mind.

9. Make follow-up calls only if you have not received a response by the date indicated. Be aggressive but not badgering.

Open a Franchise

What do McDonald's, Carvel, Mail Boxes Etc., and Gymboree have in common? They're all franchises. A franchise describes a business relationship by which you reach an agreement with a large company to run a "branch" store. Among budding entrepreneurs, franchising is becoming an increasingly popular alternative to owning a business outright. You pay the company for the right to sell its products and use its name; in return, you gain all the advantages of national advertising and product recognition. Opening a franchise is similar in many ways to opening your own independent business. The differences arise in the contract you must sign with the company and in specific issues pertaining to your relationship with it. While companies may handle franchises differently, here is a general guide to procedures that should apply in most situations.

1. Come up with a project plan. It is important to be clear on what your objectives are before you start. List them. Make sure you have the right personality, or partners, to launch your franchise successfully.

2. Evaluate different industries to decide what type of franchise suits you best. Will it be a restaurant, a retail store, a service? Each choice has specific benefits and considerations. To help you decide, attend franchise trade shows, consult books and periodicals in the library, call your local Small Business Association for pamphlets, and speak to franchise business operators in several different types of industries. Keep in mind your own needs and limitations as well as the commercial viability of the business.

3. Explore several specific franchises in your area of interest. Pay close attention to how each business will fit your requirements. What is the profit margin? What are the patrons generally like? Does this company have other franchises in the same area? What is the product like? What is the cost of buying a franchise? What sort of support will you get from the company? You may want to conduct your own market surveys to determine the answers to these questions (talk to people, sample the product) as well as consult available information. It is also advisable to meet with the company's administration; it is important that you feel comfortable with their business practices and feel able to work closely with them.

4. Narrow down your choices until you are able to decide on the business that best fits your project plan.

5. Begin contract work. You have decided which franchise you'd like to open, and you meet all the requirements set up by the corporation (mainly, that you can afford to buy franchise rights). The next step is to send the corporation a deposit and your letter of intent to buy the franchise. The franchise contract you receive from the corporation outlines your responsibilities and liabilities as well as its own and gives many of the specifics about store operation. You will want to consult with a lawyer to help you negotiate the best terms available.

6. Organize yourself. You must create a corporation of your own to start a business, and register yourself with the state. Decide what type of corporation you will be. Create a board of directors. If you are in a partnership, you must work out a partnership agreement.

7. Address the specifics of opening your store.

   Start a location search. Many franchise agreements will stipulate a limited time to find a location, so get started as soon as possible; finding a good location will be one of the most important factors in determining your future success. When looking for a location, consider the space and how it will lend itself to your business, local traffic, other similar businesses in the area, image, condition of the building, amount of work you'll have to do to prepare the space, and, of course, cost.

Sign a lease. Work with the landlord to get the best possible terms. Negotiate rent, deposit, utilities, liability, term of lease, and other lease issues (see "Read a Lease" for more information). Here again, you may want to use a lawyer. Don't sign the lease until you have signed your franchise contract—if something untoward should happen, you don't want to be stuck with a space and no business.

Locate equipment, product distributors, and contractors. Some examples are an oven and tables if you are opening a restaurant, product distributors to supply things like cups and napkins, and contractors to build and design the store. Many times the corporation will supply you with, or suggest, places to go for these things.

8. Open as soon as possible after all your contracts have been signed. To do so, you'll need to work on the store, making any necessary alterations, and bringing in equipment and supplies. You'll also want to do things like get a phone, hook up utilities, arrange for garbage pickup, and get insurance.

9. Hire a staff and purchase advertising space. Hire a payroll company. Usually, the corporation will offer training in daily operation of the store.

10. Obtain all proper permits. If the business is food-related you will need a health permit, which requires training from the Health Department.

11. Open the store. All practical and legal concerns have been met. Remember, a lease and a contract together mean that time is money. Try to open within a month or two of completing the contract. Good luck!

Request a Raise

You need to ask for a raise. How do you go about requesting one with the greatest anticipation of success? At the outset, you must make a choice: whether to request it in writing, use a person-to-person approach with your boss or a personnel manager, or use a combination of one-on-one and a written memo.

Once you have decided on the most likely form of communication, ask yourself these questions:

✓ Do I deserve a raise because I have not had one in a long time, while several of my co-workers have been given pay increases?

✓ Is a raise in order because I have steadily improved my capabilities in the company or the department?

✓ Have I recently made a distinct achievement that has been recognized and should be rewarded?

Chances are that more than one of the above will apply. Place your emphasis on the most *positive* argument(s), such as the second or the third, rather than the first. Whether you decide to submit your request in writing or voice it in person, you should first outline for yourself all the reasons why you feel you *should* deserve a raise. Detail what you can offer to the company that warrants an increased investment in your work. At the same time, be realistic and list any drawbacks to the raise. Some of these might be too little time on the job, poor decision making in the past (be sure to include a proposed remedy and positive future action), knowing that someone with your qualifications, or better, has already been turned down for a raise, or realizing that the company has had some recent financial reverses.

Most companies have policy guides for managers that help them determine whether an employee under their supervision is eligible for a raise, a promotion, or both. Ask someone you know in the personnel department to show you such a guide, if it exists, or to describe any salary guidelines that have been discussed or summarized. Company policies should not be confidential, and employees have the right to know about them.

Your formal request for a raise should be brief and to the point. Include these arguments as grounds for a raise, in this general sequence:

1. The length of time you have been with the company and in your present position.

2. Highlights of your work in the recent past, and contributions you have made to the company in general and the department in particular.

3. Any commendations or awards you have received that are directly related to your performance and skills.

4. Courses or training programs you have participated in, company-sponsored or otherwise.

5. The specific amount you feel would be acceptable and realistic as a raise.

6. Reasons why a raise is essential at this time, such as the purchase of a house, marriage, or the birth of a child. Don't concoct reasons that do not exist or that are marginal. And don't make them the main or only reason for the raise.

The timing of your request is important. Present it to your boss (or other appropriate supervisor) at the time when you know he or she is likely to be in an expansive mood—perhaps because of some personal good fortune or business success—and not under pressure and stress, overloaded with work, or harassed with budget problems.

If a raise is not deemed possible at this time, ask your supervisor for a time frame and a list of requirements whose satisfaction would make you eligible for a salary increase. Diligently fulfill them.

Leave an Answering Machine Message

Although most of us would prefer to hear a live human voice when we make a telephone call, the age of the electronic answering device is here to stay. If you feel uncomfortable or annoyed about the prospect of talking to a machine, here are a few helpful suggestions.

1. Resist the temptation to hang up. The people who installed the answering machine or voice mail system did so because they don't want to miss your call.

2. Listen carefully to the recorded message and follow the instructions. In most private homes, people use simple answering machines that require you to wait for a beep tone before you begin speaking. If the party has a more complicated voice mail system, you may be given several options. For example, you may be asked to press a particular number on your touch-tone phone to reach a certain department. If you do not have a touch-tone phone, most systems offer you the choice to stay on the line to speak to an operator. (You may decide to take this option even if you own a touch-tone phone.)

3. Speak clearly in a normal tone of voice and at your normal speed. There's no need to shout; most answering machines have a volume control in case your voice is recorded very softly. It doesn't hurt to play it safe, however. You may wish to repeat slowly any vital information, such as your telephone number.

4. Include the following information in your message: your name, the date and time of your call, your telephone number, and a brief idea of the reason for your call. Let the person you're calling know whether you need an urgent reply. If your schedule is erratic and you don't own an answering machine, let the other party know when it would be best to reach you. You can simply ask to be called back, or you may decide to leave more detailed information for the other party. For example, if you call a client about setting up an appointment and reach an answering machine or voice mail, you might find it useful to suggest a proposed date and time in your message. This will give your client the opportunity to check scheduling before returning your call. The return call you receive will thus be more likely to be efficient and productive for both parties.

5. Be brief whenever possible. Many individuals have settings on their private home answering machines that automatically hang up the telephone after a one-minute message. Others have a higher setting, such as four minutes. While this may seem rude, it is meant to deter those friends who like to leave long soliloquies from doing so. People with home answering machines often call in from the workplace to check their messages, and they may not have unlimited time for phone calls. Don't take it personally. If a machine has hung up on you and you have more to say, call back again and take up where you left off.

6. Write down any vital information you must convey in your message, in order of priority. This will prevent you from leaving out an important piece of information that may necessitate another call.

Delegate Effectively

Do you work too many hours but worry that delegating some of your burden will result in a disastrous situation and loss of control? If so, use these guidelines for delegating effectively, and you'll soon become reacquainted with the concept of free time.

1. Assess the task you wish to delegate. Make sure you fully understand what needs to be done as well as the desired results. If you can't explain the objective as well as the process to a staff member, you may be setting that person up for failure.

2. Assess the staff member you are considering for the task. Does this person have the level of skill or resourcefulness needed to get the job done? If not, can that person be taught or coached in time to complete the project? If no appropriate staff member exists, and your boss is unable or unwilling to hire additional employees, advocate short-term freelance alternatives. The pool of talented, highly skilled freelance workers has never been more diverse or accessible.

3. Let your staff know you value their work and that you'd be happy to allow them to take on more responsibility. If you're anxious about delegating, start small. Assign individual tasks associated with an overall project, giving training when needed. Clearly explain the parameters involved: your expectations, deadlines, budgetary considerations, or the appropriate people to approach for information, for example. Encourage the staff member to ask questions. Ask for progress reports. Offer praise for a job well done, and constructive suggestions for improvement when necessary. As your staff member's confidence grows, your confidence in that person, and thus your ability to delegate, will also grow.

4. As you successively delegate more complex tasks and overall projects, begin allowing staff members the opportunity to figure out how goals are to be accomplished. Remember to be clear about the nature of the problem you need solved and the desired objectives. Your staff will take pride in coming up with their own proposals as to what materials, staffpower, and money are needed to complete a project.

The more confident, trusted, and valued your staff feels, the more eager they will be to propose their own ideas for taking on greater responsibility. You, on the other hand, will realize you haven't lost control and need not perform every task yourself—you've reclaimed your life.

Find a Good Job

The right attitude and plan of action will make your job search quicker and easier.

1. Assess your skills. Before you begin to look for a specific job, determine your strengths as a worker. Make a list of your skills, particularly those currently in demand or uncommonly found.

2. Set a goal. Decide on a basic career path based on your abilities and desires. Be realistic but ambitious. Consider jobs outside of your current type of business. For instance, switch from work as a book publishing publicist to a hospital public relations position. Think about how versatile your base training makes you. Consider taking courses or doing volunteer work that would help facilitate a career change or shift in focus.

3. Create a resume. (See "Put Together an Effective Resume.")

4. Find available jobs. Do not limit yourself to advertised jobs. Most available jobs are not advertised, and those that are become flooded with applicants. Apply for positions at companies you would like to work for, whether you know about an available job or not. Contact a person of authority in the company, and arrange a meeting to talk about possible opportunities. Ask for names of contacts at other companies to build a network of potential employers who can alert you to suitable positions as they open up. Large companies hire constantly; your initiative will impress employers and keep you in their minds.

5. Figure out who needs you. Research to find companies that employ workers with skills like yours. Read trade publications, magazines, and newsletters for profiles and information on companies. Call to ask for corporate literature, catalogs, or other materials. Get a copy of the annual report to determine the company's stability, philosophy, and direction.

6. Send out resumes. Mailing a blind resume is rarely effective. Get a contact name and, if possible, a reference from someone you and the contact both know. Whenever possible, avoid personnel offices. Send your resume to the appropriate management-level person.

7. Send out supporting materials. To get the attention of a potential employer, you need to go beyond just sending a good resume. Send copies of relevant projects, constructions, reports, or other samples of your work that might attract the employer's attention. Consider volunteering your time on a project—working on spec—to show an employer your effective contribution to the company. To establish a working relationship, ask whether temporary or freelance part-time work is available.

8. Network. Employment agencies, government job services, computerized listings, and job fairs can sometimes help find you a job—but usually not. "Position wanted" ads also rarely work. The best approach to finding jobs you want is to do your research and continue to network through friends, relatives,

17

teachers, and business associates. Follow up every lead you get. If you are a freelance worker, consider printing a brochure and sending out a mailing.

9. Visit places where you want to work. Pay attention to the atmosphere and the mood of the employees. Decide whether you would want to work in that kind of physical and emotional environment.

10. Learn from everything you do. Even if you are rejected for positions or find yourself interviewing for jobs you don't think you want, don't get discouraged. The more you look, the more you will find out about yourself and your perfect job. It's out there!

See "Interview for a Job," "Buying and Selling with Classified Ads," and "Write a Thank-You Letter."

Small Business Tax Deductions

If you are self-employed or run a small business, the good news is that there are many legitimate deductions to help you cut income tax payments. The bad news is that the rules and conditions for allowable deductions can be confusing; a mistake can cost you in the long run. While you are entitled to take as many deductions as you can legally justify, keep in mind that the more questionable your deductions, the higher your chance is of being audited by the IRS. Keep good records and receipts. Start tip diaries, phone logs, daily calendars, travel and entertainment logs, mileage and toll notebooks (keep the latter in your car's glove compartment)—any kind of record that will show the expense, process, and purpose of the business performed. Include dates, names of clients, and nature of transactions.

Deductible Business Expenses

✓ Accountant/bookkeeper fees for business finances
✓ Advertising costs, including agency fees, printing costs, and giveaways
✓ Association dues
✓ Attorney fees for business affairs
✓ Bad debts, if you have already reported the debt as income or if you actually lent out money
✓ Bank fees
✓ Books used for business purposes
✓ Business cards
✓ Car expenses, including mileage, tolls, parking costs, and gas for business usage; see IRS publication 917, *Business Use of Your Car*
✓ Computer and printer costs, including software, on-line services, and instruction related directly to business; if use is split between business and personal use, you must keep a log of time used for business purposes and deduct only a percentage of the total cost
✓ Consultant fees
✓ Courses taken to improve business skills, including training tapes

✓ Employee salaries and wages

✓ Entertainment for business purposes, including dinners, parties, and events for clients (usually only 80 percent deductible); see IRS publication 463, *Travel, Entertainment, and Gift Expenses*

✓ Gifts to clients and associates; see IRS publication 463, *Travel, Entertainment, and Gift Expenses*

✓ Health insurance premiums

✓ Industry directories and listings

✓ Insurance fees for the business

✓ Interest on business loans and credit cards

✓ Licenses needed for operation of business

✓ Magazines and journals for business

✓ Office space costs, including rent, taxes, mortgage interest, and utilities; for home offices, the office space must be used exclusively for business purposes (including meetings with clients), and the deduction can only be a percentage of the total house costs based on the amount of space the office takes up in the house; see IRS publication 587, *Business Use of Your Home*

✓ Office supplies, including paper, stationery, folders, pens, pencils, tape, envelopes, and other materials

✓ Pension plan contributions

✓ Postage fees, including mail, supplies, and post office box fees

✓ Public relations costs and fees

✓ Travel expenses, including transportation (airplane tickets, car rental, train or bus costs), meals, lodging, and entertainment; see IRS publication 463, *Travel, Entertainment, and Gift Expenses*

Depreciation

Large purchases that will be used for more than one year may be written off as depreciable assets over many years or taken as a lump deduction in one year. They include cars, computers, office equipment, office furniture, and office renovations. See IRS publication 534, *Depreciation.*

Further Information

Useful free publications you can request from the IRS include publication 535, *Business Expenses*; 529, *Miscellaneous Deductions*; and 334, *Tax Guide for Small Businesses*. To order IRS publications, call 1-800-829-3676. For other questions concerning deductions and your income tax, call the IRS at 1-800-829-1040.

Simple Yoga Exercises to Do at Work

This easy yoga routine is designed for busy office workers who sit behind a desk all day. Make this a daily yoga practice, and you will find yourself more relaxed, more fit, and less fatigued.

Breathing Warm-Up

Sit upright in your chair with your arms to the side. Inhale slowly and deeply (to a comfortable level) through your nose while counting to six. Feel your abdomen and ribs extend. Hold your breath for a count of six, then exhale slowly and fully through your nose while contracting your abdomen and ribs. Pause ten seconds, then repeat. Continue this breathing pattern ten to fifteen times. Try to make the exhale gradually longer than the inhale.

Head and Neck Exercise

Rest your elbows on the desk in front of you, as close together as possible. Clasp your hands around the lower back part of your head and slowly push your head forward until your chin touches your chest. Hold for ten seconds, then turn your head slowly to the side until you can rest your chin in the palm of one hand while your other hand remains behind your head. Turn as far as you can, but take care not to push your neck too far or you may pull a muscle. Hold for ten seconds, then turn your head in the other direction and repeat. Finally, bring your head back to center. Slowly bend your neck sideways, first to the right and then to the left, so your ear approaches your shoulder. Hold on each side for ten seconds.

Back Stretch

Sit on the edge of your chair and extend your legs out straight. Slowly bend forward and grab onto your calves. Pull your body down farther by bending your elbows, and stay there for ten seconds. Relax your body completely and let your head and neck hang freely. Straighten and repeat twice.

Spinal Twist

Sit in your chair and cross your right leg over your left. Extend your left arm over your right knee and grab on to your left knee (your torso should be twisted to the right). If possible, hold the back of the chair with your right hand. Lift and twist your body as far to the right as possible and hold for ten seconds. Lift on the inhale and gently twist on the exhale. Release, switch legs, and repeat, again holding for ten seconds. Repeat the entire exercise twice.

Chest, Abs, and Hamstrings

Stand with legs together, feet at hip distance apart, arms extended straight ahead with palms up. Slowly pull your arms back and to the side to create a "T" position with your body. Bring your arms straight up above your head and join your palms. Bend back from the waist and hold for ten seconds. Be sure to tighten your abdominal muscles for support of your lower back. Lift out and back. Bend forward as far as you can, and hold for another ten seconds. Bend your knees if necessary. Repeat the sequence three times.

Relaxation Cool-Down

Recline fully in your chair or lie on your back on the floor. Rest your arms at your side and extend your legs. Relax your muscles completely. Concentrate on each part of your body, and feel your weight against the chair or floor. Remain this way for a minute or more, then rise slowly.

Lease Office Equipment

Because of the often huge investment required to purchase office equipment, and because of the all-too-common obsolescence of the latest equipment, many people choose to lease rather than buy. There are several things to consider when leasing office equipment.

Make a list of the equipment you think you'll need for your office. A basic list for most offices would include telephones, fax machine, copier, computer, and typewriter. An answering machine or voice mail is also essential, but answering machines are generally inexpensive enough to be purchased.

Next to each item on the list, estimate the volume of usage you expect each piece of equipment to have. For instance, if you have two employees and your business involves a good deal of client contact, a single-line phone is probably inadequate for your needs. How many photocopies do you estimate making each month, and how quickly do you need any copying job finished? How many faxes do you send or receive? How many computer workstations are practical? Is equipment like CD-ROM necessary? The answers to these questions will determine the type of equipment you need to rent to function at maximum efficiency and, consequently, how much money you need to spend. With a careful assessment of your needs in hand, you will be better prepared to shop around for office equipment.

Open the telephone book and call several equipment rental vendors, taking notes on the information you get from each one. If you have the time, visit electronics stores and rental houses, and ask for demonstrations of computers, faxes, and copiers. If not, request a visit to your office from the rental company's sales representative, who will be able to describe the available equipment to you and perhaps bring informational brochures.

Tell the rental houses you are shopping around for the best equipment at the lowest monthly price. Try to make package deals with vendors whereby you rent more than one piece of equipment from the same vendor. You are more likely to save money this way. Don't cut corners that will cost you valuable time, however. For example, renting a fax machine without a paper cutter may save you a few dollars but will result in the need to take a pair of scissors to long scrolls of paper—and perhaps a desire to run the machine over with your car.

Once you decide on the features of the equipment you wish to rent, make sure you ask the rental house for a cost breakdown, and make sure the lease you sign states everything in writing. Once you have struck a verbal deal, it's a good idea to then issue a purchase order to the vendor or write a letter on your company letterhead stating your understanding of the items you are renting and a breakdown of the costs. Read the lease carefully before you sign it, and feel free to question any clauses you haven't agreed to or don't understand. If the lease contains items that are clearly not part of your agreement with the vendor, cross them out and initial them. Have the sales representative counter-initial those clauses. Here are some important questions to ask while shopping around:

✓ Is there a minimum lease period? Try to avoid this, as potential dissatisfaction with a vendor or the equipment may result in your wish to terminate your contract.

✓ How is the month prorated if you return rented equipment before the monthly period is up?

✓ Is there tax on the rental? Some vendors charge tax; others do not.

✓ Don't ask whether there is a deposit, but if the vendor requires one, ask whether it can be recouped by applying it to the last month or months' rent. This is usually the case. Keep track of such deposits, and make sure you apply them so that you don't find yourself in the inconvenient position of waiting for the return of a deposit check.

✓ Is delivery and pickup of the equipment included in the price? Try to get this included as part of the deal.

✓ What sort of maintenance and repair agreement is included in your lease? How quickly is the repair response time?

✓ What supplies are included in the price? For example, are toner cartridges for your copier or printer included? if not, how long will a cartridge last, and how much will it cost you to replace it? How many copies are included in your monthly copier rental? Is it a reasonable amount for your needs? How much will additional copies cost per month?

✓ Are you insured against theft or damage to the equipment?

✓ If you are dissatisfied with the equipment, can you easily swap it for another model? How much more would the other model cost to rent?

✓ Are lease-to-buy arrangements possible? What kind of savings will you receive if you opt to buy the equipment at the end of the lease period?

Set Up a Home Office

Your home office should represent an extension of your personality, business philosophy, and work patterns. In this information age, more and more state-of-the-art businesses are run from the home. Here's a brief overview of what to consider when designing an office at home:

Choosing an Environment

Use a spare bedroom, den, basement, converted garage, or other empty space in the house. If possible, choose a room separated from the rest of the house. If you plan to have clients at the office, arrange for a separate entrance, if possible. Keep the office in a defined area—don't fragment pieces of the office throughout your house. Make sure you comply with local statutes that regulate home offices.

Layout

Determine the kind of work you will do. You may need a waiting area or conference table for meetings. You may need a drawing board or other equipment. Workstations may be required for staff or part-time workers. Plan a basic office layout before you bring in furniture and equipment. If structural alterations are necessary, you may need to bring in an architect or contractor. Choose the most efficient layout for form and function.

Lighting

Offices need stronger and clearer light than is required in a home. Install fluorescent or track lighting in the ceiling if necessary, rather than using conventional lamps.

Acoustics

Strive to keep the noise of equipment and workers confined to the office. Conversely, noise from the house should stay out of the office. Use sound-absorbing materials such as ceiling tile, carpet, drapes, wall hangings, and pads under noisy machines.

Temperature

While the office space may be heated and cooled by the house system, it may be feasible to provide separate temperature controls so you don't have to heat or cool the whole house during the day or the office at night. Keep comfort and energy efficiency in mind.

Furniture

Choose the chairs first, because you will use them most. Find comfortable, adjustable chairs. When choosing a desk, decide between a traditional desk or a larger counter unit attached to the wall. Be certain you have enough desk and table space to work on and to accommodate all necessary equipment.

Communications Equipment

Consider installing a separate telephone line for the office. Voice mail or an answering machine is a must, along with call waiting. Look into call forwarding if your business causes you to travel regularly. What extra features, such as conferencing or paging, will you require? Fax/modems are essential for quick business links and on-line networking capability.

Computer System

Get the computer that best meets your current needs. If you need more than one computer, investigate networking possibilities. Notebook computers are great if you travel or do a lot of research work out of the office. Choose office software compatible with what your clients use and what your business requires. Explore on-line services and ways to use the Internet to work more efficiently from home. Consider leasing equipment before buying. (Know what peripherals may be useful: scanners, CD-ROM.)

Other Office Equipment

You may also need a copy machine, dictation machine, television, VCR, postal meter, or other equipment. Check into each to find out the costs and models. Again, consider renting or leasing.

Wiring

Use extension power strips and surge protectors, or install more outlets in the office to accommodate electrical equipment.

Storage

Store supplies and equipment that you don't use regularly. If you don't have adequate room in the office, consider other available closets or basement space.

Supplies

Keep the office stocked with these and other materials as necessary: stationery, printed envelopes, printed mailing labels, business cards, blank paper, file folders, note pads, sticky notes, pens, pencils, pencil sharpeners, staplers, paper clips, rubber bands, scissors, tape, glue.

Research Materials

More and more research material is available on computer, cutting down the office space necessary to shelve books, magazines, and newspapers. Still, keep a reference area, such as a large bookcase, for materials you use often.

Decoration

Maintain a professional atmosphere. Licenses, diplomas, awards, artwork, and photographs are good wall decorations for offices.

Safety and Security

Keep a fire extinguisher and smoke detector in the office for fire protection. Keep valuable equipment concealed from windows. Get a safe deposit box off the premises for important documents and accounting materials. Research the best insurance policy to protect your home office from the costs of damage or injury.

Transportation

Look into leasing or buying a vehicle if your business requires deliveries or extensive travel.

See "Lease Office Equipment" and "Small Business Tax Deductions."

2. Car

Check the Front of a Car

Even for car owners who would prefer to stay as far away from their car's engine as possible, it makes both practical and financial sense to understand the car's basic needs and to be able to meet those needs before resorting to a mechanic or dealer. Here's how to make a simple, monthly check under the hood:

Note: Because all cars are designed differently, it is impossible to describe where a particular part will be found under the hood. Fortunately, these parts are usually labeled in case you don't recognize them.

1. Open the hood. Most cars have a latch or release inside the car, often underneath the steering wheel or on the floor by the driver's seat. Pull on the release to unlock the hood. In some cars the release is located in the front of the car, directly below the hood. Many cars have both inside and outside releases. After you unlatch the hood, lift it up as far as it will go. Some hoods stay raised automatically; others require you to insert a rod to prop the hood up. Check for a rod underneath the hood, and insert the rod so the hood is held securely in place. Be careful not to let the hood fall on you. *Note:* When checking under the hood do not smoke, light a match, or create sparks—you risk setting off an explosion.

2. Check the oil. Oil is measured with the use of a dipstick: a long, thin metal strip held in a long container like a sword in a sheath (Figure 1). Draw the dipstick out, and with a rag wipe off the oil currently on the stick. Replace the dipstick in the sheath as far as it will go, and pull it out again. Now, check how far oil covers the end of the dipstick. This will indicate how much oil is needed, probably one or two more quarts. Never let your car go so long that it needs more than

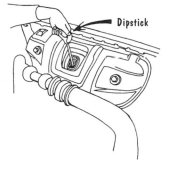

Figure 1. Checking engine oil

a quart or two of oil, or you'll risk damaging the car. If the car needs less than one quart, don't add oil. If your car needs a quart or more, unscrew the cap indicated for oil on top of the engine, and pour the required amount in. It is wise to use oil recommended by the car manufacturer; see your car manual for that information. (See "Change the Oil in a Car.")

3. Check the radiator coolant. To check for coolant/antifreeze, make sure the engine is off and cooled down. New cars have a translucent container so you can see how much coolant is present. For older cars, you may have to unscrew the radiator cap to check the fluid level. Look to see whether the liquid level is between the minimum and maximum levels indicated on the container. If the level is near or below the minimum, add a solution of half antifreeze and half water into the spout on the container (Figure 2).

4. Check the automatic transmission fluid. Like oil, transmission fluid is measured with a dipstick. The car must be running (with the parking brake on) and warm (therefore, don't check transmission fluid and radiator coolant at the same time). Pull the dipstick out, wipe it off with a rag, then replace it. Pull it out again; check to see that the fluid is pink and smooth. If the fluid has bubbles, take the car in to be examined by a technician. Then, check the level of fluid. If the dipstick indicates the level is low, add the type of fluid the car manual indicates into the same hole the dipstick goes into (Figure 3). Manual transmission must be checked by a mechanic.

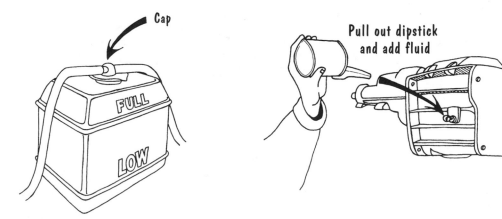

Figure 2. Translucent coolant container   Figure 3. Checking and filling automatic transmission fluid

5. Check the brake fluid. You'll find brake fluid in a small reservoir with a cap or lid. Remove the cap to check the fluid. The driver's manual should tell you how to read the fluid level. If fluid is low, add more. Make sure, though, that you add the correct type of brake fluid; the type will be indicated on the cap or in the car manual.

6. Check the power steering fluid if your car has power steering. Find the fluid reservoir and remove the cap. The cap may work like a dipstick to tell you whether fluid needs to be added. If it is low, add fluid up to the proper level and reseal the lid (Figure 4).

7. Check the windshield washer fluid. Like the radiator coolant, windshield fluid is usually in a translucent container. There's no particular level this fluid should reach; having it is not crucial to operating the car. Fill the container when low.

8. Check the battery. Most newer batteries are sealed and cannot be checked, so it's likely you won't have to worry about this step. If you have an older battery, unscrew the cell caps on top (usually four or six in all) and check to see whether there is water in the cells. If water is not covering the metal plate inside each cell, add water as needed. *Note:* the water must be distilled water, not ordinary tap water. A normal battery will last four or five years before it dies, at which point it must be replaced (Figure 5).

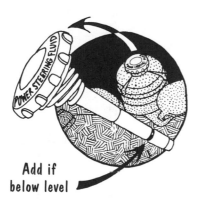

Add if
below level

Figure 4. Power steering fluid dipstick

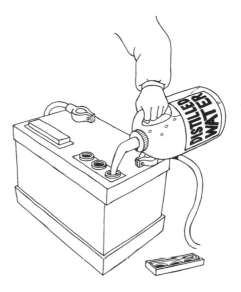

Figure 5. Adding water to battery cells

Change the Oil in a Car

Changing the oil in a car is a messy and potentially dangerous business. It's probably worth it to pay the $15 or $20 it will cost to have it done for you by a qualified car mechanic. If you insist on doing it yourself, don't wear anything you aren't prepared to ruin, and have heavy-duty soap ready to wash up afterward. Unlike *checking* your oil, which should be done every month or so, *changing* oil is necessary fairly infrequently, at the most every few months or 3,000 miles. The best time to change oil is after a long drive, when the car is warm and oil will not stick in the engine. For those who don't mind getting down and dirty, here's what to do:

1. Elevate the front of the car. Because you will need to get underneath the car, you should use ramps for elevation; don't risk using a jack, which can slip out of place. Ramps are fairly inexpensive and can be found at any car supply store. Be sure the car is on level ground. Elevate the front of the car 1 or 2 feet, enough so you can fit lying down underneath. Place cinder blocks behind the back wheels, and set the parking brake securely to make sure the car doesn't slip back (Figure 1).

Figure 1. Elevate the car's front.

2. Locate the oil pan. Slide on your back below the front of the car, bringing with you the necessary equipment: a standard wrench, a special oil filter wrench (also available at car supply stores), a new oil filter, and a bucket that will hold at least 5 quarts of fluid. Find the oil pan; it will look like a flat plate with a nut screwed on the bottom (the actual location of the pan depends on the car) (Figure 2).

Figure 2. Locate oil pan and drain oil.

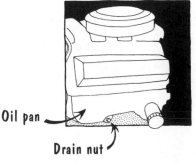

3. Drain the oil. When you have located the oil pan, use the standard wrench to unscrew the nut. Before removing the nut, position the bucket directly below it; that's where the oil will drain from. Remove the nut and allow the oil to drain completely. Be careful not to come in contact with the oil; it will burn you if it is hot. *Note*: your used oil is recyclable and may be taken to a gas station or car repair shop.

4. Remove the oil filter. The oil filter is a round cylinder that should have a brand name on it (like the oil pan, its location depends on the car). With your oil filter wrench, unscrew the filter. Keep the bucket underneath to catch any oil that might fall. Once you have removed the filter, you may throw it away (Figure 3).

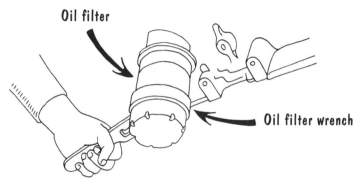

Figure 3. Remove the oil filter.

5. Replace the nut on the oil pan. Be sure to screw it on as tightly as possible so that oil will not leak from it.

6. Attach a new oil filter. The clean oil filter, available at car supply stores, has a rubber gasket around its top. With your finger, smear a little oil around the gasket to make the filter fit better and to prevent leaks. Using your hand, tightly screw the new filter into the space where you removed the old one.

7. Add new oil. Slide out from under the car and open the hood. Unscrew the cap marked for oil on top of the engine and pour the required amount of oil (about 5 quarts) into the tank. Screw the cap back on when you have finished (Figure 4).

Figure 4. Add new oil.

8. Check for leaks. Turn on the car and, with the car running, get out and look underneath to see whether any oil is leaking. If it does leak, you may need to further tighten the oil pan nut or oil filter; if problems continue, consult a technician.

9. Check the oil level. If oil is not leaking, shut off the engine and check the oil level (see "Check the Front of a Car," Step 2). If more oil is needed, add the required amount. Otherwise, close the hood and ease the car off the ramps.

Buy a New Car

You've decided to buy a new car. With today's diverse selection of high-quality models, be sure to shop around and carefully research the best type of vehicle for your needs. From a family sedan to a sporty convertible or rugged sports-utility vehicle, always consider gas mileage; safety features, such as air bags and antilock brakes (ABS); and the cost of insurance premiums and garage fees.

Before Shopping

Budget. Before you even begin to look, determine what monthly payment you can afford and how much of a down payment is possible. Research cars, trucks, or vans for the best deal in your financial comfort zone.

Research. Learn about the cars you are interested in before you visit a showroom. You can get excellent information on models, features, options, prices, and quality ratings from many books and magazines commonly available in bookstores and libraries. Narrow the field to two or three models, and be flexible. Holding out for a particular color or feature may cost you a good deal. Consider option packages carefully—do you really need every feature a package offers? What is the trade-in or resale value of each model, and what are typical repair and maintenance costs per year?

Trade-ins. You may be able to trade in your old car and deduct its value from the price of the new car. Don't discuss a trade-in with the salesperson until you've negotiated a price for your new car; dealers inflate prices if they know you are trading in. Know the value of the car you are trading in (check used car guides) before making a deal. You are likely to get more money selling your old car on your own.

Shopping

Visit showrooms. Go to several dealers and get written quotes that will hold for a week's time. *Never* put a deposit down to get a quote. Test drive every model you are interested in. Experiment with different transmissions, option packages, and other features. Find out how great the demand is for the models you want, and how many are in stock. Popular models are not discounted as readily.

If possible, buy at the end of the model year: late summer or early fall, when dealers are looking to make room for new models. You will find less selection but incredible deals. Discontinued cars, as with late-model cars, are often discounted significantly.

Look for rebate and incentives—sales tools issued by the car's manufacturer. Rebates usually promise money back once you buy the car. Try to get the rebate issued up front as the down payment. Incentives encourage dealers to sell a certain model or a certain number of cars.

Car Pricing and Stickering

By law, every new car must list certain information on a window sticker removable only by the buyer. Be skeptical of any other sticker appearing on the car; dealer stickers include dealer-added accessories and other service charges that are generally unnecessary.

Monroney sticker. This is the official name for the mandatory window sticker (the federal law for window stickers does not include light trucks). It must provide the following information: the base price, i.e., the price of the car before any options are installed; all options installed by the manufacturer, with their suggested prices; the destination charge, for shipping the car from the factory to the dealer (this should be the only shipping charge added separately); and the car's fuel economy as determined by the Environmental Protection Agency.

Dealer sticker. This second sticker includes the total dealer's price from the Monroney sticker, additional dealer-installed options and their prices, dealer preparation costs, additional dealer mark-up (ADM), and additional dealer profit (ADP). Challenge each cost. Second-sticker fees are often superfluous and unnecessary.

Paying for the Car

Negotiating. Let dealers know that you are comparison shopping for the best deal and that you will try another dealer or buy a different car to get what you want. The rule of thumb is to try to pay no more than 2 percent above the invoice price of the car; which is the price the dealer pays the manufacturer for the car. Your research should give you a good idea of what this price should be. Consider models that are sold with a "one-price" system if you truly hate bargaining. Compare dealerships, however, to make sure the posted prices are not inflated by an individual dealer.

Financing. You may pay for the car through either dealer financing or a private loan from a bank or a savings and loan institution. Shop around to compare annual percentage rates (APR), down payments, monthly payments, and term of loan.

Trade-ins, rebates, and incentives. Cash in on these *after* you've agreed on a firm price with the dealer. Otherwise, the dealer may inflate the price of the car during negotiations.

See "Lease a New Car."

Buy a Used Car

Used-car buyers do not receive a warranty or any guarantee that the car will run satisfactorily. The main objective when shopping for used cars, then, is to determine what kind of shape the car is in. Do research to find out which models have good resale value and the best maintenance records.

Where to Go

New car dealers. Dealerships that accept trade-ins on new cars resell the used cars to consumers. These cars are often late models originally bought at the dealership, and they're likely to be in decent shape. Dealerships are unlikely to sell defective cars because their reputations are at stake; they may, though, charge more for the security and higher quality they offer.

Used car lots. Here you will likely find cars that are lower priced but lower in quality as well. Garages that sell used cars tend to be more reliable because they fix the cars themselves and will stand by *their* repairs.

Private sellers. Cars sold by individuals through ads in the paper or on bulletin boards will probably be least expensive, but they yield the least amount of protection. Check bulletin boards at senior centers and retirement communities for good deals on older cars that are likely to be well kept and little driven.

Other sources. Great deals on cars and trucks often come from public auctions, such as those conducted for bank and government repossessions.

Used Car Shopping Tips

✓ All cars sold by dealers must have a Buyer's Guide label on the window with information on price and warranty. "As is" usually means there is no warranty. Factory or dealer warranties specify the terms and indicate whether they are transferable to new owners. Service contracts are sometimes available if there is no warranty, but they will cost more.

✓ Buy a used car when it is two to four years old. By then the car has already depreciated greatly but will likely still be in good enough shape to last many more years.

✓ Conservative cars such as sedans, mid-sized cars, and station wagons tend to be the best used car buys because they are typically more durable and were handled with care by their original owners.

Inspecting the Car

Before you buy a used car, be sure to examine it thoroughly. If you are inexperienced with cars, bring a knowledgeable friend along with you or ask that the car be inspected and appraised by a professional mechanic at your expense. Ask the seller to show you previous service and repair bills.

When inspecting the car, check it all over:

✓ Under the hood, for irregularities

✓ Underneath the car, for leaks and rust

✓ The body, for dents, peeling paint, rust, and signs of extensive repair work (new welds, new paint)

✓ The glass, for cracks and scratches

✓ The tires, for correct alignment and proper wear (and see that there is a spare tire and a jack in the trunk)

✓ The suspension, to make sure all sides of the car are level (bounce gently on the car to see that it recovers quickly)

✓ The odometer, to see that its indicated mileage matches logically with the shape the car is in (tampering with odometers is against the law, but often done)

✓ The interior, to see that there are no rips in the seats and no foul odors; that all the controls, accessories, and pedals work; and that the car is comfortable

The Test Drive

Once you have inspected the car completely, take it on a test drive. Take as long as you need (at least half an hour) to get a feel for how the car runs and to test all its mechanical parts. Check these features:

✓ The steering, for wheel alignment and ease in turning

✓ The brakes, for quickness and reliability

✓ The engine, for ease in starting, power, acceleration, and speed

✓ The transmission, for ease in shifting without jerkiness

✓ The exhaust, for noise level and emissions (blue smoke is especially bad, as is a black and sooty tailpipe)

✓ The suspension, to see that it handles bumps and turns well

Consumer Protection

One drawback to buying a used car is that you have less legal recourse if the car is defective. Do check your local Better Business Bureau or a state consumer protection agency before you buy, to see whether any complaints have been lodged against a dealership or used car lot.

Make sure you get all agreements in writing, and don't sign any contracts until you are sure what you are getting. If you are buying from a private seller, be sure the title of the car is in the seller's name. Otherwise, you could be buying a stolen vehicle.

See "Lease a New Car" and "Buy a New Car."

Lease a New Car

Leasing is a hot new trend for car buyers who want the luxury of driving a new car and/or those who don't want to make the hefty down payments required to buy. *Consumers Reports* states that one in five cars in America is leased. Leases can be confusing, and they often contain hidden costs. Make sure a lease agreement makes sense before signing the dotted line:

✓ Negotiate monthly lease payments on the fair market price of the car—not the sticker price. Know what your model, with all options and extras, would cost to *buy*. Do the same research a new car buyer must do before talking to a showroom salesperson.

✓ Remember that car makers use leasing as a way to deplete stock or to boost the total number of a certain model sold. Look for low payments offered as special incentives.

✓ Avoid leases that extend more than four years, require money down, or call for security deposits. A close-ended lease means you are not obligated to purchase the car at lease end.

✓ Consider how far you drive in a year. Choose lease terms with high yearly mileage maximums (15,000 miles or more) and check for per-mile costs, which can be as much as 25 cents per mile if the maximum is exceeded.

✓ Don't agree to "end of term" fees when the lease expires. Find out whether penalties accrue if you get out of a lease before the term ends.

✓ Watch out for "excess wear and tear" fees. If you have small children or pets, or are hard on your cars, this lease clause could cost you money.

✓ Remember that you are responsible for maintaining the car, often according to a schedule and terms laid out by the lease agreement. Figure these expenses into your budget.

✓ Be wary of purchasing insurance. Many car makers will give away "gap insurance"—the difference between the value of the car and the amount owed on the lease agreement if the car is stolen or totaled—as an incentive lease.

✓ Shop around. Compare prices from more than one dealer or car maker.

✓ Do the math and assess your needs realistically. If the costs and benefits of leasing are not more advantageous than buying, don't be talked into a lease agreement.

See "Buy a New Car."

Change a Tire

If you drive regularly, the chances are that at some point you'll get a flat tire. Flats are usually caused by running over sharp objects in the road such as nails or glass, though the likelihood of a flat is increased by driving on worn or overpressurized tires or by having too much weight in the car.

The most important thing is to recognize a flat immediately and get off the road. Driving on a flat tire is dangerous and can seriously damage a car's axles. When a tire has deflated, you'll hear and feel a recurring thud each time the wheel revolves. If you get a flat while driving, keep calm and follow these instructions:

Pull Over Immediately

Without slamming on the brakes, ease the car off the road. Remove your foot from the accelerator and steer in the direction you want to go. If you are on a highway, pull over as far as you can onto the shoulder and away from traffic. If possible, pull off the road completely, but make sure you are on a hard, flat surface. Put the car in park, turn off the engine, and firmly set the parking brake. Turn on your hazard warning flashers and remain mindful of passing traffic at all times.

Changing a tire can cause physical injury. If you are unsure of the procedure, if there is danger from passing traffic, or if you have any physical disabilities, get help by calling an emergency road service or walking to the nearest gas station. On the highway, wait in your car with the doors locked for assistance from the highway patrol.

Assemble Materials

Take out your car jack and lug nut wrench. Keep other supplies in your trunk in the event of a flat: a flashlight, a hammer or large screwdriver, and work gloves. Consult your car owner's manual for any specific advice on changing a tire for your car model.

Remove the Spare Tire

It will be located in the trunk or attached underneath the back of the car. If the tire is attached underneath, you'll need to release the tire by unscrewing the nuts that hold it in place. Sometimes the spare will be a full-sized tire and can be a permanent replacement for the flat tire. Check the spare to make sure it is inflated—it should not give when you bounce on it with your foot. Other times, the spare will be a smaller space-saving tire (called a "doughnut") that must be replaced with a full-sized tire as soon as you reach a full-service station or dealer.

Remove the Hubcap

The opposite end of the lug nut wrench is specially designed for prying off hubcaps. Otherwise, use a screwdriver (Figure 1).

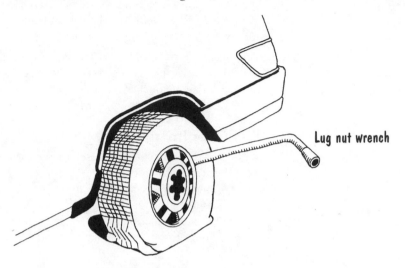

Figure 1. Remove the hubcap.

Loosen the Lug Nuts

There will be four or five lug nuts on a wheel. Many new cars have a special lug nut that is designed differently than the others and cannot be removed with the lug nut wrench alone (this is to prevent car tire theft). To remove this nut, you'll need a special key that fits on the nut and attaches to the wrench. If your car requires this key, it should have been given to you when you bought the car. Using the wrench, loosen the lug nuts, but do not remove them (Figure 2).

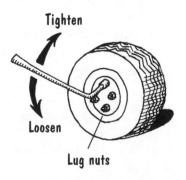

Figure 2. Loosen the lug nuts.

Jack Up the Car

Wedge a rock or solid object under the grounded tire farthest from the flat to prevent the car from shifting and rolling off the jack. Using your jack (jacks work differently; consult the instructions on the jack or in the car owner's manual for positioning requirements), elevate the car frame near the tire, far enough to bring the flat just barely clear of the ground (Figure 3). Bumper jacks should be positioned as near to the tire as possible but at least a foot from the end of the bumper.

Note: **No matter how firmly the jack seems to be in place, never put any part of your body under the car!**

Figure 3. Jack up the car.

Remove the Lug Nuts

Loosening lug nuts requires a lot of pressure and pulling, which is why you should loosen them *before* you jack up the car. Since they are already loosened, simply unscrew them completely and store them in the hubcap.

Pull Off the Flat

This may require some effort, especially if the wheel is heavy and hasn't been removed for a while. Be careful, though, not to jar the jack out of place.

Put On the Spare

Slide the new tire onto the axle, fitting the holes on the wheel onto the studs that are jutting out. Make sure the wheel is pushed in as far as it will go (Figure 4).

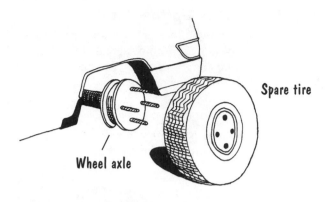

Figure 4. Put on the spare tire.

Screw Lug Nuts Back On

For the same reason you didn't loosen the nuts while the car is jacked up, you shouldn't tighten the nuts now either. Screw them on with your hands and get them as tight as you can without using the wrench. Most nuts have one rounded or cone-shaped end that goes on first and fits snugly inside.

Lower the Jack

Remove the object wedged beneath the tire.

Tighten the Lug Nuts

With the lug wrench, screw on the nuts as tightly as you can. Don't tighten the nuts in a clockwise or counterclockwise order. Rather, tighten them in a criss-cross pattern; this will keep the pressure on the wheel even. Replace the hubcap.

Pack Up

Put the flat tire in the trunk and replace your tools where you found them. Drive slowly until you are confident the wheel is secure. Have it checked at the first available service station.

Maintain Your Tires

As with all car maintenance work, the key to doing it yourself is caution. Cars are not toys, and fooling with them without knowing exactly what you are doing can be very dangerous. When it comes to taking care of your tires, some procedures are probably not worth trying, while others are relatively safe if done correctly. For instance, don't attempt to rotate your tires on your own. Not only does it require expensive equipment, it can turn out to be dangerous and troublesome. An experienced mechanic is much more familiar with the tools and the safety measures involved, and the procedure does not cost too much. Among the tire care procedures that are relatively safe and easy are these: checking your tires' air pressure and tread, and filling your tires with air if they are low. Tires should be checked at least once a month. Here's how to do it:

Check Tread

While your car is parked on a level ground but still running, turn the steering wheel to the left so you will be able to get a complete view of the front tires. Turn off the car, put the parking brake on, then come around to the tires. Check to see whether the tire tread is even. There should be an equal amount of tread on the inside of the tire as on the outside. If there is not, take your car to a mechanic or tire dealer; you may need a wheel realignment. Also measure the tread depth (the amount of tread wrapped around the tire) with a ruler or other measuring equipment. Most states have tread depth minimums, so be sure that your tread depth conforms to the requirements. If the thread measures less than $\frac{1}{16}$", or the tire begins to show "wear bars," or breaks in the tread, your tire is worn out and should be replaced. Finally, make sure there are no foreign objects wedged into the tires, such as small pieces of glass or stones, that can puncture the tires. Repeat this entire procedure for all four tires.

Check Air Pressure

To properly check air pressure, you need a quality air gauge; cheap air gauges can be way off (Figure 1). To get the most accurate reading, your tires should be cold to the touch. Remove the valve stem cover and push the mouth of the air gauge onto the valve stem of your tire. You should not hear any air leaking. The air gauge will indicate how many pounds of air pressure are in the tire. Check that the tire's air pressure is within 2 pounds of the air pressure recommended by the car manufacturer (this information will be in the owner's manual, on the car's glove compartment lid, or the left car door jamb) or embossed on the side of the tire. Repeat this for all four tires, plus the spare tire in the trunk. If the level of any tire is too low, fill the tire with air.

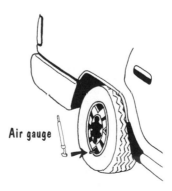

Air gauge

Figure 1. Checking the air pressure

To put air into a tire, you need an air pump. These can be found at most gas stations or auto shops. The air pump has a rubber tube to attach to the valve stem of your tire. When you push the mouth of the tube onto the valve stem, air will enter the tire. Do not keep the tube on the stem for more than two seconds at a time. Each time you remove the tube, check the air pressure, until it has reached the required amount.

Note: Good driving habits and proper upkeep of your entire car will also extend the life of your tires. Ask your mechanic to check the tires whenever you have a routine oil change.

Drive a Stick Shift

Driving a car with manual transmission requires a simple coordinated maneuvering of your feet and hands. While it will seem difficult and awkward at the beginning, rest assured that with a little practice you'll soon be shifting gears with the best of them.

Before starting the car, familiarize yourself with the clutch, brake, and gas pedals (Figure 1). The clutch, which you depress with your left foot, is at the far left. The brake, located in the center, is controlled with your right foot. The gas pedal, at the far right, is also controlled with your right foot.

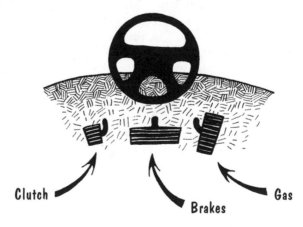

Figure 1. Car pedals

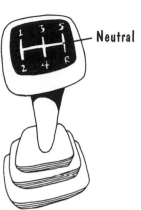

Figure 2. The gear stick

Next, familiarize yourself with the positions of the gears. All cars supply a diagram of where first gear is, but the most common configuration is illustrated here (Figure 2). The neutral position, in the center, allows the stick to move freely from left to right, and in most cars, first gear has the stick pointing forward and to the left. All gears switch through neutral. Never switch gears without first depressing the clutch pedal and keeping it depressed while switching.

1. To start a car with manual transmission, make sure it is in neutral by stepping on the clutch with your left foot, turning on the ignition, and checking that the stick is in neutral.

2. Before you shift into first, press the clutch pedal down as far as it will go with your left foot, and hold it down. Now put the gear shift into first.

3. Here's the tricky part. To get the car moving, slowly ease your left foot off the clutch as you press your right foot lightly on the gas pedal. Keep in mind that you are connecting two moving gears: when you press the clutch you are disengaging the gears, when you ease off the clutch you are reintegrating the gears, and when you give the engine gas you are setting the gears in motion. Therefore, if you are too fast off the clutch, the gears will slam together and fail to interconnect, causing the car to jerk and eventually stall. If you're too heavy on the gas before the gears connect, you'll just make the engine rev loudly, and you won't go anywhere.

    ✓ The point in the release of the clutch where the gears meet depends on the vehicle. Some cars have very deep clutch pedals. Others are shorter. Finding and recognizing that point requires familiarity with the car, so until you know the car, take it slow.

    ✓ If you are backing the car out as you start it, simply put the car in reverse gear. Depending on the car, this will have the gear stick pointing to the right and back. Once the gear is in reverse, follow the same pedal procedure.

    ✓ If you are starting on a hill, the car may drift back when you take your foot off the brakes to press the clutch. If you can engage the gears quickly, the car will probably not drift back too far. But on steep hills where there is a car close behind you, you may want to put on the emergency brake so the car doesn't drift back, then release the emergency brake once the gears are engaged and you are moving forward.

4. Once the car is in forward motion, if you are accelerating, you will soon have to shift from first gear up to second gear. There are two ways to know when it's time to shift: when the rpm gauge on the dashboard reaches around 3 (3,000 engine revolutions per minute), or when you hear the engine begin to rev loudly. To shift up, press in the clutch. Then move the gear stick to the position marked "2." Be sure the stick is firmly in place, but be careful not to be too rough with it. Then, ease off the clutch with your left foot as you give gas with your right, as in Step 3.

5. When it is time to shift again, repeat Step 4. Fifth gear, for driving at speeds of 50 mph or more, is the highest you can go.

6. When the car is decelerating, you must downshift or else risk stalling. Follow the same procedure: press clutch, shift, ease off clutch (you will not necessarily have to give gas if the car is already in motion). Do not shift down too far at once (say, from fifth to second), or you risk overloading the gears, causing the engine to rev loudly and the car to slow down too abruptly. Another method for decelerating is simply to put the car in neutral (press clutch, take gear stick out of gear so it points straight up in the middle, then release clutch) and apply brakes. If you come to a complete stop, you must either have the clutch pushed in or be in neutral. If the car stops while you are in gear, it will stall.

Parallel Park

There are probably as many techniques for parallel parking as there are people who claim to be expert parallel parkers. If a certain technique works for you, stick with it; there's no official way to parallel park. But if you've yet to find a method that works for you, try this one:

1. Position the car. Pull your car up so that it is parallel and even with the car in front of the space you wish to park in. Then set the car in reverse (Figure 1).

2. Turn the wheel. Before you begin moving backward, turn your wheel in the direction of the curb you want to park against so your car will glide back at a 45-degree angle to the curb.

3. Drift the car back. Drive back slowly, keeping an eye on the car in front. Continue gliding back until the front wheel of your car is even with the back wheel of the car in front of the space. Stop drifting back at this point (Figure 2).

4. Turn the wheel in the opposite direction. This time the wheel should be turned away from the curb, again so the car will glide back at a 45-degree angle.

5. Drift back farther into the space. Slowly reverse until the car is parallel to the curb, then stop. Check to see that the car is within 1 foot of the curb. If it isn't, you'll either have to start over (if the space is tight) or inch your way back and forth in the space until you get closer to the curb (Figure 3).

6. Straighten the wheel and center the car. If you are close enough to the curb, pull straight forward in the space, being sure to leave room for the cars in front and in back of you to pull out. Remember, don't tap the cars in front or in back of you—not even lightly—while you are attempting to parallel park. That's not only rude but can damage the cars.

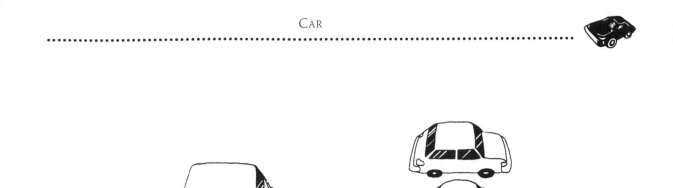

Figure 1. Pull car up parallel to car in front.

Figure 2. Pull the car back diagonally. Pull back until front tire is even with back tire of car in front.

Figure 3. Pull back into parking space and straighten out.

Three-Point Turn

The three-point turn is a simple and useful car maneuver that enables you to turn a car around quickly within a tight space. Before you attempt to perform the three-point turn, be sure there is no oncoming traffic in either direction—particularly if you are turning on a street. Most two-lane streets are wide enough to turn a car around with just "three points," or three turns of the wheel; if you have trouble because a space is too narrow, use more points as necessary to turn around.

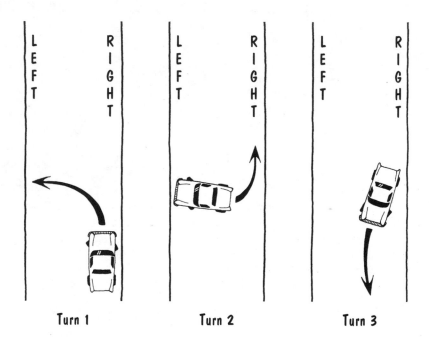

The three-point turn

Turn 1

Line your car up straight against the right side of the space in which you want to turn—the right side of a street, for instance. Turn the wheel as far as possible to the left, and pull forward slowly until the front of the car reaches the left side of the space. Come to a complete stop.

Turn 2

Put the car in reverse and turn the wheel as far as it will go in the opposite direction (to the right). Bring the car back slowly until the rear of the car reaches the right side of the space. Again, come to a complete stop.

Turn 3

Put the car in drive and turn the wheel to straighten the car on the road (if the street is two-way, you should pull away on the right side of the street). Slowly drive forward in the opposite direction from which you came.

Jump Start a Car

A battery supplies power to a car when the engine is not running. For instance, it will keep the lights or the radio on even when the car is off. Most importantly, it supplies power to start the car. A battery's power is limited. Leaving the lights on after the car is shut off will drain the battery within an hour or so, and the car will be unstartable. This doesn't mean the battery is dead; it simply needs recharging. It can be recharged by jump starting with another car battery. To do this, you need a second car with a working battery and jumper cables: two insulated wires with spring clamps at the ends, available at any car supply store. Be sure to follow the directions carefully; the transfer of power between cars is potentially dangerous and can cause a severe electric shock. Keep open flames (cigarettes, matches) away from the engine, wear eye protection, and take off any metal (jewelry, watches) on your body. Here's how to jump start safely:

1. Align the cars. The two cars (one with a working battery and one with a drained battery) should be parked close together, but not touching, and facing each other. The longer the jumper cables, the more flexibility you'll have in determining car orientation. Purchase cables at least 12 to 15 feet in length. Once the working car is in place, set the parking brake but keep the engine running. In the drained car, remove the key from the ignition, set the parking brake, and turn off all inside switches.

2. Open the hoods of both cars and locate the batteries. If the drained battery has cell caps, remove the caps to release any gases, and cover the caps with a towel or cloth.

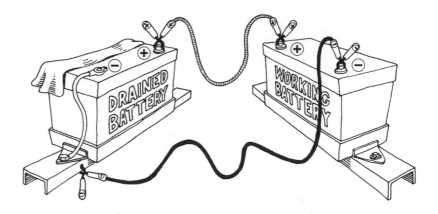

Figure 1. Hookup for a jump start

3. Hook up the jumper cables. Each battery has a positive and a negative terminal; they look like small nodes jutting from the top of the battery. They will
probably be marked plus for positive, and minus for negative. The two
jumper cables will be marked red and black. Use one color (traditionally,
red) for the plus connection and one for the minus. With the first jumper
cable, connect one end to the positive terminal of the drained battery, then
the other end to the positive terminal of the working battery. With the second jumper cable, connect one end to the negative terminal of the working
battery and the other end to a nonmoving metal part in the drained car, close
to the battery. Be sure that the cables are clamped securely and are not touching any other part of the car (Figure 1).

4. Start the car with the drained battery. Using the power of the working car's
battery, the drained car should start. If it does not, turn off both cars and
check that the jumper cable connections are secure, reconnecting them if
necessary. Then try turning on the cars again (working car first, then drained
car). If the drained car still does not start, the battery could be dead, in
which case jump starting will not work and you'll need to replace the battery
with a new one.

5. If the drained car starts, turn off the car with the working battery and let
the drained car run for a few minutes. The drained battery is recharging itself.
After a few minutes the battery should be recharged; turn off the recharged car.

6. Disconnect the cables. Remove the jumper cables in the reverse order you
put them on: the negative cable, then the positive cable. *Important*: Be careful
that the two jumper cables do not touch where they are uninsulated (near or
on the clamps), at least until the cables are completely disconnected.

Avoid Traffic

Complaints about traffic used to be voiced largely by the residents of urban areas or visitors to them. More and more, however, people in the suburbs and even rural areas are grumbling about annoying delays, gridlocks, too many cars, and too little parking. The vehicle population is simply increasing faster than the traffic solutions. Here are ways you can avoid, or at least reduce, traffic problems:

✓ Use mass transit as often as possible, and urge your friends and co-workers to do the same.

✓ Join a car pool if you commute by car.

✓ Revise your driving schedules, whether for work or for pleasure, so you are on the road when traffic is not at a peak.

✓ Listen to regular traffic reports on your home and car radios, and keep a record of the best and worst driving times.

✓ When making long trips, select departure and arrival times on days when traffic problems are minimal.

✓ Join an auto club, like AAA, and ask for regular traffic reports, both locally and for other areas you intend to visit.

✓ Make note of newspaper and broadcast reports about highways, river crossings, and city streets where major construction projects are under way. Avoid these areas.

✓ If you have to travel frequently in congested areas, know which radio stations in your area monitor traffic conditions.

✓ Change your shopping habits. Go earlier or later. Consolidate your shopping so you make fewer trips.

✓ Carry a detailed street map and, if necessary, a compass. There are usually several alternative routes that bypass the traffic. Learn what they are, and practice using them.

✓ Volunteer for community action groups whose aim is to improve local traffic and parking problems.

✓ Support legislation—local, state, and federal—to improve the nation's highways.

✓ Find out as much as you can about parking facilities at your destination *before* you leave home.

✓ Walk or ride a bike whenever you can. It's great exercise.

Develop a Sense of Direction

Sitting at home, as you look out the window, do you really know which is north, east, south, or west?

Developing a sense of direction literally begins at home. You may know that the sun comes up on one side of the house and goes down on the other. But since there are considerable variations from season to season, you really need to buy a reliable compass to distinguish the four points accurately. The easiest way to orient yourself initially is to observe the sun, which rises in the east and sets in the west. If it is before noon and the sun is on your right, you are facing north. If it is afternoon and the sun is on your left, you are facing south. Once you have gotten your home bearings firmly in mind, take the following steps:

1. Obtain a map of your town and mark the location of your house on it. Note the compass directions in relation to the house.

2. Mark the compass directions you follow to go to the places you visit most, such as your church, the supermarket, the school, your office, or the library. Note especially the directional orientation of the main parkways and thoroughfares.

3. Now, extend your directional guide by using a map of your county to establish firmly in mind which points of the compass you follow to go to nearby towns, recreational areas, sports centers, or other points of interest. Note, too, the compass relationships of these locations, one to the other. (You go east to town "B," then southwest to lake "T," then north to shopping mall "Z".) When reading a map or driving in your car, consider that even-numbered route signs travel north and south, and odd-numbered routes travel east and west. Federal highways are all marked in this manner.

4. Study your compass and note the many variations from north to south and east to west, such as north northeast (NNE) and south southwest (SSW), all determined by their location on the 360-degree circle into which the compass is divided.

5. Carry a compass in your car and visualize changes in direction as you drive from place to place. Note that built-in car compasses are not entirely accurate, since they are affected by motion, magnetic forces in the vehicle, and abrupt changes of direction.

6. When you take long drives with friends or family members, use a detailed map and assign one person as navigator. Have each person guess at directions as you approach major locations on the map. See who comes closest to the facts.

If you want to become adept at developing your sense of direction, try orienteering: the skill of finding your way with map and compass combined.

Your first step is to become familiar with compasses, and especially the points covering the instrument's 360 degrees. Then you may want to try an orienteering compass, with which you can find your bearings quickly and easily. Simply hold the compass in a level position, about waist high, with its direction-of-travel arrow pointing straight ahead. As you turn the compass housing you can see not only exactly where you are headed but how you should turn to head in any other direction on the map. As you practice with this compass and a map you will gradually develop a much better sense of direction. Don't try to perfect your directional skills all at once. Start by using both compass and a local map on hikes—even short walks—near your home. Then improve your capabilities by taking short drives in different directions.

Eventually, you will instinctively determine direction and rarely become lost. In a pinch, there's always the night sky. Take a course in star-gazing at your local community college.

10 Good Driver Techniques

Driving a car is such a common, everyday experience that we can forget how potentially dangerous it is. The utmost care should be taken when you are driving. The first safety step is to follow the law: fasten seat belts, obey all signs and rules of the road. Beyond that, there are several techniques not prescribed by the law that will help you stay out of trouble when you drive. Here are ten of them (and remember, *never* drink and drive; *never* let another person drive drunk):

1. Be awake and alert. Do not drive if you are taking prescription drugs with a side effect of drowsiness. Be conscious of your physical state. Get off the road if you are excessively tired or sick. Open the window for fresh air. Stop often; eat, drink, and use the bathroom as many times as necessary to stay comfortable and focused. Check into a motel for the night if you can't stay awake.

2. Stay calm and collected. Avoid driving when your emotions are running high, whether you are enraged, depressed, or ecstatic. Strong feelings distract you from the road and can make you a more aggressive driver. Don't play music that will wrap you up in a dream world or take your attention away from the driving.

3. Make sure your car is in good shape. Even the slightest malfunction in your car can get you into trouble while driving. Service your car routinely.

4. Treat other drivers with respect. We sometimes get trapped in the insular world of our cars and act as if we were no longer responsible for what goes on in the outside world. If lanes are merging, let at least one car in; if you arrive at a four-way stop at same time as another driver, let the other car go first.

5. Think ahead. A key technique for avoiding trouble is to spot potential problems. If you see traffic slowing up ahead, be ready to slow down if it becomes necessary.

6. Make other drivers aware of you. Don't be afraid to shine your brights or beep your horn lightly if you suspect other drivers are unaware that you are passing them or are behind them. Better to risk offending someone than risk an accident.

7. Stay away from other cars. Sometimes you are forced to come very close to other cars, particularly in heavy traffic. Whenever you can, though, leave plenty of room between your car and others on the road. This greatly increases reaction time in the event a problem arises. If you spot another car moving erratically or unpredictably, steer clear and give it a wide berth.

8. Aim your vision high. You need to see what is going on around you. The farther off into the distance you focus your vision while you drive, the wider

your field of vision will be. Check your mirrors regularly. Know the position of all the cars surrounding you.

9. Don't fix your eyes. While you look off into the distance, make sure you don't fix on a single object. Constantly survey the surroundings with your eyes; don't stare. That said, do keep your eyes on the road. Leave sightseeing to your passengers. Don't try to perform tasks inside the car like looking for toll money or changing a cassette while driving. Pull over if you need to, or wait until you reach an appropriate stop. If you have passengers, ask them for help.

10. Beware of your blind spot when turning or changing lanes. All cars have blind spots that can deceive you into thinking there is no one approaching from behind when actually there is. Besides checking your rearview mirror, it's a good idea to also make a very quick glance over your shoulder to double check. But don't lose sight of the traffic in front of you.

When to Tune Up a Car

Gone are the days when car owners could lift the hood and tune the engines themselves. What with the increasing complexity of the elements that make up a vehicle's power systems, and the use of computers and sophisticated technological devices to control them, the family car requires servicing by a well-trained mechanic. You should know, however, what the term "tune-up" refers to and how often this procedure is necessary.

A **tune-up** is described as a series of adjustments to the engine and all working parts of a vehicle to make sure it operates as efficiently as possible. There is very little difference in the scheduling and procedures between cars with standard shifts and those with automatic shifts. But consult your dealer if your car is an uncommon type or has any unusual modifications. When an inspection reveals that major parts are required, you can sometimes save money by requesting reconditioned parts—but only if they have a written guarantee.

Here are the steps performed in a typical tune-up and the frequency of each:

Engine Oil and Filter Change

Drain and replace oil. Every 3,000 miles or three months. You may still perform this function yourself. (See "Change the Oil in a Car.")

Chassis Lubrication

Grease of all moving parts in the body of the car that do not have sealed lubrication. Every 6,000–9,000 miles.

Ignition System

Check and possibly replace spark plugs, condenser, rotor, distributor caps, and coils. Every 10,000 miles or about ten months to a year.

Emission System

Check the exhaust system, mufflers, and engine emission to meet environmental control specifications and regulations. Once a year.

Brake System

Inspect brake drums and replace worn linings or other parts if necessary. On late-model cars, check antilock systems. Once a year.

Tire and Wheel Inspection

Check rotation of all tires to assure more even wear and proper traction. Once a year.

Fan Belts and Other Drive Belts

Check for wear and proper tension to assure efficient functioning. Every six months, and more often after a vehicle has reached 60,000 miles.

Steering and Suspension

Check to determine signs of wear, lack of lubrication, shock absorber performance, and proper control. Once a year.

Cooling System

Water and antifreeze levels should be checked every time a vehicle has an oil change, but especially if the vehicle is to be subjected to temperature extremes.

Battery and Wiring

With the new types of enclosed batteries that do not require regular additions of water, maintenance is seldom required.

Regular tune-ups will keep your car running smoothly and help target any major problems as they develop—not on the road!

Be Prepared for Emergencies

Anticipating car breakdowns and other emergencies related to driving, and taking steps in advance to solve these problems, will not only lessen the predicaments but let you travel with more peace of mind.

The four most important priorities for being prepared are these:

✓ Make sure you have adequate insurance to cover accidents and other casualties.
✓ Join a reliable service organization, such as AAA, so you have help on the highway when you need it most.
✓ Schedule regular maintenance on your car, suitable to its age and condition, to avoid, or at least minimize, problems and emergencies.
✓ Stay alert while driving and leave plenty of time to reach your destination. Pull over if you are tired, or cannot concentrate. Above all, don't drink and drive.

Equip your car with tools and supplies to cope with emergencies quickly and easily, and often without requiring outside help. Here is a list of the basic items you might want to keep in your car:

Tire-changing tools. Make sure you have the right ones for the job, as specified by the manufacturer. To these you might add a rubber mallet and a cross-bar lug wrench, for removing really stubborn wheel nuts; a heavy screwdriver; and a pair of work gloves. If you are not familiar with changing the tires on your car, study the manufacturer's instructions and do a "dry run" to familiarize yourself with the right steps. (See "Change a Tire.")

Jump-start battery cable. This is useful if your battery has run down. You can hook it up to that of another vehicle to start your engine. Carefully follow the steps specified on the cable (or its container); also check your car's owner manual for special instructions. Purchase a cable at least 12 to 15 feet in length. This makes it much easier to connect your car to the car supplying the jump. (See "Jump Start a Car.")

Emergency lighting. In addition to a long-life flashlight, you should have a plug-in light that attaches to the cigarette lighter and a package of flares to use as warning lights if your car breaks down in a hazardous location.

First-aid kit. You don't need anything fancy—just a compact kit you can buy in a pharmacy for less than $10.

Car fluids. If you have room in the trunk, store small containers of engine oil, radiator fluid, and steering fluid.

Maps. Before starting off on a long trip, make sure your maps are adequate and up to date. They are no longer the free handouts they used to be at almost any service station. Chart your trip plan in advance, using a highlighting marker. A small, reliable compass is also useful to help you avoid panic if you get lost.

Owner's manual. Ascertain that you have the right manual for your car, and do a little homework to familiarize yourself with its contents—especially topics related to emergencies.

Security devices. In addition to built-in security systems to prevent the theft of the car or its contents, you can buy several portable devices, like the club, that can be used when you are in remote areas or at night. (See "Security Devices.")

Survival supplies. Always carry an extra key to avoid being locked out of your car. Keep a blanket and pillow in your trunk in case you are forced to sleep in your car. Travel with a jug of water on long drives. Keep a small amount of cash, enough to handle unexpected tolls or a tank of gas, in your glove compartment. Think ahead and be prepared.

Give Your Car a Facelift

In car language, *detailing* is a relatively new term that can be defined as "a function designed to restore and enhance the physical appearance, freshness, and aroma of a vehicle" according to the Association of Service Station Managers.

There is no reason why you cannot detail a car yourself with a little work and elbow grease and two or three hours of tender loving care. However, any car in which you take pride deserves a professional detailing at least once a year—more often if it is subjected to heavy use or driving through mud, dust, or under any conditions that play havoc with its appearance or subject the car to objectionable odors, humidity, or mold.

The cost for a professional detailing job—which should be done in a properly equipped service station, car wash facility, or dealership, and not by a handyman—ranges from $50 to $90, including cleaning and renovating supplies. The cost takes into consideration the size of the vehicle being treated, its condition, and the nature of the metals, fabrics, and other surfaces that need refurbishing. A thorough detailing job includes:

✓ An exterior wash, using detergents and other cleaners formulated to remove even the toughest tars, pitches, waxes, and other accretions without damage to the finish.

✓ Subsurface waxing, followed by topcoat waxing and polishing to restore the finish to the finest degree possible.

✓ Cleaning and polishing of all chrome and other metal surfaces on the exterior, with special attention to bumpers, flashings, hub caps, wire wheels, and trim.

✓ Removal of tar, grime, and grease from the underside of the chassis, as well as from the exhaust system, axles, and suspension system.

✓ Paint touch-up to repair minor areas of chipped or scratched paint and prevent corrosion. If the damage goes down to the metal, apply a primer first. Several thin coats of paint are better than one thick one. You can purchase primer and touch-up paint from your car's dealership. Extensive paint damage should be repaired only by a professional.

✓ Removal and shampooing of all floor pads and other detachable fabrics.

✓ A thorough vacuuming of the interior, with special attention to pockets and crevices ordinary vacuum machines cannot reach.

✓ Dry cleaning to remove spots, stains, and grime from seats, walls, and other areas covered with fabric. Minor repairs, such as regluing.

✓ Cleaning and restoration of any areas covered in leather or simulated leather.

✓ Cleaning and polishing of all metals in the interior. Minor repairs, such as attention to scratches or dents.

✓ Cleaning and polishing of all plastic parts and surfaces. Minor repairs.

✓ Cleaning of all windows, mirrors, and light fixtures with detergents and glass wax.

✓ Spraying to eliminate or neutralize unwanted odors and freshen the interior.

No matter how handy you are or how determined to do a good job, you may need professional assistance because of a lack of equipment or expensive refurbishing supplies. One solution is to undertake those functions that are within your capability—such as exterior washing and polishing—and then make a deal with a detailer to handle the tougher assignments.

Security Devices

To avoid becoming a victim of crime involving your car, take steps to

✓ Prevent the theft of your car, or damage to it, when it is parked and *unoccupied.*
✓ Prevent theft, damage, or danger to the driver and passengers when a car is *occupied.*

Crime prevention focuses on devices you can install to prevent loss, damage and possible bodily harm, and preventive measures (other than product use) that you can take to minimize your chances of becoming a crime victim.

When your car is unoccupied and parked at home, on the street, or in a public parking lot, consider the following kinds of preventive installations:

✓ A top-quality alarm system, proof against false alarms and tough enough to bypass would-be burglars.
✓ A hidden, secondary ignition switch.
✓ A jimmy-proof bar that locks onto the steering wheel.
✓ A fuel shut-off device that will stop the car within seconds if not deactivated.
✓ An electronic device that tracks the car if it is stolen.
✓ An immobilizer you can use to disable the car's electrical system from up to a quarter mile away if you see your car being stolen.
✓ A canister (legal in most states) that emits a mild tear gas under the instrument panel if the lock is picked by a thief or unlocked with an illegal key.

The most effective measures you can take to insure the safety of an unattended vehicle include the following:

✓ When at home, park your car in the driveway, locked in a garage, or as close to your home as possible.
✓ Always lock your car doors.
✓ Never leave a car with the engine running or the key in the ignition.
✓ In public areas, park as close to an inhabited store or office as possible. Take note of where you are parked; forgetful and confused drivers are easy targets.
✓ When you park in attended lots, leave the ignition key only, not the trunk key or other personal keys. Some car models feature "valet" keys for this very purpose. They will only open car doors and fire the ignition.
✓ At night, park in a lighted, well-frequented area. Get an escort if possible. Many shopping centers, large garages, and office complexes readily provide assistance to help you reach your car.

✓ If you must leave your car for an extended period (at an airport parking lot, for example) remove the rotor from the engine's distributor. Get your dealer or mechanic to show you how.

✓ Make sure all windows are closed and the trunk and hood latches are tight.

When you are driving in your car, either alone or with passengers, the following devices can help to protect you from car-jacking or personal danger:

✓ A cellular telephone can be used instantly for emergency communication and help.

✓ A burglar alarm system can be activated immediately by you when you are in the car.

✓ A tiny, battery-operated alarm emits a strong, shrieking noise the instant you pull its trip-line.

✓ Flashcubes temporarily blind attackers who attempt to force their way in the door.

✓ Pepper solutions can be sprayed up to 20 feet to jolt an intruder. Some types have a dye that stains the skin and can be removed only with great difficulty. (These devices replace mace, which has a stunning effect on the person sprayed, could cause injury if seized and directed against you, and is illegal in some states.)

✓ A bullet-resistant shield can be slid up to protect the driver if he or she is threatened from the outside with a gun.

When you are driving, on the highway or elsewhere—especially in unfamiliar territory—take the following precautions:

✓ Know in advance exactly where you are going. Proceed along streets that are well lighted and well traveled. Keep maps in your car. If you do get lost, keep driving and try to find a police station or other safe public office at which to stop for directions.

✓ Notify a family member or reliable friend when starting on long trips, establish an emergency communication plan, and keep in touch.

✓ Do not stop to assist strangers, no matter how honest they may appear to be. If they seem to be in real trouble, alert the police.

✓ If you break down, place a white handkerchief or cloth on your aerial. Remain inside with all doors locked. If anyone approaches, roll your window down only an inch or two to communicate.

✓ Never pick up hitchhikers.

✓ Avoid anyone who starts asking you questions in a restaurant, or other public place, where you have stopped temporarily.

✓ Avoid situations where you have to travel late at night.

3. Do-It-Yourself

Hang Picture Groupings on the Wall

The trial-and-error method most people use results in a lopsided arrangement and a lot of needless holes in the wall. One practical solution is to use the floor as the "wall" while you decide on the most suitable arrangement (Figure 1). The steps are easy when taken in this order:

Figure 1. Laying out pictures on the floor

1. Determine the approximate size of the wall space you wish to fill, using a tape measure or yardstick.
2. Mark the same size space on the floor, directly below the wall location selected. Use coins or other small objects to mark the four corners.

3. Lay the picture frames (or other objects) on the floor space. Shuffle the arrangement around to see more than one combination. It's best to keep the bottoms aligned with the main focus of the group at eye level. Try to make the whole group fill an imaginary space or rectangle.

4. Once you've decided on an arrangement, turn the pictures over. This permits you to see exactly where the picture wires or hangers are located.

5. On the wall, measure the exact locations for the various picture hooks, from right to left and top to bottom, and hammer them firmly but gently in place. If the wall is plaster, you can prevent chipping by placing small pieces of self-sticking tape at each location where picture hooks or nails will be inserted.

If you have a great many small pictures or a complicated arrangement, place a large sheet of wrapping paper, cut to the same size as the wall space, directly on the floor. Mark the locations directly on it. Tape the paper to the wall, pound in the nails or hooks in the appropriate places, and then tear the paper loose before hanging your gallery.

One of the advantages of this procedure is that you can actually see what the wall arrangement will look like in advance. Some do's and don'ts:

✓ Do select one picture as the focal point and arrange the others around it.

✓ Do place the subjects in logical order or sequence if they collectively tell a story.

✓ Do make sure pictures are properly lighted and free of glare.

✓ Don't place pictures with small-print captions in locations where they are difficult to read.

✓ Don't place larger pictures above smaller ones in a way that makes the arrangement seem top-heavy.

✓ Avoid direct sunlight and strong heat sources.

Use a Power Drill

Power drills are quick and efficient tools for boring holes. Before you use a power drill, be certain you understand all the necessary safety precautions: wear goggles and gloves while operating the drill, turn the drill off as soon as the job is done, and keep the drill pointed away from people or objects. Electric drills can do many jobs, from boring holes to driving screws, sanding, polishing, and stripping. Cordless portable drills are probably the best bet for clueless beginners. They make simple chores like installing curtain rods fast and easy. For the rest of us, here are instructions for choosing and using a hand-held electric drill:

1. **Choose the appropriate drill.** The size of the hole you want to drill and the material you are drilling into—wood, metal, plastic, ceramic, plaster, brick, or stone—will dictate what type of drill you should use. While different drills are available for nearly every conceivable job, the main factors you need to consider for all-purpose drills are the speed type and the chuck size (Figure 1).

Drills can be single speed, turning at a set speed only, or variable speed, which can either speed up as you press the trigger or be set at a constant speed. Variable speed drills may also have a reverse feature that allows you to unscrew a screw.

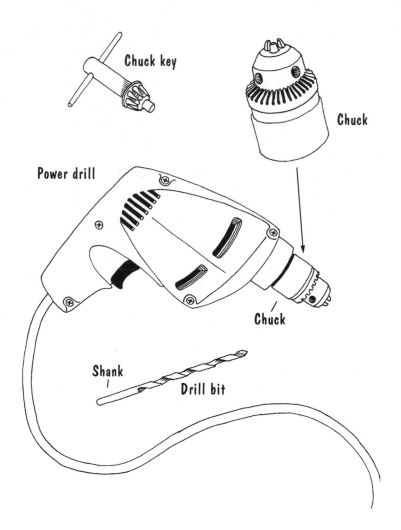

Figure 1. Power drill and parts

The chuck is the clamp at the end of the drill that spins the bit and holds it in place. Drills will be labeled as having a chuck size of either ¼," ½," or ⅜," referring to the maximum size of shank (the smooth end of a drill bit) that fits into the chuck. The larger the chuck size, the more surface area a drill has to grip a bit with; thus the more power it will have in turning the bit. For hard materials like brick, use a ½" drill for maximum power, but for softer materials like wood that require less power to drill, use a ¼" drill because it spins faster. A ⅜" drill is the best all-purpose choice.

2. **Choose the appropriate bit.** While there are many types of bits for many purposes, a standard high-speed bit is sufficient for drilling most holes. Still, you must choose its size. Buy a complete set of standard bits, ranging from ¹⁄₃₂" in diameter to ¼". Choose the bit size, which is labeled on the bit's shank, according to what size hole you want to drill.

3. **Open the chuck.** Holding the unplugged drill, turn the collar of the chuck like a dial to open the clamp wide enough to fit the bit into place.

4. **Set the bit.** Slide the shank end of the bit as far into the chuck as it will go, but not so far that the threaded part of the bit will be clamped as well.

5. **Tighten the chuck by hand.** Turn the collar of the chuck in the opposite direction you turned it in Step 3 to tightly close the chuck around the bit.

6. **Tighten the chuck with the key.** Stick the chuck key in the holes on side of the chuck and turn it clockwise to further tighten the chuck. Make sure you've tightened all the holes so that pressure on the bit is even.

7. **Set the drill at the desired spot.** Once the bit is tight, plug in the drill. With the object you are drilling securely in place, line up the drill precisely on the spot where you want to bore the hole. If necessary, punch a slight indentation in the exact location with a nail or awl to help keep the drill in place.

8. **Start the drill.** Pull the trigger to start the chuck spinning. If you have a variable speed drill, start off slowly so the bit can catch the material. Apply light, even pressure on the drill to move it into the object, making sure to keep the drill perpendicular to the surface of the object. Here are a few pointers in case problems occur:

   ✓ If the drill will not bore, check that the speed of the drill is appropriate (if variable speed or reversible), that the bit is sharp, that you have not hit a knot (in wood only), that the bit is clear of sawdust.

   ✓ If the drill gets jammed, turn it off immediately. Pull, or use the reverse feature, to remove a bit stuck in an object. If that does not work, unclamp the chuck and remove the drill from the bit, using caution, as the bit may be very hot. Try to yank the bit out of the material with pliers; as a last resort, saw off the exposed shank and get a new bit.

   ✓ If the drill begins to heat up and smoke, take some of the pressure off the bit, or shut off the drill and allow it to cool.

9. **Pull drill out.** When you finish drilling, pull the drill straight back until it is completely clear of the object, then turn the drill off.

10. **Remove the bit.** Do not leave the bit in the drill when you are not using it. Remove the bit as soon as it cools down, and return it to its proper place with the other bits. To release the bit, reverse the procedures in Steps 3 through 6.

Install a Molly Anchor or Toggle Bolt

Molly anchors (Figure 1a) and toggle bolts (Figure 2a) are used to attach heavy fixtures to a hollow wall that is too weak to hold a simple nail or screw. Both contraptions catch the inside of the wall and hold themselves in place to support a bolt or screw. Toggle bolts have spring-loaded arms; molly anchors have shoulders that expand when a bolt is screwed in them. Generally, toggle bolts give more support and can be used for heavier fixtures, and molly anchors are more versatile because they stay in place in the wall even when the bolt is removed (toggles do not). To install either, follow these directions:

Molly Anchor

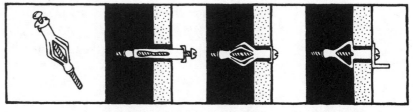

Figure 1a. Molly anchor | Figure 1b. Drill hole in wall equal to Molly anchor in diameter | Figure 1c. Tighten bolt | Figure 1d. Attach fixture and rescrew

Tools: drill, hammer, screwdriver.

1. Into a hollow wall, drill a hole using a bit equal to the diameter of the anchor (Figure 1b).

2. Push the anchor through the hole. You may need to hammer the anchor lightly to make the head lie flat against the wall. If so, be careful not to damage the wall with the hammer.

3. Screw the bolt into the anchor. Tighten it with a screwdriver until you cannot tighten any more. The anchor will be collapsing against the inside of the wall as you screw (Figure 1c).

4. Unscrew the bolt and attach the fixture you wish to hang from the wall. Screw the bolt back into the anchor to fasten it (Figure 1d).

Toggle Bolt

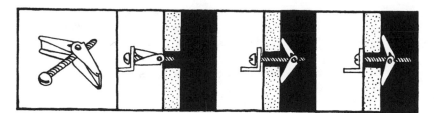

Figure 2a.
Toggle bolt

Figure 2b. Push
toggle through hole

Figure 2c. Pull
forward to catch
arms behind wall

2d. Tighten bolt
with attachment

Tools: drill, hammer, screwdriver.

1. Into a hollow wall, drill a hole using a bit equal to the diameter of the toggle arms when folded in.

2. Hold the arms of the toggle bolt folded together as you push the toggle through the hole (Figure 2b).

   Note: If the bolt has a head, you will need to have the fixture you wish to attach already in place on the bolt before passing the toggle through the wall. Then, simply tighten the bolt until it holds firmly against the wall. If possible, though, use a headless bolt.

3. Once the toggle arms are pushed through the wall, they will open up and catch behind the wall (Figure 2c). Pull the bolt forward so the arms grip against the inside of the wall.

4. Slide on the attachment (if you are using a headless bolt). This may be a hook, a shelf arm, or some other fixture.

5. Tighten the bolt to the wall by screwing until you feel resistance (Figure 2d). The bolt should hold firmly against the wall.

Refinish Wood Furniture

Refinishing a favorite piece of wood furniture can add beauty and versatility to your home. Determine first whether refinishing is possible—and whether you can do it suitably at home or would be better off with the services of a professional. Don't try to refinish fragile veneers at home.

Many procedures involved in refinishing are discussed here; use only those that apply to your furniture. Remember that the substances used in refinishing are dangerous—follow all directions on containers carefully, and protect yourself with proper clothing (long sleeves), goggles, a respirator mask, and gloves.

Work outside, if possible; if not, choose a dust-free room with good ventilation so that fumes will diffuse quickly. Cover the work area with dropcloths or newsprint to protect floors. As always, properly dispose of toxic materials—*never* flush them down a drain. Do not wash oil-soaked clothes or rags in a washer/dryer; they could start a fire.

Preparing to Refinish

1. Repair cracks in the wood and get the piece in good structural condition.

2. Remove handles and knobs, but not hinges.

3. Clean the wood. Use vinegar if the wood is only slightly dirty, and a solution of detergent and water if dirt is deep and extensive. Sponge the entire surface with the solution and scrub with a small brush. Rinse with water and dry with a cloth rag.

4. Strip the paint. There are many techniques to remove paint from furniture. Try a double-edge scraper if you are familiar with its use; improper use may gouge the wood. Heat stripping is done with a blow lamp; again, use of this tool without proper experience can be dangerous and harmful to the furniture. If you use this method, keep a fire extinguisher handy, and remove superfluous flammables from the room. Chemical paint removers, available in stores or homemade with caustic soda (lye) and water, are probably your best bet. Brush on paint remover evenly and do not splash or splatter it. Leave the room until the paint begins to bubble up, then return and scrape the paint off with a stripping knife. Apply caustic soda with a sponge and rub it in until the paint becomes frothy and dissolves. Use these chemicals with caution and read all directions carefully. Do not dispose of toxic materials improperly: read the product labels for disposal instructions. Do not allow lighted matches or smoking when using volatile chemicals.

5. Remove the varnish. Old finish will have to be taken off before you add a new finish. You may need to try more than one removal technique before you are successful. First, try to rub turpentine or a small amount of denatured alcohol or ammonia liquid into the wood with fine steel wool. Commercially available wood strippers are likely to be effective as well. Use a small brush to reach carvings and crevices.

6. Sand the wood. Stripping causes the wood's grain to raise, making sanding necessary. When the wood is dry, sand the entire surface of the wood, using a piece of coarse sandpaper wrapped in a sanding block. Sand in the direction of the grain, and be careful not to dull edges or scratch glass and metal parts. When you are finished, sand again with a fine grade of sandpaper to smooth the wood.

7. Fill in the pores. Because staining wood also causes the wood's grain to raise, it's a good idea to fill the wood's pores beforehand (unless you like the natural, rough texture). Use ready-made wood filler (or make your own with plaster of Paris) applied in circles and against the grain so it wedges into the wood. Then rub the wood along the grain to smooth it, and leave the piece to dry.

Staining

Stains color the wood but leave the grain visible. You may use either a water-based stain or an oil-based stain. Water stains are easy to use and quick to dry but can be uneven and loosen the glue on the wood. Oil stains are brushed thoroughly onto the wood, then the excess stain is wiped off. Let the wood dry, and stain it again to darken the color.

Refinishing

There are many different finishing possibilities, depending on your needs and preferences. Use oil, wax, or varnish for everyday furniture, and French polish for fine furniture. You may also choose to paint the furniture.

✓ **Oil**. Use oil alone or on top of varnish. You may have to re-oil once in a while because oil is not a very strong finish. Linseed oil mixed with turpentine is commonly used, especially for woods such as oak. Rub in the oil with a cloth until it stops sinking into the wood. Let the oil soak in for a few hours, then remove the excess and allow the wood to dry.

✓ **Wax.** Wax goes either directly on the wood or on top of a sealer. Use beeswax or carnauba wax mixed with turpentine and heated to a softened paste consistency. Apply the wax thickly on the wood, let it dry, then polish the wood to a shine.

✓ **Varnish.** Synthetic polyurethane varnish creates a strong finish on wood, while shellac allows the wood to breathe better. Brush on varnish evenly and completely, allow the wood to dry, then sand the wood with fine sandpaper or steel wool. Add more layers of varnish for a stronger finish, and polish with linseed oil.

✓ **French polish**. French polish is the most difficult and least durable finish to use, but it gives the most beautiful shine, especially to close-grained woods like ebony and mahogany. Keep a French-polished surface out of the sun, which will crack it, and away from alcohol, which will stain it. Before adding polish, make sure the wood is free of dust, well sanded, and completely sealed. Apply the polish lightly and evenly in circles. Add linseed oil if the polish does not sink in. Let the polish dry for 24 hours, then wipe the wood with denatured alcohol.

See "Repair Nicks in Furniture."

Hire a Contractor

If you plan to redo a room, build an extension, or landscape a yard, you must confront the task of hiring a contractor. Finding the right company for the job takes a good degree of common sense and caution, particularly if you're prepared to sink a large amount of money into the work. A little luck won't hurt either. Here are some ways to reduce potential problems:

1. **Ask around.** Often the best way to find a good contractor is through the recommendations of friends, co-workers, or relatives. If they have had a good experience working with a company, chances are that you will too. Consult local consumer organizations such as your area Home Improvement Commission or Better Business Bureau. Beyond that, a good place to start is the Yellow Pages.

2. **Get estimates.** Call three or four companies with experience in the work you're interested in having done. Ask each to supply you with the names of previous clients who have had similar work done. If possible, call those clients to get their input and visit them to assess the quality of the work done. Get promising contractors to come to your home or office to give you an estimate of how much they will charge for your job and how long it will take to complete. Ask for a formal written estimate with a complete itemized breakdown of services, supplies, costs, and delivery dates.

4. **Decide.** Consider all the available information when making your decision: What's the best price? Who has the best references? Who will get the job done quickest? Who seems the most professional? Weigh the intangibles: Who are you going to be most comfortable working with? Remember, it's important that you feel comfortable with the contractors you hire, especially if they will be working inside your home or workplace.

5. **Negotiate the contract.** Any contract you sign should specify price, job to be done, date of completion (with possible penalties for late completion), plus materials, design, and warranty. In addition, there should be at least a general understanding about how many workers will be allowed into your house or office, and when during the day they will work. If possible, be there while the work is being done. When you sign the contract, you have hired the contractor. Work should begin immediately unless there is a specified delay.

Get a House Inspected

If you are buying a residence of any kind, it is the responsibility of the seller to provide a basic home inspection at no cost to you. If you are selling a house, you are responsible for providing such a report if the buyer requests it. Generally, the sale is not fulfilled until the report has been reviewed and accepted. In either case, the inspection should be made by an experienced engineer who is qualified to report on the condition of all the major structural and mechanical components of the building. It is the right of the home buyer to discuss any and all aspects of the report with the inspector. Home buyers can also call in their own architect or engineer to inspect the property at the home buyer's expense. It is good practice to do so.

If you want a home inspection, either to buy or sell a house or to determine whether any of a home's features are unsafe or undesirable, get in touch with the

American Society of Home Inspectors. Almost any realtor or home builder will have names and phone numbers of local ASHI members on file.

A typical inspection covers the following:

- ✓ **Grading** around the building, including drainage, major plantings, and the condition of driveways, walks, patios, and retaining walls.
- ✓ **Sprinkler system,** if one exists, and other outside water systems.
- ✓ **Building exterior**, including the foundation, sidewalls, exterior finish, doors, windows, flashings, screens, porches, decks, and evidence of rotting or cracking.
- ✓ **Roof** and all its elements, such as peaks and valleys, ridge poles, shingling, gutters, flashing, chimneys, skylights, and downspouts.
- ✓ **Kitchen**, including cabinets, flooring, sinks, plumbing, and all appliances and other built-in equipment.
- ✓ **Electrical system** (with the exception of wiring or cables that cannot be seen or easily reached) and related components such as wall switches, outlets, circuit boxes, meters, grounding, and lighting.
- ✓ **Heating and air-conditioning equipment**, ducts, safety switches, water heaters, ventilation, fans, and related plumbing.
- ✓ **Basement**, especially interior foundations, drainage, dampness and mold, and ceiling beams.
- ✓ **Plumbing**, water distribution, piping, drains, toilets, lavatories, tubs, sinks, showers, laundry equipment, hardware, water pressure, sewage disposal, septic tanks, pumps, hose connections, and water storage.
- ✓ **Attics**, mainly with respect to ceiling leaks, ventilation, fire hazards, rafters, stairs, water condensation, chimneys, ducts, and insulation.
- ✓ **Alarm systems** for security and safety.
- ✓ **Interior room features**, including ceilings, walls, flooring, finishes, wall coverings, windows, fireplaces, carpeting, ventilation, heating and air-conditioning outlets, electrical switches and outlets, doors, tiling, stairways, hardware, and millwork.

If you are interested in specific areas of your home for your own information but do not want to hire an engineer/inspector, you can compile a considerable amount of useful data through other sources. It is more than likely, for example, that your local utility will make a free inspection of elements with which it is directly concerned, such as heating, air conditioning, water heaters, and other equipment whose energy sources are electricity, natural gas, propane, or petroleum. Utilities, particularly cooperatives, are continually interested in improving home efficiency and cutting energy demands.

Other useful information can be obtained through inspections by building contractors, architectural suppliers, and others on whom you would call for home improvements. Although many will provide useful information and suggestions, you also have to bear in mind that they have a vested interest in promoting their business and may embellish their recommendations for what needs to be done to improve your home.

Change an Air-Conditioner Filter

One of the simplest and least expensive—yet most vital—elements in any heating or air-conditioning system is the filter. Its purpose is to make sure air that enters the system and the rooms in your home is clean and free of dust or other impurities. A dirty filter can cause excessive strain on the compressor and blower motor that make up the heart of your cooling equipment, often causing the components to overheat and automatically shut down.

If your air conditioner (A/C) is used regularly during hot weather to remove excess moisture from the air, or as a heating unit in cold weather, the filter should be checked about once a month. Look for grease, lint, or a heavy accumulation of dust. Since filters cost only about $2 each and can be purchased at any hardware store and many supermarkets, replacement is advisable if the filter looks at all clogged or damaged. Filters come in standard sizes but can also be cut with scissors to fit, if the store does not carry the exact size you want. Filters are made of disposable fibers and require no gloves, glasses, or other protective devices when handled.

Most filters can be washed with soap or detergent and warm water and reused. However, washed filters must be *completely dry* before they are reinstalled to prevent moisture from being drawn into the ducts.

Where is the filter located? Your owner's manual will indicate the exact location. If the A/C is in the attic, the filter is usually housed in a grill on the ceiling or a side wall. It is about 1" thick and ranges in size from 18" × 24" to 20" × 30". The size is marked on the edge, and the internal portion is a plastic or metal mesh designed to catch dust, insects, soot, and other tiny particles. If your A/C is in the basement or a closet, the filter is often attached to the intake (or return air) duct of the unit, referred to as a plenum. You can distinguish this grill from the ones located in each room that furnish cool air—or heat in the case of heat-pump machines—because it sucks air in. If you place a piece of tissue against the grill when the A/C is in operation, it will be held in place rather than blown away.

Filters can be removed quickly and easily. Ceiling or wall units are housed in grills held in place by small catches or thumb screws. When these are loosened, the filter holder swings open like a small door. Filters attached directly to the blower unit of the A/C are generally located right behind a hinged panel. In either case, lift or slide the dirty filter out and insert the new one.

If you have a window air conditioner, the filter is small, easily accessible and probably washable. Your owner's manual will provide easy-to-follow instructions.

Clean Hardwood Floors

Wood floors either have a hard-coat varnish, shellac, or urethane finish, an oil or stain finish, or are painted. The process for cleaning and maintaining each is different.

Hard-coat Finish

These wood floors always have a high gloss and do not need to be waxed. Clean them with mild dishwashing liquid and warm water. Scrub the floor in sections with a well-wrung cloth, and wipe dry immediately to prevent spotting or warping. Do not pull furniture across a hard-coat finish; such floors scratch easily. A strong tea solution can be used occasionally in place of the dishwashing liquid to return some color to the floor.

Oil or Stain Finish

Clean these floors only when absolutely necessary with the hardwood floor cleaners available in hardware stores. Maintain them by sweeping and dust-mopping regularly and by evenly applying thin coats of paste floor wax along the wood grain and buffing with an electric buffer. Spots or stains can be scrubbed out by dipping fine steel wool in paste wax and scrubbing; buff with a soft dry cloth. Never put water or water-based products on an oil- or stain-finished hardwood floor.

Painted Finish

Wash with mild soap and water. Dry thoroughly.

Clean Carpets

As with many household furnishings, keeping carpets and rugs clean and in good condition requires a small amount of regular care and an occasional heavy overhaul. By vacuuming regularly, wiping and sweeping up messes when they occur, and shampooing every few years, your carpet should remain in good shape indefinitely. Simply follow these directions.

Vacuuming

The vacuum cleaner is the basic tool for cleaning carpets. Regular vacuuming not only keeps your carpets dust and dirt free but keeps your home healthy and prolongs carpet life. Clean carpets reduce the chance of allergy flare-ups. Use a vacuum cleaner suited for (or adjusted to) the type of carpet you have. Extension nozzles are helpful for hard-to-reach areas, and hand vacuums or carpet sweepers are convenient for quick cleanups of small areas. Vacuum as often as you find it necessary, but do vacuum at least once a week to keep dust levels low. Vacuum more often in areas of heavy traffic. Use slow, overlapping strokes.

Cleaning Stains

Sometimes stains are easy to wipe up and will not hurt the carpet permanently. Other stains call for damage control—make sure the stain is as small as possible. Work quickly to minimize any harm done. For solid stains, such as food or plaster, first scrape away the solid material with a dull knife. Gently blot the remaining stain with a moist cloth. Do not scrub the area vigorously or wet the carpet excessively—you risk making the stain sink in deeper. If the stain remains, try wiping the area with a small amount of detergent, or with liquid cleaner if it is a grease stain. If you have a spray stain remover, mist it evenly on the stain and allow it to sink in for a few minutes. Then rub the stain with a damp cloth or sponge and allow it to dry. Do not vacuum.

Shampooing

Every year or two, but not much more often than that, it is a good idea to give carpets a thorough shampooing. Do it yourself or hire professionals. Doing it yourself, though exhausting, can save a lot of money. For delicate and valuable carpets, though, it's best to leave the job to professionals.

Rent equipment to make the job easier. A carpet shampooer will help you rub in the shampoo, a task that can otherwise be back-breaking for a large carpet. A wet/dry vacuum allows you to vacuum up shampoo rather than wipe it up with a rag. A steam cleaning machine gives you an altogether deeper cleaning than a shampooing, but it can be difficult to use. Machines can be rented from home or hardware stores and sometimes from grocery stores. Be sure you understand how to operate any piece of equipment before you use it.

Before shampooing, remove all furniture from the area or wrap chair and table legs in plastic to protect them from potentially harmful shampoo chemicals. Make sure the room is well ventilated, both to provide fresh air and to speed up drying. Keep all cleaning materials away from children and out of the eyes, nose, and mouth. Follow all directions on the containers of cleaning products.

Test to make sure the carpet is colorfast by rubbing some shampoo with a clean white rag into an unseen area of the carpet. If the carpet coloring does not bleed onto the rag, begin applying the shampoo with a sponge or mop to one small section at a time. Work in the shampoo with a rag or brush unless you are otherwise instructed. Once the shampoo is sufficiently worked into the carpet, wipe away the excess lather with a rag, and allow the soap to soak in for the appropriate amount of time. This may require several hours, during which time the shampooed area of carpet cannot be walked on. If possible, leave the carpet overnight.

When the shampoo has dried, use a wet sponge to wash away the soap. Do not get the carpet excessively wet, or it could shrink or stain. Once the shampoo has been cleared away as much as possible, wipe the carpet with a dry rag to pick up excess shampoo and to help in drying. Allow the carpet to dry completely, then vacuum thoroughly to pick up any dry detergent and dirt still in the carpet.

Using Spray Carpet Cleaner

Spray or foam carpet cleaner is available in stores that sell cleaning products. It is easier to use than shampoo and more effective than simply vacuuming. Vacuum the area before using spray cleaner to clean the carpet of larger dirt particles, then follow the directions on the can for specific instructions. Most spray cleaners require you to spray the foam evenly on one small area (about 3' × 3') from a distance of about 2 feet, then leave it for two or three hours to dry. For a deeper cleaning, you can spread the foam with a mop or sponge until the foam disappears, then leave the carpet to dry. After a few hours the foam will have dried and will appear to have vanished. Vacuum the area to pick up the dried cleaner and the dirt it has loosened.

Clean Windows

Clean windows can make an entire house look brighter. Of course, some windows are a hassle to clean because they are difficult to reach. A little extra effort, though, will pay off—provided you observe precautions. If done properly, windows only need to be washed every four to six months. Here's how:

Preparation

✓ Determine how you will clean the windows. Are they removable? If not, can you reach them with an extension pole from the ground, or will you need to harness yourself out the window? Keep safety in mind: if you cannot safely reach a window, don't wash it. Hire professional window washers.

✓ Determine whether weather conditions are suitable for cleaning windows from the outside. It's best to work on a warm, dry day. At the very least, make sure it's not going to rain or snow.

✓ To prepare the windows, remove blinds and curtains if they are in the way (or simply open them without removing). Also, clear the windows of any furniture or decorations. If you are working outside, temporarily cover plants below the windows with a plastic tarp to protect them.

✓ Remove window screens if possible, and clean them separately. To clean screens, vacuum them with a brush extension, scrub them with a brush and water, and rinse them with a wet sponge.

✓ Always wear rubber gloves when working with cleaning solutions or ammonia.

Window Cleaning Procedure

For all large glass windows, whether removable or not, the cleaning procedure is essentially the same. The difference lies in how you reach the windows. This is the basic washing technique:

1. Use a strip washer (not wider than the width of the glass) to dip into a bucket of cleaning fluid. The cleaning fluid can be any reputable brand of window or glass cleaner.

2. Wring or shake the washer until it no longer drips fluid.

3. Laying the strip flat on the window glass, wash in long overlapping strips from top to bottom. Rewet the washer if necessary, but try to keep the coat smooth.

4. To dry the window, use a squeegee. Lay the squeegee flat against the glass, and wipe in straight strokes from top to bottom.

5. After each stroke, wipe off the squeegee with a cloth.

6. Wipe any corners or edges the squeegee could not reach with a dry cloth.

Removable Windows

Remove glass windows carefully, using both hands to carry them, and lay them down gently. Windows can often be removed by lifting the bottom of the sash and pulling out at the bottom. Lean the glass against a wall or table with a cloth underneath. Wash and dry one side completely, then turn the glass over and repeat on the other side. Wipe the window frame with a cloth and cleaning fluid, then dry with a clean cloth.

Nonremovable Windows

✓ Washing the outside from the inside: If you can reach the outside of the window from inside the house, wash the outside first. Open the window—from the top if possible—just far enough to let you reach your arm out to wash. Use a stepladder if necessary. Never lean on the window or stick more than your arm outside without using a safety harness.

✓ Washing the outside with an extension pole: If you have an extension pole for your strip washer and squeegee long enough to reach the windows, wash the outside of the windows from the ground below. To avoid dripping cleaning fluid, shake off excess fluid before washing, and stand clear.

Small Window Panes

For windows too small for a strip washer, use a cloth dipped in cleaning fluid to wash the glass. Wipe in a circular motion, then dry with a clean cloth. Or, wipe with newspaper to prevent streaks.

Removing Stains or Dirt on Window

If cleaning fluid is not enough to wash away difficult stains, use a solution of ammonia with water. Keeping face and hands away, pour a splash of ammonia into a bucket of water. With rubber gloves on, dip a clean rag into the solution, wring it out, and apply it to the stain. If necessary, scrub the stain with a soft brush and dry with a clean cloth. If the ammonia solution fails to remove the stain, try to scrape it off with a razor blade tool. Be careful of the blade, though, and be sure not to scratch the window.

Hang Curtains

What Kind of Curtains to Hang?

Panel curtains hang straight next to the glass of the window.

Sash curtains cover the lower half of the window.

Cafe curtains are two-tiered: one for the top and one for the lower half of the window.

Draw curtains hang on pulleys to open and close.

Valances are short, decorative curtain components that cover the tops of curtains or drapes.

Gather Supplies

✓ Curtains (valance optional)
✓ Rods for curtains (and valance)
✓ Brackets (with hardware included) to hang the rods
✓ Curtain rings or hooks, if necessary
✓ Measuring tape
✓ Screwdriver
✓ Pencil

Measure the Window

✓ Width: measure the inside of the window frame
✓ Length: measure from the top of the window to the sill
✓ Standard widths are 25," 48," 72," 96," 120," and 144"; standard lengths are 36," 45," 54," 63," 84," and 90"

Hang the Curtain

1. Decide whether you want the curtain to fall above or below the window sill. Hanging it lower than the sill prevents the edge from attracting sill dust.

2. Slip the curtain on the rod and hold it up to the window so that the edge falls at the desired place.

3. Mark the placement of the rod on the wall with a pencil.

4. Holding the rod at the appropriate height, mark on the wall the location for the brackets.

5. If you are using a valance, this rod will be placed over the curtain rod. Hold both the curtain and valance (on their rods) over the window and make marks on the wall indicating where the brackets should be placed.

6. Use a screwdriver to screw the brackets in place. You may need to make pilot holes; do this by tapping a nail slightly into the wall or using an electric drill to begin a hole.

7. Slip the curtains and valances onto their rods (or use rings or curtain hooks), making sure that all seams face the back of the rod.

8. Hang the rods on the brackets. The curtain seams should be facing the window.

9. Spread the curtain across the rod so that gathers and pleats look evenly distributed.

10. If you've purchased a "pouf" valance, fill it with lightly crumpled tissue paper.

Patch a Hole in the Wall

Whether the hole is a large break in the wall made by accident or a small nail hole, there's no reason why you should let it go unrepaired. The process is quick and easy. All you need is a spackling knife and enough joint (spackling) compound to cover the hole. Depending on the size of the hole, here's what you do:

Small Holes (Nail Holes, Nicks)

1. **Fill in the hole**. Spread joint compound into the hole with a spackling knife until the hole is filled and use the knife to smooth the compound to the wall.

2. **Let dry**. The time it takes to dry depends on the amount of compound you use; for a small hole allow a few hours.

3. **Sand.** When the compound has dried, sand it by hand until the hole is smooth and flush with the surface of the wall.

4. **Paint.** Paint over the hole with the same paint used for the wall.

Medium Holes (about 1" in diameter)

1. **Remove loose plaster.** Use a knife to clean the hole of any loose material and smooth the edges of the hole.

2. **Stuff the hole with newspaper or patching plaster.** This is not necessary if the hole is shallow, but putting newspaper or plaster into deeper holes will conserve the amount of compound you need to use. Plaster will also make the repair stronger.

3. **Fill in the hole.** Whatever space is remaining in the hole should be filled with spackling compound. Compound should be spread around the outside as well, to cover up the edges of the hole.

4. **Let dry**. Leave it most of the day or overnight.

5. **Sand**. Sand by hand until the compound is flush with the wall surface.

6. **Paint.** Paint the area the same color as the rest of the wall.

Large Holes (1" to 6"; larger holes require new wallboard)

1. **Follow steps 1–3.** See "Medium Holes," above.

2. **Apply joint tape.** Get a strip of mesh joint tape large enough to cover the hole, and press it down evenly and firmly on top of the hole. Use a joint knife to get the tape smooth with the surface of the wall.

3. **Cover with compound.** Add a thin coat of spackling compound to hide the tape. You may add another piece of tape on top for extra support, but it is probably not necessary. If you do use more tape, be sure to cover it with compound also.

4. **Let dry.** Leave the compound overnight to dry.

5. **Sand.** Sand the repair by hand, making sure not to put too much pressure on the spot and not to sand down so far that the tape becomes exposed. If the tape does begin to show, cover it with compound, and sand the area again after it dries.

6. **Paint.** If the hole is large and conspicuously located, it may be a good idea to paint the entire wall again. Otherwise, simply paint the repaired area with the same color paint as the wall.

Paint a Room

Interior house painting is one of the classic do-it-yourself home improvements. It's simple, easy, and relatively inexpensive. Safety precautions are few: Make sure there is plenty of ventilation in the room to disperse the smell of the paint fumes; consider wearing a surgical mask, gloves, and goggles if you are working with strong substances. Put on a hat and old clothes you don't mind getting paint on. If the job is big, consider inviting friends and family over to help you.

Preparation

1. Remove as much furniture as possible from the room. Take out rugs, chairs, wall decorations, and appliances. If any furniture or item is too big or too heavy to remove easily, push it to the center of the room so you can reach the walls easily (Figure 1).

2. Cover remaining furniture and unremovable wall attachments. Use a drop-cloth to completely cover everything in the room: furniture, floors, ceiling fixtures, radiators—whatever won't be painted. Dropcloths can be old sheets you don't use any more, plastic coverings available in hardware or paint stores, or simply newspaper (newspaper can smudge surfaces, so be careful where you use it).

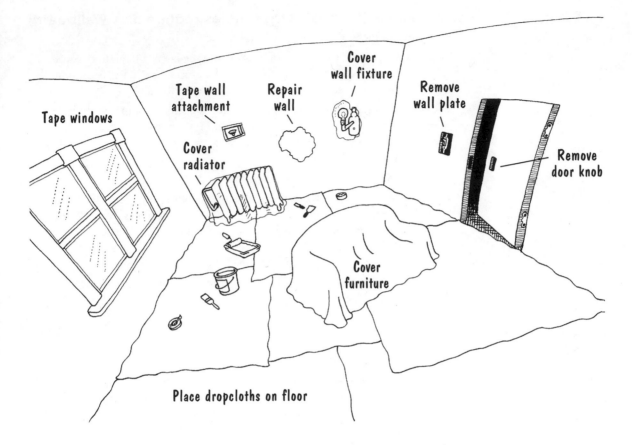

Tape windows

Tape wall attachment

Cover radiator

Repair wall

Cover wall fixture

Remove wall plate

Remove door knob

Cover furniture

Place dropcloths on floor

Figure 1. Preparation for painting

3. Remove hardware. Door knobs and electrical wall plates should be unscrewed and kept handy. Although it may seem like an unnecessary hassle, removing these items will save you from having to maneuver around them later. **Before you take off wall plates, make sure you shut off the room's electric supply (circuit breaker or fuse)**; if necessary, turn the power back on once you've removed the plates, but keep children away from the exposed sockets at all times. Also, remember to paint the wall plates separately before putting them back on the wall.

4. Repair cracks in the walls. Small nicks or bumps may simply require sanding. Small indentations can also be spackled. (For larger wall repairs, see "Patch a Hole in the Wall.") Scrape and sand wall irregularities. Any repair should be made at least a day before you plan to paint, to allow the plaster to settle and dry.

5. Dust and clean the walls. With a dust brush or dry rag, wipe the surface of the walls and ceiling to remove any superficial dirt or dust that has accumulated. For a more thorough cleaning, wash walls with a cloth rag and water (or water and a light detergent). This is probably unnecessary, but if you decide to do it, let the walls dry for a day or two before you paint. Sand any high-gloss finish before painting, to enable the new coat of paint to take hold. Dust it carefully before repainting.

6. Paint over stains on the walls. For stains that can't be wiped off, it may be necessary to prepaint these areas with a primer. Some people paint the entire room with an initial coat of primer before applying the final coat of latex paint. This is advisable only if the walls have never been painted before, if a significant color change is made, or if the walls are completely covered with stains and discolorations.

7. Tape windows and fixtures that cannot be removed. Using masking tape, cover the area where the glass meets the window frame, leaving about a $\frac{1}{16}$" gap so that when you paint you'll create an air-tight seal between the glass and frame. Tape other objects you don't want to paint, such as door hinges.

Painting

1. Collect materials: paint, rollers, and brushes. For most plaster and wallboard rooms, use a flat latex paint. In rooms exposed to moisture, dirt, or fumes, a semigloss paint provides more protection and can be wiped clean more easily. One gallon of paint should be more than enough for the average-sized bedroom. Use rollers with extensions to reach ceilings and short-napped nylon roller covers for painting smooth, flat walls. Use 1" to 3" brushes for corners and trim.

2. Mix the paint. Pry open the paint can with a screwdriver. With a wooden paint mixer, stir the paint until it is the same consistency throughout. Consider using disposable liners in your paint trays to make cleanup easier.

3. Paint the ceiling corners. Always paint top to bottom, ceiling to baseboards; and always paint the corners (edges) of a room first. Therefore, start with the edges where the ceiling meets the walls, painting a 2" margin all the way around with a brush.

4. Paint the ceiling. Using the roller with its extension, apply an even coat of paint to the ceiling in a repeating zig-zag pattern. If the ceiling is large, do one section at a time, overlapping sections as you go. Start each freshly loaded roller in an unpainted area and roll it into a painted area to ensure an even coat.

5. Paint wall corners. Use your brush to create a 2" margin, as with the ceiling corners.

6. Paint the walls. One at a time, paint each wall in the same way you painted the ceiling, moving the roller in an overlapping zig-zag pattern. Start with the top of the wall and paint down from there.

7. Paint the woodwork. Doors, baseboards, window frames, and other wood-work should be painted with semigloss paint. Use a brush for small areas; if you use the same brush as before, make sure it is thoroughly clean so as not to mix the flat and semigloss paints. Remove the door from its hinges to paint its bottom edge only if the door has never been painted before.

8. Check the walls for missed spots. Inspect the walls in the light to make sure you haven't left areas unpainted. If you have, paint them immediately before the surrounding paint dries.

9. Clean up. Be as neat as possible. Don't touch the walls. Allow at least three or four hours for paint to dry before you begin to remove coverings and tape, reinstall hardware, and return the furniture to its place.

Note: If you need to stop in the middle of a paint job, wrap the brushes and roller in aluminum foil or in plastic wrap or bags. Securely cover the paint tray with foil or plastic wrap, and reseal the paint can. For breaks of more than an hour or so, store wrapped brushes and rollers in the freezer, and pour any paint in the tray back into the paint can and reseal.

Wallpaper a Room

Before you start wallpapering, complete all washing and painting of the wood-work in the room to be papered. In that way you won't have to worry as much about an even paint job along the edges that will be covered by the paper, and you won't have to work around paper that has been freshly hung.

Another prepapering priority is to make sure the surfaces to which the paper will adhere are smooth and devoid of cracks. Sand down any rough spots. Use spack-le or some other finishing compound to fill in cracks and holes. These flaws may look trivial, but they can ruin the appearance of the paper over a long time.

When selecting the pattern, bear in mind where the new paper will be placed. If the room has uneven or slanted corners and projections, you need to calibrate patterns carefully at every seam to avoid mismatching. Use good judgment: don't select an oversize design for small wall spaces, or tiny patterns for large expanses.

When buying wallpaper, describe the size and surfaces of the room to the shop manager. Ask to see the types of paper most appropriate and the easiest to hang. Request prepasted wallpaper that is trimmed or can be trimmed at the shop. This will save you a lot of work.

You will need the following tools and items of equipment:

✓ Long work table, which can be improvised by positioning a panel of plywood over two saw horses or sturdy chairs
✓ Stepladder high enough to reach the ceiling easily and steadily
✓ Seam roller for smoothing the paper onto the wall

✓ Long scissors
✓ Metal straightedge
✓ Large sponge
✓ Razor or very sharp knife
✓ White paper toweling
✓ Water tray
✓ Yardstick or measuring tape
✓ Large T square
✓ Carpenter's level
✓ Brush

When you start the job, make sure all surfaces to be wallpapered are dry, smooth, and even. If the wall has new plaster or plaster that seems powdery, apply wallpaper sizing. This can easily and quickly be brushed on and will help the paper adhere to the wall. If the plaster or other wall surface is glossy, sand it lightly to improve adhesion.

Now comes the precision part, which will determine whether the results look amateurish or professional. Measure the exact height and width of the largest wall you will be papering. Cut sections of the paper in the correct length. Make sure the patterns fit properly as you hang the paper—generally from left to right on the wall. The easiest method for beginners is to hang the paper first with transparent tape or pushpins and mark the places where each sheet will fit against the next, working from left to right. With this method, cutting, trimming, and fitting can be done more precisely. To make sure the pattern is correct, both horizontally and vertically, use a carpenter's level. If you do not have a level, simply place a thumbtack or pushpin at the top of the wall and hang a piece of string from it with a weight at the bottom. This will give you an accurate vertical line.

Now for booking, or preparing strips for easy handling. Roll the strip of prepasted paper with the pattern facing inward. Soak it in the water tray, completely submerged, for the length of time specified by the manufacturer. Hold the corner ends of the strip and gently pull it out of the water tray. Drain excess water.

Lay the paper stretched out, adhesive side up, on your prep table until half the paper covers the table. Fold one end into the center, adhesive to adhesive, and align; don't press or crease the paper. Repeat with the second half of the paper strip. Double the paper once more, folding over the folds.

To hang wallpaper, take one end of the booked strip, open the top fold, and place it even with the top of the wall. The edges should fold over at least 2" onto the ceiling, over the bottom onto the baseboard, and around the corner to the adjacent wall. Smooth with the brush from the ceiling line to the corner and down to the center, removing all air bubbles. Peel the bottom half loose, align, and brush from center to bottom. Add new strips by matching patterns; trim at ceilings and baseboards with a knife or straightedge. To roll seams, wait at least 15 minutes, then, roll up or down from the center. Sponge off excess adhesive.

Unclog a Drain

Maintain your drains by cleaning them regularly. Install a stopper in the bathroom drains to block hair and soap and in the kitchen to block food. If a clog does begin to form, clear it immediately before the problem gets worse.

Boiling Water

1. Check other drains to determine whether the clog is local or in the main drain of the house. If other drains are not stopped up, the clog is probably in the drainpipe of the sink or tub, and not far enough into the plumbing system to disturb other pipes.
2. Pour boiling water down the clogged drain. This is a quick and often effective way to break simple blocking caused by grease buildup—it may be all you need to do. Be very careful not to burn yourself. If the boiling water does not clear up the clog, try one of the techniques explained below.

Plunger

A plunger is the safest and easiest device for unclogging a drain. For the plunger to be effective, its suction cup must be large enough to cover the drain completely, and the water level of the backup must be above the top of the suction cup.

1. Remove the drain plug or strainer from the drain.
2. Block off the overflow, and any other outlets to the same drain.
3. Line the rim of the suction cup with petroleum jelly to ensure a tight seal.
4. Place the suction cup of the plunger into the water at an angle to prevent air from being trapped underneath.
5. Cover the drain with the plunger cup.
6. Holding the plunger handle straight up, pump the plunger ten to twenty times with short, fast, forceful strokes.
7. On the final stroke, pull the plunger away and out of the water quickly.
8. Repeat a few times if the first attempt is unsuccessful. If the clog persists, try another technique.

Chemical Drain Cleaner

Chemical drain cleaner can be very dangerous if used improperly, so read all directions carefully (both here and on the container) before you begin. Chemicals should not be used if the clog is complete—caustic chemicals could back up into your sink or tub and ruin the finish, and they should not be used often because they will damage pipes. Be sure the room is well ventilated; keep your eyes, nose, and mouth away from the chemicals; and keep your hands protected with rubber gloves.

1. Use the correct type of cleaner. Alkalis are good for cutting grease, while acids work best for unclogging soap and hair. Never mix alkalis with acids—you risk creating an explosion.

2. Read the directions for use on the container.

3. Pour the required amount of chemical cleaner down the drain.

4. Let the cleaner settle for a while.

5. Check to see whether the chemicals have worked by running water down the drain. If the clogging continues, call a plumber.

As always, it is best to avoid using harsh chemicals in the house whenever possible. To keep your drains clear, flush the drains each week with 1 cup of baking soda followed by 1 cup of vinegar. While they are foaming, turn on the hot water and rinse it through.

Unstuff the Toilet

No plumbing task is very pleasant, but unclogging a toilet is perhaps the least desirable of them all. Take heart, though: most toilet clogs can be repaired quickly and easily, using either a plunger or a closet auger (snake). If your toilet clogs, don't try to flush it or it may overflow. If the toilet does overflow, turn off the water or raise the flush mechanism to stop the water flow. Here's how to handle the clog.

Using a Plunger

A plunger should be your first tool for trying to unstuff the toilet. Plungers with funnel cups on the end are specially designed for toilets, though regular plungers will work as well. There should be enough water in the bowl to cover the cup of the plunger.

1. Fit the lip of the plunger over the flush drain.

2. Use a firm and steady up-and-down motion to pump the plunger ten to fifteen times in rapid succession. This will often be enough to push the blockage through and fix the clog. If the water in the toilet flushes, the clog has been cleared.

3. If the clog has not cleared, continue pumping the plunger over the drain for five to ten more minutes. If the water level is slowly falling, continue plunging—you are making progress. If the clog remains, try to use an auger, or call a professional plumber.

Using a Closet Auger (Snake)

Unlike other augers, the closet auger is specially designed not to scratch the toilet bowl.

1. Feed the end of the snake into the flush drain until it won't go any farther.

2. Crank the handle of the auger clockwise to push the snake farther into the drain. Keep cranking until you push the blockage through. Tighten the handle screw on the auger as you crank.

3. Occasionally jiggle the snake back and forth while cranking in order to loosen the block.

4. When you think you have cranked far enough to have reached the clog, turn the auger handle counterclockwise to pull the snake back. If the clog has been pushed on through the pipes, the bowl will flush. As you pull the snake out of the drain, you may bring some of the blockage out with it. Have a bucket ready to catch the blockage material when you pull the snake out of the toilet.

5. If you are still unable to unstuff the toilet, the problem may be deeper in the pipes. Call a professional plumber.

Preventive Tips

✓ Never flush feminine hygiene products or paper products other than toilet tissue unless the product packaging indicates it can be flushed safely.
✓ Place a foil-wrapped brick or an empty quart-size glass jar in the bottom of the tank to conserve water usage.
✓ Don't try to loosen clogs with wire hangers. Wire can scratch the bowl and create permanent stains.

See "Unclog a Drain."

Repair Nicks in Furniture

Unlike furniture made of metal or plastic, wood furniture is highly susceptible to nicks by sharp objects. If the nick is not much more than a scratch, it sometimes can be sanded away without making a noticeable change in the surface. If the nick is deeper, though, you may need to take further action. There are two main ways to repair nicks in wood. Both are fairly simple and inexpensive.

Repairing Nicks with Wood Putty

Materials: putty knife, wood putty (available at hardware stores), sandpaper, stain or paint.

1. Use the putty knife to scoop some putty out of the container. Put more than enough putty on the blade to fill up the nick.

2. Apply the putty into the nick, filling in the entire area. Allow the putty to cover above the surface of the wood.

3. Let the putty dry for a few hours (according to the directions on the putty container).

4. Sand the nick down to flatten the surface. The putty should become flush with the wood.

5. Finish the area with stain or paint to match the rest of the wood. If the furniture piece is small, it may be a good idea to refinish the entire piece to ensure an even coat.

Repairing Nicks by Patching

Materials: chisel, scrap wood, pencil, wood glue, weight, sandpaper, stain or paint.

1. Cut a small wedge of wood out of a scrap that is the same kind of wood as the nicked furniture. Cut so that it is close to the same size as the nick, and also so the grain moves in the same direction.

2. Lay the wedge on top of the nick to match its size. It may be necessary to chisel the nick to make it larger so the wedge will fit. Use a pencil to trace the wedge around the nick so you know how much to chisel.

3. Chisel the wood, being careful not to scratch the wood or cut too much.

4. Apply a small amount of glue to the bottom of the wedge. Too much glue will cause leaks on the wood surface and create a mess.

5. Place the wedge into the dug-out nick area. Hold down the patch with a heavy weight.

6. Allow a few hours for the glue to dry completely before removing the weight.

7. Sanding may be necessary to smooth the surface completely.

8. Use stain or paint to match the color of the area to the rest of the piece. Refinish the whole piece, if necessary.

See "Refinish Wood Furniture."

Prepare for and Respond to a Blackout

While power failures occur most often during heavy electrical storms, they can also happen as a result of a technical problem at your local power company or even from a freak accident involving workers in the neighborhood. You can never really know when a blackout will occur.

How to Prepare

Have flashlights handy. Strategically place several flashlights around the house. At the very least, have flashlights in the bedrooms, in the kitchen, and in the basement. Attach them to the wall, or keep them in a drawer or closet where they are easy to reach and you won't forget about them.

Have a supply of batteries. All flashlights, of course, should have strong, fresh batteries in them. Put batteries in any other appliances that will accept them, such as radios, clocks, and small televisions. Check these batteries every month or two, especially if you normally run the appliances with electricity. Keep a few unopened packs of good batteries in an easily accessible place at all times.

Program important numbers into the phone. Remember, there's always 911 in case of an emergency that threatens your life or safety.

How to Respond

Keep the family together. This is particularly important if you have young children, for the whole family must stay together during a blackout. Children might be afraid and need comforting, and allowing them to roam around in a dark house could be dangerous.

Check the circuit breaker. If all the power has gone off in your house, chances are the problem does not lie in a jumped circuit breaker. Still, it doesn't hurt to check. Retrieve your flashlight. Go down to the basement and make sure all circuits are connected. If you have a fuse box, make sure none of the fuses have burned out. (See "Change a Fuse.")

Call the neighbors. Look outside at other houses to see whether the power failure affects your whole street. If you're not sure, call a neighbor and ask if their power has gone out. If it has, you can be fairly certain the blackout is due to wire trouble outside your house.

What to Do If the Blackout Continues

Ignite fire lamps or candles. Use a safe fire lamp or lantern, if you have one, for a more permanent light source than a flashlight. If you must use candles, do not leave them unguarded. Place them in jars or clear glass cups where they can burn more safely and without dripping.

Build a fireplace fire. If you have electric heat the house may start to get cold. If you have a fireplace, start a fire for heat, a good light source, and entertainment for the family. (See "Build and Light a Fireplace Fire.")

Have an activity prepared. Blackouts can occasionally last a long while. Read children a story, play a board game, or play cards to pass the time. Whatever you do, include everyone.

Have dry food available. If a blackout lasts more than a few hours you will need to eat. Avoid opening the refrigerator or freezer as long as possible so cold air won't escape, and close it quickly if you do need to open it. Have foods in the house that do not need preparing, such as fruit, vegetables, crackers, and peanut butter.

Change a Fuse

A fuse is a safety device found on electric circuits. When an electric current becomes too strong, a fuse will melt and disconnect the circuit. In a house, a shorted fuse will cause some or all of the electricity to go out until the fuse is replaced. Thanks to the modern circuit breakers in most newer houses, though, fuses are a dying breed, and as fuses become less and less common, fewer people know how to change them. But people who live in older houses need to know how to change a fuse. If you are ignorant about circuit breakers, read carefully: you never know when you'll find yourself in an old house during a power failure.

1. Locate the service box. The service box stores the fuses (or circuit breakers) for all the electrical circuits in the house. It is usually about a foot tall and has a door or cover. In a house, it is almost always located on a wall in the basement.

2. Inspect the fuses. Open the box and look at the fuses. Most fuses in homes are plug fuses, which look like small, flat, round pieces of glass with a metal strip inside. Other fuses may be cylinder-shaped cartridge fuses. These must be removed with fuse pliers, available at hardware stores.

3. Locate the burnt or melted fuse. A burnt fuse has a smoky, dark appearance. This indicates a short circuit, which may mean faulty wiring. In this event, you may want to have an electrician do a home inspection to isolate any hazards or problems in the making. A melted fuse, whose metal strip is disconnected, indicates an overloaded circuit and must simply be replaced. If the circuit has been overloaded, use fewer appliances in the same electrical outlet or circuit. Turn off electrical switches before replacing the fuse.

4. Disconnect the main switch. To avoid electrocution, make sure your hands and the floor under you and your hands are completely dry. Disconnect the main circuit by pulling the fuse blocks labeled "main."

5. Unscrew the fuse. It should not be hot. Don't touch it if it is.

6. Replace the fuse. Into the same spot where you removed the burnt fuse, screw in a new fuse. Be sure that the new fuse has the appropriate rating for the circuit; it must have whatever rating the burnt fuse had. Fuses will be labeled according to rating and can be bought inexpensively at most hardware stores. Be sure to keep plenty in the house in case of an emergency.

7. Reconnect the main switch. The circuit should now be working.

8. If problems persist, call an electrician.

Change the Washer in a Sink Faucet

Common kitchen and bathroom faucets, if they have separate hot and cold twist-on controls, are compression faucets. Compression faucets are generally trouble free and long lasting. A problem is often something as minor as a drip at the spout or a leaky handle. Usually, a leak simply means that a rubber piece in the faucet—either a washer (if the leak is at the spout) or an O-ring (if the leak is at the handle)—is worn and must be replaced. The process is quick and easy. Here's what to do.

Tools: screwdriver, pliers, utility knife, wrench, heatproof grease.

Parts: replacement washer or O-ring (from a universal washer kit).

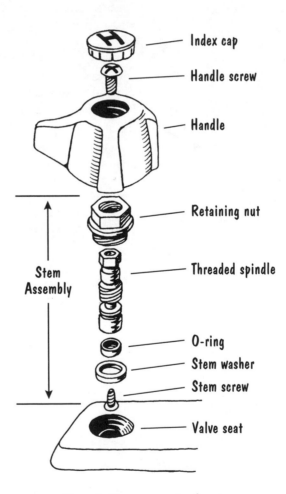

Figure 1. The compression faucet

Turn Off the Water Supply

Take the faucet apart. With the right tools, taking apart the faucet should be fairly simple. Remember where all the parts go, and make sure you don't end up with parts left over (Figure 1).

1. Remove the index cap with a knife or screwdriver. You may need to either pry it off or screw it off.

2. Unscrew the handle screw with a screwdriver.

3. Remove the handle. If the handle is stuck, you may need a special tool called a handle puller to force the handle off, but you should be able to pry it loose without too much effort.

4. Remove the stem assembly. This part consists of the retaining nut, the spindle, an O-ring, a washer, and a screw.

Replace the Necessary Piece

In the universal washer kit, available at hardware stores, find a piece that is exactly the same shape as the worn piece, either the O-ring or the washer. The kit will have many different types of neoprene (rubber) washers, O-rings, and screws. Apply a small amount of grease to the new part, and then use it to replace the worn part.

Reattach the Faucet

Simply reverse the process of taking the faucet apart. Make sure all the pieces fit back together tightly and correctly. When the faucet is back together, turn the water supply back on and test for leaks. If problems persist, the faucet may be damaged in other ways. Consult a plumber.

Lay Floor Tiles

Installing 9" and 12" vinyl composition or solid vinyl square tiles has become much easier in recent years because of the availability of self-stick backings and easy-to-apply adhesive.

1. Make sure the surface floor to which the tiles will be attached is clean and smooth. Level any low spots with filler. If the floor is made up of strips or planks, you should add an underlay of plywood, leveled and attached firmly.

2. Find the square footage of the room by multiplying the length by the width. Add 5 percent for extra tiles you may need for mistakes or odd shapes that will need to be cut.

3. Determine the midpoints of the width and length, and snap a chalk line between each of the opposing sides. Make sure that the lines intersect at right angles. Lay the tiles out dry in one area, starting at the chalk intersection, and adjust the border rows so that each will have the same width.

4. If the tiles are self-adhering, simply remove the protective backing and put the tiles down, starting at the intersection of the chalk lines. If you are laying the tiles in adhesive, follow the instructions on the container. Work in small areas and butt the joints tightly together.

5. Bold solid and composition tiles can be cut with a utility knife. Use a straightedge to keep the cutting lines even.

6. When working with odd-shaped pieces that have to fit around pipes or basins, cut a template piece from cardboard and adjust it to fit before transferring the shape to the tile. In any case, work slowly, particularly on lines that curve.

7. After the tiles are set in place, use a floor roller or even a rolling pin to firmly bond the tiles and cement. Work the roller in both directions.

8. Clean off any excessive adhesive as soon as possible, using the directions on the adhesive container as a guide.

4. Education

Improve Your Vocabulary

Tips for Building Your Vocabulary

✓ Don't gloss over unfamiliar words that you read or hear. Look them up in the dictionary.

✓ Keep a notebook of new words and definitions; record their etymologies and Latin roots to help you remember them.

✓ Quiz yourself on words in your notebook until you have their meanings committed to memory.

✓ As your vocabulary and familiarity with Latin roots increase, you may be able to guess the meanings of new words—try to do so before looking up a word in the dictionary.

✓ Do crossword puzzles and word games, but don't leave any spaces blank. Look up the answers in order to learn new words.

✓ Read, read, read! This is perhaps the best way to build your vocabulary (provided, of course, that you consult a dictionary for each word you don't know).

✓ Use vocabulary books.

✓ Use newly learned words in conversation and writing. Make them not just words you recognize but words you actively use.

Get Free Information

A vast treasury of free information from a disparate array of sources is available to the general public by telephone, fax, and mail. In this information age, the answer may be no further away than your home or business desk.

The first step in almost any kind of research is to contact your local public library. While the on-site materials available to you may be limited in smaller libraries, their personnel have the know-how to facilitate your search. Try university or college libraries—even the local high school. They may have research programs set up to assist patrons.

Almost all libraries have essential references on hand: telephone books from around the country, directories listing professional and trade associations, indexes of major newspapers and magazines, books listing information about public companies and government offices, basic subject dictionaries, encyclopedias, and almanacs. Before visiting the library yourself, call. A reference librarian may be able to locate your information quickly, and convey it to you over the phone or by fax. Of course, courtesy requires that you confine such a request to a single question. Do more extensive library research yourself.

But the library is only your first stop. Many other sources of free information are currently available. Tenacity is all–important in tracking down free information, particularly if your subject is complex. Keep a record of the phone calls you make, and note the names and addresses of the people to whom you speak in the course of your quest. This will become a valuable directory of information sources to consult for later searches; and it will enable you to thank them later. Here are several rich sources of free information:

Toll-free 800 telephone numbers. Companies often provide free information about their products and services. Request a toll-free directory from your local phone company; it should be free. 800 assistance is also available by dialing 1-800-555-1212 and is also free of charge.

Government agencies and the Government Printing Office (GPO). Consult government agencies like the Environmental Protection Agency (EPA), the Food and Drug Administration (FDA), or the National Institutes of Health (NIH) for statistics and cutting-edge studies on issues of controversy or public interest. If you don't know which agency to call, contact your senator or congressional representative's office for help in reaching the proper source. The Library of Congress and the National Archives are excellent sources of photographic and other archival materials. General statistics and trends are available from the National Census Bureau.

The Government Printing Office publishes a directory known as the GPO Catalogue, which is stocked by most libraries. It lists and cross-references most of the information available from the government under various headings.

Trade and professional organizations. From the American Medical Women's Association to the United Auto Workers, trade and professional organizations are expert sources of specialized information. Local chapters or members in your area may provide information relevant to your state or home town.

Businesses and manufacturers. Annual reports and product surveys may contain the information you need. While companies won't reveal trade secrets, they will be delighted to supply information to enhance their profile or support their products.

Research centers and universities. Think tanks and university-sponsored academic studies are often good sources of controversial information. Ralph Nader's Center for the Public Interest is a perfect example.

CD-ROM, on-line services, and bulletin boards. The information superhighway promises to be an international source. The Internet, a worldwide collection of computer networks, is largely funded by the government. If you are a student, you can probably log onto the Internet through your college or university without paying a fee. If not, you will have to pay a monthly fee to a "gateway" service provider. While this technically means that the Internet is not a free source, logging onto it will connect you with people all over the world whose interests range from rock music to astronomy. Other general on-line services, such as America Online, CompuServe, and Prodigy, are more limited than the Internet but can offer you some access to it, are easier to navigate, and offer quick networking forums with others who share your areas of interest. Most services charge a monthly fee and offer a minimum amount of free browsing time and downloadable materials.

See also "Choose an On-Line Service and Use the Internet."

Apply for a Grant

In this country alone, $5 billion is given away in grants each year. Grants are awarded by private organizations, individuals, and government agencies to people with a specific goal. They are commonly given to small businesses that promote ethnic, gender, or racial equality within communities; individuals or groups in the arts and humanities; scientists performing new research; and others whose altruistic endeavors could not be accomplished without outside funding. The application process can be exacting. You may want to engage the services of a professional grant writer. Here are some pointers to get you started.

Come Up with an Idea

Ideally, know what your project will be before you consider applying for a grant. The more specific your ideas are, the more easily you'll find a funder with similar goals and aspirations.

Research Grant Possibilities

Most groups award grants to applicants who are doing work in their community or area of interest. It would be inappropriate, for example, to apply for a grant from a civil rights organization in New York to fund a project dealing with Amazon plant life. Some funders specify the work they want done. To research organizations that give out grants in your state or interest area, begin by contacting your senator or representative to find out which state and federal agencies award grants suitable to your project or field of interest. Contact the dean of students office at a local college or university for leads on private sources of grant funding. Call the local chamber of commerce for a list of grants available to small businesses. Look in your library and bookstores for catalogues that list grant opportunities along with the specifics for applying to them. Consult with representatives from professional, trade, or academic organizations and groups, like the American

Medical Women's Association or the National Poetry Society, or talk to other members to find out about grants they sponsor or recommend.

Evaluate Your Qualifications

As you gather grant information, determine carefully whether you are eligible and suitable for the grant. Find out whether there are time, money, racial, or professional specifications that applicants must meet for eligibility. If you can, rethink your idea to fit a particular grant—but *never* apply for grants you are not suitable for. Make sure you fulfill *all* criteria before applying.

Begin the Application Process

Applying for a grant differs from organization to organization. You may need to complete an application form, make a presentation to a board, or be interviewed. Make sure you know exactly what you need to do from beginning to end *before* you start applying.

Create a Proposal

Most applications for grants will require you to construct a proposal. A proposal is a formal report on your idea that includes as much specific information as possible and explains why you should be awarded a grant. As noble as your goals may be, the proposal is essentially a work of salesmanship. Do not underestimate its importance. The report is the essential statement of intent on which your application reviewer will assess your idea's worthiness.

A basic proposal will usually not exceed ten pages, although it can be much longer. Lengthy proposals may require a separate title page, table of contents, introduction, summary, detailed report, list of goals, list of participants, budget, and schedule. Any proposal, though, should have an explanation of your project, goals, and expenses. You might want to ask if sample grants are available to read so that you can better approximate the reviewer's standards for success.

Gear your proposal to the audience reading it. These are the grantors who potentially will give you money. They are often experts in your field. Focus on how your project will further an organization's cause or fulfill its members' needs and interests. Your tone should be formal, courteous, and above all enthusiastic. Set attainable goals, but don't be afraid to be ambitious as long as you can inspire confidence in the reader. Be clear, complete, concise, and well organized. Be sure to meet any mailing or deadline prerequisites for your grant application. Don't let lateness disqualify your hard work.

Get a Scholarship and Financial Aid

Paying for college can be difficult these days. Tuition continues to rise along with the cost of living on campus. But even if you find yourself overwhelmed by the cost of the school you wish to attend, do not let that discourage you from applying. Any school that accepts you will try to arrange a way for you to afford the tuition and other expenses, whether through scholarships, grants, loans, or a work-study program. Your ability to pay has nothing to do with the admissions process.

How to Search for College Financing

1. Visit your school guidance counselor or the financial aid officer of a college you'd like to attend. Do this early in your senior year of high school to discuss your plans for college and ways to finance it.

2. Read publications concerning financial aid. You'll find them in the library, your school's guidance office, or a college's financial aid office.

3. Fill out the financial aid form. The **Financial Aid Form (FAF)** is available in your guidance office or college financial aid office. This form, which is administered by the College Scholarship Service (CSS), asks you questions about your family's income, size, assets, debts, expenses, and number of children in college and uses your answers to determine the amount your family is able to pay for your education. The college that accepts you will use this information to formulate your financial aid package. The package may include gift aid, such as grants and scholarships, and self-help aid, like work-study, loans, and entitlements. However your package is assembled, it will cover the cost of college minus your family contribution.

4. Fill out other financial aid applications. The **Free Application For Federal Student Aid (FAFSA)** is available at the same locations as the FAF and will determine your eligibility for federal aid. In addition, investigate further financial aid forms administered by your state or by the college you wish to attend.

5. Visit a library to do research on private scholarships and grants available to you. Keep in mind that many scholarships will call for certain qualities, characteristics, skills, or interest areas in students, and they may or may not be needs-based. There are thousands of scholarships just waiting to be given out—the trick is to find them.

6. Write to scholarship information services, which match students with many of the scholarship opportunities they qualify for. Be wary, though: the information you are given is often not worth the cost of the service, and may be no more than is obtained by your college's financial aid office.

Types of Financial Aid and Scholarships

State scholarships. Ask your guidance counselor or write to your state's education department for information.

Federal grants and loans. The U.S. government offers two main types of assistance to students: Pell Grants and low-interest Perkins Loans. The FAFSA will determine your eligibility for these funds.

Bank loans. Every student is eligible to get a low-interest Stafford Loan (also called Guaranteed Student Loan) from a bank. Ask your bank how to go about applying for it.

Work study. Many colleges offer students part-time jobs as a way to pay for college and expenses. These jobs are mainly on campus and do not require a huge time commitment, though you may be able to make more money at a job off campus.

Reserve Officer Training Corps (ROTC) scholarship. The U.S. military offers scholarships to students who join their training program. You will be required to serve in the armed forces for a specified number of years in return.

Private scholarships. Many schools, churches, community groups, youth groups, employers, and unions offer scholarships. Inquire in your community for scholarship opportunities.

See also "Select a College."

Take a Standardized Test

Most aptitude tests, particularly scholastic ones, are structured similarly. The SAT, PSAT, LSAT, MCAT, GRE, and GMAT all attempt to test how well suited you are to a particular type of education. The following tips apply most directly to these tests but can also apply to other standardized tests such as the Civil Service Exam.

Preparation

1. Find out as much as you can about the test. What type of questions will be on it? How long is it? How is it scored?

2. Take practice tests. Sample tests appear in test-prep books available at local bookstores or through the company that administers the test.

3. Take a course. If you have the time and money to dedicate to the process, courses are offered to help people raise their scores on many of these tests.

4. Get a good night's sleep the night before the test, and have a good breakfast in the morning. Wear comfortable clothes and shoes.

5. Bring with you several appropriate, familiar, and functional writing implements.

Taking the Test

1. Pay attention to the directions—they can be misleading. If possible, get the directions before you take the test so you don't have to waste time reading them during the test.

2. Develop a system for answering questions. Consistency will help keep you focused.

3. Use what you know about the test to your advantage. For instance, if you know that the questions increase in difficulty as you progress, but count the same amount, concentrate on answering the easier ones more quickly.

4. Pace yourself. Time is very important on these tests. Don't let yourself fall behind.

5. Guess the answers only if probability is in your favor. Many of these tests are designed so that it's beneficial to guess only if you can eliminate one or more choices.

6. Stay physically relaxed and alert. Good posture and abundant energy will help you think more clearly. Take occasional deep breaths. If you feel yourself panicking, take the moment needed to refocus.

7. Don't do any more work than you need to. People who excel on these tests are often those who know the shortcuts and understand both what a question is asking and how the test-makers want you to approach the problem. Often the first answer that comes to your mind will not turn out to be the right one, and the first method that you think of to do a problem will not be the best or the most efficient.

See also "10 Strategies for Taking Multiple-Choice Tests."

Look Up Information at the Library

What the Library Looks Like

Most libraries are divided into several sections.

✓ Reference room: contains dictionaries, encyclopedias, almanacs, atlases, and other reference books, which can be used at the library but not checked out
✓ The main book section: nonfiction is shelved according to the Dewey Decimal or Library of Congress cataloguing system; fiction is shelved alphabetically by author's last name
✓ Periodical section: contains magazines, journals, and newspapers
✓ Audiovisual section
✓ Children's room

Things to Make Your Search Go Smoothly

✓ Checkout and return desk
✓ A card catalogue
✓ Computers for searching sources
✓ Microfiche machines for viewing newspapers on film
✓ Librarians who will help you!

The Modern Electronic Library

The electronic age has made it fast and easy to find what you need at the library. If your library is on-line, there's no need to flip through endless cards in the card catalogue. Just log onto a computer and you're ready to begin your search.

To Search Books

1. Most libraries post instructions next to the computer terminals, but if you do not see or understand them, don't hesitate to ask a librarian for help.

2. Log onto the computer and choose a search by title, author, subject, or key word.

3. The screen will display a list of entries for whichever category you choose; view each entry by highlighting it and pressing RETURN.

4. Each entry will show the author, title, publication date, number of pages, a brief synopsis, and a call number.

5. The monitor will give instructions for scrolling forward or backward, displaying other nearby items, or choosing a new search.

To Search Articles

Use on-line databases in a similar way as the on-line book catalogue to search for articles published in journals or books. The entries will show you the title of the article, author, source in which it appears, a call number for that source, the date of publication, and a brief synopsis of the article. Some common databases include

✓ **MLA Bibliography:** Modern Language Association literature and linguistics index
✓ **ERIC:** Educational Resources Information Center
✓ **PsycLit:** psychological literature database
✓ **Social Science Index:** literature in the social sciences
✓ **Reader's Guide Abstracts:** the Reader's Guide to Periodicals online
✓ **General Science Index:** literature in the sciences

See also "Get Free Information," "Choose an On-Line Service and Use the Internet," and "Use a Microfilm Machine."

Use a Microfilm Machine

To save space in research libraries, and to provide continued access to aging material, many old books and periodicals are stored on microfilm. One roll of microfilm can store a large book in several volumes or an entire year of a magazine by reducing the pages to tiny pictures on film. Because the pages are made to be so small, the film can be viewed only on a microfilm projector that enlarges the pages onto a display screen.

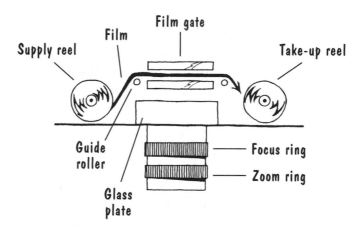

Figure 1. Microfilm projector

Loading

1. Slide the microfilm reel onto the supply side spindle, which may be either on the left or the right side; usually it is on the left. The other side should already have an empty reel on its spindle.
2. Turn the machine on.
3. Thread the film over the guide roller and between the film gate. The film gate should be made of two glass plates. There may be a switch or lever to separate the pieces; otherwise, do it by hand.
4. Continue to thread the film past the film gate and over another guide roller.
5. Insert the end of the film into the slit on the hub of the takeup reel. You may need to make a quarter-inch fold at the end of the film to hold it in the reel.
6. Close the film gate. The film should run smoothly between the glass and remain secure (Figure 1).

Viewing

1. Use the buttons or knobs on the machine as marked to advance and reverse the film. Older machines may require you to advance the film manually with a wheel or crank.

2. Focus the image on the display screen, using the focus ring on the lens.

3. To rotate or center the image, adjust the scan. This will probably require shifting or turning the entire apparatus.

4. Turn the zoom knob on the lens, if available, to enlarge or reduce the image.

Removing

1. Use the rewind button to return the film entirely to the supply reel.

2. Pull the reel straight off the spindle. Be sure you are pulling off the supply reel, not the takeup reel.

3. Turn off the machine and return the film to the librarian.

Improve Your Spelling

General Spelling Rules

As with rules of any kind, there are usually exceptions. The English language has such irregularities of sound and spelling that spelling rules cannot be strictly applied, but they can help in a general way. Be sure to learn the spellings of the words that don't conform to the rules.

✓ *I* before *e* except after *c*, or unless pronounced *a* as in *neighbor* and *weigh*; and except *seize* and *seizure* and also *leisure*; *weird*, *height*, and *either*, *forfeit*, and *neither*.

✓ Every verb ending in *r* preceded by a single vowel and accented on the final syllable forms its noun with *-ence*. For example, *prefer* and *preference*.

✓ *-Ify* vs. *-efy*: only four words require *-efy*: *rarefy*, *stupefy*, *petrefy*, *liquefy*. All others take *-ify*.

✓ *-Able* vs. *-ible*: use *-able* if the base is a full word (*accept* + *able*); use *-ible* if the base is not a full word (*compat* + *ible*).

✓ *-Able* vs. *-ible*: use *-able* if the base ends in *i* (*enviable*) or hard *c* or *g* (*amicable*, *navigable*); use *-ible* if the base ends in *ns* (*responsible*) or *miss* (*admissible*).

✓ *-Ally* vs. *-ly*: use *-ally* when an adjective ends in *ic* (*academically*, *basically*); when an adjective ends in *l* or silent *e*, keep the final letter and add *-ly*.

✓ Drop the final silent *e* before a suffix beginning with a vowel; keep the final *e* before a suffix beginning with a consonant.

✓ Add a *k* to words ending in *c* before adding a suffix beginning with *e*, *i*, or *y*. For example, *picnic*, *picnicking*; *panic*, *panicky*.

✓ For words of one syllable and those with the accent on the last syllable: when they end in a consonant preceded by a single vowel, double the consonant before adding a suffix beginning with a vowel. For example, *acquit*, *acquitted*; *forget*, *forgettable*.

✓ When a prefix ends with the same letter with which the main word begins, include both letters: *dissatisfy*.

✓ When the main word ends in the same letter with which a suffix begins, include both letters: *accidentally*.

✓ When combining two words and the first ends with the same letter with which the second begins, include both letters: *misspell*.

Tips for Becoming a Better Speller

✓ Sound out the word slowly and carefully. We often drop sounds in everyday speech.

✓ Note irregular spellings when you read. Keep a notebook of such words and review them each day until they are committed to memory.

✓ Have someone quiz you on the spellings of words from your notebook, or use a tape recorder to record a list (be sure to pause between each word to allow time for you to write the spelling).

✓ Use dictionaries and thesauruses judiciously.

✓ Examine the etymology of words. Knowing their origins and roots will help you to remember the spelling.

✓ Reread everything you write, using a dictionary to check questionable spellings. When you come across a misspelled word, record it in your notebook.

✓ Use the mnemonic method: devise a trick or saying—an association that is meaningful to you—to help you remember the spelling of a word. For example, "Sepa*rat*e contains a rat" or "*Al*right is all wrong" or "Stationery is used to write letters."

Solve Crosswords

One of the most celebrated names in crosswords, Margaret Farrar, once said that solving crosswords was "part science of deduction, part mother wit, part erudition." Veteran crossword puzzle fans know there are several trial-and-error tactics and letter frequency possibilities that can make solutions easier and faster.

✓ Almost every answer will have a vowel. The likely order of vowel possibilities in puzzles is generally *e, a, i, o, u*.

✓ Most often, when an answer ends in *g*, the preceding two letters will be *in*. If the clue suggests a plural, try filling in the last letter as *s* or *ies*. If a clue implies a verb in the past tense, you can usually try a *d* or *ed* at the end of the word. Likewise, a clue that suggests an adverb might have an answer that ends in *ly*.

✓ Puzzle editors sometimes use a verb clue to suggest that the answer is a verb. Often you can try a noun and be surprised at how quickly you come up with the right answer. The reverse may also be true: a noun clue may have a verb answer.

✓ Puzzlemakers are often forced to use certain obscure words when constructing puzzles because they are the only ones with certain necessary letter combinations. Sooner or later words such as *oast*, *oona*, *baht*, *ewer*, and *dyer* become a regular part of a puzzle solver's vocabulary. A list of over 1,000 such words can be found in *The New York Public Library Desk Reference* and some puzzle dictionaries.

There are two schools of thought about using crossword puzzle dictionaries, almanacs, and other reference books to help find solutions. One school falls adamantly on the side that says "never use a reference book of any kind." The other school argues that puzzles are meant to be both work and play, as well as a great learning opportunity. As Ms. Farrar also said, "the solvers may learn something in the process of looking words up."

✓ "Free think" the clue. This simply means to first concentrate on the clue and then let your mind come up with as many associated concepts and synonyms as you can think of. Often the answer will pop into your head. If it doesn't, move on to the rest of the puzzle and come back to the clue later on.

✓ The more sophisticated the puzzle, it seems, the more the clever the clue. For example, if a four-letter clue is "a type of pen," you might automatically consider synonyms for writing instruments or an enclosure. When you freely associate about the clue, you might come up with an answer such as *bull*.

✓ For plural words, crossword puzzlemakers often seem to find Latin plurals that end in *ae*. Puzzle editors will also try to make a clue appear to have a singular answer when it is actually a plural. For example, the clue "crop blessing" might have the answer *rains*.

✓ A working knowledge of prefixes will make you a much better solver. Words in the clue can be a tip-off to the prefix of the answer. Once you think of the prefix, you can often figure out the answer word. For example, the clue "preamble" might evoke the answer *preface*.

The best way to learn how to solve crossword puzzles is to do them every single day and build up experience through practice. You can leave a puzzle for a while, come back, and find that inspiration strikes on words that stumped you before. Be persistent and open-minded.

10 Strategies for Taking Multiple-Choice Tests

1. Read the directions carefully. Determine whether only one answer choice is correct, or more than one or none may be correct.

2. Read the questions carefully. Know what you are looking for, and read all the choices completely.

3. Eliminate answers you know are wrong.

4. Be wary of deceptive choices that seem correct but are slightly wrong. They may resemble the correct answer.

5. Recognize common types of wrong answers. Often one answer will be way off, too simplistic, or inappropriately worded—those will invariably be incorrect.

6. Use short cuts, such as working backward from the answers on math problems, if they help you get answers more quickly. Sometimes a test will require you to use short cuts to finish in time.

7. Don't leave any answers blank. Guess if you do not know the answer (except on a test such as the SAT, where wrong answers count against you).

8. Don't waste time on questions you don't know; go on and come back to them at the end.

9. Be systematic. If there is a group of similarly styled questions, develop a method for answering each in the same way. This will keep you focused and successful.

10. Pace yourself. If you have a time limit, be aware of how far you've gone and how much time remains.

Select a College

Choosing a college is a pivotal and important decision. The academic and social environment of the school will shape and inform your career choices and many of your friendships long after your college days are over. From a state university to a small liberal arts school, from Ivy League to art institutes, colleges have programs tailored to fit a myriad of possibilities. Here are some guidelines on deciding which colleges are best suited to your needs and goals.

Self-Analysis

Ask yourself what you are looking for in a college. Try to picture your ideal environment: urban/rural, large/small, old/modern, liberal arts/specialized/technical. Having an idea of the kind of college and curriculum you prefer will help narrow down the field. Keep an open mind; you may find yourself surprised by a college you never thought you'd be interested in.

Research

Find out about as many colleges as you can. Attend college fairs, where you can meet college representatives and obtain literature. Consult books that rate colleges and list their strong departments and academic focus. If you have not received information on a particular college and you'd like to, call or write to the college's office of admissions and request brochures. Ask a favorite teacher in your field of interest for colleges that might be advantageous for your particular talents.

Consider all these factors to determine how well each institution matches your needs and wants:

Size. Colleges range from a few hundred students to many thousands.

Location. Decide whether you want a school in a city, near a city, in a small town, in the same or a different state or part of the country from where you live.

Cost/financial aid. Compare the tuition and housing costs of a college with the amount you and/or your family are prepared to spend. Check on the availability of financial aid. Do not disqualify a college because you consider it too expensive; a college that accepts you will try to arrange enough financial aid to make it affordable to attend school there.

Degrees/majors offered. Determine whether the school offers courses, majors, and degrees in an area you'd like to study. Find out whether that department is highly regarded in the field.

Faculty/alumni. Find out the faculty-to-student ratio, whether there are any distinguished faculty you might be interested in learning from, or whether there are alumni who have become highly successful after graduating.

Services/facilities. Look into the career placement service, and the kinds of educational, recreational, living, health, and food facilities available.

Atmosphere/affiliation. Evaluate how well the school's atmosphere fits with your lifestyle. Check if the school is connected with a particular religion, race, or organization.

Academic standards. Look for colleges within your reach. While you should without doubt aim high, don't waste time applying to a school that is out of line with your academic qualifications.

Visit

Never choose a school until you've visited the campus. Spend a day at the college to get a feel for life there; if possible, go for a few days. Take a tour of the campus, sit in on some classes, speak to students and faculty, and even stay overnight in a dorm. This may also be a good time to have your admissions interview if one is required.

Apply

From the scores of colleges you should receive information on, narrow down your choices to only the colleges you would gladly attend if you are accepted. Apply to at least one school you are fairly certain of being accepted to, and one or more schools slightly out of reach. Apply to twenty schools or three, as long as you are willing to do the work called for on each application. Some applications simply require an information form, whereas others ask for essays, academic references (teacher or counselor), and perhaps even outside writing samples. Many applications come attached to the college brochure; others must be requested by mail or phone. Be sure to complete the application before the due date. Include the required application fee.

Choose

It may be several months before you hear back from colleges. Once you've heard from all accepting colleges, decide which school you will attend. Reconsider all the factors above when you choose. Notify all the schools of your decision as soon as possible.

Read Music

Music notation communicates to the performer the intentions of the composer or arranger. Notes, symbols, and terms are used to convey how a piece of music should be played on an instrument. When learning to read music, use your instrument to translate the written page into sound. Just as a dictionary can provide word definitions but not teach you how to read, the following reference can offer only the basic elements of music notation as a first step in the learning process.

Note: numbers in the illustration correspond to explanations.

1. **The staff.** Nearly all music is written on a staff, which consists of five parallel lines. Where a note is placed on the staff—on a line, on a space, or on a ledger line above or below the staff—indicates the pitch of the note. Which note corresponds to which line or space depends on the clef, or system of notation, that is being used. The diagram on page 103 shows the letter assignations of the treble and bass clefs.

2. **The clef.** This figure indicates which system of notation is being used. The treble clef generally shows notes above middle C (on a piano, the C key nearest the middle of the board) and the bass clef shows notes below middle C. While there are other clefs, these two are by far the most common. Higher-pitched instruments use the treble clef, and lower-pitched instruments use the bass clef; the piano uses both.

3. **Key signature.** These marks indicate which notes will be sharp (raised one-half step) or flat (lowered one-half step) throughout the piece. The key signature also tells you what key, or grouping of notes, the piece will utilize. Any changes from the key signature in the music is noted by an accidental, or mark in the music directly in front of the note to be changed. These marks are either sharps, ♯; flats, ♭; or naturals (which cancel a sharp or flat in the key signature).

4. **Time signature.** This figure indicates what the beat or rhythm of the music will be. The top number tells how many beats there are per measure, and the bottom number tells what kind of note receives one beat. For instance, music with a 3/4 time signature will have three beats in a measure (counted as 1-2-3, 1-2-3) with a quarter note getting one beat. Common time signatures include 2/4, 4/4 (which can also be signified with a C), 3/4, and 6/8.

5. **Notes.** The pitch of a note is determined by where it is placed on the staff, but the time value of a note (how long the note is played) is determined by what the note looks like. The note stem will tell you how long to play a note, but a note's time value is ultimately relative to how fast or slow the piece is meant to go (Figure 1).

Figure 1. Notes

6. **Rests.** Like notes, rests come in different shapes and time values. They indicate how long to sustain a silence. A dot after a rest (as well as after a note) means that the time of the rest should be increased by a half (Figure 2).

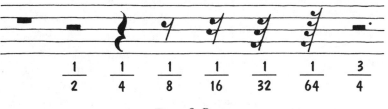

Figure 2. Rests

7. **Other symbols.** A double bar (7a) indicates the end of a piece of music (see Figure 3). A double bar with two dots to the left of it (7b) tells you to go back to repeat a section; return to the measure that comes after a double bar with two dots to the right.

A dot on the top or bottom of a note indicates it should be played *staccato* (7c), with a short and choppy character; a curved line connecting notes indicates the notes should be played *legato* (7d), or smoothly.

A short arrowhead under or above a note means the note should be *accented* (7e). A long sideways vee pointed left marks a *crescendo* (7f), to play gradually louder, while a long sideways vee pointed right marks a *decrescendo*, to play gradually softer.

8. **Terms.** Occasionally a piece of music contains words or abbreviations to indicate a specific way to play, such as

ff (fortissimo): very loud
mf (mezzoforte): half loud
pp (pianissimo): very soft
accelerando: getting faster
stringent: faster and stronger
tempo primo: original tempo
grave: slow, solemn
andante: walking, moderate
andantino/allegretto: slightly fast

f (forte): loud
p (piano): soft
fz (forzando): accented
ritardando: getting slower
morendo: dying off
largo: broad, sustained
adagio: slow
presto: fast

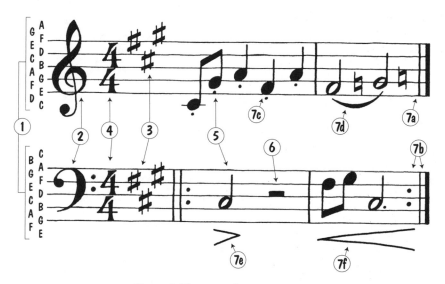

Figure 3. Elements of music notation

1. staff	7a. double bar
2. clef	7b. repeat
3. key signature	7c. staccato
4. time signature	7d. legato
5. notes	7e. accent
6. rests	7f. crescendo

Speed Read

Speed reading is a procedure you can begin to develop on your own, or perfect by enrolling in a class. The degree of "speed" is dependent upon the course you select. Speed reading is most effective when it is used for nonfiction, particularly texts the reader is familiar with, such as professional articles, business summaries, long news accounts, financial reports, and informative books. It is not appropriate for articles and books of literary essays, poetry, short stories, or fine novels, read for enjoyment. You will want to savor those to the fullest.

Speed reading requires a high degree of concentration and commitment. It takes substantial practice. To speed read well, you must

1. Establish time limits for any given read.
2. Skim passages from which you want general ideas.
3. Judge in advance, or as you proceed, what is likely to be the most important information in the text at hand.
4. Focus more slowly on passages that contain data or information you want to absorb.
5. Concentrate on the job and avoid distractions.
6. Cover the entire text in one sitting. If it is too long, divide it into workable segments, preferably by subject categories.
7. Take advantage of printed guidelines to topical passages, such as chapters, headlines, subheads, and statistical listings.
8. Preview condensations or excerpts whenever possible. Experienced speed readers, especially in the business and professional worlds, also keep tabs on colleagues who may already have read lengthy texts, so they can zero in more readily on the most important sections and passages.
9. Use a highlighter to mark key words and phrases for later reference.
10. Practice.

How fast can you speed read? The average reading speed is 300 to 350 words per minute, or the equivalent of about three-quarters of a page of *The Reader's Digest*. Speed readers who have received professional training can double that rate.

You would do well to read this article in one minute.

10 Tips for Taking Good Notes

1. Buy a pad designed for note-taking, with easy-to-flip pages and good-quality paper that yields the best clarity on the page even when you apply the least amount of fine detail.
2. Use a pen or pencil you are comfortable with—one that will not fail part way through the job. Carry extras.
3. If you know in advance which related topics you will be covering or which speakers you will be hearing, allocate specific note-pad pages to them ahead of time.

4. Before taking notes in a course or at a lecture where questions are permitted, jot down some questions of your own on your note pad. Concentrate and focus.

5. Take a cue from experienced note-takers who learn elementary speed writing (shorthand) or create their own symbols and abbreviations to replace words and phrases. You will obtain notes that are more complete.

6. When you are about to take notes in a roomful of people, arrive early enough to get a seat up front where you can hear more clearly. Nothing interrupts good note-taking more than trying to make out what the speaker is saying. If it's appropriate, ask the speaker to repeat information that has been missed or to speak more slowly.

7. Consider using a small tape recorder (if permitted), but bear in mind that it should be an adjunct and not an alternative. The act of writing information down helps to ensure your mind will retain it and understand it through focused processing.

8. Reserve one sheet of your note pad for listing any suggestions made about reference materials on the subjects at hand: articles, reports, books, tapes, and the like. If you are not sure where any of these may be obtained, ask for more information.

9. Compare your notes with those of one of your peers, particularly if there are any segments you found unclear or for which you did not make as many entries as you would have liked.

10. Review your notes as soon as possible after you have completed your note-taking session. Use a highlighter to focus on key points. Add any further ideas or relevant comments while the subject is still fresh in your mind.

Bonus Tip: Consider purchasing a notebook computer. Make sure the batteries are fully charged. Take note of available electrical outlets in your study environment, just in case the batteries fail or run out.

See also "Speed Write."

Understanding Sign Language

American sign language (ASL) is a beautiful language based on spatial relationships and pictorial contexts. Its syntax comes from natural gesture. Anyone can begin to learn sign language by using the body, hands, and facial expressions to communicate (Figure 1). For instance, when we are happy or are attracted to something, we move forward. When we are afraid or repelled, we pull back. Above all, remember to be observant and maintain eye contact—looking away is a sign of rudeness in the deaf community.

There are over 22 million deaf or hard-of-hearing people in America. As the deaf community becomes more outspoken and politically active, ASL has also begun to enter our mainstream culture. Deafness is no longer considered a disability by members of the deaf community.

Remember these basic concepts when learning to sign:

✓ Relax your physical inhibitions and make full use of body gestures.
✓ Use facial expressions to enhance meaning. The same sign can have subtle differences of meaning depending on the facial expression of the speaker.
✓ Use natural gestures. As in a game of charades, many formal signs actually look like what they mean. Practice conveying ideas without using words.
✓ In sign language, it is not impolite to point!
✓ Mouth movements aren't always used to make English words. Use mouth movements as adjectives—a pucker for sourness, for example.
✓ To communicate in ASL, you must draw pictures that show spatial relationships. You must "set the stage" before you will be understood.
✓ Practice! Volunteer at a school for the deaf or other place where you can observe the language as it is fluently spoken by members of the deaf community.
✓ Study! Take courses at a local college or university.
✓ Be patient! The transition from spoken English to ASL is difficult. The languages operate differently and cannot be interchanged word for word. Learn the distinct rules of grammar, style, and usage as you would for any foreign language.
✓ Enjoy! Enter the flow of this beautifully expressive language. Let it move you.

I   Love   You

I Love You

Figure 1. Two ways to say "I love you" in American Sign Language

5. Electronics

Hook Up a VCR

How you hook up a video cassette recorder (VCR) to your television will depend on what kind of television and what kind of antenna you have. The first thing to do when you unpack your VCR is to make sure that all the appropriate cables and wires are present. You should have at least a coaxial cable with an antenna adaptor for the VCR to television connection (Figure 1). Most VCRs also come with a remote control, and audio/video connection cables in case you want to hook your VCR up to a stereo or another VCR. Read your manual carefully for important safety instructions and further information on the VCR's special features. To simply install your VCR, follow these steps.

Connection to Antenna (No Cable TV)

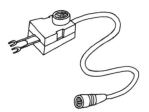

Figure 1. Coaxial cable with antenna adaptor

1. The wire from the antenna should be connected to the television. Disconnect the antenna wire from the back of the television and connect it to the appropriate terminal on the back of the VCR (it should be marked "Antenna," "Ant" or "In From Ant").
   - ✓ If the antenna wire is a round coaxial cable, it should screw right onto the VCR's round antenna terminal.
   - ✓ If the antenna wire is flat with two fork-shaped metal connectors, use the antenna adaptor supplied to connect it to the VCR (it will probably not be supplied) (Figure 2).

2. Connect the round screw end of the coaxial cable (with antenna adaptor) that came with the VCR into the appropriate terminal on back of the VCR (it should be marked "TV" or "Out to TV").

3. Connect the other end of the coaxial cable to the 75-ohm antenna input on the back of the television.
   - ✓ If your television does not have a terminal to accept the coaxial cable, you must use an antenna adaptor to attach the cable to the screws (Figure 3).

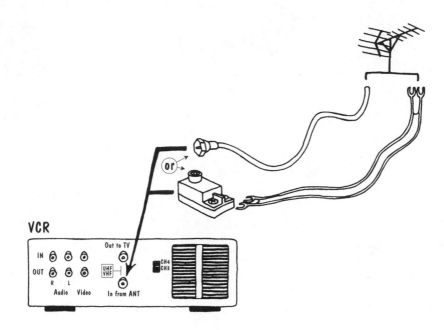

Figure 2. Antenna to VCR connection

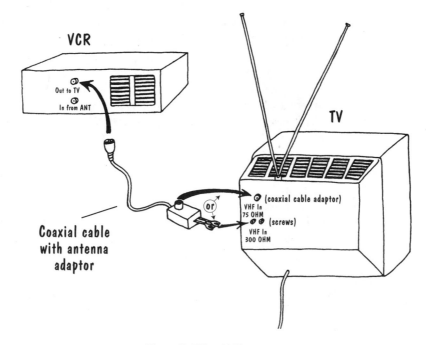

Figure 3. TV to VCR connection

Connection to Cable TV

1. The round coaxial cable that carries the cable TV signal from the wall or cable box should be screwed into your television. Unscrew the cable from the television and screw it into the terminal marked "Antenna" on back of the VCR.

2. Connect the round end of the coaxial cable that came with the VCR into the terminal marked "TV" on the back of the VCR.

3. Connect the other end of the coaxial cable to the VHF antenna (75-ohm) on the back of the television. If you have a cable converter with an A–B switch, connect the cable to the converter and then the converter to the television (Figure 4).

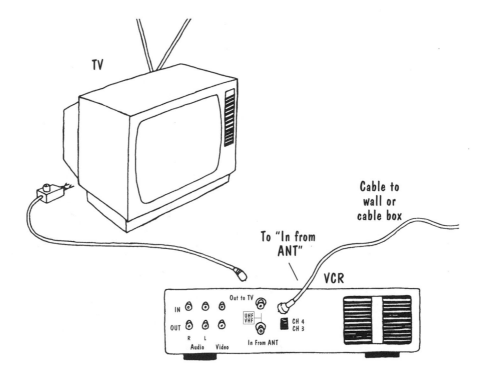

Figure 4. TV to VCR connection with cable TV

Set Up a Computer and Printer

What do you do with all those impressive-looking boxes of high-tech computer equipment? Where do you begin?

1. Check the packing slip or invoice to make sure you've received all of the equipment ordered, then unpack one box at a time. A typical basic system will consist of the following items: the computer or central processing unit (CPU), which is the guts of the system. It's a box-like object and usually has a monitor sitting on it (Figure 1). Some Macintosh computers combine computer and monitor into one unit. There will also be a monitor, a keyboard (and possibly a mouse as well), and a printer. Everything will come with its own cables. To make set-up easier, unpack the CPU cables and place them next to (or on top of) the CPU, the monitor cables with the monitor, and so forth. Double-check the boxes to make sure everything has been unpacked. Move the empty boxes out of your way, and assess your desk space to figure out how best to configure placement of the equipment. Avoid placing your computer by a window. Aside from the dangers of providing would-be thieves with an enticing view, direct sunlight may harm the system. Keep the computer in a cool place, avoiding both heat and extreme cold. Make sure the built-in air fan on the computer isn't up against a wall or otherwise blocked from proper ventilation. Avoid placing the computer in kitchen areas, where it will be subjected to the hazards of oils, food, and water.

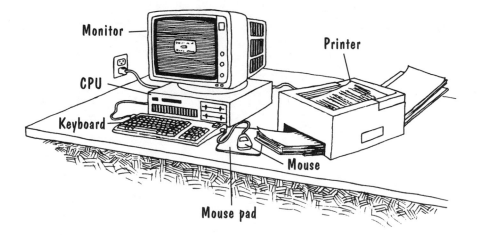

Figure 1. Front view of a typical computer/printer set-up

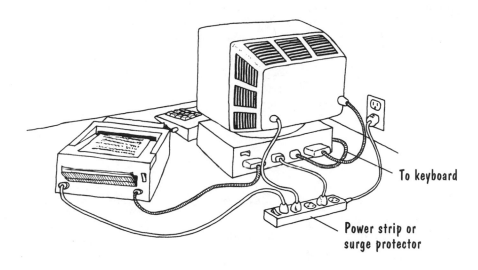

To keyboard

Power strip or
surge protector

Figure 2. Rear view of a typical computer/printer set-up

2. Locate the manuals that come with the computer for set-up instructions. If you can't understand the instructions, it's not because you lack intelligence. Many manuals are translated from another language—and not very well, either. At the very least, find a diagram in the manual that points out the placement of switches, cabling, and connectors (also called ports). Cables are plugged into, or connected to, ports (Figure 2). Although the placement and configuration of computer equipment and cabling varies, the following basic instructions will be helpful if you can't make sense of the manual. Look for customer service support telephone numbers in the manual, and don't hesitate to call if you have questions.

3. Set up the CPU. It may be placed on your desktop or underneath your desk, depending on the amount of space you have and your personal preference. Find its power cable. It will have one end that looks like a standard three-prong wall socket cord, and another end that plugs into the back of the computer. Find the port in the back of the computer that appears to fit the power cord, and plug in the power cord. If it doesn't fit, chances are you've chosen the wrong port. Be patient and try again until you've got it. You may plug the computer into the wall outlet now, but don't turn it on just yet. Connecting the other pieces of equipment to the computer while the computer is on may damage the system. Make sure this power cord, and any other power cords connected to computers or printers, are plugged into a grounded wall socket, a grounded power strip, or surge protector.

Power strips are recommended, since they are equipped with several three-prong sockets and filter harmful "noise" from power lines. Surge protectors offer a greater degree of protection but are more expensive.

4. Set up the keyboard. One end of the keyboard cable is either permanently attached or plugs into one side of the keyboard itself. The other end plugs into the keyboard port (usually round) in the back of the computer, where you may find a label, "keyboard" (Figure 3). If you have an IBM-compatible PC, look for the port that has the same number of holes as the number of pins in the keyboard cable. On the Macintosh, match up the symbol (also called an icon) on the keyboard cable end with the corresponding icon above the keyboard port. As with all cables, the holes in the port and the pins on the end of the cable must be lined up perfectly for the connection to be made. Again, don't force it; line it up properly, and it will go in without a problem.

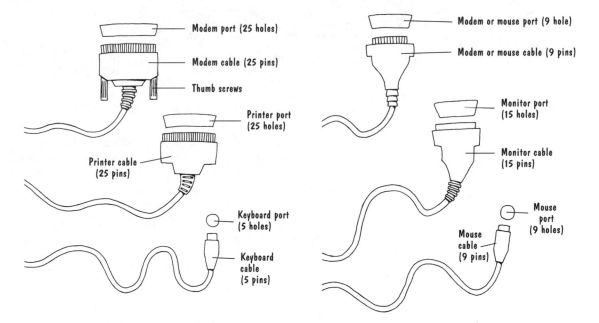

Figure 3. Possible types of IBM-compatible PC ports and cable ends

If your system comes with a mouse, plug the free end of the mouse cable (the other end is permanently attached to the mouse) into the other side of the keyboard. On some systems, the mouse cable is plugged into a mouse port in back of the computer. If you own a Macintosh, match up the icon on the cable end with the icon above the port on the keyboard, and plug it in (Figure 4). When in doubt, count the number of pins on the mouse cable end and find the matching number of holes in the port. The mouse can be placed atop a mouse pad to help it glide freely during use.

5. Set up the printer. The printer has two cables: a power cable and a cable that connects it to the computer. One end of the power cable fits into the back of the printer, and the other end looks like a standard three-prong wall plug.

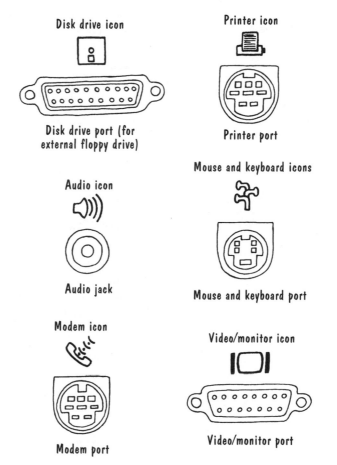

Figure 4. Typical Macintosh ports and icons

Check with your dealer to make sure your printer comes with a cable that fits into the back of your brand of computer. If it doesn't, you can easily purchase one. Find the printer port that appears to match the printer cable, and plug the printer cable into the computer. Again, when in doubt, count the number of pins in the printer cable end, and find the matching number of holes in the printer port. If there is more than one port in the back of your IBM-compatible PC, look for the one labeled "LPT1" or "PRN" or "First Printer," and use that one. You may have to tighten a couple of screws on the cable end with a small screwdriver to make it stay put, or there may be thumbscrews that are tightened by hand. On a Macintosh, match up the symbols on the printer cable and above the printer port, and plug the printer cable in. Plug the wall plug end into your power strip or wall socket, but don't turn anything on yet.

Your printer will also come with either ribbons or cartridges, depending on the type of printer. Follow the printer manufacturer's instructions to install them, and to load either single-sheet or fan-fold, continuous form paper.

6. Set up the monitor. You may place this on top of the CPU, next to it, or on the desktop alone. Find the monitor's power cable and make sure it's connected to the back of the monitor and a grounded power source. The other cable will go from the back of the monitor to the monitor port on the back of the computer. On an IBM-compatible PC, this connector may be labeled "Video" or "VGA." If your Macintosh has a separate monitor unit, match up the icon on the monitor cable end to the corresponding icon above the monitor port, and plug it into the back of the computer.

7. If your equipment includes the increasingly popular CD-ROM, it may be an additional internal disk drive in the CPU, or it may be an external drive that plugs into the CPU. If your CD-ROM drive is external, it will plug into the port labeled SCSI (pronounced "scuzzy"). All current Macintosh models and some IBM-compatible PCs come with SCSI ports (recognizable on the Macintosh by the SCSI icon above the port), and the newer Macintoshes have sound cards already installed. Of course, listening to CD-ROMs requires computer speakers (which look like small stereo speakers) and/or headphones that are plugged into a sound jack, usually found in the back of the computer. If your computer doesn't come with an internal CD-ROM drive, you may be able to upgrade your computer to accommodate it. Consult your dealer or manufacturer.

8. Now you'll need to install the programs you've bought: word processing, spreadsheet, or whatever (not to mention those all-important computer games). Instructions for installation vary from program to program, so follow the step-by-step procedures that are outlined in the software manual.

9. If you're tearing your hair out and wondering whether the cables can be used for macramé or a noose, don't despair. Call your computer-literate friends, manufacturer's customer support, or dealer's customer support for help.

Hook Up Nintendo

The Nintendo entertainment system is the most popular of the home video game players. The system and a television set allow you to play any of the extensive list of game cartridges (sold separately) made for use with the Nintendo unit.

Your Nintendo system should come with the following parts:

✓ the main NES Control Deck
✓ two game controllers
✓ AC adaptor
✓ RF switch
✓ audio/video cables

Plug In the System

To connect the system to a power supply, simply plug the AC adaptor into a wall socket and the other end of the adaptor into the jack on back of the control deck.

Connect the Game Controllers

Plug the two game controllers into the sockets on the front of the control deck. It doesn't matter which controller you plug into which socket, though you must use the controller in socket 1 (on the left) for a one-player game.

Connect the System to the Television

If your television has a VHF cable connector on the back:

1. Plug the RF switch into the RF switch jack on the back of the control deck (Figure 1).

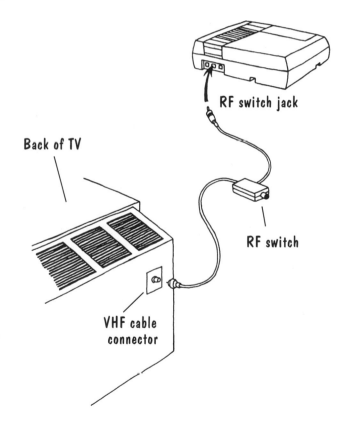

Figure 1. Connection to VHF cable connector

2. Screw the other end of the RF switch to the VHF cable connector on back of the TV.

If your television has two VHF screws on the back:

1. Plug the RF switch into the RF switch jack on the back of the control deck.

2. Screw a 75/300-ohm converter onto the VHF screws on the television. The connector is not included with the system, though one may already be present on the TV. If not, they are available at electronics stores (Figure 2).

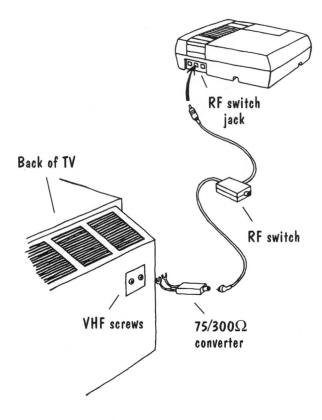

RF switch jack

Back of TV

RF switch

VHF screws

75/300Ω converter

Figure 2. Connection to VHF screws

3. Attach the other end of the RF switch to the cable connector on the converter.

If your television (or a VCR attached to the television) has audio/video jacks:

1. Plug the audio/video cables into the audio/video jacks on the right side of the control deck. Plug the red cable into the audio and the yellow cable into the video (Figure 3).

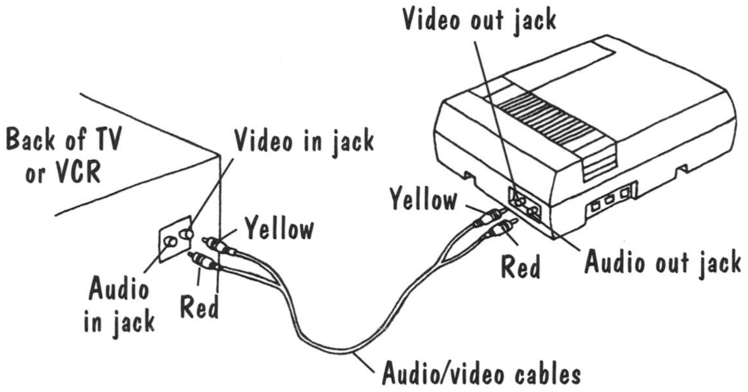

Video out jack

Back of TV
or VCR

Video in jack

Yellow

Yellow

Red

Audio out jack

Audio
in jack Red

Red

Audio/video cables

Figure 3. Connection using audio/video cables

2. Connect the other ends of the cables to the audio/video jacks on the back of the TV (or VCR). Again, red into audio and yellow into video.

Replace the Cable TV or Antenna
Hook-Up for Normal Television Viewing

✓ If a cable already was hooked up to the television or to an attached converter, unscrew it and screw it into the cable connector on the RF switch (Figure 4).

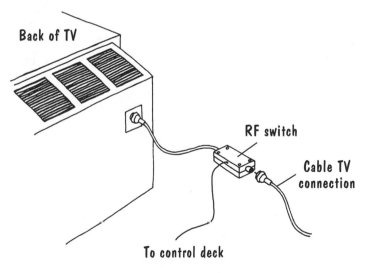

Back of TV

RF switch

Cable TV
connection

To control deck

Figure 4. Cable TV hook-up

✓ If an antenna with a twin lead wire was attached to the VHF screws on the television, unscrew the wires. You will need to get a 300/75-ohm converter (not included with system, but available at electronics stores). Screw the twin lead wires onto the screws on the converter, then attach the cable connection on the converter to the cable connector on the RF switch (Figure 5).

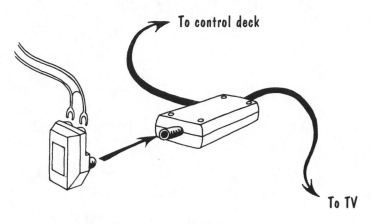

Figure 5. Antenna hook-up

Operate the Nintendo System

1. Turn on the television.
2. Set the television to channel 3 (or channel 4 if 3 is used for broadcasting; if so, set the switch on the back of the control deck to 4).
3. If you are using audio/video jacks into a VCR, set the TV/VCR switch on the television to "VCR".
4. Open the chamber cover on the front of the control deck.
5. Slide the game cartridge face up into the chamber, push it all the way in, and push down to lock it in place. Close the chamber when the cartridge is in place.
6. Press the power switch on the control deck to turn the system on. Do not turn the power on before you have loaded the game cartridge, and be sure to turn the power off before unloading a cartridge.

Hook Up a CD or Stereo System

Here are quick and easy directions for attaching basic stereo components, as well as some tips to enhance performance:

Components

Most systems feature a receiver, cassette tape deck, and CD player. Others may still include a turntable, while other new systems include hook-ups for stereo TV, a digital audio tape (DAT) player, or a digital compact cassette (DCC) player (Figure 1). Arrange the components close together, stacked if possible. Do not place components on top of a receiver that has ventilation slots to release heat. Connect the components to the receiver with stereo (or phono) cable. Cables usually come in pairs for stereo hook-up with color-coded input jacks at the ends. Often one is white, the other red.

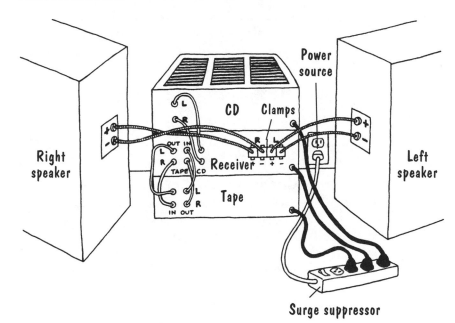

Figure 1. Stereo hook-up

Connecting the Tape Deck to the Receiver

Four connections need to be made to hook up the tape deck—two lines in (for stereo recording on the tape deck from other components) and two lines out (for playing tapes in stereo). Be sure the cable connections are secure.

1. Locate the appropriate jacks on the back of the tape deck and the receiver. They will be marked "left input," "right input," "left output," and "right output" (or something similar). The jacks on the receiver should specify that they are for the tape deck.

2. Connect the cables for playing the tape deck. Using the first phono cable of a pair, connect the left output on the tape deck to the left input on the receiver. With the other cable of the pair, connect the right output on the tape deck to the right input on the receiver.

3. Connect the cables for tape deck recording. With another pair of phono cables, connect one from the left input on the tape deck to the left output on the receiver. Connect the other from the right input on the tape deck to the right output on the receiver.

Connecting the CD Player to the Receiver

Because the CD player does not record, there is no need for an input line; therefore, only two connections are made.

1. Locate the appropriate jacks on the back of the CD player and receiver. They will be marked "left line out" and "right line out" on the CD player and "CD left line in" and "CD right line in" on the receiver (or something similar).

2. Connect the cables for playing the CD player. With one phono cable from a pair, connect the left line out on the CD player to the left line in on the receiver. With the other cable, connect the right line out on the CD player to the right line in on the receiver.

Connecting Other Components

Hook up components that record (such as a DAT player) the same way as the tape deck; hook up components that only play (such as a turntable) the same way as the CD player.

Connecting Speakers to the Receiver

Use insulated speaker wire, not phono cables, to hook up speakers. Instead of sliding a cable input jack onto the stereo equipment, you will need to clamp or screw the exposed speaker wire in the appropriate place, but the principle is basically the same. Like stereo cable, speaker wire comes as two attached insulated wires distinguished by slight differences in color or by markings on the insulation.

1. Locate the speaker connections. On the back of the receiver there will be a series of four clips marked "right +," "right -," "left +," and "left -." Push the clips to open a small hole to insert the speaker wire into, then release to clamp shut. On the back of each speaker there will be two similar looking clips marked + and - or two screws marked + and -.

2. Arrange the speakers. For a complete stereo effect, place the speakers so you are between them and facing them when you listen. Make sure the speaker to your right is the right speaker and the speaker to your left is the left.

3. Connect the right speaker. Attach an exposed (uninsulated) end of the paired speaker wire to the speaker, one wire onto the + screw or clamp and one wire onto the - screw or clamp. Connect the other end of the same wire to the speaker connection on the receiver. The wire you connected to + should connect to the "right +" clamp, while the wire connected to the - connects to the "right -" clamp.

4. Connect the left speaker. Follow the same procedure as with the right speaker but connect the speaker wire to the "left" clamps on the receiver.

Tips on Connections

✓ Do not plug stereo equipment into an electric supply until you have hooked up all the components.

✓ Do not open up components to look inside. If you have a technical problem, consult a specialist.

✓ Do not tangle wires when connecting them. Having different wires touch will take away some sound quality.

✓ Keep the wires as short as possible to maximize sound quality. Keep long wires rolled up and tied.

✓ It may be necessary to attach other wires and accessories. Turntables often require a ground wire to attach to the receiver. Receivers may have antennas for radio reception.

✓ Don't overload electrical sockets with too much equipment. Plug stereo equipment into a surge suppressor for protection.

✓ For additional advice on acoustics, consult books or stores that sell stereo equipment.

Hook Up a Telephone Answering Machine

Since telephone answering devices (TADs) come in a wide variety of types and capacities (see Figure 1), you need to consult the owner's manual supplied by the manufacturer at the time of purchase. However, the installation steps have a commonality and follow this general pattern:

1. Locate the two small cassettes that come with each instrument. The cassettes are identical—one for incoming messages and the other for the announcement you compose.

2. Insert the cassettes in the channels into which they fit, with the full reels to the back. (If you have one of the newer models, it may be a digital type, which uses a single cassette—easily inserted in the right slot—for both purposes.)

3. Select the **telephone line cord**, clearly marked in an installation diagram in the owner's manual. Plug one end of the cord into the telephone lines (or tel line) jack in the back of the message machine.

4. Plug the other end of the telephone line cord into a **modular wall jack**, which is the same jack you would plug a telephone into directly if you had no answering machine.

5. Take the **telephone set cord** (the same one that is on your telephone itself) and plug it into the **telephone set jack** located on the back of the message machine.

6. Insert the **power cord** into the **power jack** located on the back of the machine, and plug it into the nearest convenient electrical outlet. Make sure that the outlet is not controlled by a wall switch. If you must use such an outlet, tape the switch open.

7. Your message machine is ready for operation. After you have plugged in the power line, you will notice that the cassettes will automatically rewind.

8. Your final step is to follow the manufacturer's directions (usually imprinted on the cassette cover itself) and record the message you want callers to hear when they reach the machine instead of a person.

One final caution: Although the line cord and telephone set cord are standard equipment for all modern telephones, you should use only the **power cord** supplied by the manufacturer of your answering machine.

Depending on the complexity and caliber of the answering machine, you may have other installation options, such as a clock, a message window, and remote message gathering and control. These functions are all easy to activate and will be explained clearly in your user's manual. TADs can also be used in conjunction with fax machines and other telephonic devices to convey information and alert users to messages.

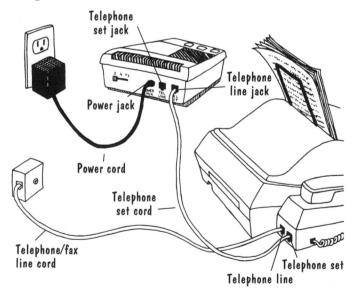

Figure 1. Telephone answering machine hook-up with phone/fax

Dial Direct Overseas

Making an international call involves dialing more numbers than calling long distance in the U.S. or Canada. While each U.S. state or Canadian province (or part of a state or province) has an area code, foreign countries have country codes and city codes. The procedure is quite simple, but finding the correct codes can be confusing. The following explains how to dial and provides some often-used country and city codes. For codes not listed here, refer to a phone book or call the international operator by dialing "00." For more information, contact your long distance carrier.

1. Dial 011. (This, like 1 for some calls in the U.S., must be dialed before all direct overseas calls).

2. Dial the country code. It will be a two- or three-digit number.

3. Dial the city code. It will be a one- or two-digit number.

4. Dial the phone number. Remember that foreign phone numbers often contain fewer digits than the seven we are used to in the U.S.

Argentina 54
  Buenos Aires 1

Australia 61
  Melbourne 3
  Sydney 2

Brazil 55
  Rio de Janeiro 21

Czech Republic 42
  Prague 2

Denmark 45
  Copenhagen 1 or 2

Egypt 20
  Cairo 2

France 33
  Nice 93
  Paris 13, 14, or 16

Germany 49
  Berlin 30

Greece 30
  Athens 1

Haiti 509
  Port au Prince 1

Hong Kong 852
  Hong Kong 5

India 91
  Bombay 22
  New Delhi 11

Iran 98
  Tehran 21

Ireland 353
  Dublin 1

Israel 972
  Jerusalem 2
  Tel Aviv 3

Italy 39
  Florence 55
  Milan 2
  Naples 81
  Rome 6

Japan 81
  Tokyo 3

Jordan 962
  Amman 6

Korea 82
  Seoul 2

Mexico 52
  Mexico City 5

Morocco 212
  Casablanca: no
    code required
  Tangier 99

Netherlands 31
  Amsterdam 20
  The Hague 70

Nigeria 234
  Lagos 1

Norway 47
  Oslo 2

Pakistan 92
  Islamabad 51

Philippines 63
  Manila 2

Poland 48
  Warsaw 22

Russia 7
  Moscow 095
  St. Petersburg 812

Saudi Arabia 966
  Riyadh 1

South Africa 27
  Johannesburg 11

Spain 34
  Barcelona 3
  Madrid 1

Sweden 46
  Stockholm 8

Switzerland 41
  Geneva 22
  Zurich 1

Taiwan 886
  Taipei 2

Turkey 90
  Istanbul 1

Ukraine 7
  Kiev 044

United Kingdom 44
  Glasgow 41
  London 71 or 81
  Manchester 61

Venezuela 58
  Caracas 2

Dub a Tape

To the technologically deficient, using the tape deck on a stereo system correctly can seem like a major scientific achievement. The following instructions will help the hopeless (and not-so-hopeless) learn how to record a tape onto another tape and how to do it well.

1. Set the receiver to the tape player. This may not be necessary to record, but otherwise you won't be able to hear what is being recorded.

2. Put the tapes into the tape deck. If you have a double cassette deck (one component with two tape decks), one deck will have a record function and the other will not. Put the blank tape into the recordable deck and the tape you want to record from into the other deck. If you use two separate components to dub, put one cassette into each tape deck and set to play the deck with the blank tape.

3. Set the deck to tape dub. For a double cassette deck, turn the tape dub function on.

4. Set the recording level. On some double cassette decks it is impossible to set the recording level when dubbing a tape. If you can set the level, 5 or 6 is a good place to start. Set the level so that the dB meter on the recording tape deck reads 0 or slightly above.

5. Set the tape speed. Some double cassette decks offer high-speed dubbing, which allows you to dub a tape faster than it would take to play it. On a good cassette deck, the sound quality at high speed should be the same as at regular speed. For high-speed dubbing, press the appropriate button on the tape deck. Do not switch back and forth between high speed and regular speed while recording or you will warp the recording sound.

6. Allow the record tape to run for a few seconds. Cassettes normally contain a small piece of unrecordable lead tape (often clear) at the beginning of the reel. Press "record" on the blank tape to let it run a few seconds so the lead tape will pass. Then press "pause" to hold the tape in place.

7. Press "play" on the play tape.

8. Release "pause" on the record tape to begin recording. Do this immediately after the play tape has begun so as not to miss any of the recording. Once the recording begins, you may need to readjust recording levels. Simply adjust the levels, then rewind both tapes to the beginning and go back to Step 6.

9. Make the recording. Leave the tape decks alone while recording. If you do not want to hear what is being recorded, turn down the main volume on the stereo.

10. Press "pause" on the record tape to end taping. This will stop the recording silently, without the harsh noise that results from pressing "stop". Hit "pause" before the play tape ends to avoid recording the sound of the play tape stopping. Once you have pressed "pause," you can then press "stop" on the record tape without creating noise on the recording. After you have stopped the record tape, you may stop the play tape as well.

11. Remove the tapes from the decks and label them. To keep track of sound quality, indicate on the dubbed tape that it is a second-generation recording (recorded from another recording), or a third-generation recording if the play tape was itself a second-generation recording. A small amount of clarity is lost with each generation. Store tapes in a cool place and away from magnetic fields such as those generated by microwave ovens.

Choose a Computer and Printer

With all the new technology flooding the market, buying a new computer and printer can be daunting. There are so many factors to consider, and any new computer today may turn out to be a dinosaur within five years if you don't keep it current with the latest peripherals. Still, the only true concern you should have when buying a computer is that it meets your current needs and requirements. Compare models and brands, and consider mail-order companies with on-site service guarantees. Subscribe to a computer magazine before making your purchase to discover more about the latest trends and developments.

Budget

Figure out how much you want to spend before you shop. Like buying a car, computers come in economy and luxury models. Look for the best price for the most features and support services. Research exactly what your money can buy, and get advice from a computer expert in the office—don't rely on the salesperson's advice alone.

Used vs. New

Used computers and printers are often cheap to pick up and can be a good way to start out. But they can be costly to repair and service, and often they cannot be easily upgraded. The higher quality, capabilities, and service guarantees of a new computer or printer may be more important.

Type

From desktops to laptops, choose the best option for your circumstance. If you travel a lot, choose a laptop, but remember that they are costly to repair and are much more fragile. Always choose a laptop with a removable upgradable hard drive, and purchase an extra battery pack. A good home system can support more power and peripherals like CD-ROM. When deciding between Macintosh and DOS/Windows systems, opt for whichever system gives you the most flexibility of use and access. Printers come in dot matrix, ink-jet, and laser formats. Laser printers should be used when reproduceability must be at its greatest—600 dpi (dots per inch) is the minimum acceptable level for ink density. For home use, ink-jet printers are a cost-effective quality choice. Small office networked systems can easily share one printer.

Comfort and Usability

Choose a computer design you feel comfortable with. Keyboard comfort is especially important. Special boards are now available to reduce the chance of your getting repetitive stress syndrome in the wrists from heavy use. Choose a computer and printer that fit easily into your available space. Laptops are great for studio apartments or college dorms.

Memory and Hard Drive Space

The more random access memory (RAM) a computer has, the more programs you can load and the faster they will run. Likewise, the more hard drive space a computer has, the more data it will store. Data space is measured in megabytes, or MBs. Find a computer with enough megabytes of memory and drive space to run your software and store your files. 8 MBs of RAM is recommended for Windows-based word processing programs. Get at least a 120-MB hard drive.

Features

Investigate built-in fax/modems for going on-line and for sending or receiving large batches of information. CD-ROM opens a whole world of graphics and sound capabilities with interactive "edutainment" and computer games. Scanners allow computer users to program images into the computer and reproduce them in document files. Consider which, if any, peripherals you may need for your home or office work.

Compatibility

If you will be working on more than one computer—at home and at work both, for instance—you will likely want to buy a computer compatible with the others you use. Compatible computers read the same computer language and can be used interchangeably.

Expandability

Research the upgradable features available for your computer and printer. Be aware of the costs to upgrade. Sometimes it is cheaper to get a feature built into the computer if you are reasonably sure you will use it. Do not buy equipment that is not easily upgradable.

Hardware

Be aware of what equipment the computer comes with, and the quality of that equipment. If the computer comes with a monitor, find out about its resolution, color capabilities, and screen width. If you are buying a printer, consider whether you want a dot matrix, letter quality, or laser output. Can your printer perform with your software and with the additional fonts (typefaces) available? If you get a modem, look into the modem's baud rate (the speed it communicates at) and the communications software it comes with.

Software

Some manufacturers offer software packages as bonuses. But never buy a system for the software; consider it a nice perk and look for packages with programs you are interested in. If you already own software, make sure the computer and printer you choose are powerful enough to run it. Conversely, now may be the time to purchase a more powerful word processing or spreadsheet program to take full advantage of a system's capabilities. Avoid pirated or second-hand software. You don't get the support and upgrades that ownership of a legitimate license makes possible, and you could risk importing viruses or other problems related to the bootleg programs.

Programmability

If you plan to program on the computer, find out how easy it is to do and what language the computer understands.

Support

Don't buy a system if it does not come with a toll-free help line and comprehensive manual. Take the same precaution with software. Proper technical support can make all the difference in customer satisfaction.

Repair and Warranty

Many new computers and printers come with a limited warranty and an opportunity to buy an extended warranty for service. Choose a company that offers timely, on-site service guarantees and loaner equipment. Used systems, of course, will probably not be covered by warranty.

See also "Set Up a Computer and Printer."

Format a Disk

Before you can store any information on a computer disk, you must format it. Formatting is a process that prepares the disk to receive data. You can save yourself some time by buying preformatted disks, but unformatted disks are cheaper. If you do the formatting yourself, make sure the disks you choose to format are blank, and the right size and type for your disk drive. When in doubt, refer to the manual that came with your computer, or enlist the aid of your local computer supply store. Remember, if there's any information already on a disk, the process of formatting will erase everything.

How to Format a Disk On an IBM-Compatible PC Using DOS Commands

Turn on your computer. If DOS is not installed on a hard drive, or if you have only a single-drive computer, you may also have to insert the DOS disk to access the FORMAT command. Insert a disk in drive A. At the prompt on your screen: C:> or C:\> if you have a hard disk, A:> or B:> if you have no hard drive, type FORMAT A:

Floppy disk drives, A and B

Drive C hard disk

Figure 1. A dual disk drive computer with a hard disk

Be sure to leave a space between FORMAT and A. Press ENTER or RETURN. You've just told the computer to format a blank disk in the A drive. This is the left-hand or upper disk drive in dual disk drive computers, or the name of the disk drive in single disk drive computers. The right-hand or lower disk drive in dual disk drive computers is called B drive, and if you wish to format a disk in that drive, then you must insert the disk in drive B and amend the above command to FORMAT B: The hard disk is referred to as the C drive (Figure 1). *Never, ever type FORMAT C:* This will erase all information on your hard disk!

The computer will now ask you to insert a disk and press ENTER or RETURN. If you use 3.5" disks, just push it in all the way. If you use 5.25" disks, you may also have to press a lever on the disk drive to lock the disk in place. If you have a single disk drive and no hard disk, you may have to remove the DOS disk at this point. Insert the blank disk and press RETURN or ENTER.

The computer will ask you if you want to give the disk a volume label, which is the computer's way of asking you to give the disk a name. This is an option; if you don't wish to name the disk, just press RETURN or ENTER.

The computer will ask you if you wish to format another disk. If you don't, type N and press ENTER or RETURN. If you do, type Y and press ENTER or RETURN.

How to Format a Disk on an IBM-Compatible PC Using Windows

If your PC has Windows, a program that makes your IBM-compatible computer work a bit more like a Macintosh, you can format disks in two major ways.

The first way is to use the DOS commands outlined above when your screen displays the C prompt (C:\ or C:\>). If Windows loads automatically when you turn on your computer, you can get back to the C prompt (and the DOS environment) by double-clicking with the mouse or highlighting with the arrow keys and pressing ENTER on the MS-DOS icon on the Main Windows window (Figure 2).

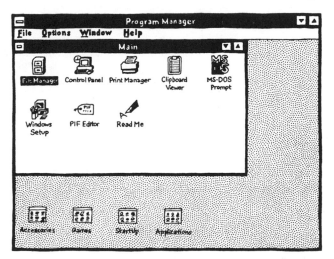

Figure 2. Main Windows window

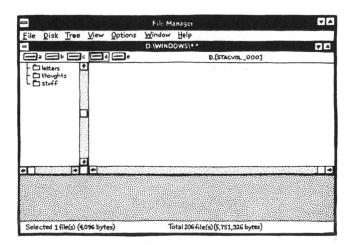

Figure 3. Windows File Manager window

To format a disk in using Windows' Format Disk command in File Manager, insert a disk in drive A (we are formatting in drive A for this particular example). Double-click on the File Manager icon, which will display the File Manager window on the screen (Figure 3). Click and hold on Disk at the very top of the File Manager window, move the mouse's arrow down to Format Disk, and release the mouse button. (Or type D and ENTER to get into the Disk menu. Then type F and ENTER to select the Format Disk command.) A Format Disk window will appear on the screen (Figure 4). Make sure it says Drive A in the Disk In box. If it doesn't, click on the arrow next to the Disk In box and select Drive A with the mouse. Once Drive A is displayed in the Disk In box, you can click on OK to commence formatting.

Figure 4. Windows Format Disk window

Note: Formatting will erase any data on the disk in drive A, and the screen will flash a warning to this effect, giving you the chance to cancel the format command.

The Format Disk window will also display the following options. Quick Format will perform formatting faster if the disk has been formatted before, but it won't check the disk for errors. Make System Disk will copy MS-DOS files onto the formatted disk, just in case you need these files to access your data on another computer, or in case your hard drive meets with an unfortunate accident. It also leaves you less room on the formatted disk for your data files. Label gives you the option to name the formatted disk.

How to Format (or "Initialize") a Disk on a Macintosh or an Apple

Insert a blank disk. The computer will give you a message that the disk is unreadable and will ask if you want to initialize it. If your disk is high density, the computer will offer you two choices: EJECT or INITIALIZE. Some Macintosh computers will offer you three choices: EJECT, ONE-SIDED, or TWO-SIDED (800K disks are two-sided; 400K disks are one-sided). If you want to cancel formatting, click on EJECT. If you want to proceed with formatting, click on either INITIALIZE, ONE-SIDED, or TWO-SIDED. Apple computers will ask you to click on the disk's capacity (800K or 400K) before proceeding with initialization.

If you're unsure what type of disks you're formatting, check the disk manufacturer's packaging.

The Macintosh will warn you that the process of initialization will erase all information on the disk. If you still wish to proceed, click on ERASE.

The computer will ask you to name the disk. Type in a name and click on OK. Now initialization (formatting) occurs.

When formatting is complete, the disk icon (a picture of the disk) appears on the screen with the name you assigned to it.

Back Up a Disk

There is nothing more upsetting than losing your computer programs and data files via a crashed hard disk or a damaged floppy disk—that is, unless you also neglected to make backup copies of your files. If you use an IBM or IBM-compatible PC, make a backup copy of your AUTOEXEC.BAT files and CONFIG.SYS files as well. These files contain valuable information about the setup of your computer. Make backing up your data files a daily ritual; it's like buying insurance or peace of mind, and it's a lot cheaper.

How to Back Up Disks on an IBM-Compatible PC Using DOS Commands

There are three DOS commands you can use to make backup copies: COPY (to copy ...

entire disk), or BACKUP. The third choice, BACKUP, is not explained here because the files created by the BACKUP command are not usable by themselves. To use BACKUP files, you must first copy them onto your hard disk using a command called RESTORE. The COPY and DISKCOPY commands create files that are immediately usable, either on your computer or on any other compatible computer.

The first thing to do is to determine the location of your source disk (the disk containing the file to be copied) as well as the location of your target disk (the disk where the copy will be placed). Drive A is the name for the drive in single disk drive computers, or the upper or left-hand drive in dual disk drive computers. Drive B is the name for the lower or right-hand disk drive, and Drive C is the hard disk (see Figure 1 on page 128).

The COPY command consists of the following information to be typed at the DOS prompt (A:>, C:>, or C:\>, depending on your computer). At the DOS prompt, type the word COPY, followed by a space, followed by the source drive and a colon, followed by the source filename. Then type a space, followed by the target drive and a colon, followed by the target filename (if the copy is to have a different name). The target filename can be the same name as the source filename, as long as the source file is not being copied onto the same disk. If you wish to duplicate a file on the same disk, you must assign the duplicate a different filename.

Sample Copy Commands

To copy a file called CONTRACT from drive A to drive B, type the following: COPY A:CONTRACT B: Note that there's no need to retype the filename after indicating the target drive as B, unless you wish to name the backup copy something else. Press ENTER or RETURN. The computer will ask you to insert the disk for drive B and press ENTER or RETURN (it may also tell you to strike any key) when ready.

To copy any files found in hard disk subdirectory \LETTERS to drive B, type the following: COPY C:\LETTERS*.* B: Note that typing *.* is a time-saving device that indicates all files. This can be varied, for example, by typing COPY C:\LET-TERS*.TXT, which would copy only those files in subdirectory \LETTERS that have the file extension TXT.

To copy an entire disk from drive A to drive B, type the following: COPY A:*.* B:

Note for computers with only one disk drive: When you copy files from one floppy disk to another in single drive computers, the computer will ask you to place the source disk in Drive A. This gives you the chance to eject the DOS disk, if it's in the disk drive, and to replace it with the source disk. The computer will prompt you to alternately remove and replace the source disk with the target disk, and may call the single drive "A" when referring to the source disk and "B" when referring to the target disk. This note also applies to the use of the DISKCOPY command.

To determine whether the copy has been made, type in the command DIR followed by the target drive name and a colon, and press ENTER or RETURN. All the files on the target disk will be displayed, including the backup copy you just made.

The DISKCOPY command is used to copy the entire contents of one disk to another disk. This command saves time, as it automatically formats (and thus erases!) anything on the target disk before it makes the backup copy. To use the DISKCOPY command, type in the following information at the DOS prompt: the word DISKCOPY, followed by a space, followed by the source drive and a colon, followed by a space, followed by the target drive and a colon. Press RETURN or ENTER.

To copy a disk in Drive A to a disk in Drive B, for example, you would type DISKCOPY A: B: You are then prompted to insert the source disk in A, insert the target disk in B, and strike any key (or ENTER or RETURN) when ready.

A single drive computer user simply types DISKCOPY and press RETURN or ENTER, or may also type DISKCOPY A: A: A message appears on the screen asking you to insert the source disk in drive A and strike any key when ready. As with the COPY command, you'll be prompted from time to time to swap the source disk with the target disk. Again, your version of DOS may refer to the single drive as Drive B when the target disk is to be inserted.

The screen sends you the message that the copy is complete, and asks if you wish to copy another. Type Y if yes, or N if no, and RETURN or ENTER.

How to Back Up Disks on an
IBM-Compatible PC Using Windows

If your PC is equipped with the Windows program, you can either use Windows' File Manager to back up files or disks, or use DOS commands at the C prompt. (See "Format A Disk: How To Format Disks on an IBM-Compatible PC Using Windows" for instructions on switching from Windows to DOS.)

To back up with Windows' File Manager program, double-click on the File Manager icon in the Main Windows window (or highlight the File Manager icon with the arrow keys and press ENTER). The File Manager window will appear on the screen (Figure 1). Note that the upper part of the File Manager window displays the various disk drives on your computer, and that the one currently in use has a box drawn around it. On the left side of the window are all of the directories (groups of files) contained on that disk. Clicking on one of these directories will display all of that directory's files on the right side of the window.

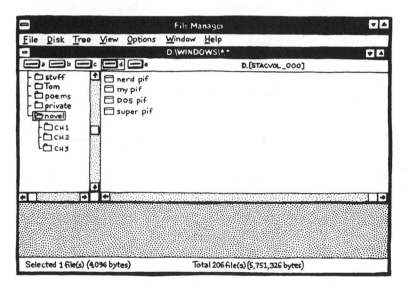

Figure 1. Windows File Manager window

Let's say you want to back up a file or directory from C drive to a disk in B drive (or A drive). Insert a disk in the destination drive (in this case, B drive). Click on C drive at the top of the File Manager window. Click (without releasing the mouse button) on the file or directory in C drive that you wish to copy onto drive B. Drag the file or directory icon up to the B drive icon and release the mouse button. The program will ask you if you're sure you want to copy the file to this particular location. If you do, click on the YES button.

You can also back up (or copy) an entire floppy disk from A drive to B drive. Note that to copy from one floppy disk to another, the disks must be the same size or capacity. To copy an entire floppy, use the Copy Disk command in File Manager. Put the source disk (the disk you wish to copy) in drive A and the destination disk in drive B.

Important note: Because Copy Disk will erase everything on the destination disk in drive B before it copies the data from drive A, be sure to use either a blank disk in drive B or one with data you can afford to lose. (Don't worry, though. The computer will flash a warning on screen and give you a chance to cancel copying if you make a mistake.) Click and hold on Disk at the very top of the File Manager window, move the mouse's arrow down to Copy Disk, and release the mouse button. (Or type D and ENTER to get into the Disk menu. Then type C and ENTER to select the Copy Disk command.) A Copy window will appear displaying where you are copying from (make sure the From box says A) and a To box. Type B: in the To box or click on the button next to the To box to display the choices of destination drives. In any case, make sure the To box says B. Click on OK to start the copying process. While copying takes place, the name of each file being copied onto the disk in drive B flashes on the screen until copying is complete.

You can also copy a disk from A drive to A drive, or B drive to B drive. Just click on the drive in File Manager, choose the Copy Disk command as described above, and designate the same drive as both To and From (or source and destination). The source disk will be inserted into the drive first. Follow the instructions on the screen as to when to remove the source disk and replace it with the destination disk, until copying is complete.

How to Back Up Disks on a Macintosh

Quit any programs you're using so that the screen's desktop, with all its files and folders, is displayed. If you wish to copy a single file, group of files, single folder, or group of folders from the hard disk to a floppy or vice versa, do the following. Click once on the target file or folder, which highlights it on the screen. If you wish to copy additional files or folders, point and click while pressing SHIFT for each additional item you wish to copy, until all your selections are highlighted. Using the mouse, collectively drag the selected files onto the icon (or picture) of the target disk.

If you have two disk drives and would like to copy the entire contents of one disk onto another disk, do the following. Insert the source disk into one of the drives, and the target disk into the other drive. Drag the icon of the source disk onto the icon of the target disk (Figure 2).

In any case, if the target disk already has a file with the same name as the file you're trying to copy, the computer will ask if you want to replace the existing file with the selected items. If you don't need the old version, click on OK. If you do need the old version, click CANCEL, and copy the file onto a different disk.

My File

To copy an entire Macintosh disk, use the mouse to point to the icon of the disk you wish to copy.

Drag the icon of the disk you wish to copy onto the icon of the back-up disk.

Figure 2. Back up procedure for Macintosh

Use a Fax/Modem

A fax/modem is a communication device that allows you to send and receive messages directly from your computer, and links you to networked databases. Most computer systems are now delivered with a preinstalled fax/modem. This commonly used peripheral can be added to a system or upgraded for minimal cost. Even notebook computers use fax/modems no bigger than credit cards that can be invaluable when you are traveling away from home, school, or office. Remember, however, that you can't receive fax messages unless your computer is turned on. You'll need to have a good fax/modem before you can go on-line or cruise the Internet.

Modem speed is important in uploading and downloading data, particularly graphics files, which can be large and complicated. A fast modem will save you time and money. Choose the 9600 bps or 14.4 bps (bits per second, or baud rate) models, and consider upgrading if your modem is a 1200 bps or 2400 bps. Faster technology, such as the 28.8K-bps speed, is not yet standard and may cause more problems right now than it will solve.

See also "Choose an On-Line Service and Use the Internet" and "Set Up a Computer and Printer."

Send Electronic Mail

Electronic mail, or e-mail, is fast becoming the way we communicate with each other in the information age. It's faster than sending regular mail and cheaper than a phone call. As intercomputer communications systems like the Internet grow larger, more and more people are gaining access to networks capable of sending e-mail messages. All you need is a computer with a modem (and communications software, if necessary) and access to a computer network such as the Internet (computer networks at universities and government offices, as well as many private and commercial networks, can communicate through the Internet).

See also "Choose an On-Line Service and Use the Internet."

How to go about sending e-mail depends on the system you use, but all e-mail communications share these common features:

The Header

Certain information must accompany your e-mail message to ensure it gets to the right person and can be identified. An e-mail header will usually include:

1. The date and time of the message.
2. The sender's e-mail address.
3. The recipient's e-mail address.
4. A slug or subject reference for identification purposes.

Most systems ask you to supply some of this information before you send your message and will automatically supply the rest.

Addresses

Every e-mail user must have an address where he or she can receive or send messages. The format of an e-mail address is standard and is arranged in a hierarchical order; it is *user@host.domain*, where "user" refers to the name used by the individual on the mail account, and "host" and "domain" refer to the networks the individual uses to communicate, from most specific to least (more than two components can be arranged here). All information should appear without any spaces, with all components of the address separated from each other by a period except the initial name, which is followed by the symbol @. The addresses of others can be difficult to find if you don't already know them, though mailing list directories are available to help you. Whenever possible, get the e-mail address of someone you wish to communicate with in advance.

The Body of the Message

Once the header is complete, you will be able to fill in the body, or actual text, of your message. Type this in the space provided, or upload an existing file to send.

Sending the Message

When your message is complete, you may send it to the appropriate address. The procedure for sending depends on the system, but often it is as simple as pressing one key on the keyboard or clicking on an icon.

E-mail Etiquette

As with any form of communication, e-mail users follow unwritten rules of etiquette in addition to all the applicable rules of everyday courtesy:

1. Don't use all uppercase letters. It looks loud and angry.
2. To communicate a smile, draw it sideways with the characters :-) or :). For a wink, use the characters ;-) or ;). For a frown, use :-(. For a laugh, use :-D. For no comment, use :-x .
3. Remember that unlike phone calls, e-mail messages can be saved and sent to others. Don't say anything you will regret later. Insulting, rude, or angry messages—called flames—are to be avoided.
4. When you send a message, stick to one topic per communication. That way, messages are easier to organize and relay if necessary.
5. Frequently used phrases are often abbreviated. Among many others, they include

IMO	in my opinion
FAQ	frequently asked question
BTW	by the way
LOL	laughing out loud
RTFM	read the f**king manual
MSG	message
BFN	bye for now
JIC	just in case
CUL	see you later
OIC	oh! I see

Use New Phone Company Services

Today, a whole array of customized phone services is available for home and office environments. They can be used separately or in combinations suited to your individual needs.

Caller ID

Allows you to identify the number of the caller before you pick up the phone or to find out what numbers have called while you were out. To use Caller ID you need to supply your own display unit, available at any electronics or phone store.

1. When you receive a call, the phone number of the caller will appear on the display unit after the first or second ring. If the caller has restricted the

number, the display unit will indicate "Private" or "P." If the number is outside the Caller ID access area, the display unit will indicate "out of area."

2. Accessing the calls you have missed depends on the model of your display unit. Some models hold more numbers in memory than others.

3. To restrict your own number from being identified by Caller ID, consult your local phone company.

Call Forwarding

Lets you automatically transfer incoming calls to another telephone number.

1. To forward calls, dial 72# from the number you want forwarded, and wait for the dial tone.

2. Dial the number where you want your calls forwarded. You'll hear two short tones, then normal ringing. When the line answers, Call Forwarding is in effect. If you forward calls to a number that is not your own, be sure to inform the proper person or office that they will be receiving your calls.

3. If the line is busy, or there is no answer, hang up and try Steps 1 and 2 again. No answer is needed this time to establish Call Forwarding.

4. If a call comes when Call Forwarding is in effect, your telephone will ring briefly as a reminder, but you cannot answer the calls. You, not the caller, will be charged for the call from your phone to the forwarding number. You can still make outgoing calls from your phone.

5. To cancel the service, dial 73# from your phone. You'll hear two beeps and a dial tone, indicating that Call Forwarding has been canceled.

Call Return

Allows you to call back the last number that called your number, whether or not you answered the phone.

1. Get a dial tone, then press *69. You will automatically call back the last number that called you. Some numbers will be out of the calling area; you will not be able to access them.

2. Unlike Caller ID, you cannot restrict your number from this service.

Call Waiting

Lets you receive a call while you are already on the telephone.

1. The phone beeps, indicating another caller. If you do not respond immediately, a second beep will sound after ten seconds. The new caller hears only the normal ringing of your phone.

2. If you'd like to end the first call, hang up. The phone will ring with the second call.

3. To answer the new call without ending the first, press and release the receiver button (the "hang-up" button or "hook"). Your first call will be on hold while you talk to the second caller.

4. To return to the first call, again press and release the receiver button. You can switch back and forth between calls as often as you'd like. If you hang up the phone while you still have a line on hold, the phone will ring you back.

Repeat Dialing

Allows you to automatically redial busy numbers.

1. If you call a number and it is busy, hang up the phone.

2. Get a dial tone, then press *66. Hang up the phone. Your number will call the busy number every minute for 30 minutes or until the line is no longer busy. During this time, you can make and receive other calls. When the line becomes clear, your phone will call the number automatically and ring you back to indicate that the call is going through. A special ring (usually a double ring) will let you know this is your Repeat Dialing call, not an incoming call.

3. Pick up the phone. Remember, you are the caller, not the callee.

Three-Way Calling

Allows you to add a third party to an existing call.

1. Press and release the receiver button, putting your call on hold. You'll hear three beeps, then a dial tone.

2. Dial the third party's number. You can talk before including the first party. (If the line is busy or there is no answer, you can return to the first call by pressing and releasing the receiver button.)

3. To begin the three-way call, press and release the receiver button. All three parties will be able to talk.

4. To add a new party if the first caller hangs up, repeat Steps 1, 2, and 3. To disconnect the third party, press the receiver button twice. You can add a new third party by repeating Steps 1, 2, and 3.

Message Services

Many phone companies now offer automatic messaging, such as voice mail, that do away with the need for an answering machine. Instructions on how to use this service will vary. Call your local phone company for costs and availability.

Note: Some of the following services are limited or unavailable in some areas. You'll need to check with your local phone company. Fees are charged for each of these services. Call Waiting, Call Forwarding, and Three-Way Calling require a monthly charge and must be requested. The rest are accessible to everyone and incur a cost each time you use them. In some calling areas, however, services are limited or not available. Consult your local phone company for specific prices and availability.

Understanding Multimedia and CD-ROM

Multimedia is creating a cultural revolution. By combining media—sound, video, still photography, graphics, touch, and data processing—multimedia gives its users unprecedented possibilities for accessing and using informational databases for professional, educational, and recreational uses. Available on compact discs, CD-ROM resources allow users to learn foreign languages, play the piano, travel the globe, explore an art gallery, or venture to other places and interests unknown and waiting for discovery.

One CD-ROM disc holds 600 megabytes of data—an electronic bookshelf. You can't save information from your computer onto a CD-ROM disc, but you can download information from a CD-ROM source. Databases of periodicals, academic studies, medical information, business statistics, and more can be searched and accessed for fast, in-depth research results. Your local university library can provide you with an excellent introduction to CD-ROM references and resources and tell you how to conduct efficient information searches.

CD-ROM drives can be either internal or external. A multimedia system's quality depends upon its speakers, sound card, and drive speed (faster is better). Buy a system that comes bundled with a CD-ROM package or get an upgrade kit; don't attempt to purchase separate components. And welcome to the twenty-first century!

Choose an On-Line Service and Use the Internet

To use an on-line service or link up to the Internet, you'll need a modem. A CD-ROM drive can also be useful for accessing sound capabilities but is not absolutely necessary.

On-Line Services

Subscribership to computer on-line services has increased dramatically in the 1990s. Services allow users to join bulletin board discussions on special interest topics, do personal banking, shop from home, take educational classes, access domestic or international newspapers and periodicals, get the current stock market figures, read sports results, and take advantage of other services. Some of the most popular services are America Online, CompuServe, Prodigy, and Delphi. LEXIS/NEXIS and Dow Jones News/Retrieval are notable services directed at businesses.

On-line services generally charge a monthly base fee for a set amount of usage hours per month; extra hours cost more. Additional fees are charged for downloading information to your computer. For the home, school, or office, on-line services can provide invaluable super-fast information resources. Users can also hook up instantly with other on-line subscribers to share information. Many on-line services offer limited access to the Internet.

Cruising the Internet

The Internet is a global telecommunications link of over two million computers on 30,000 networks in more than 75 countries. It was created during the cold war by the Pentagon to connect it with defense researchers in academia and business. In the late 1980s, scientists around the world promoted lay usage of the Internet, spawning a global academic community. Today, the Internet links users to a countless array of users, services, resources, and activities—a cyberspace smorgasbord.

For the uninitiated, Internet access provided by on-line services is probably more than sufficient. For the user with more sophisticated computer literacy, local universities and networks often offer direct links for a minimal monthly fee. To avoid being labeled a "clueless newbie" or getting "flamed" (inundated with hate e-mail), the new user would be wise to consult one of the many good Internet books on procedure, resources, and "netiquette." Once you are on the net, the possibilities are endless—happy cruising!

See also "Use a Fax/Modem" and "Understanding Multimedia and CD-ROM."

6. Food, Kitchen, and Entertaining

Use a Fish Knife, Sauce Spoon, and Other Special Utensils

The array of silverware you may find at your place setting for a formal dinner can be quite intimidating. Here are some basic rules of thumb to help keep your focus on enjoying the food and company.

The pieces of flatware to be used first are located on the outermost edges of the place setting, where they are most accessible to your hands. As each course is served, work your way closer to the plate. Keep this in mind and you'll never pick up the wrong piece of flatware.

For example, if soup is the first course, you'll find your soup spoon on the outermost edge of the right side of the place setting. If you are served salad before the entree, your salad fork should be found to the left of the larger dinner fork. If it is to be served after the entree, it should be found to the right of the larger dinner fork. Your dessert spoon and fork may either be found above the dinner plate or else brought to the table when the dessert arrives.

There are two basic methods for using a knife and fork, which may be applied to eating with the dinner fork and knife, salad fork and knife, and fish fork and knife. Feel free to use whichever method is most comfortable to you. In the American method, the fork, tines down, is held in the left hand to hold the meat in place while the right hand cuts the meat with the knife. The knife is then laid down on the plate rim, usually at the 11 and 2 o'clock position (Figure 1). The fork with the cut piece is then transferred to the right hand, tines up, and the piece is eaten.

In the European or Continental method, the fork stays in the left hand, tines down, while the knife remains in the right hand to cut the food and push it onto the fork. The knife may also be rested on the plate rim from time to time.

To rest both knife and fork on the plate before finishing a course, put the handles out to either side, with the tops of the knife and fork near the top of the plate, fork tines down (Figure 2). When you have finished a course, place knife and fork parallel to each other, with the handles at the 4 o'clock position, and the tips at the 10 o'clock position (Figure 3). Never rest the used end of a piece of flatware on the table; always lean it on your plate or place it in your bowl.

To use a soup spoon, hold it at the end of the handle, thumb on top, and dip it sideways into the soup. Lean forward very slightly to avoid spilling anywhere but inside the soup bowl, and sip from the side of the soup spoon. When only a small amount of soup remains in the bowl, slightly tilt up the soup bowl rim that is closer to you, and spoon up the last of the soup. When you have finished, place the soup spoon either on the right side of the underplate, or inside the center of the bowl if there is no underplate.

The small three-pronged oyster fork is used for clams, oysters, or mussels served in the shell and for shrimp cocktail. Use one hand to steady the shell on the fish plate, and, with the oyster fork, extract and eat the shellfish in one bite. Mussel shells may be picked up with one hand while the oyster fork pulls out the mussel. Once the clam, oyster, or mussel is extracted and eaten, you may pick up the shell and (quietly) sip the juice from it. If a shrimp is too large to eat in one bite, pierce it with the oyster fork and eat part at a time, redipping the shrimp in your cocktail sauce, if desired, before each successful bite.

A fish fork and knife are used to eat fish, which may be served either filleted or whole. If fish is served whole, use the knife and fork to slit the fish from tail to gill (you may opt to first cut off the head and tail), fold the skin back, and remove and eat bite-sized pieces. When the backbone is exposed, use the fish fork to remove it while the fish knife blade is inserted underneath one end of the backbone for leverage. Place the bone on the fish plate and resume eating with the fish fork. Remove fish bones from your mouth with your fingers and place them on the rim of your fish plate.

If salad is served as a separate course, use your salad fork to eat it. If salad is served with the entree, it is acceptable to use the large dinner fork and knife to eat both the salad and the entree. If salad leaves and other vegetables are too large, it is perfectly all right to cut them up with the salad knife. Rest the knife on the salad plate rim after each piece is cut.

If dessert is served with both a dessert fork and a spoon, use the spoon for eating and cutting while you use the fork for holding food in place or pushing it onto the spoon. If using both feels uncomfortable, it's all right to use just the spoon for fruit desserts, or just the fork for desserts such as pie. It is acceptable to eat cake or pie served with ice cream with both the dessert spoon and fork or with the dessert spoon alone.

A sauce spoon is an old-fashioned item reappearing at individual place settings. It is meant for spooning up and eating sauce or gravy from the plate, for those who would rather avoid the more calorie-laden method of dipping bread into gravy. If

Figure 1. Knife only: resting position

Figure 2. Knife and fork: resting position

Figure 3. Knife and fork: finished position

you do wish to use bread for eating the rest of that delicious sauce, break off a small piece of bread with your hands, press it into the sauce, and then use a fork to pick up and eat the moistened bread.

When in doubt, take your cue from either the host or a confident-looking fellow diner. Observe which piece of flatware they pick up and how they use it.

Above all, if you make a mistake, don't make a fuss and don't panic. Be an observant diner and practice at home, and before long the mysteries of flatware usage will become second nature. If you do find yourself eating with the wrong piece of flatware, either put it down and pick up the right one, or continue eating as unselfconsciously as possible with the wrong one. You won't be judged for this minor infraction.

Set the Table

Through custom and practicality, rules for table settings have developed over the years into a standard etiquette. While conforming to these traditions will surely impress those who know the difference, how you decide to set and decorate your table depends upon how formal the occasion is, what you are serving, and how much latitude you're willing to grant yourself with the rules.

Formal Dinner

Understated elegance and symmetry are the guiding principles for a formal table setting (Figure 1).

Tablecloth. A white linen damask tablecloth is the most traditionally appropriate choice for a formal dinner. You may choose instead a colored tablecloth of damask or cotton, or an elegant lace tablecloth over solid cloth or over a bare table.

Napkins. Again, you can't go wrong with napkins of white damask, but you may also choose a color to match the table covering. Fold the napkin into either a squared-off triangle or a rectangle with the thicker fold facing to the right. In the most formal of settings, the napkin rests to the left of the forks. It may instead be placed on the service plate for a touch of informality.

Centerpiece. The centerpiece is often a beautifully arranged, elegant bouquet of fresh cut flowers. Silk flowers or fruit is also acceptable, arranged in crystal or fine china. Place the centerpiece in the center of the table for symmetry, and make sure it will not obscure your guests' view of one another.

Candles. Long white candles set in elegant candle holders or small candelabra should be placed at both ends of the centerpiece and lighted before your guests arrive at the table.

Silverware. Silverware should be sterling silver whose pieces match, although extra silverware, such as dessert utensils and butter knives, need not match in design.

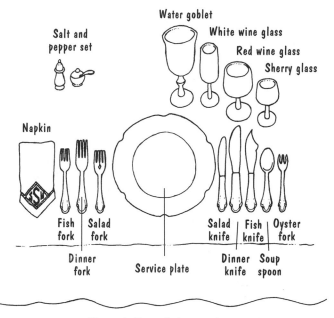

Figure 1. Formal place setting

China. All plates, saucers, and teacups should be of matching fine china, at least during each course. The exception is the service plate, which is larger than the dinner plate and upon which the first-course plate rests. The service plate has a design different from that of the main china service.

Place Settings

✓ Settings should be at a comfortable distance from one another, with the picture on the plate (if there is one) facing the diner.

✓ To the right of the service plate, place knives (teeth toward the plate) in the order of their use, with the first to be used on the outside, and so on. Place separate knives for salad, meat, and fish courses, depending upon what you are serving. To the right of the knives, lay spoons (also in the order of first use), and a small fork for shellfish (often referred to as an oyster fork) if necessary. Never have more than three forks, three knives, or three spoons on a side at one time.

✓ To the left of the service plate, place separate forks for salad, meat, and fish courses, with the first to be used on the outside. If there are only a dinner fork and a salad fork on the left side, you may place the oyster fork (if shellfish is the first course) on the outermost left side of the setting. Salad is always served after the entree at a formal dinner, and the salad fork is therefore placed to the right of the dinner fork.

✓ Dessert forks and spoons are not placed on the table at a formal dinner until dessert is about to be served. They are laid vertically on the left and right plate rims of the dessert plate. Coffee cups are not brought out at this time, as coffee is served

145

after dessert at a formal dinner, often in another room. When coffee is served, the coffee cup should be placed on a saucer, with a teaspoon on the saucer.

✓ Place glasses above the knives to the upper right with the water goblet on the left and the wine glasses in any order, either in a line or in a grouping, so long as no tall glass obstructs a smaller glass behind it.

✓ Butter plates and salad plates are not used in formal place settings.

✓ Salt and pepper sets are either placed at each place setting or shared between two place settings.

Informal Dinner

In contrast to the conservative whites and strict rules of formal settings, an informal table allows for more creative license (Figure 2). Settings may be minimalist or elaborate, rustic or sophisticated, depending upon the occasion or theme. Brighter colors and bolder designs or patterns on plates, tablecloths, and candle holders can be used. You may use place mats in addition to or instead of tablecloths, or even set an elegant candlelit dinner on a bare wood table. Silverware need not be sterling.

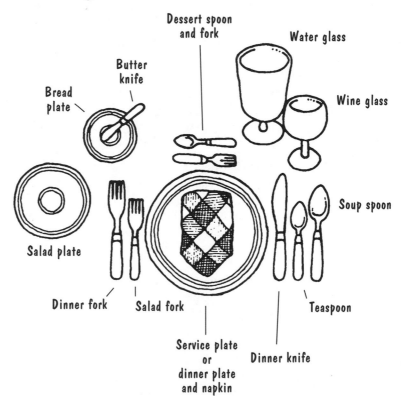

Figure 2. Informal place setting

Make the Perfect Martini and 15 Other Alcoholic Drinks

In mixing drinks, there's no strict way to combine ingredients. The recipes below are standard mixtures, but feel free to experiment with drinks until they taste the way you want them to. Try to use fresh ingredients, particularly when mixing fruit juices. Shake or stir ingredients thoroughly, but don't shake carbonated drinks. Above all, drink safely and responsibly.

Alabama Slammer

Shake
1 oz. each of Southern Comfort whiskey and amaretto
Top with orange juice, and add a dash of grenadine.

Bloody Mary

Shake
1½ oz. vodka
3 oz. tomato juice
juice of 1 lemon
1 dash each of Worcestershire and Tabasco sauce
pinches of salt, pepper, and celery salt

Champagne Cocktail

Mix
1 oz. brandy
1 teaspoon sugar
2 dashes Angostura Bitters
Top with champagne.

Daiquiri

Shake

1½ oz. rum
juice of 1 lime
1 teaspoon powdered sugar
fruit juice (strawberry, peach, or other)
Add crushed ice for a frozen daiquiri.

Fuzzy Navel

Stir
½ oz. peach schnapps with orange juice

Long Island Ice Tea

Stir
½ oz. each rum, triple sec, vodka, tequila, and gin
2 splashes margarita sour mix
Serve over ice and top with Coke (or cream to make a Long Beach).

Mai Tai

Shake over crushed ice
2 oz. rum
1 oz. curaçao
½ oz. each grenadine and almond syrup
juice of ½ lime
1 teaspoon of sugar

Manhattan

Stir in ice
1½ oz. whiskey
¾ oz. sweet vermouth
dash of Angostura Bitters, maraschino cherry (optional)

Margarita

Shake
1½ oz. tequila
½ oz. triple sec
juice of ½ lime
Pour with ice in a salt-rimmed glass, or add crushed ice for a frozen margarita.

Martini

Stir (unless you are James Bond)
2–6 oz. gin, depending on your taste (the more gin, the drier it will taste)
1 oz. dry vermouth
Strain into a glass (ice optional) with an olive or a twist of lemon. Some people
    prefer to substitute vodka for gin to make a vodka martini.

Pina Colada

Pour over ice
½ oz. each dark and light rum
1 oz. each lime, pineapple, and orange juice
dash of grenadine
Top with coconut milk; use crushed ice for a frozen pina colada.

Sea Breeze

Pour over ice
1 oz. vodka with equal parts cranberry and grapefruit juices.

Singapore Sling

Shake
2 oz. gin
½ oz. cherry brandy
juice of ½ lemon
1 teaspoon powdered sugar
Pour over ice and top with seltzer water.

Tennessee Lemonade

Stir with ice
1 oz. each triple sec, Jack Daniels whiskey, and margarita sour mix
Top with 7-Up.

Tequila Sunrise

Stir
1½ oz. tequila
3 oz. orange juice
Add 1 oz. grenadine and do not stir.

Tom Collins

Shake
2 oz. gin (or vodka to make a vodka collins)
juice of ½ lemon
Stir in a teaspoon of sugar, add seltzer water, and pour over ice.

See also "Give a Cocktail Party."

Make the Perfect Cup of Coffee

Follow the manufacturer's instructions for your particular type of coffee maker, be it automatic drip, manual drip, French press, or espresso maker. Avoid the old-fashioned percolator, which boils the coffee, often resulting in a bitter taste. Regardless of the type of coffee maker you use, the following method will ensure a perfect cup, every time.

1. Buy best quality beans or ground coffee. The first and most important ingredient for the perfect cup of coffee is the coffee itself, which comes from various regions of the world, each with its own particular taste. Some coffees have added flavors such as vanilla, chocolate, or hazelnut. Visit specialty coffee shops and do some taste-testing to decide which type to buy. Feel free to experiment with mixing types and flavors together.

2. Store coffee properly to ensure a fresh taste. Coffee beans that come in vacuum-packed containers will stay fresh, if unopened, for months at room temperature. Whole beans, once the container has been opened, may be stored in the freezer in an air-tight container (such as Tupperware) for a month or so. Grind daily for maximum freshness, or take out enough beans when brewed up to two weeks after grinding. Store ground coffee in an air-tight container at room temperature. If you live in a warm climate, keep it in the refrigerator. If you don't own a coffee grinder, vacuum-packed containers of ground coffee will stay fresh for weeks if unopened.

3. Measure to your individual taste. Usually 2 tablespoons of ground coffee per 7 ounces of water (which yields about 6 ounces of coffee), or 1 tablespoon of espresso per 2 ounces of water (which yields about 1½ ounces of espresso), is

a good start. If you like the strong taste of espresso but don't have an espresso maker, you can also brew ground espresso in an automatic drip machine. Use 2 rounded teaspoons of espresso to each 6 to 8 ounces of water.

4. Use fresh, good-tasting water—the kind you'd enjoy drinking. If your tap water tastes bad and is full of additives, it will affect the taste of your coffee and clog your machine with mineral deposits. Consider using bottled spring water. If your brewing equipment is manual rather than electric, use water that is just off the boil to avoid a burnt-tasting coffee.

5. Serve your coffee as soon as it is made. Throw out any leftover coffee that sits on the burner longer than 20 minutes, as it will have a bitter taste. Don't even think about reheating coffee or reusing coffee grounds, as the resulting drink will taste terrible.

6. Clean out your coffee machine about once a month or so to avoid a bitter taste from any accumulated coffee residue or mineral deposits. Run white vinegar through the equipment as if you were brewing coffee, then run pure water through several times until any vinegar smell is gone.

7. Grind the coffee as fine or as coarse as your coffee-making equipment requires. Most grinders in coffee specialty shops and supermarkets have settings for each type of coffee machine. Preground coffee is generally the proper grind for most drip machines.

Open Champagne

The first thing to remember when opening a bottle of champagne is to avoid potential injury and lawsuits, which could ruin an otherwise festive occasion. In all seriousness, do keep the top of the bottle pointed away from any nearby persons or breakables while opening champagne, as a champagne cork can fly out of the bottle at an amazing speed.

There are two ways to open champagne after the wine braces have been gently pushed down from the cork.

The first, and more foolproof way to open champagne, is to grasp the cork firmly with one hand, and the bottle, wrapped in a tea towel, in the other hand. While keeping the bottle as stationary as possible, use the hand holding the cork to gently but firmly turn the cork around and around while gently pulling it up at the same time with each turn. This method allows the pressure in the bottle to be more slowly released than in the second method, and will result in fewer incidences of projectile corks.

The second way, for those with a good strong arm, is to grasp the cork firmly with one hand while pulling the bottle firmly away from it with the other hand. Keep a dish or tea towel wrapped around the bottle to avoid slippage. If this does not work, or if the top of the cork should break off, use a corkscrew to carefully remove the rest of the cork.

Have champagne glasses at the ready so as not to waste a drop of that precious bubbly, which will be in a rush to leave the bottle.

Sharpen a Knife

There are three basic ways to sharpen a knife: grinding, honing, and steeling.

Many sharpening tools are available on the market today. Electric sharpeners make quick work of the process and usually include all three basic processes. Use these appliances according to the manufacturer's instructions.

Grinding is actually that and should *not* be done often because the process literally grinds away some of the knife. A good knife will only need grinding once or twice in a decade, or if it gets chipped or badly dulled. A roll-type sharpener also grinds the knife and should not be used often.

Honing is the process of fine-tuning a knife. It can be done once or twice a year. A brand new knife may need honing before it is used.

Honing is best done with a fine carborundum stone, available in hardware and kitchen equipment stores. Many stones have two sides: a coarse surface and a fine surface. Place the stone on a damp towel to keep it from sliding. Use the coarse side first and then the fine side. Hold the knife firmly in your right hand and place the heel of the blade against the right corner of the stone. Use your other hand to hold the tip of the knife against the stone at a tilted angle so the beveled cutting edge makes contact. Gently drag the knife across the stone from right to left. Then turn the knife over and repeat the process from left to right. Do both sides of the blade a couple of times on the coarse side. Then, turn the stone over and repeat the process on the fine-textured side. Reverse the entire process if you are left-handed. Be patient and you will have to do this only a couple of times a year!

Steeling is really a cleaning process and does not actually sharpen the knife. It simply makes a sharp knife more efficient. It should be done often, depending on how much you use the knife. A professional chef will steel every 15 minutes of use. Home chefs can steel every month or so.

Steeling is done with the long poker that comes in most knife block sets or that can be purchased separately. Professional chefs hold their steels in the air and make quick work of the process. Beginners should try a safer method by bracing the steel on a cutting board. Hold the steel handle firmly and put the tip of it on the cutting board as if you were going to pound it into the board. Place the heel of the knife at the top of the steel by the handle. Gently drag the knife down the steel, keeping the blade at a slight angle. Do this on the other side also. You will probably notice the residue that comes off the knife. This cleans the blade and makes it a safer and more efficient tool.

Always remember . . . a *dull* knife can be very dangerous!

Microwave Timing

Microwave ovens are great for defrosting, cooking fresh vegetables, and warming precooked foods and leftovers. To find out more about how to use a microwave oven and to learn recipes designed for microwave cooking, consult a special microwave cookbook. Listed here are the cooking times of some foods commonly prepared in the microwave.

Defrosting Meats, Fish, and Poultry

While it's possible to cook meats in the microwave, the best way to use it with meats is to defrost them. To defrost meat, place it in a dish or a wrapper (punch holes in the wrapper). Turn over and separate the pieces of meat halfway through defrosting. Make sure no part of the meat begins to cook. The center may remain slightly frozen, so let the meat stand for 10 minutes afterward.

One Pound of	Defrosting Time
Steak	8 to 10 minutes
Hamburger	8 to 10 minutes
Hot dog	5 to 7 minutes
Chicken breast	10 to 12 minutes
Chicken pieces (thighs, wings, drumsticks)	6 to 8 minutes
Bacon	5 to 7 minutes
Sausage	6 to 8 minutes
Fish fillet	6 to 8 minutes
Fish steak	6 to 8 minutes
Crabmeat	10 to 12 minutes
Shrimp	6 to 8 minutes

Cooking Vegetables

To prepare vegetables for microwave cooking, simply wash and slice them as usual (for vegetables kept whole, pierce holes in them to allow steam to escape). Place the vegetables in a deep dish, add the appropriate amount of water, and put a lid on the dish. Microwave on high. Stop once, half way through the cooking time, to stir. Cook until the vegetables reach the desired tenderness, then let stand before serving.

One Pound of	Cooking Time
Broccoli, ¾ cup water	8 to 10 minutes
Carrots, ¼ cup water	6 to 8 minutes
Asparagus, ¼ cup water	5 to 7 minutes
Green beans, ½ cup water	10 to 12 minutes
Cauliflower, ¼ cup water	6 to 8 minutes
Zucchini, ¼ cup water	6 to 8 minutes

One Pound of	Cooking Time
Peas, ¼ cup water	5 to 7 minutes
Potatoes, ¼ cup water (no water for whole potato)	6 to 8 minutes
Corn, ¼ cup water (no water for corn on the cob)	8 to 10 minutes

All About Barbecues

Barbecues are one of those American culinary traditions that appeal to everyone, from those with sophisticated palates to the youngest children. A barbecue can be as simple as a backyard picnic with a few hamburgers and hot dogs tossed on a grill, or a gala event with everything from soup to main course to desserts containing grilled ingredients. The choice is yours.

As with any type of entertaining, the key to a successful barbecue is preparation. At least two days before beginning, make up a menu and grocery list, and include paper goods if you will be using them. Be sure to note which elements in each dish need to be grilled for a separate grilling order. Except for grilled foods, plan to serve cold or lukewarm dishes that can be prepared in advance.

The traditional American side dishes are potato salad, coleslaw, and green salad, but do not feel you have to limit yourself. Bean-and-grain salads are always excellent choices. Besides being highly nutritional, they can marinate at room temperature or in the refrigerator overnight.

When planning appetizers and entrees, do not depend solely on red or white meat. You can also grill fish, vegetables, and even fruit for an unusual dessert. In these cholesterol-and-fat-conscious times, you are sure to have at least one guest who refuses to indulge in grilled meat. Be ready to please him or her with other options.

When making up your shopping list, don't forget condiments: mustard (try to have at least one spicy and one mild), guacamole, salsa, barbecue sauce, ketchup, and relish. If you plan to have guests create their own sandwiches, you will want to put out platters of tomato, onion slices, pickles, lettuce, and other toppings. Fresh fruit is often a satisfying follow-up to a grilled meal on a hot summer day.

A word about grills: the most effective, best-tasting food is cooked on a covered charcoal grill (usually kettle-shaped). Covered gas grills are also available, but they don't impart the same charred taste to food. Braziers are inexpensive flat grills (a hibachi is a small brazier) that are less useful because the heat cannot be adjusted on them. Indoor gas and electric grills are a good substitute if you live in an apartment and have no outdoor space, although they too do not give that distinctive charred taste to the food. *Never use an outdoor grill indoors; it can cause asphyxiation.* Maintain your grill carefully, and clean it thoroughly after each use.

Be sure you have enough fuel for your grill. The choicest steaks will go to waste if you run out of charcoal or lighter fluid. The key to good grilling is a hot fire.

When using a charcoal grill, be sure to start your fire with plenty of time to spare, and do not place any food on the grill until the briquetes have turned gray and begun to ash.

A plain chop grilled to perfection can be delicious on its own, but when you want to add something special, try marinating meat, fish, or vegetables in a vinegar- or wine-based marinade beforehand. You can then baste them by brushing on the remaining marinade while they are on the grill, or if you prefer not to marinade but still wish to add flavor, baste with a flavored butter made by combining butter and herbs. One caveat: do not salt the meat until it has almost finished cooking, since presalting tends to dry the meat out. If there is room on the grill, try toasting buns or other bread alongside the meat.

Once the fire is blazing, you will need some equipment to keep things under control. A pair of long tongs and a long-handled fork are good for turning the food. If you are cooking hamburgers or fish, have a spatula nearby, as they are more delicate to handle than steaks or chops. An oven mitt will protect your hand from the heat. If you are using a very large grill, you may want a leather barbecue glove, which will cover your forearm and is flame resistant.

Several other instruments, while not crucial, can make barbecues easier. Kitchen stores sell handy hinged-wire grilling baskets that can be used to hold fish, vegetables, and other more delicate—or smaller—foods over the fire. Herb- and mesquite-flavored wood chips are also available. Tossing them on the fire will give everything you cook a distinctive flavor.

Serve Wines

The elaborate etiquette associated with serving wine has evolved over centuries. There is a defined way to pour wine, specific wines to serve with certain foods, and even a sequence for serving different wines. All these rules are fine if you are a traditionalist—many of them are based on good manners and common sense. But never let the rules take complete precedence over your own customs and instincts. Try various wines to determine which ones taste best with different foods. Experiment. Still, it's good to know the customs before you decide to break them. You may even find yourself in complete agreement.

Preparation Before Serving

While wine bottles are best stored on their sides to keep the cork moist and tight, stand any bottle you plan to serve upright at least an hour before opening to let the sediment settle to the bottom. Open the bottle about an hour before serving to allow the aroma to emerge. Smell the cork to make sure the wine has not soured. If you wish to chill it, stand the wine in an ice bucket until you are ready to serve.

Wine Glasses

Use cocktail glasses for before- and after-dinner wines or dessert wines. Use regular clear wine glasses for white wines, and either a wine glass or a goblet for red wines. For champagne or other sparkling wines, use champagne glasses.

Wine with Food

White wine traditionally is served with fish, seafood, and poultry; red wine with meat, cheese, and nuts. However, follow your individual tastes or those of your guests. When you purchase the wine in advance of a meal at home, ask the wine merchant to suggest a vintage that will perfectly complement your menu.

Order of Wines

When serving more than one type of wine at a dinner or sitting, serve the newest wines first and work toward the older (and presumably better) wines. Serve drier wines first and reserve the sweetest wine for dessert. In general, white wine is served before red, and light wine before heavy.

Temperature

Usually, red wines or rich sherries do not need to be chilled and should be served at room temperature. White wines, pink wines, dry sherries, and sparkling wines should be chilled slightly in the refrigerator or freezer, to about 40 degrees.

Serving Wines

At a dinner, wine should be poured immediately after the food has been served. Guests should be able to see the wine bottle's label (perhaps pass it around) when you pour. Fill your own glass first, though only slightly, to taste the wine. If satisfied, fill each guest's glass three-fourths full unless a guest asks for less or declines completely. At formal dinners, wine glasses are removed and replaced with new glasses before a second wine is served.

Wine Tasting

Taste, of course, is a matter of taste. Don't let all the experts and "wine snobs" intimidate you and keep you from enjoying the fun of wine tasting.

Cleanse the Palate

To taste a wine accurately, you should have no other flavors in your mouth. If your sole purpose is to taste wine (as opposed to drinking it with dinner or socially), avoid eating or drinking foods with a strong flavor directly before tasting. Foods containing garlic, onion, or hot peppers linger in the mouth and keep you from experiencing the taste to its fullest potential. Cheese goes well with many wines but also impedes taste. To cleanse your palate, try a small piece of unflavored bread or a few sips of untreated (bottled) water.

Look at the Wine

Pour one-half ounce of wine into a clear glass. Inspect the wine's appearance against a white background to see its true color. Wine should be clear, not cloudy, and free of sediment (red wines should stand for over an hour before serving to allow sediment to settle). White wines feature gold highlights; red wines glow a dark ruby color with traces of brown that develop with age (excessive browning in younger wines is a sign of poor quality).

Smell the Wine

The bouquet should smell flowery, as if the grapes had just been picked from the vine. The more complex and varied odor of a wine, the better—very flowery wines are said to have a "nose." With the best wines you will be able to detect the scents of specific flowers like lilacs or violets, or certain herbs and spices, though the ordor will remain well balanced and subtle. Because the bouquet of older wines will diminish and pass quickly, don't let old wines breathe excessively. While this practice implies that bouquet is not always an indicator of a wine's quality, a bad-smelling wine is probably a bad-tasting wine as well.

Taste the Wine

Taste is where subjectivity enters the experience. Generally, a wine should taste balanced and complex—that is, full flavored and light as opposed to thin or heavy. A wine should exhibit the characteristics of its type: a Beaujolais should be fruity, a white Burgundy almondy. To determine taste qualities, try different wines together and compare them. Bring out the full flavor of the wine by holding a sip in your mouth for a few seconds, swishing it around, and breathing in before you swallow. If you are tasting many wines and do not wish to drink too much, spit the wine back into the glass instead of swallowing.

The Aftertaste

Certain qualities of a wine come out only after it is gone from the mouth. Like taste, aftertaste can be subtle, so be extra sensitive and allow the wine to leave its impression.

Choose, Butcher, and Carve Meat

The most important rule in butchering or carving meat is to use a knife that is the right size (about 9" long) and well balanced, comfortable in your hand, and *sharp*. You also need a strong, two-tined fork with a steel guard to protect your hand from the knife blade. A cutting board is the preferred surface on which to work.

Meats should be cut "across the grain," preferably in thin slices, especially ham, pork, tongue, and lamb. The technique to use depends upon the nature and shape of the meat, the size and position of the bone if any, and the end use of the pieces you are cutting. When selecting a large piece of meat, tell the butcher how you intend to prepare and carve it, and ask whether you have the right cut. The following guidelines will be helpful.

Boneless Cuts

With the meat as flat as possible and held firmly with the fork, cut at right angles to the board, starting at the larger end. Cut downward, directly across the grain, pulling the knife slightly toward you as you do so to prevent tearing the fibers and assuring more even slices. If you are slicing a rolled roast, leave the string in place until you reach it. Remove the outside fat first, as well as any excess pockets of fat you encounter along the way (Figure 1).

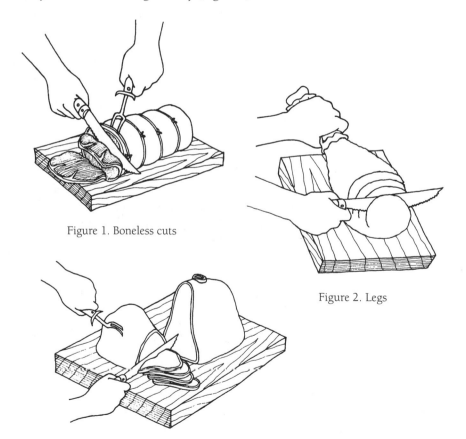

Figure 1. Boneless cuts

Figure 2. Legs

Figure 3. Ham

Legs

When slicing lamb, mutton, ham, or venison, place the small end to your left (if you're right-handed), pointing upward. Hold it steady, either with a fork or with your hand (preferably protecting your hand with a paper towel). Cut away from your fork or hand in **diagonal** slices, bringing the knife right down to the bone. When the downward slicing is complete—as many pieces as you need for the moment—run your knife under the slices, with a gently sawing motion, to release them from the bone. Depending on the size and shape of the meat, you may need to turn it over and repeat the process (Figure 2).

Ham

Carving ham is quite similar. First, cut a lengthwise slice off the bottom to make a flat base and hold the meat steady. Cut thin slices. For the next set of slices, turn the ham on its side and slice down to the bone, vertically, back to the butt. Or turn the ham over and make thin slices lengthwise (Figure 3).

Roasts

Rib. Place the meat in the standing position, with the ribs on your left and the crust side on top. Then slice horizontally across the grain from right to left until your knife reaches the bone.

Crown. Slice down between the bones to make chops, holding the meat with your fork firmly stuck between the ribs to keep the meat steady as you cut. A rack roast can easily be cut into chops in the same manner.

Loin. Remove the backbone first, then cut straight down between the ribs.

Saddle cuts. When you order a saddle of lamb, mutton, or venison, the bone is T-shaped. Place the roast with the T upside down and slant the roast toward you as you slice all the way down to the backbone. Remove the meat in two chunks, which you can carve either crosswise or lengthwise.

Shoulders. In pork, venison, and lamb, the shoulder bone makes a V. Slice the meat diagonally down the bone, then turn the shoulder over. Holding the bone with a paper towel in your hand, cut other similar slices from the bottom side.

Steaks. First, cut the steak from the bone by running the point of a small, very sharp knife along the edge of the bone. Then cut the meat into sections of the desired width, starting at the wider end and slanting your knife slightly, following the grain. If part of the steak is more tender, make sure that your guests receive equal shares of the more desirable portions.

Filet a Fish

Most fish sellers will clean and filet any whole fish you buy from the counter. If you prefer to try it on your own, or if you have caught rather than bought the fish, the process, while a bit messy and smelly, is quite simple.

To clean the fish, start with a sharp, sturdy knife, preferably a fish knife with a scaler on the back of the blade. Use a cutting board (either wood or plastic) that sits securely on your counter top and will not slip. Remove the fish head by using a diagonal stroke, slanting from the back of the head to the underside of the fish. The gills, located under the flaps behind the head, will come away too. Do not remove the tail, because it is often handy to hold onto during the fileting operation. Now follow these steps:

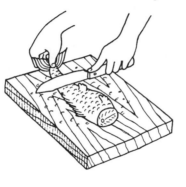

1. Scrape off the scales, using the back of the fish knife or a fish scaler (which resembles a coarse file). Work against the grain from the tail to the front.

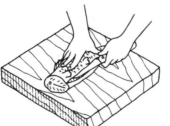

2. Remove and discard any remainders of the gills (some cooks like to leave the head on, but always remove the gills). Moving from the head end with your knife, slit the belly and scrape out the internal organs from the belly cavity. Carefully scrub the belly free of all blood, and flush the cavity under the faucet. Fish sometimes literally throw up their stomachs when caught.

3. Drain the fish thoroughly. Blot it with a paper towel to make it less slippery.

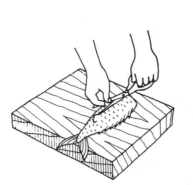

4. Snip off the fins with a pair of heavy-duty scissors.

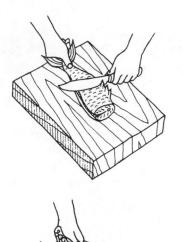

5. Holding the knife diagonally, cut off bony edges and the dorsal (top) fin.

6. In a slitting motion, cut along the backbone from the front to the tail.

7. Roll back one side of the fish, leaving the entire backbone on the other side.

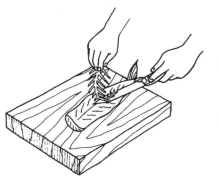

8. Cut the backbone out, carefully removing all fragments of bone, again working from front to tail.

9. Remove the skin by holding the tail end and sliding the knife under the flesh, working neatly toward the front.

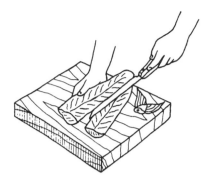

10. Slice off the tail, using a slightly diagonal stroke with your knife.

You can leave the two filets as they are, if the fish is small, or cut each one into smaller portions.

You may prefer to leave the fish whole (except for the head, tail, and internal parts to be removed) so it can be stuffed. In this case, simply remove the backbone without severing the two sides to yield plenty of cavity for stuffing.

If you have an overabundance of fish—perhaps from a successful catch of your own—freeze what you are not going to cook immediately. Most kinds of fish, whether from fresh water or salt water, can be frozen successfully, wrapped in standard freezer foil. Properly frozen fish will retain its flavor and texture for three to four weeks.

Tell Whether a Hamburger or Steak is Rare, Medium, or Well Done

The quickest and most efficient way to tell when any meat is cooked is to use a meat thermometer, which is available in housewares stores. The thermometers are clearly marked with the type of meat—from tender ham to veal, lamb, and poultry—along with the proper temperature for full cooking. Follow recipe instructions for individual cuts of meat; cooking times and oven temperatures may vary. Meat on the bone will take no longer to cook than boneless, skinless meat. An open or covered dish also affects cooking time. In general, follow the chart below; meat is done when it reaches the proper temperature, usually about 20 minutes per pound. Keep in mind that your 325-degree oven may actually be hotter or cooler than your neighbor's. A meat thermometer is the best method to gauge doneness.

Roast Meat Temperatures For Doneness

With an oven set for roasting at 325 degrees:

Meat	Temperature
Poultry	190 degrees
Fresh pork	185 degrees
Lamb	180 degrees
Cured pork, veal, well-done beef	170 degrees
Medium beef	160 degrees
Tender ham	150 degrees
Rare beef	140 degrees

If you don't have a meat thermometer, here's an easy way to feel a steak or hamburger to check for doneness. Touch the skin in the curve between your thumb and forefinger and notice the softness, which resembles the feel of rare meat. Push your fingers together and touch the same spot for the feel of medium-cooked meat. Make a fist for well done. To check the meat, simply make a small incision in the steak or hamburger, and compare. Also check the color: the redder the meat, the rarer it is. To prevent unnecessary illnesses from undercooked meat, particularly hamburgers, avoid serving rare-cooked meats to small children, the elderly, or people with depressed immune systems. Always wash your hands after handling raw meat; germs can spread to countertops and other foods prepared for the meal.

Use Chopsticks

Figure 1. The first chopstick remains stationary.

Figure 2. The second chopstick moves like a pencil.

Chopsticks are the correct utensil for eating Chinese food. It takes only a little know-how and practice to master them. Pick up a chopstick and note that the upper end is thicker. Hold the chopstick in a stationary position, with the upper end resting at the base of your thumb and forefinger (Figure 1). Hold the lower end firmly with the tips of your little finger and ring finger.

The second chopstick is held with the tips of your thumb, index finger, and middle finger. Eat by using a pincer-like motion so the pieces of food can be grasped by bringing together the tops of the moving chopstick and the stationary chopstick (Figure 2).

Make sure the slender tips of the two implements are even so they can pick up small bits of food more easily. To do this, simply tap the tips lightly on your plate from time to time.

Before sitting down to a Chinese meal, adjust the way you hold your chopsticks several times until they seem snug, but relaxed, in your fingers. Then practice picking up various small items of food, such as grains of rice, cereal bits, and peas. You'll be a pro in no time.

If you simply cannot get the hang of it, try this: Wind a small rubber band around the upper ends of the two chopsticks. Squeeze a small wad of folded paper between them. Then slip one loop of the rubber band below the wad of paper. You have created a hinge to use the chopsticks the way you might employ a pair of tweezers—But it won't be as much fun!

Cook an Omelet and Prepare Eggs

If you learn to cook only one thing, learn to cook an omelet. It's possibly the simplest, quickest, least expensive meal you'll ever enjoy for breakfast, lunch, or dinner. Stuffed with just about anything you could imagine, omelets are dynamic, practical, and nutritious.

Omelet

9" or 12" frying pan or omelet pan (non-stick pans are ideal)
spatula
2 or 3 eggs
water
margarine or butter
Extras: cheese, tomatoes, onion, pepper, broccoli, spinach, bacon, sausage, ham, hot dog, banana

1. Prepare the ingredients. The most common added ingredient for an omelet is cheese, and just about any kind of cheese tastes great with eggs. Besides cheese, vegetables such as onions, green peppers, and tomatoes are popular omelet ingredients. Add as many or as few ingredients as you want, and don't be afraid to be creative. Remember, though, that omelets are as healthy or unhealthy as what you put in them. Using low-fat cheese is one good way to make the omelet better for you (you'll find another health tip in Step 2). Whatever you choose to put in your omelet, have it prepared before you start cooking the eggs. Slice all ingredients into small pieces, keeping them the same size as much as possible. If you want your ingredients raw, put them to the side for now. If you want them cooked in the omelet, add them to the pan before you add the eggs (before Step 4). Cheese should be added when the omelet is nearly done to keep everything from sticking to the pan.

2. Prepare the eggs. The number of eggs to use for your omelet will depend on the size of the omelet pan and on how thick you want your omelet to be. An average-sized pan is designed to cook a two- or three-egg omelet. Crack the eggs into a bowl. For a low-cholesterol omelet, pour only the clear egg whites into the bowl, throwing the yellow yolks away (you'll need to use more eggs this way). You may want to add about one-half ounce of water into the bowl for every two eggs you put in; while this is optional, it will thin out the eggs so they spread more evenly in the pan and appear smoother. With a fork or an egg beater, beat the eggs (and water) in the bowl until they are of uniform consistency (the yolk and whites should mix completely).

3. Prepare the omelet pan. Put the pan on the stove and turn the heat to medium. Heat settings may vary from stove to stove so adjust accordingly. Keep in mind that too low a heat level will not cook the eggs, and too high a level will burn them. Now add a pat of margarine or butter to the pan and allow it to melt until it thinly covers the entire base of the pan.

4. Cook the eggs. As soon as the margarine has melted, pour the beaten eggs into the omelet pan (if you decided to cook your ingredients first, you should add them to the pan and allow them to cook. Once cooked, remove them and set aside while you cook the eggs). Let the eggs spread evenly over the bottom of the pan; don't touch them. When the eggs begin to solidify, use a spatula to make sure they are not sticking to the pan. You may also jiggle the pan to move the omelet around. If some of the egg remains liquid on top, you may tilt the pan and let the liquid run off to the outsides of the omelet.

5. Add the ingredients. If you decided not to cook the ingredients, add them now. Put all ingredients onto one half of the omelet (a semicircular area). Do not add so many ingredients that the omelet cannot be folded neatly.

6. Fold the omelet.This is the most delicate maneuver. With your spatula, fold the empty side of the omelet onto the side with the ingredients. Be careful the omelet does not rip when you fold it. Allow the ingredients to warm and the cheese to melt for about a minute, making sure that the omelet is not burning on the bottom.

7. Slide the omelet onto the plate. When the omelet has finished cooking, lift the pan off the stove. Tilting the pan, allow the omelet to slide onto the plate. Do not try to lift the omelet with your spatula; it may fall apart.

8. Serve. Add salt, pepper, or whatever you'd like on your omelet. Make sure you've turned off the stove before you begin to eat. Enjoy!

Scrambled Eggs

1. Turn the stove burner to low heat.

2. Cover the bottom of a frying pan with a thin coat of vegetable oil, margarine, or butter.

3. Break eggs into a bowl and blend them with a fork or whisk to an even consistency. Use one to four eggs for a regular-sized frying pan.

4. If you'd like, mix a small amount (one teaspoon per egg) of milk or water to the eggs. This is often done to extend the eggs and create a smoother texture.

5. Pour the eggs into the frying pan.

6. Allow the eggs to solidify, stirring occasionally to break the eggs and create the scrambled texture. Let the liquid parts run to the bottom of the pan.

7. When the eggs have solidified completely, remove the pan from the heat. Cooking time will be about two or three minutes.

8. Do not remove the eggs from the pan if they have not cooked completely. Instead, let them finish cooking off the heat of the pan. This will ensure that the eggs do not overcook and dry out.

9. Once the eggs finish cooking, serve them immediately. Scrambled eggs cool quickly.

Fried Eggs

1. Turn the stove burner to low heat.
2. Pour a thin coat of vegetable oil, butter, or margarine in a frying pan. To avoid greasy eggs, use only a small amount.
3. Break an egg directly into the frying pan or crack the egg onto a small plate first, then slide it into the pan (this will ensure the egg lands smoothly into the pan).
4. Add a tablespoon of water to the pan, then cover the pan with a lid for two to three minutes. This will let the egg steam-fry.
5. Fry until the whites thicken and the yolk develops a thin white membrane. For a "sunny side up" egg, serve as is.
6. For an "over easy" egg, use a spatula to flip the egg carefully. Be sure not to break open the yolk. Fry the turned-over egg for a few seconds, then serve.

Poached Eggs

1. Crack one fresh egg onto a small plate (or two eggs onto two plates).
2. Fill a shallow pan with about half an inch of water, then boil.
3. Use a spoon to swirl the boiling water, creating a small whirlpool in the pan.
4. As the water is swirling, slide the egg (or eggs) into the pan. The water should cover the egg completely. If you used more than one egg, they should not touch each other.
5. Let the water return to a simmer, but not to a boil. Lower the heat before the water boils again.
6. Leave the eggs in the water for three to four minutes.
7. When the yolks develop a thin white membrane and the whites look like jelly, remove the eggs with a slotted spoon.
8. Serve immediately or refrigerate in cold water to reheat later.

Baked Eggs

1. Preheat the oven at 300 to 350 degrees.
2. Break an egg into a muffin tin (or similar container) that has been coated with vegetable oil, margarine, or butter to keep it from sticking.
3. Cover the tin with aluminum foil to keep moisture in.
4. Place the tin in a shallow pan of hot water (not higher than the side of the tin).
5. Bake for 7 to 12 minutes, until the whites are milky and the yolks are soft but solid.
6. Remove from the oven and pop or scoop the eggs out of the tin.
7. Serve immediately.

Make a Toast

Many people are self-conscious and uncomfortable when expected to make a toast at table. If you are one of them, know you are not alone. Remember that the true focus of the toast is its recipient; it is an experience you will both share. Toasts should be reserved for special occasions, such as birthdays, anniversaries, and wedding receptions, and confined to those present who are key figures in the occasion. The main reasons for giving a toast are these:

1. To congratulate a person(s) for accomplishments.

2. To offer good wishes to one or more people about to embark on a venture or personal relationship.

3. To express an appreciation for assistance or support by the person toasted.

4. To remember someone who may not be present.

5. To give assurances of one's blessing to a person who has made an important decision.

Follow these simple rules when asked or expected to make a toast:

1. If possible, prepare your toast in advance of the occasion and practice it in front of a mirror. You may even want to do a dry run with your partner or a close friend.

2. Stand up at what seems like the appropriate moment, before, during, or at the end of the dinner. Raise your glass, whether it's an alcoholic beverage, soda, or plain water, and announce firmly, "I propose a toast to . . ."

3. Refer to the person in formal ("Dr. Smith"), informal ("Sally"), or colloquial ("Sis") terms, depending upon the forum of the occasion and your relationship to the person toasted.

4. Keep your remarks brief and to the point, especially if you feel awkward. If you are a raconteur or are adroit at telling jokes, feel free to use the occasion to make a pertinent point. However, be sensitive in choosing your remarks. This is probably not the best time to bring up embarrassing anecdotes. Use common sense. Confine your remarks to no more than three minutes out of consideration for others.

5. When you finish your remarks, raise your glass and wait until others do the same. Then take a sip. Everyone else will follow suit with their beverages.

6. If two or more toasts are in order, either make them yourself while you have the attention of those assembled or say you are turning the floor over to someone else who has a few words to say. If appropriate, encourage a "speech" from the toastee.

Incidentally, the term *toast* became popular in the 18th century when guests at dinners in England raised their glasses and praised their hostesses for being as tempting as a favorite gourmet dish of the day: spiced toast.

Pasta Basics

Pasta is among the world's favorite foods. It's inexpensive, easy, versatile, tastes great, and can be prepared in so many ways: with sauce, in a salad, baked. You can easily purchase fresh pasta in supermarkets today. If it is not available, and you don't have the time to make your own pasta from scratch, use boxed pasta imported from Italy. Boxed pasta is sometimes preferable to fresh because it retains more heat, which can contribute to the final cooking of the sauce. Spaghetti is pasta's most familiar form, but it comes in quite a few other shapes and sizes as well. Here are some common pasta shapes; choose the one that best complements the flavor and texture of your sauce.

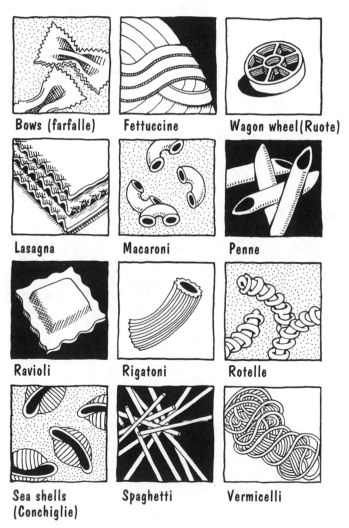

Bows (farfalle)   Fettuccine   Wagon wheel(Ruote)

Lasagna   Macaroni   Penne

Ravioli   Rigatoni   Rotelle

Sea shells (Conchiglie)   Spaghetti   Vermicelli

To Cook Pasta

1. Boil water. For every 8 ounces of pasta, bring 3 quarts of water to a rapid boil in a pot large enough to hold the pasta.

2. Add salt and oil to the boiling water. Salt and oil ensure the pasta won't stick together; both also add flavor.

3. Add pasta. How much you use depends on the number of people you are serving and the serving sizes. An average pasta serving is about 1 cup cooked, equal to about 2 ounces of dried pasta. Submerge the pasta totally in the boiling water.

4. Cook. Keep the pasta in the water until it has softened to your liking. It is suggested that pasta tastes best *al dente* (literally "to the teeth"), when it is tender but still firm enough to sink your teeth into. Others prefer it softer. Keep the pan uncovered while the pasta is cooking, and stir occasionally to separate. Fresh pasta should be completely cooked after only 30 seconds of immersion in boiling water; boxed pasta will take about 10 to 15 minutes, depending on its shape.

5. Drain. When the pasta is ready, drain the water out, using a strainer. Some people like to rinse the pasta with warm water to wash away excess starch, but that is not necessary.

6. Serve with the sauce or meat of your choice.

Eat Lobster, Shrimp, and Crab

Sometimes it seems as if half the pleasure in eating certain foods lies in the very difficulty of getting to their edible parts. Would we enjoy artichokes as much if we did not have to get past their spiky crowns to reach their tender meat? Likewise, would shellfish be as enjoyable if it were not so much work to crack their shells and extract the rich meat? The process itself is enjoyable and rewarding.

Lobster

The gleaming red shell of a freshly steamed lobster can be prohibitively hard to penetrate and intimidating to novices. From each pound of fresh lobster, you can expect to garner three or four ounces of cooked meat, equal to one-third to one-half cup.

Of course, it goes without saying that you want to eat the freshest lobster possible. Purchase precooked lobster extremely carefully, and only when the tail is curled tightly against the body. It is far preferable to purchase a live lobster and store it in the refrigerator until just before cooking, or to order it in a reputable restaurant.

To begin, first gather the tools. You'll need a nutcracker, a knife, and a long, thin fork or other utensil for digging out meat. In shellfish restaurants that abound in

Maine, Massachusetts, and other states where lobster is a local delicacy, paper bibs are provided for patrons, but with some patience and skill you should be able to manage a lobster without splattering. Of course, if you are extracting the lobster meat in your own kitchen—to use in lobster salad or soup, for example—do wear an apron.

Lobster

Claws

Smaller claws

Tail

Cut the lobster from head to tail. Pull shell apart.

Discard gills and stomach sac. Remove intestinal vein. Leave roe in place. Twist off head from tail.

Remove meat from shell.

Suck meat from shell.

Crack the claws.

Lobster is most commonly served back up to show it at its most attractive. Break off the two large claws—they should snap off easily when you turn them—and crack them with the nutcracker. Do so firmly, right at the center, and you will be rewarded with large, smooth pieces of pink meat. Using the long fork or pick, poke the meat out through the holes where the claws were initially attached to the lobster's body. Dip the succulent pieces into hot, melted butter.

The lobster also has eight smaller claws, sticking out from its center; they resemble large insect legs. Break those off as well. You can then either break these legs at their joints and suck out the somewhat stringy meat inside, or simply leave them on your plate.

Turn the lobster over and slice it vertically down the center of its bottom shell, which is somewhat brittle and should crack easily (in a restaurant, this cut will probably already have been made). From there you can easily remove the tail and the main piece of meat.

You can determine the sex of a lobster by inspecting the two swimmerets—the oar-shaped appendages used for swimming—on the lobster's underside at the base of the tail. A female's swimmerets have soft, feathery hair, whereas a male's are smooth. While eating a female lobster, you may discover some pink roe underneath the tail. If so, you are in luck: these are the lobster's unlaid eggs, and they are as tasty as the priciest caviar. If you do happen to be extracting the lobster meat for use in a soup, reserve the roe and stir it in just before serving for an extra dose of flavor and an attractive pink color.

Another odd lobster product remains: the tomalley. This is the green-gray, mushy substance in the lobster's chest—the lobster's liver. As is true with so many types of liver, some people love it and others detest it. It is entirely edible and is certainly worth a taste.

Shrimp

Shrimp must be peeled and deveined. Since it is more often sold frozen than fresh, you won't be able to freeze the shrimp again.

To peel shrimp, take off the feet inside the curve, push back the shell, and carefully pull off the shrimp tail.

To devein, locate the two veins, one on the outside of the shrimp curl and one on the inside. The veins may be dark or may be hardly visible. If the vein is exposed at the head end, pull it out from there. If not, make a small incision at the back of the shrimp and remove the vein that way.

Crab

Steamed hard crabs are a Maryland delicacy. To crack crabs, you'll need a mallet and a small knife or fork to pick out the meat.

First remove the spindly side claws. There isn't much meat here; suck it out by chewing down on the claws.

Break off the large front claws. Crush the claws with the mallet and remove the meat with your fingers. You can try to pull the joints apart to remove the meat in one clean motion; this takes practice and patience.

Turn the body of the crab over and remove the apron, breaking it completely off. Insert your thumb and finger into the body of the crab, and force apart the upper and lower shells to expose the inner body. Remove all innards; they will make you sick if you eat them.

Break the remaining shell down the middle to leave you with two shell-encased units of crabmeat. With a paring knife, cut across the shell and pull it open to expose the meat. Or, crush the shell with your mallet. Pull the crabmeat out in large lumps with your fingers, and enjoy.

It is far easier to buy already picked meat for preparing crab dishes, such as crab cakes or Imperial crab, than to pick the meat yourself. Sift through crabmeat to remove shell fragments before cooking.

Choose a Melon

The two basic classes of melons are watermelon and muskmelon. The latter group includes the typical grocery store varieties of cantaloupe, honeydew, Crenshaw, Persian, casaba, and Christmas melon.

One of the best ways to choose ripe and tasty muskmelon is by the smell. If it smells sweet and perfumy, it will be sweet! The right place to smell is at the blossom end of the melon. Press your finger at this end, and the melon should give slightly. Then, take a whiff!

You should choose melons that are heavy for their size. Obviously, avoid fruit with bruises, soft spots, mold or shriveled areas. Melons are picked when ripe, so unripe melons will never really reach ripeness when you get them home. One sign of an unripe melon picked before its time: If the stem end has jagged edges the melon was picked too young.

Slightly unripe melons can be encouraged to ripen by placing them in a paper bag with an apple and storing at room temperature. The apple releases ethylene gas, which speeds ripening. Check often to make sure the melon doesn't ripen too fast. You can also poke some holes in the bag to allow some of the gas to escape. Once the melon has ripened, store it in the refrigerator for as long as several days.

Cantaloupes should have a thick, cream-colored netting over a golden green rind.

Casabas will have an even-colored yellow rind and can be slightly wrinkled in appearance.

Christmas melons are oval, yellowish-green melons with stripes.

Crenshaws have a golden-green, smooth rind.

Honeydews are fairly smooth and are creamy yellow.

Persian melons should be pale green with a soft netting.

Watermelons can be large or small, round or oval, and yellowish-green to dark green, depending on the variety. Superior-quality watermelons are always symmetrical.

Avoid watermelons that have soft spots, bruises, gashes, or shriveled areas. The best way to choose a ripe watermelon is the old-fashioned method of thumping it. If it sounds hollow, the watermelon is ripe. Cut melons should have a bright color and firm flesh. Avoid those that are water-soaked or mealy.

Choose Fresh Fruits and Vegetables

As you select fresh produce, bear in mind that organic fruits and vegetables may not look as colorful or smooth as inorganically grown vegetables. However, they often taste better.

Apples. Avoid bruises or blemishes, look for bright color.

Bananas. Firm and yellow with no dark bruises.

Beets. Firm, round, slender main root, smooth surface, rich red or gold flesh.

Broccoli. Dark green florets, crisp, no yellow flowers.

Carrots. Well-shaped, smooth, firm, and bright. No splits or wilting.

Cauliflower. Firm white heads with no dark spots.

Celery. Light green crisp leaves.

Cherries. Dark sweet cherries are deep red, almost black; bruise easily. Perishable; use quickly. Fresh May to August.

Corn. Fresh husks, with bright color and silk ends. Plump, but not mature, kernels.

Cranberries. Deep burgundy color indicates ripeness. Avoid blemishes. Bright color indicates unripeness. May be frozen for up to one month. Fresh October to December.

Cucumbers. Firm, green to white green color when ripe. Shriveled ends yield bitter, tough taste and texture.

Garlic. Plump, firm bulbs.

Lemons and Limes. For more juice, choose smooth skin and a thin peel that gives easily to hand pressure. For zest, or slicing, choose firm, rough-skinned fruit. Avoid yellow spots on limes.

Onions. Look for brittle paper skin. No soft or moldy spots. Sprouting or woody center indicates spoilage. Store in dry place at room temperature.

Parsley. Fresh-looking and not wilted. Trim an inch off the stem bottoms and store the bunched parsley in a glass of water in the refrigerator to keep it fresh.

Pears. Ripen in closed paper bags at room temperature with no light. Color depends on variety.

Peas. Sweetest when plump. Choose full pods and pale green color. Fresh February to September.

Potatoes. Firm and smooth, without sprouts. Store in a cool dark place.

Raspberries. Berries mold rapidly and crush easily. Prepare and use within a 24-hour period. Fresh May to January.

Strawberries. Deep, bright color when ripe, with full green caps.

Tomatoes. Color depends on variety. Choose tomatoes that appear firm, plump, well-shaped, and smooth with no blemishes. To ripen them evenly, place in a closed paper bag.

Good Garnishes

Garnishes make a delicious meal a visual treat. There are many simple ways to garnish plates before bringing them to the table. You will find that tasteful presentations add pleasure to your guest's eating experience.

The simplest garnish is a sprig of fresh herbs. Although parsley has become something of a cliché, it serves a useful purpose. Chewing it after a highly flavored meal can freshen the breath. Other good herbs for garnishes are fresh sage, rosemary, and thyme. Try to make such herbs compatible with the flavor of the dish. If you have used a fresh or dried herb in cooking, that herb becomes the natural choice. If not, make an attempt to harmonize flavors. You can simply place a sprig on the plate rim or be more creative. Many chefs serve dishes piled as high as possible; try standing up a sprig of rosemary for eye-catching appeal.

Other simple and edible garnishes can be made from raw vegetables. Although some highly skilled chefs can carve roses from radishes, you need not go so far. Four thin slices of cucumber arranged in an overlapping pattern, an artichoke heart sliced into quarters, or a few carrot curls grouped together will suffice.

Lemon is the most common garnish for fish. A wedge of lemon is both attractive and useful for squirting onto the fish to season it. Or take a thin slice of lemon, make a cut that goes from the outside edge to the center, and twist the slice along the cut so that the two corners face in opposite directions. The same can be done with oranges or limes. Other fruits such as a few strawberries or a small bunch of grapes are a refreshing garnish for light entrées and desserts.

Edible flowers like borage and violets have become quite popular lately. Some flowers are poisonous when eaten, so this is not an area in which you want to exercise your creativity unless you are well informed. Serve only those flowers clearly marked "edible" or so designated in a reliable cookbook and purchased in a food store or grown in your own garden. Flowers will wilt on hot plates, so sprinkle them over salads or desserts just before serving. Sometimes, edible flowers have hard centers. In this case, tear off the petals, discard the center, and sprinkle the petals separately.

Soup benefits from a dash of fresh herbs right before serving. Dill in particular melds well with broths of all types and has an attractive fernlike appearance. A good option with puréed soups is to reserve a handful of one of the ingredients and add it in small pieces at the end. For example, if you are making a carrot-ginger soup, sprinkle a handful of chopped carrots—either cooked or raw—on top before serving.

When preparing cream-based soups, reserve a small amount of the cream, about one teaspoon per portion. Right before serving, pour the cream into the center of each soup-filled bowl. Then, stand a knife in the center of the cream at a 90-degree angle and pull it out toward the edge of the bowl. Repeat this several times in different directions, always beginning from the center, to create an attractive swirled effect.

Desserts are often the prettiest and most tempting dishes and—not coincidentally—the easiest to garnish. On a chocolate dessert, try chocolate shavings (made by pressing a hard block of chocolate against a grater) or simply sprinkle the top with cocoa powder. A dry cake, such as a sponge cake, becomes a delightful confection when you lightly place a doily on top, sprinkle powdered sugar over it, then remove the doily to leave behind a snowflake design. In cake-decorating stores and bakeries, you can purchase all sorts of attractive edible decorations.

Polish Metals

There are commercial cleaners designed for all household metals. But if you want to save time and expense you can use some simple household products to clean and polish almost everything. In either case, check the labels of the substances you intend to use and opt for the ones that are environmentally friendly. The important thing to remember is this: once the metal is clean, rinse it in warm water and wipe it *dry* with a soft, clean cloth. Also, do not try to polish lacquered metals. You would have to remove the lacquer first.

Baking soda does a fine job as an all-purpose metal polisher because it has some scouring power but is gentle enough not to harm the metal. You may want to try it before using harsher alternatives.

Brass

Household ammonia works best. Just rub it on and wipe dry with a clean, soft cloth. A piece of lemon dipped in salt will also do the job of scouring tarnished areas.

Copper

Anything acidic will do the job: vinegar, lemon juice, even tomato juice! Rub any of these on and wipe off. Let the liquid sit on the metal for a while if it does not work immediately. Or add some flour to any of these to make a paste, spread it on the area, let it sit for a while, and then rub off. Add some salt to the paste if you need extra scouring power. Or coat a lemon wedge with salt and rub it on the area until the metal is clean.

Pewter

Pewter is not supposed to shine as brightly as silver, so don't try to polish it too hard. Here's a traditional treatment: polish pewter with cabbage leaves, or use wood ashes moistened with water. You can also make a paste of denatured alcohol and whiting, which is a fine abrasive powder available in hardware stores. If these don't do the job, use extra-fine steel wool dipped in olive or vegetable oil.

Silver

Ammonia also works on silver. Or try toothpaste (the nongel type works best). When cleaning fine silver, be careful not to harm the finish with harsh cleaners.

You can buy a cleanser that consists of a metal plate and some Arm & Hammer cleaner. Or use the homemade version of aluminum foil and baking soda. First heat some water in a pot until it just simmers. Remove from the heat and put some crumbled-up aluminum foil into the bottom of the pot. Add a couple of table-spoons of baking soda to the water, and then add the piece you want to clean. The baking soda will foam up and react with the silver. Then the aluminum foil will attract the tarnish. If you need to, add some more baking soda. Be careful not to do this too often on fine silver or plated pieces, because it removes some of the sil-ver! Again, be sure to rinse the metal and wipe it dry completely.

Platinum and Gold

The instructions for silver are applicable to other precious metals as well. A jewel-er should be consulted, however, if you want to clean jewelry that combines two or more precious metals.

Stainless Steel

Other than commercial cleaners, plain old ammonia works just great. Rub it on with a clean cloth and then dry the metal completely. Toothpaste (nongel type) also works for quick cleanups in the bathroom.

To Remove Rust from Metals

Make a paste of hydrogen peroxide and cream of tartar, and rub on rust stains in sinks and appliances. Or soak corroded pieces in vinegar until the rust begins to dissolve. This works effectively on shower heads and tools!

Give a Cocktail Party

So you want to host a cocktail party! Here are the most frequently asked ques-tions about planning and organizing the perfect afternoon or evening, along with all the answers and information you'll need.

What is the best day of the week to schedule the affair? Friday and Saturday are the most popular, but it really depends on the age group and the preferences of your guests. On these evenings, you can count on more late-stayers. If you want people to go home at a reasonable hour, choose Sunday or a weekday.

What hours should the invitation specify? If you desire definite time span, specify 6 to 8 P.M. or whatever two-hour period is most convenient for your intended guests. If you don't care about a cutoff time, it is acceptable to say sim-ply "from 6:30 P.M. to . . ." Consider also an open house party, which can be more informal and less costly and conventionally scheduled from 1 to 4 P.M. or 3 to 6 P.M. on a weekend or holiday. It is perfectly proper to stagger the hours, so you can invite some people for an earlier period and others for later. More people are accommodated with minimal effort.

How many should I invite? Inexperienced party-givers tend to over-invite, leading to internal "gridlock" where too many people create too high a noise level, and too much drinking compensates for the difficulty in carrying on sociable conversations. If your space is small, it is better to schedule two parties, or a series of small ones, rather than one large blast.

How should dress for the occasion be specified? Cocktail parties encompass all styles, from ultra formal black tie to bathing suits by the pool. Consider the environment and the time of day the party will take place. Also take into account the nature of the occasion—is it an anniversary, graduation, business dinner, reunion of old friends, or holiday event?—and the mood you'd like to set. Specify a dress code that will be comfortable for your intended guests. State dress on the invitation as "black tie," "formal," "casual," or other specific description.

Do I need a bartender? What beverages should be served? For more than an intimate get-together, hire a bertender unless you are experienced at mixing sensible drinks and have friends or family members who are capable assistants. When hiring a bartender, firmly set the ground rules regarding the types of potencies of drinks, the services expected, the cutoff point, the hourly or package rate, and any other pertinent details. Let the bartender advise you on which drinks are most popular in your neighborhood or among the kind of people who will be attending, unless you already have some ideas of your own. Purchase alcoholic beverages from a dealer who will let you return unopened bottles. In this way you will be sure not to run out. Most important these days, provide plenty of alcohol-free beverages, such as sparkling waters, fruit juices, sodas, and nonalcoholic beer. Many guests want the option of selecting those drinks without being conspicuous about their abstinence. When your party takes place late in the day, coffee and tea are a *must*.

What kind of food should I serve? If your guests are likely to be hearty drinkers, provide hearty foods to absorb the alcohol. Otherwise, the fare can be anything you choose, depending upon your talents as a chef, the limitations of your budget, and the nature of the occasion. Give your party a **theme** and serve hors d'oeuvres and basic foods that are Mexican, Italian, vegetarian, or whatever suits your fancy. Investigate having a caterer if the affair is large.

What are my responsibilities as host? Make sure your neighbors are aware a party will be in progress, especially if it is to end late.

Anticipate any potential parking or other transportation requirements. Make sure guests know the phone number where the party will be held, in case they get lost or need assistance.

Look out for any of your guests' special needs, particularly couples with small children, elderly people, or anyone who is disabled.

Introduce people you feel may hit it off well; you're now the social director.

Most importantly, you *must* keep in mind that *you* are the one responsible for any problems that arise from underage drinking associated with your party. And, in the event some tragic accident occurs because one of your guests has imbibed too much without being restrained, *you* might be held legally responsible. Never let your guests drink and drive, arrange rides or offer a bed for the night.

One last thing: enjoy!

See also "Make the Perfect Martini and 15 Other Alcoholic Drinks."

Give a Tea Party

"There are few hours in life more agreeable than the hour dedicated to the ceremony known as afternoon tea," wrote Henry James.

The occasion is just called "tea" or "afternoon tea." Saying "high tea" might sound fancier, but it's incorrect. In England, high tea is more like an early farmhouse supper, not the culinary equivalent of "high church."

Whether serving tea for two or entertaining a larger party, the same basics apply: enough hot, strong tea to perk up your company (Darjeeling is flavorful but not too strong) and a variety of sandwiches and sweets to accompany the brew.

Prepare your sandwiches and cakes first. One basic tea sandwich is just thin brown bread, spread with butter and cut into small triangles. Another easy tea sandwich is the cucumber sandwich. Wash and peel a firm cucumber, cut it into very thin, even slices, and let it drain on paper towels for about an hour. Or, salt the cucumber slices, put them in a bowl, refrigerate and drain after an hour. After the cucumber slices are drained and dried, arrange them on thin, dense slices of white bread spread with dill butter (allow butter to soften, and mash in some dill). Add a sprig of watercress, cut off the bread crusts, and make more small triangle sandwiches. Serve about four types of sandwiches, allowing about two of each per person.

For sweets, choose petit fours from the bakery and accompany them with thin slices of rich pound cake spread thinly with plum or raspberry jam. The classic British tea includes scones with jam and thick clotted cream.

"Hot the pot" before you make the tea. Run the hottest available sink water, or boiling water, into the empty teapot (stoneware or silver) and let it sit, covered for about a minute. When the water boils in the kettle, pour the hot water out of the teapot, dry it completely with a lint-free tea towel, add the tea leaves or bags, and then pour in the boiling tea kettle water. Let the tea brew undisturbed for a few minutes without pressing the tea bags or stirring the leaves.

On an attractive tray, set up your teapot, a sugar bowl, a saucer with very thin slices of lemon, and a creamer. A gracious host may pour the guest's tea, place a teaspoon in the saucer, and allow the guest to take the sugar, cream, or lemon as desired. Naturally, none of your guests will put the common serving spoon or sugar tong in their cups.

Use silver teaspoons for stirring. To protect delicate china cups from almost boiling water, place the silver teaspoon in the cup to deflect the heat and keep the teacup from cracking.

Now, welcome to civilized company in a relaxed, refreshing setting.

Key Table Manners

Table manners for the most part are self-explanatory. When you are an invited guest at a meal, you do not want to do anything to offend your host or another guest. But you need not become so obsessed with manners that you feel stiff and uncomfortable. Simply do what's natural to the circumstance while remaining considerate to others. An informal barbecue and a dinner party for business associates require different etiquette. Some rules, however, are universal. Here's a short list of good table manners.

✓ Sit upright, with correct posture.
✓ Keep your chair legs on the floor.
✓ Try not to cause unnecessary noise: don't clang your silverware against your plate or screech your chair along the floor.
✓ Keep your napkin on your lap. Do not tuck your napkin in your collar (unless, of course, lobster is the entrée and your host is handing out bibs), and be discreet when wiping your mouth.
✓ Do not eat until the blessing or prayer has been said, if one is said. Follow the custom of the house as to whether you stand or bow heads during the blessing.
✓ Wait until everyone has been served before eating. This isn't necessary at a large dinner party, at which the guests wait until the host or hostess invites them to start. At a buffet dinner, wait until at least three people have served themselves before you begin eating.
✓ Do not stretch to reach for food. If you cannot reach something easily, ask someone closer to "please pass" it to you. Remember to say "thank you."
✓ Take what is offered to you. If the host or hostess offers you a dish you do not want, take a very small portion and either suffer through it or mix it unobtrusively into your leftovers. If you cannot eat a dish for dietary reasons, politely say "no, thank you."
✓ Do not take huge portions. Take seconds if you'd like, but give others a chance to be served.
✓ Eat slowly. Besides being rude, eating fast is unhealthy.
✓ Be neat.
✓ Do not stuff food into your mouth. Take small, manageable bites.
✓ Keep your mouth shut when you chew.
✓ Don't talk with your mouth full.

✓ Swallow your food completely before you drink. It's good manners and good for your health.

✓ Do not pick your teeth at the table. If you have food stuck in your teeth and it is noticeable, you may discreetly remove it. Otherwise, wait until after the meal to use a toothpick.

✓ Keep your arms and elbows off the table while you are eating. You may rest your arms on the table once the meal is over, but always keep to your own space.

✓ Keep your hands away from your face. You shouldn't be blowing your nose, picking your teeth, rubbing your eyes, or doing other such things while at the table.

✓ Don't primp. The table is not the place to comb your hair or apply makeup.

✓ Ask to be excused before leaving the table. Simply taking off is rude to the host and the other guests.

7. Health and Exercise

Tighten Your Abs

The exercises given here will help tone and strengthen both your lower and upper abdominal muscles, the stabilizing source of the body's power. Do them for ten minutes every day for a flatter, toned stomach. To be truly effective, these exercises must be combined with aerobic exercise and a proper diet. Stretch well before and after each exercise, and be careful not to overexert yourself.

Bicycle for Lower Abdominals

1. Lie on your back with your legs straight out and your toes pointed. Place your hands behind your head with your elbows out. Keep your shoulders from creeping up toward your neck, and keep your chest lifted.

2. Bring your right leg up to your chest while your left leg remains straight a few inches off the floor. Touch your right knee to your left elbow by raising your back and head slightly and turning your upper body. Pull your navel down into your spine. Hold for one second.

3. Switch legs, extending your right leg and bringing your left leg up to your chest. Touch your left knee to your right elbow by turning your body the other way. Hold for one second.

4. Repeat this exercise 20 times. Inhale as you release, and exhale as you pull up (Figure 1).

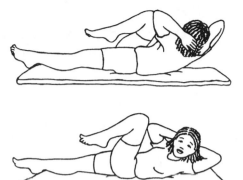

Figure 1. Bicycle for lower abdominals

Situps for Lower Abdominals

1. Lie on your back with your knees bent and your feet flat on the floor about one foot apart. Place your hands behind your head with your elbows out.

2. Lift your upper body, using your chest and stomach muscles (not your arms), and bring your head and upper back slightly off the floor, making sure that the effort is coming from your stomach muscles and not your back. You need not come all the way up to your knees—this can be bad for your back. Hold for one second.

3. Release your stomach muscles, and lower your back to the floor.

4. Repeat at least 20 times, and work up to more, day by day, as you become able. Inhale on the way down; exhale on the way up (Figure 2).

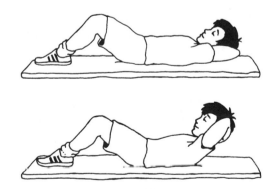

Figure 2. Situps for lower abdominals

181

Crunches with Legs Extended for Upper and Lower Abdominals

1. Keep your upper body in the situp position, as in the previous exercise. Pull your legs in toward your chest, and keep your knees bent so your toes point upward. Your lower back should touch the floor.

2. Lift your head and upper back, using your stomach muscles. Then bring your arms to your side and reach out past your legs. Hold for one second.

3. Release your stomach muscles, and lower your back.

4. Repeat 20 times (Figure 3).

Figure 3. Crunches with legs extended for upper and lower abdominals

Scissor Kicks for Upper and Lower Abdominals

1. Keep your upper body in the situp position.

2. Lift your head off the ground, and pull your navel down toward your spine.

3. Move your legs back and forth a few inches in each direction with a scissor motion; swing the front leg around so it is directly in front of the back leg as you kick.

4. Alternate your legs from back to front with each count as you count to ten, then stop.

5. Release your stomach muscles as you lower your head.

6. Repeat the exercise five times. Keep breathing; never hold your breath. Breathe out during exertion, in on release (Figure 4).

Figure 4. Scissor kicks for upper and lower abdominals

Natural Remedies

Natural remedies and exercises can help treat a variety of common ailments. If you do not exercise regularly, be sure to have a complete physical examination before you begin a workout regimen. When you are in doubt about how to use a particular natural remedy, consult sourcebooks as well as experts in the relevant areas.

Acupressure

This treatment involves pressing particular points on the body that correspond to various body parts to treat ailments and relieve tension and pain. You can easily perform acupressure on yourself or have a partner press the points for you. Consult a good sourcebook (see Bibliography) that tells you which points correspond to which ailments, as well as the contraindications for this treatment.

Aromatherapy

Aromatherapy is the therapeutic use of essential oils to promote health and even to treat many pathological conditions.

✓ Stimulating oils: cardamon, cedar, cinnamon, fennel, lemon, ylang-ylang.
✓ Sedating oils: chamomile, melissa, peppermint.
✓ Antiseptic oils: lemon, thyme, orange, bergamot, juniper, clove, citronella, lavender, peppermint, rosemary, sandalwood, eucalyptus.
✓ Antispasmodic oils: lavender, marjoram, lemongrass, cypress, anise.

183

To Use the Oils

1. Test essences for adverse reactions by applying them to a small area of your body first. For example, soak your hand or foot in water with a drop or two of essence.

2. Mix a few drops with plain massage oil to use in massage.

3. Soak a compress in a diluted essence and apply to the body.

4. Put a few drops of essence into your bath water.

Exercise

1. Have a complete physical examination and consult with your practitioner before beginning a new exercise regimen.

2. Always begin your workout with ten minutes of gentle stretching for arms, legs, sides, back, shoulders, and neck.

3. Do 30 minutes of aerobic exercise at least three times a week to improve your circulation, respiration, endurance, and strength. Try walking, bicycling, jogging, aerobic dance, step aerobics, or swimming, or a stair machine, treadmill, exercise bike, ski machine, or rowing machine.

4. Always cool down with 5 minutes of slower-paced movement and 10 minutes of gentle stretching.

5. If any exercise causes pain, nausea, shortness of breath, or dizziness, stop immediately and consult your health care practitioner.

Training Pulse Rate

Use your first three fingers to feel the pulse in your neck or temple. Count the beats in 15 seconds and multiply by 4.

Age	Beats/minute
20	138–158
25	137–156
30	135–154
35	134–153
40	132–151
45	131–150
50	129–147
55	127–146
60	126–144
65	125–142
70	123–141
75	122–139
80	120–138
85	119–136

Herbal Remedies

Herbs can be used in many forms of:

✓ Ointments, lotions, oils, poultices, syrups
✓ Inhalation of boiling herb steam
✓ Tisane: tea made from various parts of the plant
✓ Infusion: tea made by steeping herbs in boiled water
✓ Decoction: tea made by boiling herbs and straining them
✓ Capsules, tablets, or drops to place under the tongue
✓ Herbal baths
✓ Tinctures: herbs are infused in alcohol

You can purchase herbs at a health or natural foods store, or visit a trained herbalist for his/her diagnosis and suggestions for herbs to try. As illustrated in the list above, there are several ways to use herbs, and some herbs can be toxic if used in the wrong amounts. It is best to consult with an herbalist before using herbal treatments, but if you decide to treat yourself, be sure to seek advice from books about herbs and from someone who is experienced in their use. Store herbs in tightly capped glass bottles in a cool, dry place.

Common Herbs and Their Uses

Aloe vera: helps heal burns and skin rashes
Anise: relieves digestive discomfort
Bayberry bark: relieves sore throats and congestion
Chamomile: soothes the nerves
Echinacea: treats fevers and infections
Fennel: reduces flatulence, aids digestion, and relieves colic
Ginger: relieves bowel and stomach spasms
Ginseng: improves circulation and sexual function
Goldenseal root: treats internal infections and ulcers
Jojoba: soothes skin and scalp problems
Parsley: a good diuretic, useful for treating gallbladder problems and expelling kidney stones
Peppermint: aids digestion and reduces fever
Sage: treats sore throats and mouth sores
Valerian root: relieves nervousness and aids sleep disorders
White willow bark: relieves arthritis and other types of pain

Hydrotherapy

Use water, internally and externally, to treat various ailments.

✓ **Cold or ice water** rejuvenates, acts as a diuretic and anesthetic; use for burns and pain/swelling from injuries.
✓ **Warm or hot water** relaxes, induces perspiration.
✓ **Steam** opens pores, increases perspiration, relieves congestion.

Therapeutic Bath Additives

Oatmeal relieves itchiness, skin problems.

Salt has a relaxing effect.

Apple cider vinegar fights fatigue, relieves sunburn, itch.

Pine increases perspiration, softens skin, relieves rashes.

Epsom salts increases perspiration, relaxes muscles.

Chamomile soothes skin, opens pores; in tea form, relieves insomnia and
digestive upset.

Corn starch and bicarbonate of soda act as an antiseptic.

Massage Techniques

✓ Make rhythmic strokes with open hands to soothe muscles.

✓ Lift, roll, press, and squeeze the skin to stimulate muscles.

✓ Use your thumbs, fingertips, and heels of your hand to make small pressured circular movements.

✓ Gently pummel with your fists, hack with the sides of your hands, clap with your open palms, and pluck the skin to stimulate circulation.

Tips for Good Nutrition

✓ Eat whole foods; avoid processed foods.

✓ Avoid foods that contain dyes, additives, or preservatives.

✓ Limit your intake of fat, salt, sugar, and cholesterol.

✓ Eat a diet rich in fiber.

✓ Take a multivitamin supplement daily.

✓ Base your diet on the U.S. Department of Agriculture Food Pyramid (Figure 1).

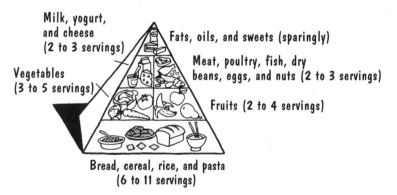

Figure 1. The Food Pyramid

See also "Simple Yoga Exercises to Do at Work," "Plan a Healthy Diet," and "Plan an Exercise Regimen."

Test Your Drinking Water

The quality of tap water varies widely from area to area, and even from house to house in places where each home has its own well. If you or a family member should become sick from drinking your water, contact your state health department immediately. It has the resources to do an in-depth chemical analysis. You can also do some preliminary tests yourself if you suspect problems with water purity.

To clear the pipes, run the water for two minutes with the faucet open all the way. Then, reduce the water pressure to about one-third and run the water another two minutes. Fill a clean, clear glass with water and observe it carefully. Your senses of sight, smell, and taste can tell you a great deal about your own water supply.

If foam is floating on top of the water, your water supply may have detergent residue in it, or if your water source is outside your house, your septic system may be leaking slightly into the water. Call a plumber to examine the tank.

As obvious as this may sound, water should be clear. Hold the glass in front of a white surface. If the water appears murky or cloudy, the filter assigned to clean your water may not be functioning. If the coloring is reddish rather than black, your pipes could be rusty. A plumber can determine pipe damage more accurately. Any type of discoloration in the water indicates that it is not being treated correctly.

A chlorinated or eggy taste or smell is unpleasant and can indicate that the chemicals used to clean the water are being applied too liberally. Attaching a filter directly to your faucet or using a filter pitcher (both available in hardware and housewares stores) should eliminate most of the "off" odor or flavor.

Hardware stores and some pharmacies sell kits for testing water. These kits instruct you to take a sample from one or more faucets in your home. When doing so, use a sterilized bottle. Be sure there are no leaks around the faucet and no attachments (such as a hose, shower head, or filter) and that the faucet is clean. Fill the bottle after running the faucet as described above, and test it immediately, following the kit's instructions, or take it to a laboratory to be tested.

Should such testing reveal any dangerous impurities, drink and cook with bottled water until the problem has been fixed. It is the responsibility of your state health department to handle any serious water problems. The solutions and actions to be taken vary by state. For less serious abnormalities, contact a qualified plumber.

Do a Breast Self-Examination

With breast cancer a leading cause of death in women, second only to lung cancer, it is crucial that you detect the first signs of abnormalities. Early diagnosis and treatment save lives. If you are an adult woman, you should do a breast self-examination once a month. Do it a few days after you've ended your period, when the breasts will be least tender and swollen. If you no longer menstruate, choose a day you'll remember, such as the first of the month, to do the exam. If you detect any abnormalities, such as lumps in your breasts, see a doctor immediately.

1. Undress to your waist and either sit or stand in front of a mirror with your arms at your sides. Look at your breasts in the mirror to see if you can detect any irregularities in the texture or size of your breasts, or if you have any discharge from your nipples.

2. Clasp your hands behind your head and press them forward so your arms pull back. Check for any changes in the shape of your breasts, and for any unusual differences between the two.

3. Put your hands on your hips and pull your shoulders and elbows back. Again, check for irregularities in appearance. Then move your shoulders and elbows forward, checking once more.

4. Raise one arm above your head, and with the other hand inspect the breast opposite to it. Using three fingers, press down firmly on a spot in your breast. Rub the area in a circular motion, feeling for lumps under the skin. Continue pressing spots until you have inspected the entire area of the breast, including the area near the armpit and the armpit itself (Figure 1).

5. When you have pressed around the breast completely, pinch the nipple softly and check for any liquid discharge (Figure 2).

6. Repeat Steps 4 and 5 with your other hand and breast.

7. Lie on your back with one arm folded under your head. This will flatten the breast; stretched tissues make lumps easier to feel. Again pressing your hand firmly, slide your hand around the breast in a circular motion and feel for lumps under the skin (Figure 3). Start at the outside of the breast and move toward the center in a circular motion. Also feel the area at the top of the collarbone and the armpit.

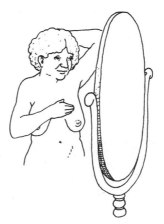

Figure 1. Raise one arm.

Figure 2. Check for discharge.

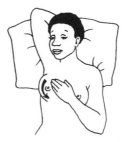

Figure 3. Lie on your back with one arm folded under your head.

8. Repeat with your other hand and breast.

Women with a family history of breast cancer should begin receiving mammograms by age 40. All women should receive the test after age 50. Screening tests using mammography, according to the American Medical Association, have reduced death rates from breast cancer in women over 50 by 30 percent. Have regular gynecological checkups at least twice yearly.

Plan a Healthy Diet

"Diet" has come to connote a weight-loss plan usually followed until the goal weight is reached, and then discarded. Truly successful long-term weight loss, however, relies on a permanent change in eating habits and on slow and continued slimming. Despite the claims of various marketers of diet programs and equipment, it is not recommended that anyone lose more than 2 pounds per week. Before beginning any diet or weight-loss program, always consult your

189

physician, and try to start at a low-stress time so that you can focus on your goal. It will increase your chances of success.

Your doctor can tell you whether it is appropriate for you to begin a diet and will have charts to guide you in determining your optimum weight, taking into account your gender, height, build, and age.

It would be unhealthy and possibly dangerous to attempt weight loss simply with a change in diet and no program of physical exercise. Your doctor can also recommend appropriate activities for your health and fitness level. Swimming and walking are two exercises that most people in reasonably good shape can do without concern for overexertion or injury. You may want to choose more than one sport or activity to keep up your interest, since the goal is to continue exercising long after your goal weight is achieved. Alternate between such activities as jogging, tennis, or bicycle riding to keep you motivated. While organized exercise classes like aerobics or stepping are great calorie-burners, you should seek out ways to fit informal exercise into your day. Park the car a few blocks away from your destination or at the far end of a parking lot, take stairs rather than elevators, garden or do lawn work, chop vegetables by hand instead of using a food processor.

Keep a food diary for a week or two before starting your diet. In a notebook, mark down when, where, and how much of everything you put in your mouth. This can help you identify situations that cause you to overeat—such as late-night television watching—show you exactly what kinds of food you are eating, and reveal how much food it will take to satisfy you.

Weights of Men* Ages 25–59

Height	Small Frame	Medium Frame	Large Frame
5'2"	128–134 lbs.	131–141 lbs.	138–150 lbs.
5'3"	130–136	133–143	140–153
5'4"	132–138	135–145	142–156
5'5"	134–140	137–148	144–160
5'6"	136–142	139–151	146–164
5'7"	138–145	142–154	149–168
5'8"	140–148	145–157	152–172
5'9"	142–151	148–160	155–176
5'10"	144–154	151–163	158–180
5'11"	146–157	154–166	161–184
6'0"	149–160	157–170	164–188
6'1"	152–164	160–174	168–192
6'2"	155–168	164–178	172–197
6'3"	158–172	167–182	176–202
6'4"	162–176	171–187	181–207

Height includes shoes with one-inch heels. Weight includes five pounds of indoor clothing.

Weights of Women* Ages 25–59

Height	Small Frame	Medium Frame	Large Frame
4'10"	102–111 lbs.	109–121 lbs.	118–131 lbs.
4'11"	103–113	111–123	120–134
5'0"	104–115	113–126	122–137
5'1"	106–118	115–129	125–140
5'2"	108–121	118–132	128–143
5'3"	111–124	121–135	131–147
5'4"	114–127	124–138	134–151
5'5"	117–130	127–141	137–155
5'6"	120–133	130–144	140–159
5'7"	123–136	133–147	143–163
5'8"	126–139	136–150	146–167
5'9"	129–142	139–153	149–170
5'10"	132–145	142–156	152–173
5'11"	135–148	145–159	155–176
6'0"	138–151	148–162	158–179

Height includes shoes with one-inch heels. Weight includes three pounds of indoor clothing.

Courtesy of Metropolitan Life Insurance Company, *Statistical Bulletin.*

To figure how many calories your body *really* needs, you need to know your metabolic rate. This will depend on your age, sex, degree of activity, body fat, and other factors.

The Food and Nutrition Board of the National Academy of Sciences has developed a simplified formula for figuring out daily caloric needs: Your weight × 11 (for women) or 12 (for men) – 2 percent of the total for every decade of your age past 20 = your basal metabolic rate (BMR), or the basic amount of calories needed to run your body. For example, a 30-year-old woman who is 140 pounds would calculate her calorie needs this way: 140 × 11 = 1540 – 30.8 (2 percent of 1540, for one decade over 20) = 1509.2. Individual activity levels also influence the ideal amount of calories any person should consume. Generally, you can figure that the average person requires about 15 calories per day per pound of weight (less if inactive or underweight, and more if active or overweight).

Use a calorie guide to discover the exact calorie counts of the foods you've been eating. You may be surprised! Then, with your doctor's supervision, plan out low-calorie menus for each week and follow them. You should schedule breakfast, lunch, and dinner, as well as two snacks per day. (Unbuttered popcorn and fruit are both good healthy snacks.) Allow yourself to consume unlimited amounts of leafy green vegetables such as spinach, kale, and lettuce, but use a cautious hand with dressings, oils, and other fats.

If you are uncertain about getting all the necessary nutrients while dieting, you may take daily vitamin pills, but it is far preferable to plan a diet that provides for your vitamin and mineral requirements. As the recently revised FDA Food Pyramid demonstrates, a healthy diet is based mainly on vegetables and grains. You do not need large amounts of protein—a serving of beans is a good source, as is a small piece of fish. (One ounce of American cheese is equivalent to 10 cups of kidney beans or 25 cups of long-grain rice) Fruit will satisfy your craving for something sweet and boost your fiber intake. Choose skim dairy products over whole or low-fat, white meat over red. Be cautious about eating in restaurants, where you have much less control over food preparation. Watch your fat and salt intake carefully, particularly animal fats (those from meat and butter).

Although it is always dangerous to mark certain foods off limits (this usually backfires and results in your craving and bingeing), allow yourself small amounts of whatever your weakness is. If you have a sweet tooth, eat a cookie, or even a small ice cream cone, once a week. If red meat is your downfall, an occasional lean grilled hamburger or even a small portion of steak will not completely do you in. Remember that the object is to learn a new way of eating that will last, not simply to drop the weight and revert to old unhealthy habits.

Low-fat, low-calorie food need not be bland fare. Grilling, steaming, and poaching are all good methods for preparing delicious meat and vegetable dishes with little or no fat. Learn to use fresh and dried herbs, flavored vinegars, and mustard to add flavor.

Remember, you really are what you eat. Healthy nutrition and a balanced exercise regimen will boost your energy level and leave you feeling fit and better than ever.

See also "Plan an Exercise Regimen."

Stretch Before Exercising

Warming up your muscles and rendering them supple can make the difference between injury and enjoyment. If you stretch carefully for a short period of time before attempting any heavy-duty physical workout, you greatly reduce the chances of feeling stiff, sore, and out of sorts the next day. Stretching exercises should not cause you to sweat or breathe heavily. Perform them slowly and calmly, with deep even breaths. Jerky motions will only hurt you. Hold the positions for a few seconds; this is more beneficial than bouncing. Do five sets of the following exercises, or do them until you feel loose.

1. The best stretching exercise is the one you probably perform instinctively each morning. Stand as straight as possible, lift your hands over your head, and clasp them together, keeping your shoulders down. Then, pull up onto your toes. Imagine a string running between your fingers to the top of your head, pulling you upward.

2. To stretch out your torso, stand with your feet about shoulder-width apart and rest your hands on your hips. Slowly lean forward as far as you can with a flat back, then lift yourself up and lean backward as far as you can, keeping the pelvis tucked under. With your hands still on your hips, turn to the right as far as you can and hold that position for a few seconds. Repeat on the left side. Move from the waist; keep the lower body still. Finally, place your hands at your sides with the palms facing inwards. Lean down and to the right, letting your right hand slide down your right leg. Repeat on the left side. Keep your chest lifted, resisting the urge to lean forward.

3. Groin muscles are rarely considered, but they are easy to pull when running or biking. To stretch them, stand with your legs shoulder-width apart and your hands at your sides. Tilt your right thigh in while holding your left leg straight until you feel a tug in your inner right thigh. Repeat on the left side.

   To finish stretching your thighs, face a wall and lean your left hand against it. Grasp your right toes with your right hand. Your leg will be bent up behind you, and you will feel some stretching in the front of your thigh. Repeat with your left leg. Keep the pelvis tucked under.

4. Place your feet about 24 inches from the wall flat on the ground, hip distance apart. Lean up against the wall with your palms flat and at shoulder level. Slowly lean in toward the wall by bending your elbows. Now place your left foot slightly ahead of the right one, and bend your left knee. Continue pressing against the wall with your hands. You should feel some stretching in your right calf. Repeat on the other side. Then, bend over from the hips until your back becomes a table top, stretching your palms to the wall. Look down at the floor. Hold for a few seconds and release (Figure 1).

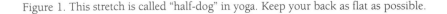

Figure 1. This stretch is called "half-dog" in yoga. Keep your back as flat as possible.

5. Sit on the floor with your legs straight out in front of you, feet together. Slowly reach forward and grasp your toes (or, if you cannot reach your toes, hold onto your shins or a towel slung around your feet). Let your body and head fall forward, and hold that position for a few seconds. Spread your legs as far apart as you can. Massage your inner thighs briskly. Place your hands on the floor between your legs and lean forward until you feel some pull in your inner thighs. Sit up straight. Lean out over your right leg, grasping your toes with both hands if possible, or just holding onto the right shin. Repeat on the left side (Figure 2).

Figure 2. Grip your toes with one hand to stretch leg muscles.

6. To stretch your arms, in a standing position bend your right arm while letting your right hand drop down behind your shoulder. Do the opposite with your left arm, reaching up toward the right hand behind your back (Figure 3). If you cannot make your hands meet in the middle, try holding a belt or other strap in your right hand and grasp it with the left one. Hold your right arm as vertically as possible. Switch arms and repeat.

Figure 3. Clasp your hands behind your head to loosen up your arms.

7. While you probably do not rely consciously on your neck muscles, they hold your head up no matter what you are doing and can be pulled easily. Rolling

and cracking your neck is not as effective as this simple exercise. While standing or sitting, hold your head up straight with your chin parallel to the floor. Drop your chin to your chest, then slowly lift your head and drop it back. Drop your chin to your chest, then slowly lift your head and drop it back. Now, lower it to the right side, letting your ear fall as close to your shoulder as possible. Repeat on the left side. Finally, turn your head until you are looking over your right shoulder. Gently lower your head until your chin touches your shoulder, then turn to the left and repeat.

No matter what kind of stretch you are doing, pay attention to your body's limitations. Work only to the point of pain, not beyond. Do not force a stretch. Use your breathing to help relax the body and direct the movement.

Plan an Exercise Regimen

Regular exercise helps us live longer, more productive lives. There are mental benefits (stress reduction, clarity of thinking, general well-being) and physical benefits (muscle tone, increased lung capacity, proper digestion, stable blood pressure). When developing an exercise regimen, choose sports and activities that conform to your lifestyle, personality, and fitness level.

Considerations

Physical condition. Factors such as age, weaknesses, medical conditions, and previous injuries must be considered realistically before you begin exercising. Consult your doctor for a stress test to measure the amount of exercise your body can handle (this is mandatory for anyone over 35 and advisable at any age), and have a full exam to determine whether any medical conditions will prevent or limit your activity.

What do you hope to get out of exercising? Do you want to lose weight? Reduce stress? Improve your endurance and flexibility? Tone your muscles? Improve your body's fat-to-muscle ratio? Or simply heighten your overall health and well-being? While stretching may reduce stress and improve flexibility, it may not improve endurance as more strenuous activites do. Know what you hope to achieve.

Personality. Do you like the competitive atmosphere of team sports? Or prefer the solitary activity of swimming? Do you crave high-intensity exercise such as basketball or less intense, low-impact activities such as walking?

Schedule. It's crucial that you stick with the exercise you choose. Set a regular schedule that is realistic and fits your lifestyle. Don't exercise if you are overly fatigued or ill.

Age. Young children are naturally active, but good exercise habits should be taught from childhood. Medical studies show that regular exercise performed before the age of 25 can affect the way our body ages as we go past 50. No matter when you start an exercise program, the benefits to health and longevity are palpable.

Workouts with a purpose. For stress reduction: High-intensity sports such as basketball, racquetball, and karate let out aggression; relaxation techniques of breathing and stretching are found in dance, yoga, and meditation.

✓ For muscle toning and building: Isometric exercises such as weight lifting, body sculpting, climbing, or rowing. Try golf to improve upper body strength.

✓ For flexibility: Exercises that require muscle control, balance, and stretching such as yoga, karate, ballet, or gymnastics.

✓ For endurance: Exercises to increase duration and intensity, such as running, swimming, tennis and biking. Try walking the golf course instead of riding a cart.

✓ For weight loss: Highly aerobic exercises such as calisthenics, stepping, aerobic dancing, jogging, or biking—combined with a healthy diet.

✓ For increased lung capacity: The disciplined breathing of yoga and meditation or aerobic activities such as running, dancing, or skating.

✓ For increased cardiovascular fitness: Get blood pumping with aerobic activities—running, stepping, football. Try swimming or biking for less intensity. Know your limits. If you can't breathe comfortably, you've pushed too far.

Your Program

Balance. Condition all parts of your body—heart, lungs, legs, stomach, back, and upper body. Work on becoming strong *and* flexible.

Regulate. Take your pulse before and after every exercise sequence. If you find yourself struggling, lower the intensity and work on building up endurance. Keep breathing smoothly and rhythmically.

Intensity. To gain the maximum cardiovascular benefits from exercise, you want to elevate your heart rate to about 75 to 80 percent of your maximum heart rate (the fastest your heart can beat). Figure your estimated maximum heart rate by subtracting your age from 220. Raising your pulse far above 80 percent of the maximum can be dangerous; not raising it at least to 75 percent will not be truly exercise.

Frequency. Exercise at least three times a week, though more is fine if you have the time and are able. Avoid burnout, though—you're in this for the long term.

Duration of workout. The best exercise sessions last for 30 minutes of sustained activity. The cardiovascular and fat-burning benefits of aerobic activity will *not* take effect if you are not moving and breathing through this time period— whether that means simply walking or a high/low dance class. Don't overexert; don't stop; do keep breathing and moving at a comfortable, confident pace.

See also "Plan a Healthy Diet," "Tighten Your Abs," "Stretch Before Exercising," and "Jog."

Jog

The advantages of jogging are clear: better circulation, a stronger heart, muscle tone, higher energy, and a general sense of well-being. Before you start, get a checkup and ask your doctor for a stress test to determine how much of a workout your body can handle. Know what your heart rate should be, the maximum it should be allowed to reach, and how to measure it. Don't overexert yourself; build up your fitness level gradually.

Techniques

Speed. How fast you run is not so important as long as you get a good workout. Forcing yourself to run faster than you can handle is dangerous. Know your limitations and build from there.

Time and distance. Most runners set a distance (2 miles, 10 miles) to run each time, and complete it even if it they must walk part of the way. Others decide to run for a set amount of time (20 minutes, half an hour). Determine what's best for you, and stick to it.

Location. Whether on a track, neighborhood sidewalks, or cross-country nature trails, a combination of environments provides needed variety in your runs. Avoid hard surfaces such as concrete; they can stress the knees and shins.

Schedule. Keep a regular schedule for jogging. Sporadic runs will not improve your fitness level. Start off with about one hour a week, divided into three or four days (about 15 minutes every other day). As your endurance grows, jog longer.

Recording progress. Keep a log to monitor your progress. Write down the date, time, and distance of each run; your beginning and ending pulse rates; and any notes you may want to add about how you are feeling.

Outfitting

Shoes. The type of shoe you wear depends on the surface on which you run. Whatever shoe you get should be designed specifically for running. Wear the shoes only when you jog. Consider fit, comfort, material, shock absorption, and flexibility.

Clothes. Clothes should always be comfortable, loose enough to allow your body to move freely, and appropriate for the weather.

Headwear. Wear sweatbands if you sweat a lot. Tie your hair back if it is long. Use waterproof sunblock and a hat to protect your skin from the sun.

Style and Form

Form. Don't worry about correct running form—just do what feels comfortable. To avoid difficulties or injury: run upright (back straight, shoulders up), keep your body solid but your muscles loose, keep your arms bent to some degree (whatever is comfortable), keep your hands loose (not clutched), and land on the heel and push off the ball of your foot.

Breathing. Regulate your breathing. Most runners breathe through their mouths, but to keep your breathing steady you may find it helpful to inhale into your mouth and exhale through your nose. Make sure you never deny your body the oxygen it needs, or you may hyperventilate.

Stride. Your running motion should be solid and comfortable. Strive to keep it regular.

Workout

1. Allow at least two hours to digest food. Before you leave, take a small drink to prevent dehydration, and go to the bathroom if necessary.

2. Stretch your muscles, especially those on the back of your legs, your lower back, and your neck. Stretch a muscle until you feel an uncomfortable tension, but don't strain.

3. Start with a slow run to warm up. When you feel ready, increase your speed to a regular pace.

4. As you increase your speed, establish a stride for the duration of the jog. Exert yourself, but don't push yourself to the point of pain.

5. Slow down as you reach the end of your run. When you have stabilized your breathing, you may return to a walk. Continue walking until your pulse rate has normalized and your breath is regular.

6. Stretch again when you have completed your jog. Running will tighten your muscles; stretch to reduce the soreness and stiffness you may feel later.

See also "Stretch Before Exercising."

Choose a Doctor

You may one day need to find a new doctor. Perhaps you have moved to a new town, or your doctor has retired; perhaps you require the attention of a specialist. Elderly people, whose care is often especially complex and important to monitor, may find themselves rushed by a doctor who does not want to see Medicare patients or stranded when a trusted family doctor stops practicing. Maybe you are simply dissatisfied with your current doctor. For whatever reason, finding a new doctor you trust and like is not always easy. Where can you go to find a good doctor? And what should you look for in a doctor? These tips will facilitate your search.

1. Ask friends, relatives, or trusted co-workers. The best recommendations always come from people you trust. If you are not satisfied with a doctor, ask people close to you if they are satisfied with their doctors. If they are, try going to them.

2. Call a hospital. Particularly if you are new in a town, the local hospital will refer you to doctors affiliated with them, no matter what the specialty. Remember, though, that because hospitals refer you only to the doctors working in house, you won't get a complete picture of all the doctors available. Still, the hospital is a good place to start, and it's wise to choose a doctor with admitting privileges at the hospital.

3. Call referral lines. Many medical associations will run, or sponsor, toll-free or local referral lines. They can direct you to a doctor anywhere in the country. Check your phone book under the appropriate medical category, or call information for toll-free 800 numbers. Some prominent groups include the American Medical Association, the American Medical Women's Association, the National Institutes of Health, and the American College of Physicians.

4. Ask other doctors. If you like and trust your current doctor but need medical care in an area he or she doesn't handle, you may want to ask that doctor for advice in choosing a specialist. Your doctor deals with many other doctors and will probably be able to recommend a known and respected specialist. If you are moving to another town, your doctor may have contacts there for you to pursue.

5. Contact consumer health advocacy groups. These organizations may help you find doctors whose expertise fits your specific needs and viewpoints. Some noteworthy sources are the National Women's Health Network, the American Association of Retired Persons, the People's Medical Society, and the Center for Medical Consumers in New York City. Call information for the toll-free 800 number.

6. Visit a doctor. Set up an appointment to go see the doctor you've been referred to. During your visit, observe the things you like and dislike about the doctor:

   ✓ How hard is it to set up an appointment?
   ✓ How easy is it to reach the doctor or the secretary by phone?
   ✓ How comfortable do you feel in the office or waiting room?
   ✓ How personable is the doctor?
   ✓ How well does the doctor answer your questions, both clearly and thoroughly?
   ✓ What course of treatment does the doctor suggest for your condition?
   ✓ Has the doctor involved you in the decision making process for treatment?
   ✓ How long did you wait to see the doctor? Did the doctor hold a private conference with you after the examination? Did you feel rushed?
   ✓ While money should never be the ultimate factor in deciding on a doctor, if you are not covered by health care insurance, keep in mind how affordable the doctor is.

7. Decide whether to return to the same doctor. If you are unsatisfied by the doctor's care, or do not feel comfortable with the doctor, do not hesitate to find a new one. The important thing is that you feel good about your

medical care. Keep in mind, though, that a doctor's effectiveness often depends on how well he or she knows you. If you keep switching, you never get the chance to develop the kind of doctor-patient relationship that will promote good health.

8. Older people may require special care. Find out whether major teaching hospitals in your area have special geriatric clinics or centers. For instance, Johns Hopkins in Baltimore has a world-renowned medical facility.

9. If you know you have a specific condition or illness, try contacting national organizations devoted to that particular problem. The National Heart Association, the Cancer Association, and the Arthritis Foundation are a few examples. Ask a local librarian to help you do research to find organizations that may be helpful in finding the right doctor or treatment.

10. Be as well informed as possible. The more you know about your condition, the better you will be able to choose a doctor effectively and receive the best possible care.

When to See a Doctor

It is a good idea to receive yearly physical exams from a family physician or internist. This doctor should take baseline x-rays, cardiograms, and blood work, and compare the results over time as you age or if a health problem is suspected.

Visit the dentist every six months for a good cleaning and checkup. Regular cleanings help prevent gum disease as you grow older.

Visit the ophthalmologist every year if your eyesight is bad or you have an eye problem. Others can hold to visits every other year.

Women should see their gynecologist every six months. Regular examinations are the best prevention against breast and cervical cancer.

Visit specialists for specific health care problems and conditions according to the schedule supplied by the doctor. Maintaining good health often hinges on regular examinations and evaluations. Don't put them off or rationalize follow-up examinations as unimportant—they may save your life.

Cure Insomnia

Insomnia, or difficulty sleeping, can occur for many reasons and come in many forms. It can be medical—the result of illness, pain, asthma, aging, stress, or depression—or it can arise from problems with eating or drinking or simply from jet lag. Insomnia can take the form of trouble falling asleep, waking frequently at night, waking too early in the morning, or not sleeping deeply enough. Almost always, the best cure for insomnia is to treat its cause. Remember, though, that sleep patterns depend on the individual; what is insomnia for one may be normal for another. Here are some suggestions for treating insomnia. If problems persist, be sure to consult a doctor before taking further steps.

✓ Exercise regularly. Being active helps keep the body on schedule.

✓ Set regular hours for sleep. Stick to what your biological clock tells you; working against it and disrupting your natural sleep pattern will get you into trouble.

✓ Sleep only when you're tired. Don't bother getting in bed if you're just not tired, you'll only toss and turn until you do get tired. Instead, do something constructive that will inevitably make you sleepy.

✓ Avoid naps during the day. Obviously, sleeping during the day will keep you up at night. If you find you need a nap, perhaps you're not getting enough sleep at night and should readjust your schedule.

✓ Get plenty of fresh air, both during the day and when you sleep at night. Good air circulation is important to maintaining healthy sleep.

✓ Relax in bed. Everyone has techniques to help relax at night, such as counting sheep or thinking of waves in the ocean. Try anything that will get your mind away from the concept of falling asleep and focused on relaxing your body.

✓ Read before bedtime. Other media, like television or radio, may work, but more likely they will just keep you awake and tuned in.

✓ Regulate the room temperature. Some sleep better in a cool room, others in a warm room. Set the thermostat to whatever is most comfortable to you, but keep in mind that extreme temperatures may be unhealthy.

✓ Sleep in a comfortable bed. Sometimes insomnia can be traced to a lumpy or excessively hard bed. Again, make your bed suit you. If your mattress is too hard, try a feather bed; if it is too soft, place a board underneath it.

✓ Sleep in comfortable clothes. Generally, loose-fitting clothes that don't irritate the skin promote the best sleep.

✓ Drink hot milk. It's not just an old myth; hot milk really does contain a chemical that helps induce sleep.

✓ Stay away from caffeine or other stimulants, particularly at night.

✓ Avoid late-night eating binges. A full stomach can lead to restless sleep.

✓ Once in a while, have a glass of wine before bed. For some, alcohol causes drowsiness; if this works, it's fine to do in moderation. Often, though, alcohol disrupts sleep. Never mix alcohol and sleeping pills.

✓ Take sleeping pills with caution. Use them only according to the directions and for short-term problems. Don't use sleeping pills for more than two weeks at a time. After that, pills can actually harm sleep patterns, causing increased insomnia and restlessness. Read all warning labels. Consult a doctor before resorting to pills.

✓ Stay up when jet lagged. If possible, it is best to simply stay awake and assume the natural rhythms of your new environment.

10 Ways to Quit Smoking

Everyone knows the harmful effects of smoking cigarettes, but many smokers just can't seem to quit. Finding the right method or combination of methods may make the process a bit easier. Here's a list of quitting techniques:

1. **Cold Turkey.** While this is the most popular and the most effective way to quit, it can also be one of the toughest. The first few weeks, when the urges for nicotine are strongest, are the worst. If you can stick it out, though, this method will last—and it won't cost you a cent. The most important key to success is not to let yourself think you've been so good that you "deserve" a cigarette.

2. **Progressive Quitting.** Try cutting down little by little, at a pace you feel comfortable with. Smoke one cigarette less a day every day, or one less every week. Eventually you'll dwindle your cigarette intake down to nothing. Be careful—it'll be easy to break the rules when you are the one setting them.

3. **Relaxation Techniques and Exercise.** Many people smoke to relieve stress. Relieving stress in other ways, such as meditation, may do away with the need to smoke. (See also "How to Meditate.") You can also release nervous energy through exercise.

4. **Hypnosis.** In recent years, hypnosis has become a popular way to rid yourself of the urge for nicotine. While this process has proved effective, it can be expensive. If you decide to try it, make sure you go to a reliable hypnotist, or get a book on autohypnosis.

5. **Nicotine Patch.** Another recently devised method, patches have also proved effective. A skin patch will supply your body with the nicotine it craves. Physicians generally prescribe the highest dose for the first three weeks, with lower doses tapering off over the next three weeks. You must not smoke while using the patch—the strength of the high dose patch should satisfy your body's craving for nicotine. The patch, however, cannot satisfy your social cravings for a cigarette or replace cigarette smoking as an oral habit. Try sucking on hard candy; carry a pen or pencil to hold in your hand. Nicotine patch therapy is most successful when combined with psychological counseling.

6. **Nicotine Gum.** As with the patches, you can supply your body with nicotine through chewing nicotine gum. It will also let you quit gradually—in six to eight weeks if used correctly as prescribed.

7. **Behavioral Modification.** Some people need to smoke at specific times: after a meal, with coffee, when under pressure, or when about to perform. If you can identify what situations give you the urge to smoke, you can anticipate or simply avoid them. You'll be less likely to want to smoke. Maintaining a constant blood sugar throughout your day helps to avoid dangerous "crave" times. Eat several small meals a day that focus on fruits and vegetables, proteins, and complex carbohydrates. Stay away from sweets.

   Try regular Epsom salt baths to help remove nicotine and tar from the body. Use one-half pound of salt in a full tub; rinse off afterward in the shower.

8. **Avoid Temptation.** Many people smoke when they are around other people who smoke. If you are like that, avoid places such as bars or restaurants where you know people will be smoking.

9. **Avoid Caffeine and Other Stimulants.** Stimulants like coffee increase the craving for cigarettes. Try to cut back or do without them. Get energy from fruit drinks or sport beverages like Gatorade. Eating and drinking in a healthy way will help your body adjust and keep your energy level high.

10. **Eat.** People often complain that ever since they quit smoking, they can't stop eating. Well, that's okay if you are eating healthy, low-fat foods. Carry fruit or raw vegetables as quick snacks. Chew sugar-free gum if you must have something to hold in your mouth. Now is the perfect time to improve your diet and live healthy!

Recognize and Treat Common Allergies

Allergies are reactions your body experiences to substances generally harmless to most people. Substances causing allergic reactions, called allergens, can be just about anything but are usually pollen, grass, chemicals, dust, smoke, animal dander, mold and certain foods. While definitive treatment of allergies is not always possible, lessening the symptoms can provide relief. The treatments described here for hay fever, asthma, and food intolerance, three of the most common types of allergic reaction, are suggestions based on what has been known to work for many people. They may or may not work for you. Before taking any medicine or altering your diet, consult an allergist or a general practitioner to determine what you are allergic to and the proper strategy for treating your condition.

Hay Fever

A very common seasonal allergy, hay fever generally strikes people under 40 during the spring and summer months and affects more women than men.

Symptoms

Itchy, watery, red, and/or swollen eyes; itchy, runny or stuffy nose; sore throat; headache.

Causes

Pollen (tiny flower seeds) in grass, trees, and weeds, dust, and other airborne substances.

Treatment

✓ Reduce exposure to allergens: stay away from open fields; close windows in the house; stay inside after dark, when pollen levels go up; keep the house clean and vacuumed; avoid smoke-filled environments; and bathe and groom animals, and vacuum pet hair, regularly.

✓ Use eye drops, nose drops, and over-the-counter allergy medicines for temporary relief of symptoms (Caution: long-term use of nose drops can irritate the nasal passages and aggravate some chronic conditions.) Follow all directions on the package.

✓ Wash your face often to clear it of pollen in the air.

✓ Alter your diet. This offers nominal help: avoid grains, alcohol, and milk; increase your intake of vitamins B_6, B_{12}, C, and E; carotene; and magnesium. Also try botanical medicines such as licorice root, angelica, Chinese skullcap, ephedra, skunk cabbage, onions, garlic, chili peppers, or mint tea.

✓ Go to a doctor. Prescription antihistamines are effective but cause jitteriness and insomnia after prolonged use. If your symptoms are especially severe, you may need to receive allergy injections.

Asthma

Asthma generally begins in childhood and decreases in severity or disappears in adulthood. It can, however, develop at any age, and heredity is a factor.

Symptoms

Recurrent but not constant wheezing, attacks of breathlessness, and difficulty breathing.

Causes

Can be triggered by many factors, including a variety of allergies, irritations, infections, over-activity, fatigue, and emotional factors such as stress or anxiety.

Treatment

✓ Avoid the factors that trigger asthma. This may require a visit to an allergist to determine the exact cause of your asthma.

✓ Doctor-prescribed medications, including injections for severe cases, cortisone in limited use, or bronchodilators, which open up bronchial passages and are commonly taken with the use of an inhaler (these should be used sparingly to remain safe and effective).

✓ Vomiting, while not recommended as a regular practice, can ease the symptoms of asthma.

✓ Alter your diet. As with hay fever, this may help in part; see the vitamins and natural medicines specified in the section above.

✓ Exercise and physical conditioning in the appropriate amount can lessen the likelihood of an asthma attack. Relaxation techniques such as yoga, and non-stressful exercise such as swimming, can be helpful.

Food Allergy or Intolerance

A dislike or distaste for a food does not constitute an allergy or intolerance. Food intolerances cause distressing medical conditions or physical reactions.

Symptoms

Nausea, heartburn, swollen lips, vomiting, headaches, diarrhea, gas, hives, itching, eczema.

Causes

Particular foods, most commonly milk products, eggs, fish and shellfish, wheat, additives, strawberries, and cereals.

Treatment

✓ Avoid the allergen food. This may require testing by an allergist to determine exactly what food is causing the allergic reaction—for example, lactose intolerance to milk products.

✓ Antihistamines, in some cases, can relieve symptoms.

✓ Over-the-counter medicines such as antacids and diarrhea treatment can provide temporary relief but should not be thought of as a cure.

5 Ways to Relieve Fatigue

If you feel abnormally tired for an extended time, your fatigue could be the result of various physical and psychological factors. A disease like diabetes or tuberculosis can be a physical cause of fatigue, which must be treated along with the disease. People recovering from a virus will sometimes experience chronic fatigue syndrome, which can be debilitating but will eventually go away. Extreme or persistent fatigue that shows no somatic (physical) origin can be a sign of clinical depression. Depression can be treated. Consult your family doctor or licensed psychologist or psychotherapist, who can provide helpful counseling and possibly drug therapy.

Here are some strategies you can try at home to beat a cycle of fatigue:

1. **Sleep less.** Fatigue builds on itself. Beyond the required amount, the more sleep you get the more tired you will be. Sleep only as much as you need to

function, try to sleep the same amount every night, and avoid resting during the day.

2. **Increase your activity level.** Exercise is the best activity for reducing fatigue. Try an aerobic exercise like walking or jogging to improve your circulation and stimulate the body's production of mood-enhancing endorphins. But even if you don't get a lot of physical exercise, just keeping active in any way will make you too busy to be tired. Take up a hobby or join a club—anything to avoid boredom and stagnation. If your fatigue is a side effect of a serious physical illness, consult your physician before beginning any exercise regimen.

3. **Improve your diet.** As you know, what you eat and drink has a great effect on how you feel. Eat and drink more or less, depending on your needs, and pay attention to the types of foods you put in your body. Eat carbohydrates like pasta for quick energy, fresh fruit for natural sugar and vitamin C. Take a multivitamin daily. *Don't* take sleeping pills or overdose on caffeine drinks; they will only exacerbate a fatigue-insomnia cycle.

4. **Analyze your problems.** If depression is the cause of your excessive fatigue, you can cure your fatigue only by treating your depression. Think about any situations or issues that may be troubling you; discuss them with a friend or a professional if necessary.

5. **Relax.** Excessive stress and tension will wear you out. Try various relaxation techniques to help alleviate your feelings of fatigue.

See also "Relieve Stress," "Simple Yoga Exercises to Do at Work," and "Meditate."

8. Holidays

Wrap a Present

Get scissors, tape, wrapping paper, and ribbon, then find a hard, flat surface to work on. Follow these directions for the conventional, and not-so-conventional, gift wrappings.

Box

1. Place the package in the center of a sheet of wrapping paper.
2. Cut the paper so it will overlap a few inches when wrapped around the width of the box. Also, be sure the amount of excess paper on the ends of the package is at least two-thirds the height of the package.
3. Wrap the paper around the width of the box smoothly, and tape where the paper overlaps itself. Fold the overlapping side to create a smooth edge before laying it down (Figure 1a).
4. Fold the end paper around the height of the box to lay flat. Create triangular flaps at the top and bottom. Fold the top flap end down over the sides. Then, fold the bottom flap up over the top flap and tape it (Figure 1b). Crease the bottom flap to create a smooth edge.
5. Repeat Step 4 with the other package end.
6. To wrap a ribbon around the package, turn the package over and lay a long piece of ribbon across the midsection of the side that should face up. Bring both ends of the ribbon entirely around the width of box until they meet on the other side. Cross the ribbon, turn each end 90 degrees, and continue to wrap it around the length of the box and back around to the front, flipping the box over to do so. Tie the ends of the ribbon in a bow (Figure 1c).

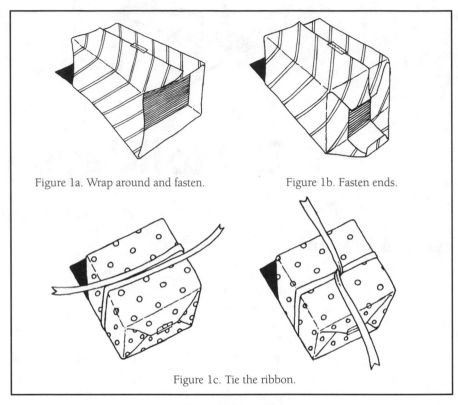

Figure 1a. Wrap around and fasten.   Figure 1b. Fasten ends.

Figure 1c. Tie the ribbon.

Figure 1. Wrap a box

Bottles, Spheres, Odd-Shaped Objects

1. Place the object on top of two sheets of square wrapping paper (tissue paper works best), both at least twice as long as the object. Turn the sheets diagonally so they form an eight-pointed star.

2. Lift all eight points up over the object to meet at a point above the package.

3. Tie the area where the points meet with ribbon, and let the excess paper blossom out (Figure 2).

Figure 2. Wrap odd-shaped objects

Flat Objects

Flat objects such as thin books, records, or calendars are done the same way as box packages until Step 4. Instead, fold down triangular-shaped pieces from the corners of the excess ends, then fold the entire flap down and tape it. Repeat with the other end. Follow step 6 for ribbon-tying.

See also "13 Gifts for Just About Anyone."

Assemble a Gift Basket

With a minimum of effort and imagination, anyone can design and assemble a gift basket that will charm and delight the most mainstream or the most eccentric recipient, for any occasion under the sun, and within the confines of any budget.

Consider the person's interests and tastes, the nature of the occasion, and your relationship to that person. Gift baskets can be as conventional as an Easter basket filled with chocolate eggs, a small stuffed rabbit, and jelly beans for a child; or as unusual as a birthday gift basket filled with incense cones and sticks, an incense burner, essential oils, a deck of tarot cards, and a book on meditation. Those who like rich foods and good wines might enjoy a basket filled with champagne, a pair of champagne glasses, and fine imported chocolates. Gift baskets need not contain such calorie-laden items, however. A diet-conscious person might enjoy a selection of coffees, teas, or mineral waters as well as fresh fruit. A gift basket need not contain anything edible at all; it can be filled with various combinations of toys, jewelry, or even sexy lingerie. The only limit is your imagination.

Now that you've decided on the basket contents, the next thing you'll need is the basket itself. Baskets are available in a large variety of materials, shapes, sizes, and colors, and range in price from a dollar or two on up. Five-and-dime stores, variety stores, florists, party supply stores, novelty shops, discount imported goods shops, and craft shops often have a large selection of baskets to choose from, as well as supplies for decorating. Choose a basket that pleases the eye and is the right size to accommodate the items without appearing too overcrowded.

You may wish to decorate your basket. Basket handles and edges can be wrapped or otherwise adorned with colorful ribbon, lengths of gauzy or opaque fabric, dried or silk flowers, tiny craft shop items such as birds, or gift wrapping decorations such as metallic paper shapes on colorful wire. If you need to anchor a gift item or decoration in place, use floral foam blocks and floral pins, or floral wire and tape. Decorations may also be glued to the basket with a hot glue gun or with another type of strong glue. Baskets can be unlined, lined with fabric cut to the proper size, or lined with colored wood fibers, natural straws, moss, wrapping paper, or iridescent plastic straw. Lining a basket is not only decorative but can also help fill up empty spaces in your gift arrangement and balance the composition. You may wish to wrap the entire gift basket in colorful clear cellophane and tie off the top with a bright ribbon. Be on the lookout for decorative items you may use at a later date—seashells and pine cones are just a couple of the possibilities provided by nature's bounty.

In decorating as well as in filling a gift basket, arrange the gift items and decorations with an eye for balance. Although the arrangement need not be symmetrical, the overall appearance should be pleasing to the eye. Experiment with juxtaposing different colors, shapes, sizes, and textures while assembling and decorating the basket until you are satisfied with the result. Above all, let your individuality and the joy of gift-giving be your guide.

Hassle-Free Holiday Shopping

✓ Make lists of ideas for each person, and prioritize the choices. If your first choice is too difficult to find, go to the next item. Purchasing the items you can find easily may help you stumble upon those you're still looking for.

✓ Keep a notebook with the names of people you buy for, and whenever you think of an appropriate gift for someone, record it. When the holidays roll around, you won't say, "Now what was it I wanted to get for Bill?"

✓ Begin shopping early—right at the end of this year's holiday for next year, if you wish, when prices are lower.

✓ If your list is long, divide the number of people you buy for by twelve months, and make it a point to buy that many gifts each month.

✓ Start a holiday fund to ease the financial burden. See if your bank offers a Christmas Club savings plan, or do it yourself. Estimate the amount of money you will spend on gifts, divide that number by twelve, and deposit that amount in a separate savings account each month.

✓ If you don't like going to crowded stores and shopping malls, shop at home from television shopping networks or mail-order catalogues.

✓ When you see a gift that's just right for someone on your list, pick it up—no matter what the time of year—and put it away until the holiday. Keep a list of the specific gifts bought for each person, and remember where you've hidden them!

✓ When in doubt about size or taste, give a gift certificate.

✓ For someone who has just about everything, consider offering your services as a gift: an evening of babysitting or a home-cooked meal.

✓ A gift of money is always an easy way out, but give it along with a small present—like a Christmas tree ornament, a key chain, or a money clip—to make it more personal.

Celebrate Birthdays and Anniversaries

✓ Send a bouquet of flowers or balloons, or hire a "Birthday-gram" service that will have someone deliver a birthday greeting in person.

✓ Make a video or cassette tape of yourself offering birthday or anniversary wishes.

✓ If the person you are celebrating has a particular hobby or interest, throw a theme party. For example, if he or she likes to cook, throw a gourmet potluck party, and ask guests to bring food-related or cooking-related gifts.

✓ Instead of a party, go for an excursion. For instance, to honor a baseball fan, take a group jaunt to a game, complete with a pregame tailgate party.

✓ For the person who has everything, why not offer your services as a gift? Prepare a home-cooked dinner, pack a picnic basket lunch, offer an evening of babysitting.

✓ If you have a particular artistic talent, use it to create a special gift: a painting, sculpture, poem or story, or cassette tape of musical selections you play.

✓ For a special birthday or anniversary, put together a photo album or scrapbook with pictures, captions, and other mementos.

15 Gifts For Just About Anyone

Finding the right gift for the right person can be very difficult. You don't want to buy something someone already has, but you're not quite sure what is appropriate. For the perplexed gift giver, here are some suggestions for can't-go-wrong gifts that just about anyone would like and could use, from family to friends to co-workers:

1. Overnight travel bag or tote
2. Make-up/toiletry case
3. Picture frames/photo album
4. Address book/organizer/Filofax or stationery/envelopes
5. Travel alarm clock
6. Gift certificate
7. Donation to a favorite charity
8. Useful book (like *this one!*) or a CD of favorite music
9. Flowers/candy
10. Magazine subscription
11. Antique with some significance to the recipient's life or interests
12. A decorative knick-knack to go with the recipient's collection
13. Gourmet food item/kitchen gadgets
14. Computer accessories
15. Tickets to a show or event

Select and Decorate a Christmas Tree

Buying a Tree

Whether you cut down your own or choose one from a selection of precut trees, look for the following:

✓ The appropriate size of tree for the room it will stand in
✓ Symmetrical shape
✓ Healthy green color
✓ Pleasing fragrance
✓ Needles that don't shed when you shake the tree
✓ Strong limbs to support decorations
✓ Springy branches that will fall into place when you set it up

Easy Tips for Keeping Your Tree Healthy

✓ When you purchase the tree, have the trunk trimmed to the desired length.
✓ Ask if the tree seller offers disposal bags for easy removal of your tree after the season.
✓ Make sure your tree is secure in a tree stand.
✓ Keep the stand tray filled with water at all times to prevent the tree from drying out quickly.
✓ Place the tree in a cool room and out of direct sunlight if possible.

Decorating Your Tree

1. Place the tree near an outlet if you will use lights.
2. Drape the lights first, beginning at the top and working downward, and letting them rest on the branches.
3. Drape the garland next, beginning at the top and working downward.
4. In general, place larger ornaments on the bottom and smaller ones on top, so that the tree does not look top-heavy or lopsided.

Trees with a Festive Theme

Decorate your tree with a particular theme in mind:

✓ Victorian
✓ A single color
✓ Teddy bears
✓ Angels
✓ Snowflakes
✓ Country
✓ Toys
✓ Birds, houses, feeders, feathers
✓ Bows
✓ Cookie ornaments

Decorations You Can Make

✓ Use needle and thread to string cranberries and popcorn for an old-fashioned garland.

✓ Bake sugar or gingerbread cookies and decorate them with frosting and other decorations (be sure to poke holes in the dough for hanging them).

✓ Collect pine cones; spray them silver, gold, or a color; sprinkle them with glitter.

✓ Use styrofoam balls, felt, sequins, glitter, beads, and a hot glue gun to make your own Christmas balls.

✓ Did you collect lots of seashells on your summer vacation? Try using them to decorate your tree.

✓ Drape your tree with wide ribbon instead of traditional tinsel or garlands.

Carve a Pumpkin

A simple jack-o'-lantern has geometric features.

Carving expressive, scary, or silly faces can be somewhat more complicated.

Jack-o'-lanterns perched on front stoops herald the coming of Halloween. While some are so creative they become a form of temporary sculpture, most are simple scary or silly faces.

To begin, choose a large, sharp knife that will slice easily through the thick skin and flesh of the pumpkin.

Spread newspapers over a flat surface to avoid leaving a mess. Draw a circle with a diameter of about 5 inches around the stem of the pumpkin. Insert the tip of the knife at one point on the circle, with the blade running along the line you have drawn. Pierce the skin sharply in that spot until you feel the tip of the knife enter the hollow space inside the pumpkin, then follow the line with the knife as well as you can until you have cut around the entire circle. Pull on the stem to remove the circle. Set it aside.

With your hands, remove the seeds and pulp from inside the pumpkin. If you wish, the seeds can be cleaned and roasted for a snack.

Draw the design you plan to carve on the front of the pumpkin. A good, simple face consists of two triangular eyes, a triangular nose, and a wide, grinning mouth. Remember that it is more difficult to cut curved lines than straight ones.

Depending on the size of the pumpkin and the features you have drawn, you may want to use a smaller—but always sharp—knife to carve out the eyes, nose, and mouth. Remove those pieces when you have done so. Replace the stem with its circle of skin on top.

Once carved, the pumpkin should last a week or two. Jack-o'-lanterns are particularly spooky at night when a small votive candle is lit and placed inside.

9. Home

Sell Your House

Reasons to Sell

✓ You need a bigger or a smaller home.
✓ Your job has been transferred to a new location.
✓ You've already bought another home.
✓ You want to move.
✓ You have undergone a divorce or a death in the family.

When to Sell

✓ Spring and fall are the boom seasons.
✓ December is considered the worst month to put your home on the market, and July and August are slow real estate months.
✓ Given the climate of your area, consider when your house will be most accessible and appealing.
✓ The availability of mortgage money, interest rates, and the overall economy can affect when you decide to sell.

Setting a Price

✓ Get the tax assessment for your property as well as for other homes in your area from your local tax assessor's office.
✓ Consider having a licensed real estate broker do a fair market appraisal of your home. This is the highest price a willing buyer will pay and the lowest price a willing seller will accept.
✓ Do a competitive market analysis of recently sold homes that are comparable to yours in location, size, style, features, and price. Do this yourself, or call a few realtors and ask for their help.

Prepare the Property to Sell

1. The entire house should be clean and should smell fresh.

2. Get rid of clutter. Leave just enough furniture and accessories to make the house look finished but with a sense of spaciousness.

3. If necessary, give the interior a fresh coat of paint and lay new inexpensive carpet.

4. Make sure all light switches, doorknobs, locks, and faucets work.

5. Clear kitchen counters of appliances, and clean the sink, stove, refrigerator, and dishwasher.

6. Clean bathroom mildew, hang a new shower curtain if necessary, and make sure the toilet flushes smoothly.

7. When you expect a visit from prospective buyers, make sure the beds are made, clothes are put away, and closets are neat—people will look inside of them.

8. Clean the exterior siding of your house and repaint the trim if necessary. Trim foundation shrubs and cut the lawn short.

9. If you're selling an empty house, it is especially important for it to be freshly painted and clean.

10. Measure each room in the house and keep a list of the sizes handy in case visitors ask.

Sell Your Own House

1. Make a "listing" sheet giving the specifics: price, style, age, number of rooms, taxes, lot size, heat type, garage, basement, water, sewer, and description of the rooms on each floor. Model this list after the multiple listing system that realtors use.

2. Get a map and familiarize yourself with routes from the major roads to your house so that you can give directions to visitors.

3. Be knowledgeable about your town and such features as businesses, schools, shopping, community centers and activities, construction in the area, and proposed zoning changes.

4. Determine how much down payment you will require, and calculate what the buyer's income and savings must be in order to purchase your home. You can do this by calling a bank mortgage department and asking for the amount of monthly payment for principal and interest on $000,000.00 (the price of your house minus the down payment) for a 30-year fixed-rate mortgage. Add one-twelfth of the annual taxes to this figure to get a monthly payment. Multiply this figure by twelve. To get a rough estimate of the yearly income the buyer must make, consider the mortgage lender's rule of thumb: that mortgage payment plus taxes should not exceed 28 percent of income.

5. When you find a buyer, draw up a Purchase Agreement binder, which will be followed by a formal contract to be drawn up by your lawyer. The Purchase Agreement should indicate the date, location of home, names of seller and

buyer, agreed price, amount of earnest money (a good-faith deposit), the amount of down payment agreed upon, the type of mortgage the buyer will apply for, the closing date, and signatures. Include a statement that says: "This Agreement is subject to formal contracts to be drawn up by a reputable attorney and executed by the parties involved within five days of this date."

6. Advertise your home in the real estate section of the newspaper. Friday, Saturday and Sunday are the most effective days to advertise.

7. Answer phone calls, and show your property by appointment.

8. Listen to what people have to say about your house—you might be able to address some of the criticisms to make your house more appealing to other visitors. For example, if someone complains that the toilet doesn't flush, adjust the internal mechanism or replace it with a new one. If someone else complains that the basement feels damp and musty, put a dehumidifier in the room.

9. Think about how you want to present your house and the neighborhood: stress the major advantages and appealing features in your conversations with prospective buyers.

10. Before you begin to sell your home, find a lawyer that you feel comfortable working with and keep her/him involved and up-to-date on your endeavors to sell.

Arrange Flowers

Like any decorative art, flower arranging has rules, but they can be broken. As you follow a few basic principles of flower arranging, trust your instincts about what is pleasing to your own eye. Flower arranging can be a delightful form of personal expression. Experiment!

The arrangement container is an integral component of the design—as important as the flowers and foliage. Arrangement containers can be shallow or tall and made of terra-cotta, crystal, or any other type of material. Vases and containers can be as standard or as unconventional as your own personal style and resourcefulness. You may choose anything from a classic tall cut-crystal vase to an antique cup and saucer or an old wooden drawer from a discarded desk. If the container you choose isn't waterproof, you may arrange the flowers and foliage in a plastic container containing water inside it. Choose the shape, material, and color for the container that will most advantageously complement its flowers and foliage.

Conventionally, the height of your arrangement should be designed in direct proportion to the height of the vase, if it's a tall one, or to the width of the container, if it's a shallow one. Although you should trust your own eye, the height of the flowers above the top of a tall vase should be one and a half to two times as tall as the vase itself. The height of the flowers above a shallow container should be one and a half to twice the width of the container. Remember, these are only conventions.

You will also need sharp shears or scissors to cut and trim flowers, foliage, and branches to the desired heights and shapes. If you are using shallow containers for arrangement, you will need a pinholder or a foam block that absorbs water. The stems and branches of the flowers and foliage can be stuck into the foam or the pinholder to hold them in place. Foam may be anchored on florist spikes, which are in turn held in place in the arrangement container with waterproof floral clay. Moss, rocks, shells, or driftwood can be used to hide the foam or pinholder. You do not need foam blocks or pinholders in tall vases, as the stems are naturally held in an upright position by the walls of the vase. Flower arranging supplies are easily obtainable at a florist or craft supply shop.

Decide what kind of effect you'd like to create with your arrangement: dramatic, subtle, bold, or muted, and choose your colors, shapes, and textures accordingly. When designing the overall shape of your arrangement, you can aim for either symmetry or asymmetry. If your arrangement is symmetrical, simply put the same types, colors, and sizes of flowers and foliage on both sides. If your arrangement is asymmetrical, make sure that neither side is more eye-catching than the other. You may choose to shape your arrangement as a line, triangle, cone, curve, or circle, as well as any other shape that strikes your fancy (Figure 1).

Choose the focus or feature flowers: the most eye-catching or important flower or flowers in the arrangement. Feature flowers may consist of one to three large flowers or several small flowers of the same basic size and color. Choose additional foliage or flowers that will complement, rather than overpower, the feature flowers. Aim for interesting contrasts, alternating tall and short flowers, bright and soft colors, big and little flowers, rough and velvety textures. For example, contrast shiny leaves with downy petals, or delicate white baby's breath with a brilliantly colored large flower.

When choosing colors for an arrangement, it is helpful to understand the relationship of primary and secondary colors (Figure 2). To achieve a soft, harmonious effect, choose a primary color as the focus color of the arrangement, and use adjacent colors on the wheel as accents. When referring to any color on the color wheel, include all of its associated shades. Red, for example, includes shades such as pinks, crimsons, and burgundies. To create a dramatic effect, you may wish to pair colors to their opposites, or complements, on the wheel: purple/yellow, red/green, orange/blue.

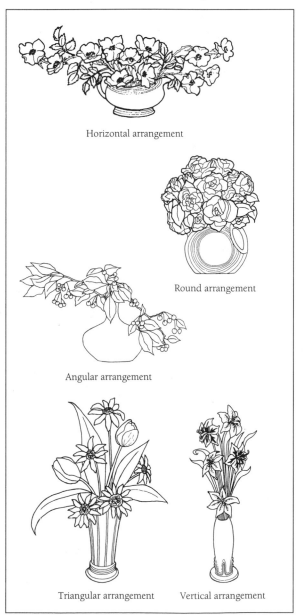

Horizontal arrangement

Round arrangement

Angular arrangement

Triangular arrangement   Vertical arrangement

Figure 1. Arrangements for flowers

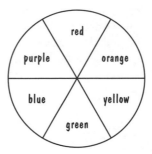

Figure 2. Using color contrast to select flowers

Primary Colors	Secondary Colors	Complementary Colors for Dramatic Accents
red	purple	green/red
yellow	orange	blue/orange
blue	green	purple/yellow

If you have only a few flowers, augment them for a fuller-looking arrangement by adding branches or driftwood with interesting shapes. These can provide a dramatic backdrop to even one or two flowers, forming strong diagonals, sweeping arcs, or arresting patterns. Try to avoid too many complicated or crossing lines when using branches, and trim them to the desired line. Dried branches, as well as rocks, shells, or pine cones, may be used as the foundation or backdrop for semipermanent or permanent arrangements. Various types and numbers of fresh flowers may be combined with these items and replenished as they fade.

Remove Stains

The first rule of stain removal is this: a spot is *on*, while a stain is *in*. If you put off removing a spot, it may soon become a stain and thus require extra work. Don't count on a spot remaining a spot just because it is on a surface treated with Scotchgard, Stainmaster, or other commercial stain repellent.

In order of priority, take the following steps as soon as you spill something or detect a spot or stain:

1. Determine what made the spot and whether there is more than one type of substance to remove (such as grease and tomato juice). You need to know which enemies you are attacking.

2. Get rid of everything that is loose and that can be extracted without intensifying the stain, using a vacuum, brush, or scraper before applying any cleaner or solvent.

3. Remove as much of the stain as you can with porous white cloth (like terry cloth) or absorbent paper towels. Avoid using old rags that may simply smear the substance in deeper. *Blot*—don't rub or scrub!

4. To avoid leaving a ring, work on a stain from the outside in during all stages of the process.

If all the substances in a stain can be removed with water and detergents but are stubborn, try pretreating. Make a paste of the detergent and spread it over the affected area. Let it sit for half an hour before flushing the area with warm water. Avoid hot water, since heat will set many stains.

If stain treatment requires something other than water, test the remover on an unseen area of the stained object to make sure that it does not change the color or bleach it out. Read the manufacturer's stain-removal instructions and follow them carefully. Whenever possible, use stain removers that are environmentally safe. Small stains on clothes can be spritzed with hair spray and rinsed out with soapy water.

Alphabetically, here are some of the most common producers of spots and stains, and tactics for eliminating them:

Acids. Rinse the affected area immediately, even if no discoloration is evident to prevent damage to fibers. Use *cool* water, then apply ammonia. Ordinary household ammonia is generally safe but should be diluted with water (half and half) if used to flush silk or wool.

Adhesive tape. Use the edge of a dull knife to scrape off as much gummy substance as possible. Then sponge the spot with a grease solvent, like carbon tetrachloride.

Beer. For washable fabrics use warm, soapy water and rinse well. For nonwashable materials, rub the stain lightly with a sponge that has been wrung out with warm, soapy water. Repeat if necessary, and blot out the moisture with white paper towels.

Blood. Blot as much as you can if the stain is still moist. For an old stain, soak the fabric in salt water for an hour, then blot with ammonia, rinse, and bleach with hydrogen peroxide, if necessary. Test a hidden part of the fabric first to see whether the peroxide causes a further problem.

Butter and other grease. Scrape up as much as you can from the surface, working from the outside toward the center of the spot. Blot—don't scrub—with purchased dry-cleaning fluid. Then blot with a detergent solution in warm water. Rinse. If a grease stain is old and has yellowed the fabric, try using diluted bleach, and then, if necessary, a stronger bleach solution. Rinse immediately in cool water.

Candle wax. Use a dull knife to scrape off as much wax as possible. Place the affected area between two clean white blotters or layers of paper towels. Press with a warm, not hot, iron. Repeat until the wax has vanished. If there is a residual stain, use a mild grease solvent.

Chewing gum. Place the fabric in your freezer in a clean plastic bag. When the gum has frozen, it will lift off. If the fabric is too large, pack the gummy area with ice cubes. That will harden the gum until it is brittle enough to pick or scrape off.

Chocolate. Scrape off as much as possible, then wash the fabric thoroughly. If the chocolate is greasy, use a grease solvent before washing. If the fabric is not washable, sponge the area with cool water and then use the solvent. Tough stains may need hydrogen peroxide: apply, blot, and rinse.

Coffee. Make a paste with detergent powder and water. Work it into the stain after soaking the immediate area with cool water. Blot with a little vinegar. Rinse. Resort to diluted bleach or dry-cleaning fluid if the stain persists.

Egg. Soak the stain in cold (never hot) water. If gentle sponging does not do the trick, work in full-strength detergent that is fabric-safe. Rinse and blot the area.

Fruit and berries. If it is safe for the fabric stained, stretch the affected portion across a large bowl and pour boiling water through the stain from a height of 2 feet. Repeat until the stain disappears. If the stain is stubborn or boiling water would injure the fabric, work in a detergent. Try hydrogen peroxide as a last resort.

Grass. Sponge rubbing alcohol on the stain. Blot with paper towels. Repeat as necessary. If the stain persists, sponge with diluted bleach or with hydrogen peroxide if bleach would damage the material.

Gravy. Remove as much of the spill as possible with a dull knife. Soak the area in cool (not hot) water. Wash in warm suds and rinse thoroughly. If the stain remains after the material has dried, apply a grease solvent, such as carbon tetrachloride.

Grease. See **Butter**.

Ice cream. See **Gravy**.

Ink, ballpoint. Treat the stain with acetone (nail polish remover). Blot, and repeat as needed. Old stains may require the use of bleach. Start with diluted bleach and then use a stronger solution if the fabric is not affected.

Ink, India. Treat stains immediately, since they can seldom be removed once the ink dries. Force cool water through the area to loosen the pigment. Then wet the spot with household ammonia (diluted if the material contains silk or wool). Work a detergent into the dampened stain if discoloration persists. Rinse thoroughly in cool water. Repeat if necessary.

Lipstick. Sponge the stain with a grease solvent. Rub detergent directly into the stain. Wash the material in warm, sudsy water, and rinse thoroughly.

Liquor. Treat fresh stains by soaking the fabric in cool water, then working in a detergent. Old brownish stains can sometimes be removed with diluted bleach. If the alcohol has caused any loss of color in a dyed fabric or results in a ring around the stain, restoration is impossible.

Makeup. Brush away any surface particles. Rub in a detergent, starting from the outside and working toward the center. Wash and rinse. For nonwashable fabrics, treat the stain with a grease solvent.

Meat juice. See **Gravy**.

Metal. Tarnish from brass, copper, tin, and other metals can usually be removed by blotting the stained areas with white vinegar or lemon juice. Allow it to stand

20 minutes and then rinse. If the fabric is stained by this process, moisten the affected area with household ammonia.

Mildew. Launder the fabric thoroughly and allow it to dry in the sun. If the stain remains, try diluted bleach, blotted onto the affected areas. An old mildew stain may be permanent, since the mold will have weakened the fibers. Nonwashables need the services of the professional dry cleaner. Do not attempt home treatment.

Milk. Sponge the stain with cool water. Work in a detergent. Rinse thoroughly and allow to dry. If residue remains, use a grease solvent.

Mustard. Rinse with cool water. Work in a detergent. Immerse the material in hot, sudsy water, and let it soak for several hours. If the stain has not disappeared, use bleach in whatever strength the material can handle safely. For nonwashable materials, treat the stain with rubbing alcohol, diluted two parts water to one part alcohol.

Nail polish. Treat the stain with nail polish remover or acetate. If the material contains synthetic fibers, test a hidden section to make sure no damage occurs.

Oil (vegetable, fish liver, etc.). Wash the material in hot, sudsy water. If the oil persists, work in detergent, then rinse with hot water. A persistent stain may require a grease solvent (see **Butter**).

Paint, oil-base. Treat promptly, since paint is almost impossible to remove after it has dried. Scrape the area with a dull knife. Blot with paper towels. Soak the area in whatever kind of paint thinner is recommended on the paint can. Sponge in a strong detergent. Rinse immediately in hot, sudsy water. If the stain persists, soak the material in the thinner for an hour. You have nothing to lose, since the material will be spoiled anyway if you cannot remove the paint.

Paint, water-base. Stains are relatively easy to remove and will probably come out with normal washing. Light rubbing may be required, followed by soaking, then laundering. For nonwashables, place paper toweling under the material and sponge with warm, soapy water. Blot dry immediately.

Perspiration. Sponge the stain with detergent and warm water. Launder, and rinse well. If the perspiration has altered the color of a dyed fabric, treat the area with white vinegar or household ammonia. If perspiration has left an odor, freshen the material by soaking it in warm salt water, using five tablespoons of salt to each quart of water.

Rust. Mix 1 tablespoon of oxalic acid (available at drugstores or hardware stores) with 1 cup of warm water. Test the fabric in an inconspicuous area for color fastness. Moisten the stain with the solution, allowing 15 minutes for it to work. Rinse the fabric at least twice in hot water, since the acid can damage fibers over a period of time. For heavy, persistent stains, apply a paste of the oxalic acid, made with a spoonful of hot water. Rub this in with a spatula (not with your fingers unless you use a rubber glove). Rinse several times.

Shoe polish. See **Lipstick**. If the stain persists, try bleach or hydrogen peroxide, depending upon what the material will handle without damage.

Syrup (maple, honey, molasses, etc.). Soak the material in cool water after scraping away the residue. Wash it in warm soapy water. Sponge detergent over the area if the stain is stubborn. If the stain is an old one, soak the material overnight in soapy water.

Tar, asphalt. Scrape off all you can with a dull knife. Blot with paint thinner, dry-cleaning fluid, or turpentine. Sponge with detergent and warm water. Rinse thoroughly. If an odor is present, soak the material in water and baking soda (one part soda to four parts water) for several hours. Then rinse.

Tea. See **Coffee**.

Urine. Whether the source is human or animal, prompt treatment can make the difference between success and failure. If the stain is still liquid, blot with paper towels until all the moisture has been absorbed. Sponge the area with cool water. Continue blotting. Repeat. Sponge with a solution of 2 tablespoons of household ammonia to 1 cup of water. Blot dry. If this is not entirely successful, repeat the process using full-strength white vinegar. Rinse with cool water.

Vegetable juices. See **Fruit and berries**.

Wine, red. Use paper towels and blot as much liquid as possible. Pour boiling water through the stain from a height of 2 feet after spreading the material across a large bowl. Sponge in a detergent. Rinse with cool water. Repeat the process as necessary. If the stain persists and the fabric can handle it without damage, use a diluted bleach or hydrogen peroxide.

Wine, white. See **Liquor**.

Lay Out a Floor Plan and Use It to Decorate

Laying out a bird's-eye-view floor plan to help you decorate can save you endless hours of rearranging furniture (not to mention a strained back) and trips back and forth to the store to buy the piece that fits. Take your finished floor plan with you when you go shopping.

If blueprints are available, use them. If not, make your own floor plan, one room at a time, using these supplies, which are easily obtainable in stationery or art supply stores: tape measure, ruler or architectural scale, pencil with eraser, and tracing paper with printed quarter-inch grids. A quarter-inch on the paper and ruler will equal 1 foot of actual space. An architectural scale will convert feet to quarter-inches for you, making it easier to draw the plan (*make sure to use the side that reads ¼", not ¼" size*). If you're not using an architectural scale, simply divide the total inches of each dimension by 12. For example, a 36"-wide doorway would translate to three ¼"-grid boxes on the plan.

Using your tape measure, determine the total length and width of the room. Then, using your ruler, draw the outline of the room on the grid paper at a ¼" scale. If the room is irregularly shaped or has niches or alcoves, measure them too, and add them to the drawing. For easy reference, make a note next to each ¼"-scale item on the floor plan of the actual dimension.

Measure the dimensions and placement of doors, windows, and closets (plus the height and width of the trim); fireplaces; and any built-in features that take up space or that you don't plan to remove, such as heating units, built-in bookshelves, and cupboards. Add these items, at ¼"-scale, to the drawing.

Measure the height of the ceiling, the distances between the tops of windows and the ceiling, and the distances between the bottoms of windows and the floor, and make notes of these on the plan.

Create templates for each room that approximate the furniture, fixtures, and plants you already have or might plan to acquire (Figure 1). Move the templates around on the floor plan, experimenting with various placements. Experiment with dramatic and unusual configurations. There's no risk at this stage; it's only paper. Imagine yourself sitting, eating, playing, sleeping, or working in the room, taking into consideration the light and the space needed between objects.

Once you've decided on a configuration, trace the templates onto the floor plan. If you change your mind, either erase the original plan or put another piece of tracing paper over it. You can then reconfigure the furniture in another way. Keep as many versions of the plan as you wish until your final decision is made.

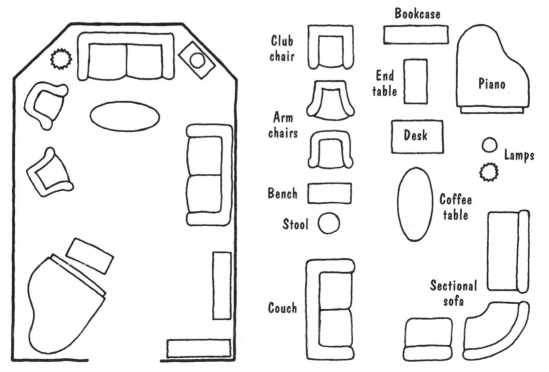

Figure 1. Living room and/or family room templates

Keep Flowers Longer

After you've spent time and money to buy a beautiful bunch of flowers or grow them in your garden, the last thing you'll want to do is see them wither and die within just a couple of days. Follow these instructions to help make flower arrangements last longer.

From the Garden

1. Cut garden-grown flowers and greens early in the morning, when they are dew-covered and revitalized by the cool of the night. Whether you are in the garden or at the florist, choose blossoms with tight, but not overly tight, buds that can open in the vase and thus last longer than a fully opened flower. Use sharp clippers to cut stems cleanly at a 45-degree angle. Avoid jagged, bruising cuts to the stems; such cuts will hinder the cut flower's ability to absorb water. Immediately put the cut flowers into a pail of enough room-temperature water to cover about three-quarters of the stem. This prevents flowers from drying out while you are cutting. Mist the blossoms with cool water.

2. Take a cut flower out of the pail and place it into another container of room-temperature water. Keeping the stem under water, cut another 1 or 2 inches off the stem bottom at a 45-degree angle, then scrape some of the green off the bottom 2 inches of the stem with a knife to expose a greater area for water asbsorption. Remove all lower leaves that would otherwise be under water in the arrangement vase. For roses, make a slit from the bottom of the stem up to about 1 inch, and pound the stem end with a mallet to help it absorb water. (Florist's roses can first be wrapped in layers of wet newspaper before the slit is made.) If the flowers have woody stems, pound the end with a mallet, then make a longer slit, up to one-third the total length of the stem. If the stems are hollow, do not scrape the ends. Instead, remove the hollow-stemmed flower from the water, recut the stem, and sear the end with a flame. After removing the excess leaves as described earlier, put the hollow-stemmed cutting back into the water. Repeat the appropriate process for each flower until all cuttings have been recut and treated. Mist the blossoms with cool water.

3. Wait a couple of hours. If any of your garden flowers have wilted, repeat the recutting and appropriate stem treatment process. If the flowers look fresh, place them up to the neck in cool water. As a preservative, put one or two drops of chlorine bleach and 1 teaspoon of sugar into each quart of water. Mist the blossoms with cool water, then store the cut flowers overnight in a dimly lit, cool room before arranging. If you used a commercial preservative such as Floralife, follow the package instructions. When you are ready to arrange your flowers, add Floralife to the water in the container in which you make the floral arrangement.

From the Florist

1. Flowers that come from a florist generally need less conditioning than garden flowers. Unwrap and untie them as soon as you get them home. As directed in Step 2 earlier, cut off the ends of the stems and treat the stem ends when appropriate. Then, put the flowers in a container of water to keep them constantly irrigated while, or until, you arrange them in a separate vase. If you don't plan to arrange them until several hours later, put the interim container of cut flowers in a cool, dimly lit room until you are ready to begin.

2. After your flowers are arranged, make sure to keep the water level high, adding water once a day as it is absorbed, and misting daily. Keep the arrangement in a cool place, out of direct sunlight and away from heat sources. Recutting the stems after several days while the flower stems are under water, then rearranging the flowers, also prevents wilting and helps make the flowers last longer. If a rose in your arrangement starts to wilt, floating the entire rose in tepid water may help to revive it.

10 Ways to Make Your Bed Look Like a Store Display

The bedroom is a private, luxurious place where we retreat to rest and restore ourselves. Beautiful bed linens and accessories enhance this very personal environment and add to its comfort.

1. Choose mattress pads or feather beds to add buoyancy and softness. Mattress pads also protect your mattress from stains.

2. Dust ruffles complement bed linens and hide the underbed area from view— an especially important device if you use this space for storage. Ruffles can be a simple solid cotton, a bright accent print, or a formal damask. Coordinate dust ruffles and curtains to give the room a subtle unity and allow for more versatility in choice of spreads and quilts. A department-store trick: Use two ruffles for a layered effect. If you have a full-sized bed, choose a full and a twin ruffle.

3. Buy a good down comforter, and cover it with a decorator duvet cover. This makes washing much easier and gives you freedom of choice in alternating bed covers. Complement the comforter with a throw or cotton blanket in a neutral solid color to cover the sheets and keep the bed neat.

4. Your imagination reigns in the choice of sheets and pillowcases. Solid colors are more versatile than prints. Rotate one or two sheet sets until they wear out—this saves money, storage space, and time.

5. For guests, place a dryer fabric softener sheet or a bar of scented soap between sheets. Remove them, of course, before bedtime.

6. Choose an array of decorative pillows, and layer them on the bed or strew them randomly.

7. Decorate headboards or footboards with dried flowers or strands of artificial ivy for a romantic, Victorian look.

8. Choose minimalist crisp cotton for a breezy, no-muss look.

9. Use a lace or cut-work tablecloth over a solid sheet. Alternate sheets for variety.

10. Paint bedrooms in a neutral pastel so you won't be stuck with decorating and redecorating to match the walls. Make a decision for solid sheets and print comforter and accessories, or vice versa, to avoid clashing and to increase the number of variations and combinations on your bed.

Hire a Housekeeper

If you don't have time to do housework, you are no good at it, or you simply hate doing it, and you are willing to pay someone to do it for you, why not hire a housekeeper?

Researching Your Possibilities

Cleaning services are companies who send out qualified housekeepers to clean your house. Because they train and do background checks on their housekeepers, you are more likely to get a competent worker from a cleaning service than if you hire privately. But because a service will charge you both for the housekeeper and for administrative costs, it will likely be more expensive than hiring privately.

To find a housekeeper through a cleaning service, look in the Yellow Pages under "House Cleaning" or "Cleaning Services." You'll see a list of companies that offer cleaning; some will specify commercial or residential, interior or exterior. For a house, you want a residential interior cleaning service. Call several of these companies to compare prices and services. Specify exactly what you want done. A basic cleaning usually consists of dusting, vacuuming, mopping, and scrubbing the kitchen and bathroom. Other services, such as window or wall cleaning, may be extra. Also make sure the housekeeper's schedule fits with yours.

Independent housekeepers hire themselves out, usually at a lower price than cleaning services. Keep in mind, though, that if you pay independent housekeepers regularly and directly (unlike cleaning services which you pay directly only), and they work under your supervision, they will be considered your employees and you must pay taxes for them. In addition, hiring privately requires you to do the background research yourself and gives you less recourse if you are unsatisfied with a cleaning job.

To find an independent housekeeper you can look in the classified section of a newspaper under "Household Help," ask friends for recommendations, or browse through the bulletin board at your local community center. If you answer an ad in the paper or from a bulletin board, be sure to get references as well as information on price, services, and available days. Answer several ads and compare. If friends are happy with them, it's a good idea to hire one of them rather than risk hiring a stranger.

Trying Out Candidates

Before you decide on any housekeeper, have a few candidates come over for a try-out. You will need to pay tryouts for any work they do satisfactorily, whether or not you plan to hire them permanently. Interview applicants and try to judge how comfortable you'd feel having them in your home or office regularly.

If you are unsatisfied with a cleaning service or do not feel comfortable hiring the housekeeper it sent, you can ask the service to send a new housekeeper, or you can find a new service. If you feel a housekeeper has not done the specified job, do not pay the company.

Judge independent housekeepers by their thoroughness, promptness, disposition, and price. Do not feel compelled to hire anyone you are not 100 percent happy with.

Hiring the Housekeeper and Setting a Schedule

Hire the housekeeper you feel completely comfortable with. Unless you plan to have your house cleaned only sporadically, set a regular time, price, and list of jobs you want done at each cleaning. Only when you have grown to trust the housekeeper completely should you consider giving out your house or office key and allowing the housekeeper to work when you are not there. Until that time, supervise the cleaning.

Cleaning services will bill you for each visit. You will pay the company, not the housekeeper. For independent housekeepers, set a policy for payment: after each visit, or once a month. Inform yourself about withholding income and Social Security taxes on all employees you hire to do work for you regularly.

Recycle and Reduce Waste

So many resources can be conserved by recycling that it's no longer just a good idea—it's an imperative. Today, with local governments passing laws that require recycling and special collection services, it is easier than ever before to do your part. Recycle and reuse household materials whenever you can. Contact local sanitation authorities for more information, community programs, or specifics on area laws and pickup.

To Recycle

Create separate receptacles in your kitchen. Have distinct containers for glass, metal, paper, and plastic materials, plus another for food scraps. Get in the habit of separating your trash.

Arrange for the collection of recyclable material. Some areas collect recyclable material in much the same way they collect trash, while other communities do not have the resources to offer a pickup service. If there is no home pickup in your area, you may need to drop material off at designated locations. Call local authorities for more information.

Use food scraps to make compost. If you have a yard and a garden, keep a compost heap for scraps of food. Pile the scraps in a designated area in the yard, and sprinkle garden dirt over each layer of scraps. In several weeks, the food will break down to form an excellent fertilizer.

Buy only recyclable material. Check the products you buy to make sure the packaging is recyclable. Avoid foam packaging, and buy only recyclable plastics.

Buy returnable bottles. Don't forget to return them!

Recycle oil. If you change the oil in your car yourself, take the old oil into a gas station or garage to be recycled.

Recycle batteries. Many communities collect old batteries. Batteries contain hazardous waste materials—*never* throw them in with household trash and thus allow harmful chemicals to enter our air, soil, and water.

To Reduce and Reuse

Buy products with the least amount of packaging. Bulk products are cheaper, and waste less packaging material.

Reuse grocery and shopping bags. Bring bags with you when you go shopping. Strong cloth bags can be reused.

Avoid paper products that get thrown away after each use. Use glass and ceramic dishes and cups, and cloth napkins.

Save containers for reuse. Collect jars, bottles, and boxes to use for other purposes. Jars make good snack containers, bottles can be used as flower vases, and boxes can be saved for storage and moving. Reuse padded mailing envelopes.

Recharge batteries. Investing in a battery recharger will save money on batteries in the long run and reduce the amount of hazardous waste in the environment.

Use scrap paper. Always recycle paper in your home for use as scrap. Then recycle. Don't throw paper in the household garbage. Conserve the world's trees!

Take proper care of materials. Many things, such as plastic tableware and glasses, can be used again if handled properly. Proper care of your clothing and other belongings will help them last longer.

Dispose of toxic materials properly. Household cleansers, paint, paint thinner, and other hazardous materials should not be thrown in the trash and *never* thrown down the drain. Contact your local sanitation department to find out how to properly dispose of these materials. Some communities collect unused paint for use in public schools and other public facilities.

For more information on recycling and conservation, call the Environmental Defense Fund at 1-800-CALL-EDF.

Choose a Long-Distance Telephone Service

Once upon a time your telephone left you with few choices beyond the color of the receiver. Not so anymore. Long-distance carriers offer an array of services, discount programs, and customer incentives that make it well worth while to shop and compare. Consider these features of each service:

✓ Service provided. Does the company provide worldwide, 24-hour service?

✓ Rates. What are the charges per minute? Most companies have different rates for daytime, evening, and nighttime calling. Are there lower charges for weekends? Holidays? Compare the discount scheduling blocks of each service.

✓ Plans. Does the company offer a variety of plans? Look for unlimited calling (if you make a lot of calls), discounts overseas or to a specific area code, small business plans, calling cards, and budget plans.

✓ Special offers. Introductory offers often include reduced charges on the number you call the most, frequent flyer miles, or cash back. Be wary—these incentives may not last, but they can save a lot of money in the short term.

✓ Your calling needs. Determine where you call the most, and at what times you make calls. Look for services that offer deals that best accommodate your calling habits and pattern of use.

✓ Customer service. How responsive is the company to complaints? How willing is it to help find the best plan for you? Are the bills easy to understand?

✓ Extra charges. Is there a monthly fee or an initial hookup fee?

✓ Sound quality. The sound quality of most phone services is certainly good enough, but if you are sensitive or hard of hearing you'll want to find the very best sound available.

✓ Reliability. Does the phone service ever malfunction or disconnect? Be sure the company you use doesn't cause you inconvenience.

See also "Use New Phone Company Services."

Keep Electric Bills Down

We use electricity constantly and could hardly manage without it. But the cost of using electricity is going up, and as responsible citizens we should investigate and pursue ways to use energy more efficiently and conserve the earth's resources. Lowering your electric bill does not require you to deprive yourself of the comforts you are used to. It is simply a matter of being a proactive consumer, choosing energy-efficient products and technologies, and guarding against wasteful overuse. Here are some general tips for conserving energy.

Insulation

The best way to cut down on electric costs is to reduce the amount of energy expended on heating and cooling—the single largest cost of energy in your home. Insulation reduces energy costs by keeping heat in during winter and heat out during summer, thus allowing your heating and cooling system to work less hard to make your house comfortable.

✓ Thermal insulation for walls, ceilings, and floors can save you enough on electricity bills to recoup the necessary cost of materials in one or two years. Insulation comes in a few different materials and in a variety of forms. To determine which type will provide the most insulation, consider only the R value and not the thickness or material. R value is a measure of insulation ability: the higher the number, the more insulation provided. Where you put the insulation also factors into how effective it will be.

✓ Storm windows, or double insulated glass, will cut heat loss drastically. You may even add a third window for further insulation. Plastic sheet window coverings are a less expensive way to keep heat in and are very effective.

✓ Weather-stripping with rubber, vinyl, or felt strips in the cracks of windows and doors will reduce the amount of air leakage in a house and is an easy process.

✓ Caulking cracks and gaps is another easy do-it-yourself method for insulating. Caulk can be applied where a window meets the window frame or where a door touches the door frame. Be careful not to seal the window or door so you cannot open it. Be sure to clean away dust and dirt before applying the caulk.

Heater/Air Conditioner

Proper use and care of your heating and air-conditioning unit will lower the amount of energy it uses to work. Here are some ways to get the maximum output from your units.

✓ Change filters on heaters and air conditioners every month or so, and keep them free of dust and dirt. Inspect units regularly as directed in the user's manual. Choose models with a good energy rating.

✓ Set units at a moderate temperature and avoid changing the setting. A low and regular output will heat or cool more efficiently.

✓ Don't block units with furniture or drapes, and install units as close to the middle of the room as possible.

✓ To keep heat outside in summer, close draperies to reduce solar warming; to let solar heat in on winter days, open draperies.

✓ If you spend most of your time in one or two rooms, turn down the house thermostat and use space heaters for those rooms during cold weather.

✓ Keep doors, windows, and fireplace flues shut when running heaters and air-conditioning units.

✓ Investigate ways to improve heating and cooling efficiencies. New and effective energy-saving methods have been developed that are not yet widely used. Ask your electric company about adding a heat pump to your furnace or about techniques like geothermal heating and cooling or electric thermal storage.

✓ Of course, using fans in summer is far more energy-efficient than constant use of air-conditioning units. Be sparing in your use of high-energy-consuming appliances. Trees planted on the sunny side of a house or a porch awning can cut heat down dramatically.

✓ In summer, make a pitcher of iced tea, open the windows and sit by the pool!

Water Heater

The heating of water in your house is a costly process, so using hot water more efficiently can potentially save you a large amount of money.

✓ Make sure no faucets are leaking water.
✓ Insulate your hot water heater and the pipes that water travels through.
✓ Lower the thermostat level on your water heater; it will often be much higher than you need it to be. If you find the heater set at 150°F, lower to 140°F if you have a dishwasher and even lower if you do not.
✓ Use colder water whenever possible, such as when washing dishes or clothes.
✓ Turn off the water heater if you plan to be away for an extended time.

Lighting

While lighting requires much less electricity than heating and cooling, proper energy conservation measures in this area will noticeably lower your bills.

✓ Turn off lights whenever they are not in use. The same, of course, goes for appliances like televisions and computers.
✓ Fluorescent light bulbs use significantly less energy than incandescent bulbs and should be used whenever possible.
✓ Except in areas where good lighting is essential for reading and seeing, use bulbs with lower wattage. Use 40 or 60 watts, for instance, instead of 100. Buy the newer energy-efficient types of bulbs.
✓ Install dimmer switches.

Energy-Efficient Technology

✓ Contact your local utility company about products and services they can provide to help you, and your community, conserve energy.
✓ Always choose energy-efficient appliances—from hairdryers to refrigerators to washers and dryers.
✓ Write your senator or representative in Congress and let him or her know that energy conservation is important to you.
✓ Consumers have the ultimate power. If we demand clean, energy-efficient technology for the products and services we buy, businesses will supply them. Let's make some demands!

Plan for Emergencies

The best way to plan for home emergencies is to become familiar with the layout of your house in detail and in all of its components. Use the builder's plan as your visual guide. If a plan is not available, make reasonably accurate sketches, showing the locations of the elements. These include heating and air-conditioning units, water heaters, other water storage containers and processors, major appliances, small appliances, plumbing fixtures and pipes, pumps (if any), gas lines and valves, electric outlets, alarm systems, circuit panels, switches, phone lines and connections, message units, computers, TV sets, radios, and other communications equipment.

Keep a list of emergency phone numbers for each type of component that could break down or have problems, so you are adequately covered for failures in plumbing, electricity, equipment, heating, and communications. Maintain a reference file of owner's manuals, with a paper clip or bookmark in the sections marked "troubleshooting" or the equivalent. Familiarize yourself with troubleshooting instructions, so that when a problem arises you will already be aware of what should be done.

Keep a pair of heavy-duty rubber gloves near the main circuit box or in a quickly reachable location.

Here are the most common kinds of problems you can expect to encounter in a residence:

Plumbing. Burst water pipes, clogged drains, toilet tank failure, overflowing toilet, water-pump stoppage, lack of hot water.

Electricity. Power failure, blown fuses or circuit breakers, defective switches, bare wires, overheating motors.

Heating systems. Furnace shutoff, overheating, low heat output, circulation failure, gas leaks.

Air-conditioning systems. Poor efficiency, clogged drainage pipes, noisy fans, weak circulation.

Appliances. Poor refrigeration and failure of ice maker, water leakage, failure of dishwasher to clean the dishes, leakage, washing machine failure or inability to clean clothes properly, clothes dryer cutoff, ranges that are smoky or have poor temperature capabilities, microwave units that require more time than specified to cook properly.

If an appliance, electric outlet, or any piece of equipment that is wired gives off sparks or smoke, act quickly to prevent a possible fire. If unplugging a cord at the scene of the trouble does not solve the problem, throw the master switch in the circuit box. Use rubber gloves if you see any exposed wiring.

Regular inspections and proper maintenance of equipment will avoid unnecessary damage and tragedies.

Often, the problem is very minor—such as a blown fuse or tripped switch—and can be corrected in a matter of minutes, thus eliminating substantial, and unnecessary, service fees. Make sure you know how to turn off the electricity, stop the flow of water, or close a faucet to prevent damage or neutralize a potentially dangerous situation. In particular, know the exact location of these important devices:

✓ The fuse box or circuit breaker, to cut off electricity in danger of fire or shock

✓ The main water valve leading from the street into the house, to prevent flooding if a water line has broken or been cracked open in a freeze

✓ The cutoff valve if you use gas and there is danger of explosion or fumes from a leak

Problems are usually detectable by noticing unusual sounds, silence when there should be sound, odors, smoke, steam, dripping water, electric shock, or, in some cases, warning bells and buzzers installed in household equipment.

Pack for Moving

Packing Boxes

1. Start far in advance of moving, anytime from a few days to a few weeks beforehand.

2. Find a large open room to set up headquarters. Here you will assemble the boxes and store them until the move. Choose a room near the exit for this operation.

3. Set out boxes, cartons, packing paper, bubble wrap, markers, scissors, and strong tape. Boxes should be new and as big as possible to still facilitate carrying. Used supermarket boxes are fine if they are not old and damaged, and liquor cartons are sturdily constructed. Markers should be thick and black. Beware of wrapping articles in newsprint, which smudges; consider buying blank newsprint or crepe paper for delicate items.

4. Label boxes and keep an inventory. As you pack boxes, keep a list of every item and its cost, in case of loss or damage. This is particularly important if you have hired a moving company. Mark on the outside of the box what is packed inside. Pack boxes according to the room they will go into in the new home.

5. Pack first the things you won't need. Old relics in the basement and out-of-season clothes should be packed first, with the most necessary items saved for the last minute.

6. Don't overpack boxes. Make sure no box is too heavy to carry or at risk of falling apart. Pack heavier materials in smaller boxes.

7. Wrap glass, china, and ceramics in paper or bubble wrap before you pack them tightly and securely in boxes.

Packing the Truck

1. Use a blanket to help slide heavy items onto the truck.

2. Load large and heavy appliances such as refrigerators, bed frames, couches, bookcases, and washing machines first.

3. Stand mattresses and box springs on their sides, against the wall of the truck. Slide well-wrapped mirrors and breakable flat items in between them for safe storage.

4. Secure to the walls of the truck any furniture you fear may slide. Wrap furniture in blankets and secure with heavy tape, or cover upholstery by wrapping a chair or sofa in plastic wrap.

5. Break down shelves and tables if possible.

6. Pack smaller loose items between the large pieces to save space. Use pillows and blankets as padding.

To Remember

1. This is a good time to have a yard sale or donate old furniture to charity. Divest. See also "Set Up a Garage Sale."

2. Keep track of moving expenses such as truck rental costs and packing supplies. Save your receipts; they may be tax deductible if your employer has transferred you.

3. Be careful when lifting heavy boxes and furniture. Keep your back straight and bend at the knees. Do not overexert yourself.

10 Ways to Make the Most of Cabinet and Closet Space

From the kitchen to the workroom to the bedroom, here are 10 ways to increase storage space:

1. Use over-door pantry racks, which can be hung on the back of any shelf door without screws or other hardware.

2. Install hooks or utility racks, which can be selected according to the objects to be stored, such as long-handled tools, vacuum hoses, mops, brooms, ironing boards, and dusters.

3. If the spaces between shelves are too deep, intersperse them with shelf dividers. These come in a great variety of sizes and types and are usually made of rubberized wire. They hold such frequently stored objects as blankets, plates, canned goods, and small boxes.

4. Use multitiered can dispensers for canned goods, bottles, medical supplies, and other small containers that clutter up your shelves.

5. Consider the numerous kinds of wardrobe organizers you can buy through catalogues. They hang on ordinary closet rods and provide specialized space for all kinds of clothes, including jackets, sweaters, shoes, shirts, ties, belts, and undergarments as well as blankets, sheets, towels, and other bulky items.

6. Install compact shoe shelves, which can extend along the floor, fit vertically in narrow spaces, or hang from the clothes pole. Some types are expandable.

7. Double your closet's hanging space by adding an extra rod. Two sets of short items, like suits, jackets, or skirts, can be hung above and below. Build in an extra rod or use a tension rod. Don't hang heavy items on a tension rod.

8. Buy closet cubes, which come in various sizes and widths and are stackable.

9. Use sports racks to store athletic gear that takes up a lot of space. Check sporting goods stores for racks specifically designed to hold skis, bicycles, tennis rackets, skates, in-line skates, balls of all sizes, bats, baseball mitts, weights, and many other such items.

10. If you are really pressed for closet space, move some of the bulkier contents into rollout boxes on wheels, which are wide but shallow enough to slide right under your bed. Alternate summer and winter wardrobes in this fashion. Always use moth balls or cedar chips for protection.

10 Ways to Secure Your Home

Too often a burglar's best accomplice is the homeowner. By providing opportunities for a break-in, a homeowner can encourage burglaries. The solution, therefore, is not to give the potential burglar the chance to even attempt a break-in. The extent to which you secure your house is a matter of personal preference; certainly you don't want to turn your house into a prison in order to keep others out. While no method is 100 percent certain to work, there are many methods anyone can use to better protect a house and property. Some require a money investment, others require only a little time, and all will help keep your house safe. Here are ten of the best precautions:

1. Install locks on all doors and windows. All doors to the outside should have at least a key lock and a second latch lock. It's a good idea to also have a chain lock inside. Sliding doors should have a lock at the handle and a metal bar to block the door when not in use. Windows should also have secure latches or locks. Be sure to keep at least the ground floor windows shut whenever you are not home.

2. Install outdoor lighting. All sides and corners of your house should have a light that can be switched on from inside the house. Keep at least one light on, perhaps at the front door or driveway, while you sleep. For added security and your own convenience, it's a good idea to have motion detector lights for the driveway or front door. They will turn on when something moves in the light's detection range.

3. Install a fence. Some people consider a fence too restricting for their tastes and would rather go without, but fences either keep burglars away or at least send the message that you are concerned about security. Fences can be expensive, depending on the material you use (wire, stone, or wood), but they provide an added layer of protection for your house.

4. Install bars on windows. As with a fence, some people see window bars as a drastic precaution, but having them—at least on your ground floor windows—can be very practical. Bars should be made of steel and firmly fastened to the house so they cannot be cut or ripped out. They should be close enough together to block anyone from entering but not so close together that they prevent you from seeing out. Bars are particularly effective in urban neighborhoods. Some cities require them by law under certain conditions.

5. Install peepholes in doors. Most outside doors already have a peephole. If they don't, install one right away. You can also use a window next to the door to see who is outside, but then you too will be seen. Of course, never open the door to strangers before they have identified themselves to your satisfaction. If a stranger continues to knock after being asked to leave, call the police immediately.

6. Post warning stickers. Whether or not your house is protected by an alarm system, a ferocious guard dog, or membership in a neighborhood watch, it's not a bad idea to have a sticker on your front door that says it is. These stickers are sometimes provided by the local police department, or you can find them in home and hardware stores.

7. Discourage climbing. A popular technique of burglars is to climb up the side of the house and enter through a less secure upstairs window or through the chimney. You can discourage this by making sure there are no trees with branches that come close to the roof, and no ledges or vine gratings to climb up on the side of the house.

8. Keep an interior light on. Whether you are in the house or not, keep a light on to make it seem as though you are home and awake. You may want to put the light on a timer as a further measure; it will also conserve electricity.

9. Draw the curtains. Especially at night and when you are not home, keep the curtains or blinds on your downstairs windows closed. If burglars can see inside your house, they can tell whether you are home and they can see what valuables you have to steal. Don't give them this advantage.

10. Install a central alarm system. This is the most sophisticated means of preventing a burglary but also the most expensive. If you have an alarm system already, use it at night and whenever you go out. If you do not have a system, research different alarm companies and installations to determine whether you can afford it. If so, an alarm system will probably be a very wise investment.

Note: If you ever come home and suspect a burglar may still be in the house, leave immediately and go to a neighbor's to call the police (911). Do not risk confronting the burglar, who may be armed.

For more information on how to secure your home if you plan to leave for an extended period of time, see also "12 Things to Do Before You Leave on Vacation."

9 Sewing Tips

1. For versatility and strength, use transparent nylon thread. You'll never need to change colors in your sewing machine.

2. When hemming a skirt or pair of trousers, knot the thread every 3" or 4". A small break in the hem won't mean an entire rehemming job.

3. Iron patterns before laying them down on material. Copy a pattern by tracing it on newsprint or wrapping paper.

4. A bar of soap, still in the wrapper, makes an excellent pin cushion and helps pins slide more easily.

5. Use elastic thread on waistband buttons. This is a great idea for children's clothes—it makes room for growing.

6. Velcro saves the day! No more safety pins to close gaps in blouses or blazers. Also replace buttons or zippers with Velcro to make hard-to-fasten garments easy for arthritic hands to manage, or to secure loose items like hats, gloves, and scarves.

7. Use iron-on patches to repair small rips or tears in bed linens as well as shirts or jeans.

8. Use fishing line or dental floss to sew buttons on jeans or coats, or in any sewing job where extra strength and durability are required.

9. Use empty baby food jars to store sewing supplies such as needles, thread, and bobbins, for at-a-glance retrieval and to keep supplies free of dust and dirt.

Sew on a Button

A dangling or missing button can be very annoying. Sewing one back on is one of the easiest repairs you can make yourself. Before you begin, make sure to have the right thread and needle on hand. Follow these simple guidelines for getting ready.

1. What kind of button is it? Does it have several little holes, or a ring shank attached at the base? If it has little holes, you'll need the same color thread to match what the other buttons on your garment are sewn with; a shank button is sewn from beneath, so the thread doesn't show.

2. Get the right-sized needle for the job—a thick needle with a larger eye for an overcoat, a standard mending needle for a cotton shirt, a very thin needle for a silk blouse.

3. Similarly, you'll need the correct thread to correspond to the weave and thickness of the cloth. For a shank button on a coat, you can even use dental floss for extra strength. The heavier the fabric, the thicker the thread you should choose, and of course, the larger the needle.

4. Thread the needle. Cut about 2 feet of thread from the spool with very sharp scissors. Thread that's either too short or too long can be unmanageable.

Thread one end through the eye of the needle, pulling the thread until both ends are even. Tie a tiny knot in the end by rubbing the two thread ends together almost as if you were going to twist them. Wrap the thread ends around your index finger and continue the twisting, rubbing motion to pull them around into a knot. Snip off the extra thread below the knot—about ¼" on the end is fine.

Now you're ready to sew. A simple button-sewing trick is to place a match between the button and the cloth while sewing; this allows just the right amount of "give" for the buttonhole. For thin fabrics, use a paper match; to sew a big flat button onto a heavy woolen overcoat, use a wooden kitchen match. (Don't substitute a toothpick—it's too easy to poke yourself with the sharp ends.)

1. Find the exact spot where the previous button was attached. Gently remove any remaining old threads. Now, stick your needle in from the back of the fabric to the front at that exact spot. Pull it through, around the match, and through the ring shank until the thread is taut. Poke the needle down around the other side of the match. For the multihole button, sew around the match in a cross or parallel pattern to match the pattern on the other buttons. Repeat about ten times, and bring your needle out between the button and the cloth.

2. Gently tug the match out. Wrap the thread from the needle around the slightly loose thread at the base of the button where the match had been. Circle the base threads about five times, then sew back down through the base of the thread and the cloth. Come back up and wrap a few times and sew down again.

3. Bring the needle through the thread anchor to the back of the cloth, snip the thread very close to the eye of the needle, and with the two threads, tie a close, tight knot at the base of the cloth. Snip away extra thread. The button should now be very secure.

Care for Houseplants

Temperature. Some plants are more sensitive than others; know how much heat or cold a particular plant can tolerate. Plants may require a special heat lamp or a warmer area of the house. Avoid draughts, and be especially mindful in winter, when house temperatures can fluctuate widely. Keep the room temperature stable.

Humidity. For some plants (such as cacti) humidity is not a problem, but most will become dehydrated if the humidity in the house is not high enough. Keep plants away from dry areas such as near the radiator, and stand plants that are sensitive to humidity close together so they can help each other create a moist environment. If low humidity is a problem, spray the plant daily with antitranspirant liquid or water to keep it moist.

Light. In general, keep young plants and plants with foliage out of strong and direct sunlight. Variegated (marked or striped) plants may require extra sunlight. Know how much light your plant requires.

Water. Once a week is a safe bet, but always be on the lookout for signs the plant needs more or less water. Underwatered plants, whose soil has been allowed to dry completely, will begin to wilt and dry up. Overwatered plants turn yellow and may also wilt. Let the soil dry out to a reasonable point before rewatering; and check it for dampness. Use tepid, pure water. Let tap water sit at least 24 hours to let the chemicals dissolve, or boil and cool it. Rain water is good unless the rain in your area is especially acidic. Pour the water slowly and thoroughly until it covers the top of the soil. The water should eventually sink into the soil and drip out the bottom of the pot holder; if not, give more water.

Food. Plants need nitrogen (for leaves), phosphorus (for roots), and potassium (for seeds, fruit, and flowers) to flourish. In addition, magnesium, iron, calcium, sulfur, and other minerals are important. A well-balanced compost is advisable, but fertilizer is usually also necessary as a supplement. Use the right kind for your plants. Liquid fertilizers should be administered about every two weeks in the spring and summer and used in smaller doses for young plants. Read all directions before using a fertilizer (you may need to dilute it), and never apply it if the plant needs watering.

Potting. Clay or plastic pots seem to work best—clay because it is porous, and plastic because it is light and easy to use. Be sure the pot drains water correctly. When the roots of a plant become cramped, you must repot it into a larger container. Look for signs such as pale growth and roots sticking out of drain holes. Try to repot before the growing season in early spring.

Grooming. Control the growth of your plant by supporting and trimming its leaves. Prune your plants before the growing season, and encourage plants thicken by to growing out instead of up. Cut back the longest trailers on a hanging plant to promote heavier growth at the top. Remove dead flowers and leaves by cutting them cleanly at the stem. Keep plants free of dust by wiping the leaves with a cloth and/or leaf shining formula.

Diseases and insects. Various fungicides and chemicals can cure plants of disease or insect infestation. To be safe, keep new plants away from others until you can be sure they are disease and insect-free.

3 Hardy Houseplants

Boston fern (*Nephrolepsis exaltata*). Place in semishade with no direct sunlight but moisture in the air. Water at least twice a week in spring, once a week in winter. Mist if the air is dry.

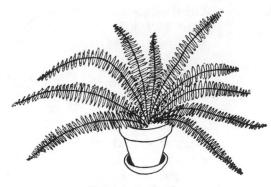

Figure 1. Boston fern

Umbrella tree *(Schefflera)*. Give bright or light shade. Water once a week; let soil dry between waterings in the winter.

Figure 2. Umbrella tree

Wandering Jew *(Tradescantia)*. Give bright, indirect sunlight. Water at least twice a week in spring and once a week during winter.

Figure 3. Wandering Jew

Build and Light a Fireplace Fire

Before central heating, knowing how to build a fire was almost as essential to surviving winter as dressing warmly. But while we should be thankful for modern heating methods, there's still no nicer way to spend a cold night than in front of a fireplace fire. A well-made fire not only warms the temperature in a room but warms the atmosphere as well. A good fireplace fire is one that gives the most possible heat to the room, one that burns evenly, and one that lasts. Perhaps the best way to learn how to make a fire is to watch others who have been building fires for years. Over time, they've developed the tricks that lead to the best fires. While the basic procedure is a simple, the difference between building a successful fire and an unsuccessful one is a matter of attention to subtle details. Follow these directions as closely as you can to get a head start in the art of fire building.

1. To avoid starting a chimney fire, make sure the chimney has been cleaned recently.

2. Open the flue. When a fireplace is not working, the chimney should be closed off with a flue to prevent the house's heat from escaping. Make sure you open the flue before you start a fire; otherwise, the entire room will quickly fill up with smoke. Most flues open by turning a knob or manipulating a handle on the inside of the fireplace.

3. Check for ash and andirons. The ash from the last fire should not have been swept out of the fireplace. A small pile of ash on the floor of the fireplace, perhaps 2" high, is good for a fire; it reflects heat back into the fire, keeps heat off fireplace walls, and partially blocks air currents from entering underneath a fire and sending heat up the chimney. The andirons, a metal rack that holds the firewood, should rest about an inch or two above the ash heap (Figure 1).

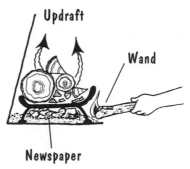

Figure 1. Lighting the fire

4. Lay the kindling. The first wood to lay on the andirons is the kindling. This is a group of twigs or wood cut small and thin, arranged in a criss-cross pattern that allows air to flow between the pieces. Kindling must be easy to light because it will be used to ignite larger logs. The best kindling is dry softwood such as cedar or pine.

5. Lay the logs. On top of the kindling, lay two or three logs. These should be roughly 6" in diameter and as long as will fit in your fireplace without touching the fireplace wall. The best logs are made of hardwood, like maple, and work best when very dry. To ensure your logs are dry, cut or buy them well in advance of using them (perhaps a year) and keep them either inside or well covered outside. Arrange the logs in the fireplace so they send heat forward into the room as opposed to up the chimney. To do this, do not stack the logs in a pyramid; rather, arrange them sideways, sloping forward with the largest log in the back. Once you've laid the logs, you may add more kindling between them.

6. Between the ash and the andirons, stuff a few balled-up sheets of newspaper. Newspaper lights easily and burns quickly, making it a good, nonobtrusive fire starter.

7. Light with a rolled-up newspaper. Take another sheet of newspaper and roll it into a tight wand. Holding it at one end, light the other end with a match or lighter and stick the flaming end into the fireplace above the wood pile. You should see the smoke rising, indicating that an updraft has been created; this limits the amount of smoke that enters the room when you light the fire (some smoke is to be expected, but a lot can be dangerous—be absolutely sure the flue is already open). Once you've created an updraft, use the wand to light the other pieces of newspaper below the wood. This should, in turn, light the kindling and start the wood burning. While some people like to use firestarters to help light the fire, dedicated fire builders view that as cheating. If you do plan to use them—with or without newspaper—place them below the logs with the kindling—and be careful.

8. Close the screen. Once the fire has started, it's a good idea to shut the fireplace screen to prevent sparks from flying into the room. Shutting the screen, however, blocks a lot of heat from entering the room. If you'd like to keep the screen open, make sure you watch the fire closely for sparks, and move rugs and other potentially flammable material far from the fire.

9. Stoke the fire. When it appears the fire is beginning to die down, stoke it with a fireplace poker or tongs, moving the logs slightly in order to stir the air around. A fire need not be roaring to give off maximum heat.

10. Add logs. About every half hour or so you can add a new log to the fire to keep it burning, but first allow the logs in the fireplace to burn sufficiently. Do not pile wood up too high, and when you add logs be careful not to burn yourself; use iron tools whenever possible. Pull partially burned logs toward the front and add new logs at the back.

11. Ending the fire. It's not a good idea to try to put the fire out yourself; let the fire burn out naturally. While this may take a while, don't leave the fire unsupervised if you don't have to. When the fire has died down, shut the screen and glass door (if there is one) of the fireplace completely, but keep the flue open for several hours until you are sure the fire is out. You may want to

sweep up some of the ash with a brush and shovel when the pile grows too high—but only when it has had ample time to cool. Live coals can lurk in apparently dead ashes for 24 hours or more.

12. To prevent the buildup of deposits that can ignite and start a chimney fire, have your chimney cleaned regularly.

Time-Saving Laundry and Hand-Washing Tips

With our automatic washing machines and superheated dryers, we forget what a difficult physical task washing and drying clothes once was. Then, as ever, the laundry just never seemed to get done.

Designate one day of the week for laundry and stick to that schedule. Find an activity to occupy your time between trips to the laundry room, or between loads: choose an evening when there is something you enjoy on television, rent a video, read a magazine in the afternoon, or do your morning workout.

If you do your laundry either in an apartment building or at a laundromat using coin-operated machines, keep a supply of quarters on hand (keep a small box on your dresser to deposit quarters from change for this purpose). A week's time should yield enough quarters to let you do laundry without begging for change from store owners or depending on change machines, which are so often broken.

Just as you keep up a supply of toothpaste, deodorant, and other household items, be sure you are always well stocked with detergent and fabric softener. Always buy these items at least two at a time. Purchase a replacement when you finish the first bottle or box.

Separate darks, whites, and light-colored clothes right in the room where your hamper or laundry bag is. If you have enough space, keep two or three different hampers or laundry bags and separate the clothes each night when you get undressed. When separating directly into the washing machine, you will inevitably miss one bright-red, never-before-washed sock, and end up with a load of "pinks," not "whites." Put machine-washable delicates in lingerie bags to protect them, and keep them together. Generally, whites are washed in hot water, and darks in cold, but carefully follow the instructions on clothing labels. Never attempt to wash something that is marked "dry clean only"—this is a sure recipe for disaster.

While the clothes are in the washing machine, hand-wash any fine fabrics that would be ruined there. Fill a sink or plastic tub with cool water and a capful of detergent (special detergent for fine washables is preferable). Let the clothing soak briefly, then swish it through the soapy water. Finally, gently rub any spots or stains together in a fold of fabric. Rinse clothing with cool water until the water runs clear, wring it out very gently, and hang it up to dry.

As soon as the spin cycle is finished, put your belongings into the dryer. Immediately hang up any clothing that cannot go into the dryer to drip dry along with the hand washables.

If you are laundering for more than one person, save folding time by insisting that everyone put clothes into the hamper or laundry basket right side out. If you have trouble dividing up everyone's clothes afterwards, set up a color-coding system, marking each person's items with a small dot on the label in a different-colored marker.

Time-Saving Ironing Tips

Ironing—not a glamorous household job—takes true skill and dexterity. The most convenient way to handle ironing hassles is to buy only fabrics that dry wrinkle-free. Should you already own a wardrobe full of silk blouses and cotton shirts however, there are some ways to reduce the time you spend ironing.

One way to save time, if not money: take these items to a reputable dry cleaner or hand laundry. Many people who wear dress shirts to work every day take them to a laundry regularly. It is an added expense but could be a cost-effective one if time is a real priority.

The best way to speed up ironing is to do it all at once. In a large household, this may mean a few hours standing over the ironing board, but each time you avoid dragging the ironing board out of the closet to iron one or two items you gain 20 minutes to half an hour of time.

Set aside an area for clothing to be ironed in the future. Place only dry clothing in that area. Fold it neatly before doing so—at least it won't become more wrinkled while waiting for your attention.

Certain fabrics, such as silk and linen, can be ironed better when damp. Place these items in plastic bags and freeze them. When you remove them a few days later, they will still be damp, somewhat pliable, and ready for ironing.

Likewise, should you pull a shirt out of your closet one morning only to find it is unwearable and you must iron it, try hanging the shirt in the bathroom while you take a hot shower. The steam may take out some minor wrinkles and will certainly make the fabric more receptive to ironing.

Certain fabrics may not need ironing if properly handled. Clothes tend to wrinkle more if the dryer is crowded. Dry things fairly loosely, and remove them as soon as possible after the drying cycle is complete. Also, ironing denim is truly unnecessary. This fabric goes almost immediately from stiff to supple when it is worn.

Air-dried items should approximate their correct shape when drying. Never hang a cotton dress shirt on a hook or a line; always drape it carefully over a plastic hanger (metal will leave rust stains) and button it. Smooth it once or twice with your hands.

Be prepared. Keep your iron clean at all times, and use only distilled water for steam ironing; otherwise, clothes will stain. Avoid miniature ironing boards. They are real time-wasters, since you have to shift them around so much while ironing one piece of clothing. Separate items by type and iron them in groups to establish a rhythm. Keep plenty of hangers handy. As you finish each item, drape it carefully and hang near by. Avoid crowding clothes into your closets; you don't want to waste your ironing efforts by wrinkling the clothes afterwards. Finally, reward yourself. You deserve it.

Dyeing and Tie-Dyeing Fabrics

Dyeing simple cotton clothing is a good way to refresh your wardrobe with a jolt of color without spending too much money. Dyeing with dark colors can save light-colored items that have been stained and might otherwise be ruined.

Certain fabrics—mostly synthetics such as polyester—cannot be dyed. One hundred percent cotton is the best fabric for dyeing because it absorbs readily. If you want to make a batch of funky tie-dyed shirts, buy a package of inexpensive white cotton undershirts and a bundle of rubber bands.

Dye comes in two forms, powder and liquid, both widely available in pharmacies and stores where household goods are sold. Both dyes need to be mixed with water. Always wear plastic gloves when dyeing an item, or your hands will be stained for days afterwards.

Fill a large tub or pot (you can do this in your own bathtub, but it will take some scrubbing to remove dye stains afterwards) with water and mix in the dye as dictated by package instructions. Be sure to leave ample space for the clothing you plan to dye. If necessary, dye articles one at a time to avoid crowding.

If you are dyeing something a solid color, place it in the tub and swish it around. When you are sure that the fabric is not folded up on itself anywhere (this will result in white or lighter-colored blotches) simply leave the item in the tub until it is two shades darker than your desired final color. The fabric will lighten slightly as it dries.

Wring the clothing out well over the tub before removing it. Allow dyed clothing to air-dry completely.

To tie-dye, take a handful of the material you are dyeing and twist it. Now encircle this twisted portion with rubber bands. Dip it into the dye and hold it there until the desired color is achieved. The more rubber bands you use, the more sunbursts the final product will have. Bleeding two colors together, say red and blue, will create other colors; here, purple. Do not place rubber bands less than 2" apart.

A final tip: newly-dyed fabric will run heavily when you wash it. Hand wash home-dyed fabrics separately the first few times. Wash them in cold water, and only with dark colors, after that.

Basic Pool Maintenance

Clean your pool regularly and run it through a weekly checkup. At the very least, you need to make sure the water is treated with disinfectant and the pool itself is clean and in good working order throughout the swimming season. For safety, don't allow swimming until you are sure the pool is properly disinfected.

Water Treatment

Most pools use chlorine to kill bacteria, algae, and other organic materials in the water. Many types of chlorine products are available; read the container and follow all directions. When adding powdered chlorine, sift it through a skimmer so the crystals will separate.

Test the water regularly with a special pool testing set to make sure it has enough chlorine and the proper pH balance. There should be between .3 and .6 parts of chlorine per million in the pool, with a slightly alkaline pH reading (7.2 to 7.6). If the pool appears grayish and smells of chlorine, there is probably too much chlorine in the pool and it is too alkaline. If the water causes skin or eye irritation, it may be too acidic and not have enough chlorine. To correct this type of chlorine imbalance, it's good to superchlorinate, or add three times the normal amount of chlorine to the pool, every few weeks. This will clear the pool of ineffective chlorine.

Pool Care and Cleaning

1. Skim the water surface with a hand-held skimmer to keep outside materials (grass, dirt, bugs) out of the pool.
2. Vacuum the pool floor and scrub the pool wall. Make sure the water level covers the skimmer. Use a cleaning system that works best for the construction materials of your pool—plaster, vinyl, tile, fiberglass, or paint.
3. Clean the leaf strainer.
4. Check and clean the pool filter and water pump.
5. Hose down the pool deck.
6. Make sure all other mechanical pool parts of the pool are clean and working.

Closing the Pool for the Winter

1. Lower the water level about 1" below the pool skimmer.
2. Vacuum the pool thoroughly.
3. Remove diving boards, ladders, and other removable pool accessories.
4. Adjust the pH to the proper level, between 7.2 and 7.6.
5. Add the proper winterizing chemicals.
6. Disconnect the pump and filter, and drain all the water out of the circulation system to prevent freezing in winter.
7. Plug all the pool inlets and outlets with winter pool plugs (available at pool stores).
8. Cover the pool with a strong vinyl or plastic cover and secure it in place with heavy stones or cinder blocks around the edges.

Opening the Pool in the Spring

1. Remove the pool cover.
2. Replace the diving board, ladders, and other equipment removed for the winter.
3. Remove the pool plugs from outlets and inlets.
4. Vacuum and scrub the walls and floor thoroughly.
5. Raise the water to the proper level.
6. Backwash the filter to clean out debris accumulated from the winter.
7. Superchlorinate, and adjust the pH to its proper level.

10. Just for the Fun of It

Play Rummy

Like poker, rummy is among the most popular of card games and is played by people all over the world. The rules are simple, and the strategies require a good memory for tracking which cards have already been played. Here are the basics:

Dealing. For a regular two-player game of rummy, deal both players ten cards each. For three or four players, deal each player seven cards, and for five or six players, deal each player five cards. Place the remainder of the deck in the center of the table face down, then turn the top card over and place it next to the deck. This is called the up card.

Card groupings. Players must use their hands to make groupings of at least three cards. Cards can be grouped either by sequence (for example, 3, 4, 5 of the same suit) or by value (three 3s).

Picking cards. In turn, players may either pick up the up card, if it helps them to complete a group, or pick a card from the deck. Whenever a card is picked, one must be discarded; discard a high card if no card grouping for it seems possible (see the score section).

Laying down. When you complete a grouping, you may put the cards face up on the table. This is called laying down. You can also choose to hold your groupings until the end and lay them down all at once. This is called "gin rummy" or "going rummy"; the pros and cons of going rummy are discussed below in the score section.

Laying off. If either player has a card or cards that will fit into one of the groupings already laid down (for example, a 6 of the same suit to match the 3, 4, 5 above), the player may lay down the card or cards during his or her turn, whether or not the player laid down the original grouping.

Duration. A round of rummy ends when a player uses all of his or her cards in groupings. This may require going through the deck more than once.

Score. The value of the cards remaining in the losing player's hand is added up (face cards count as 10, and aces as 1); the total represents the number of points the winning player gains. That's why it is better to get rid of high cards as soon as possible. Play continues to a specified point total, such as 100. A player who goes rummy (see the section on laying down) gets double points but risks being caught with all ten cards in hand.

Block rummy. In this variation of rummy, the game ends when the deck ends, and the player with the lowest point total wins. All other players subtract the winner's points from theirs to determine the number of points the winner gains.

An alternative scoring method is to add up the points you are stuck holding at the end of the hand and subtract them from what you have laid down to get your score (this could be a negative total!). Obviously, the winner of the hand will have no points to subtract. The first player to reach 100 points wins.

Poker Basics

Poker is one of the most popular card games in the U.S. Whether you are playing for fun or for high stakes, the best way to improve your poker skills is just to play. With experience, you will learn the game's rules and strategies and develop a sense for how to best play your hand. Here is some basic poker information it will help you to know before you even start:

Progression of hands. No matter what type of poker game you play, the ranking of hands does not change (except in a rare instance, which must be specified beforehand). From best to worst, they go in this order:

✓ Royal flush: ace, king, queen, jack, 10 of the same suit
✓ Straight flush: any five-card sequence of the same suit
✓ Four of a kind: four cards of the same value
✓ Full house: a pair and three of a kind
✓ Flush: any five cards of the same suit
✓ Straight: five-card sequence, not of the same suit
✓ Three of a kind: three cards of the same value
✓ Two pair: two sets of two cards with the same value
✓ One pair: one set of two cards with the same value
✓ High card: the highest value card in the hand

Types of poker. Because a dealer is free to set just about any rules he or she wants, there are as many styles and variations of poker as there are people who play the game. These are the most popular versions:

✓ *Draw.* In draw poker, players are dealt their whole hand face down (only the player can see the cards) and may exchange some or all the cards for new ones. While a five-card deal with a three-card draw is common, the number of cards dealt and drawn can vary and should be announced before the deal.

✓ *Stud.* In stud poker, some cards are dealt face up (all players can see the cards) and some down. As in draw poker, the number of cards dealt and which ones are dealt face down varies and depends on the decision of the dealer. A five-card stud with the first card dealt down is common, as is a seven-card stud with the first two and last cards down.

✓ *Spit in the Ocean.* In its most common form, this game consists of four cards dealt down to each player and one card turned up in the middle of the table. The up card is wild, and players use it to complete their five-card hands (meaning that each player has at least a pair to start with).

✓ *Cincinnati.* In this game, each player is dealt five cards down while five cards are turned over, one at a time, in the center. Each player can use the five cards in the center, which gives them ten cards in all to find the best five-card hand. In other variations, the amount of cards dealt is lowered and the center cards are arranged in a cross formation, allowing a player to use only one row of three cards to complete a hand.

✓ *High-low.* High-low is not really a game in itself but rather a rule that can be applied to many poker games. In it, the highest hand splits the pot with the lowest, or worst, hand. The worst possible hand in most poker games is ace, 2, 3, 4, 6 (or 2, 3, 4, 5, 7 if ace is high).

✓ *Lowball.* This game takes the high-low principle to the extreme. In it, the lowest hand wins the entire pot.

✓ *Guts.* In this game, two or three cards are usually dealt down, though more can be dealt. The players try to form their best poker hands, usually only a pair or high card, then hold their cards out face down by the edges. At a count of three the players either hold their cards or drop them on the table. Those who drop have folded; those who hold compete for the best hand. Any player who holds but then loses must match the pot (therefore, if two players lose, the pot is doubled). The game ends when only one player holds.

Betting. Three factors usually determine bets in poker: the ante, or what each player put into the pot before the deal; the minimum bet, or the least amount that can be bet in a round; and the maximum bet, or the most that can be bet in a round. The rules for betting should be set out before the deal.

Wild cards. To raise the level of the hands, dealers often call wild cards. These are cards that can act as any card in the deck. Jokers, deuces, or particular face cards (one-eyed jacks, suicide kings) are often designated wild and should be called before the deal.

Strategies. Poker strategy can be very involved, and it requires a lot of playing experience to truly understand. Here is a list of some of the most basic strategies:

✓ Come with enough money to play. The fear of running out of money will make you apprehensive about betting, which other players may read and exploit. As a beginner, stay away from games with expensive stakes. Play for pennies, barter for errands, or play for your favorite snack or candy.

✓ Be confident. Don't allow other players to read you. Try to show an even level of enthusiasm whether you have a good hand or not. When you decide to bet, act confident whether you have the cards or are bluffing.

✓ Watch others. Just as others will try to read your expression, you should try to read theirs. Also, watch other player's open hands; they may reveal what kind of hand a player has, or at least tell you what cards you will not be dealt.

✓ Get out unless you have a promising hand. Staying in on a long shot will sometimes pay off well, but more often than not you'll just be wasting money. Bluffing is fine, but in the end you need to have the best hand to win.

Etiquette. As in any game, there are certain unspoken rules that should be upheld. Don't count your chips or money at the table, don't pick up your cards until every one has been dealt, don't leave the table in the middle of a hand, bet in turn, and avoid table talk or "talking trash" with other players.

10 Secrets of Scrabble

1. The tiles you leave on your rack are just as important as the tiles you choose to play. For example, if you leave three tiles with the letter I on your rack, the chances are good you will cripple your next play or be forced to exchange your next turn for new tiles (thus halving your two-turn total score). If you have two or more of any letter on your rack, it is usually best to think about using or exchanging at least one of them.

2. Play defensively. Avoid opening up the high-scoring triple word score alleys (the four rows that form the perimeter of the board) unless you score many points. Similarly, if you have a choice between putting a vowel or a consonant next to a premium (colored) square, choose the consonant.

3. Try to use as many tiles as possible at each turn. This will allow you to see a maximum number of tiles over the course of the game and will improve your chances of getting the "good" tiles—the letter S, the blanks, and the high-scoring tiles.

4. Always think about how to play all of the tiles on your rack before considering alternative possibilities.

5. Don't rush. Try to think of at least three possible moves before making your play. Try to have at least two reasons why this play is the best one you can come up with. Usually the best move is the one that scores the most points or just about the most points—but not always. All the other possible moves must be considered, but don't keep sacrificing too many points or you will lose.

6. If you are behind when the game is more than half finished, take more risks for the sake of points and opening the board up for high-scoring plays.

7. If you are ahead when the game is more than half finished, do everything you can do to close up the board so that your opponent will not be able to play all of his or her tiles. True, you won't be able to either—but you are ahead, so it doesn't matter.

8. Unless you are playing with your English teacher, points are more important than showing off your vocabulary.

9. If you have a choice between playing a real word you are certain your opponent knows and one you think your opponent might challenge—and all other things are equal—play the one that might draw the challenge.

10. Use the letter S or the blanks to get very high-scoring or seven-letter plays.

Chess Moves

Chess is a game of nearly infinite possibility, in which strategy and game development require deep concentration and years of practice. Don't expect the following information to turn you into a champion overnight. What you will find here is a brief explanation of basic chess moves: some special moves certain pieces are able to perform, and a few simple strategic maneuvers. In explaining, we'll assume the reader has a basic knowledge of chess and its rules, including the movement of game pieces.

Castling

Castling is a move that involves the King and a Rook, also called a Castle. It can be a valuable strategic move if used appropriately. To castle, both the King and the Rook (either the King-side or the Queen-side Rook can be used) must be in their opening positions and have never been moved. There cannot be any other pieces of either color between the King and Rook, and the King cannot currently be in check or be castled to a spot that will put it in check. If these conditions are met, castling can be performed. It will count as one move.

To castle with a King-side Rook, move the King from its opening position two squares over (to the King's Knight's position) to stand next to the Rook. Then move the Rook two squares in the opposite direction, directly to the other side of the King.

To castle with a Queen-side Rook, move the King two squares over (to the Queen's Bishop's position) toward the Rook. Then move the Rook three squares in the opposite direction, over the King, to land directly next to the King (in the Queen's position).

Capturing in Passing (en Passant)

Capturing in passing is a rule designed centuries ago to counterbalance the rule allowing Pawns the option of moving two squares on an opening move. It works in only a very specific situation: A Pawn in starting position that is in danger of being captured by an enemy Pawn (in an adjoining file, or vertical row) if it advances one square cannot avoid capture by advancing two squares instead. Even if the Pawn advances two squares (to a position directly next to the enemy Pawn), the enemy Pawn can still capture that Pawn by moving diagonally forward one square (its normal capturing move). Two conditions: Capturing in passing must be done on the first possible opportunity or never, and the move cannot result in the King's being put in check.

Pawn Promotion

If a Pawn moves forward to the opposite end of the board (the eighth rank, or horizontal row), it can be transformed into any higher piece (except the King), regardless of whether it is already on the board. The Pawn usually becomes a Queen, because it is the most dynamic piece. Promotion takes place immediately (meaning that the King can be put in check by the transformation) but the piece cannot move until the player's next turn.

Strategic Maneuvers

The net. This move is the basic form of capture. It involves cutting off the lines of retreat so the enemy piece has no place to move. Checkmate is a net of the King (Figure 1).

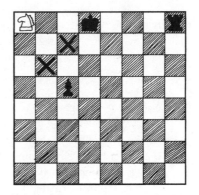

Figure 1. The net. The White Knight has nowhere to retreat. Moving the Black King forward one square sets up the Rook to capture the Knight.

The pin. This involves trapping a piece so it cannot move because it is protecting the King from check (Figure 2).

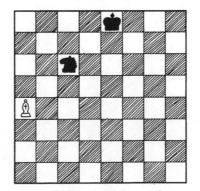

Figure 2. The pin. The Black Knight cannot move because it protects the King. It must fall to the White Bishop.

The fork. This move is an attack by one piece on two enemy pieces in different directions. The piece is positioned so it can capture either piece. To move one enemy piece means losing the other. If one of the pieces is a King there is no choice which to move, as getting the King out of check takes precedence over all other moves (Figure 3).

Figure 3. The fork. The Knight is in position to capture either the Black King or Queen. The King must move and thus the Queen is lost.

The skewer. This move is similar to the fork and, in essence, is the opposite of the pin. It involves getting two pieces in the same line for capture so that to move one will mean the capture of the other. Again, if one of the pieces is a King, there is no choice which to move (Figure 4).

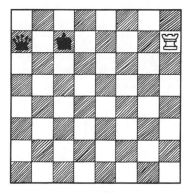

Figure 4. The skewer. The White Rook takes the Black Queen by forcing the Black King to move out of check.

The tied piece. An attack of two pieces on two enemy pieces where one enemy piece is protecting the other. By attacking the piece that is protecting, it is forced to either move (thus leaving vulnerable the piece it was protecting) or stay and be captured (Figure 5).

Figure 5. The tied piece. The Black Knight protects the Black Rook from capture by the
White Bishop. But the approach of the White Pawn means the Knight
will either have to move, exposing the Rook, or be captured.

Set Up and Play Backgammon

Backgammon is a popular board game for two players. Each player has 15 stones
(round playing pieces) of the same color. The backgammon board consists of two
sides, each with a set of 12 points (Figure 1).

The object of the game is to move all your stones around the board in the
required direction and off the board before your opponent does. This is done by
rolling a pair of dice and moving your pieces according to your roll. You may
move one stone the total amount of both dice (if you roll a 2 and 4, then move 6
spaces) or move one stone for each die (one 2 spaces and the other 4 spaces). If
you roll doubles you may move twice the rolled amount (if 3 and 3, then move
12). As before, you may move one stone the entire amount or split up your roll
among 2, 3, or 4 stones.

Stones of different colors cannot sit on the same point. If more than one stone of the
same color rests on a point, it is closed and a stone of another color cannot land
there. If only one stone sits on a point (or no stone) the point is open and a different-
colored stone can land on the point. If a single stone is present where a different-
colored stone lands, the resting stone is removed from the board. It may reenter
when the player rolls dice corresponding in value to an empty point, or a point
where like-colored stones rest; the player may not make another move until then.

The most confusing part of the game is remembering how to set up the board.
The diagram below shows how it's done. Black stones move clockwise, bottom to
top. White stones move counterclockwise, top to bottom. The end of the board
marked "1" is where stones reenter on the player's side and leave the board on the
opponent's side after completing a successful round. The end marked "12" is
where stones travel around the board.

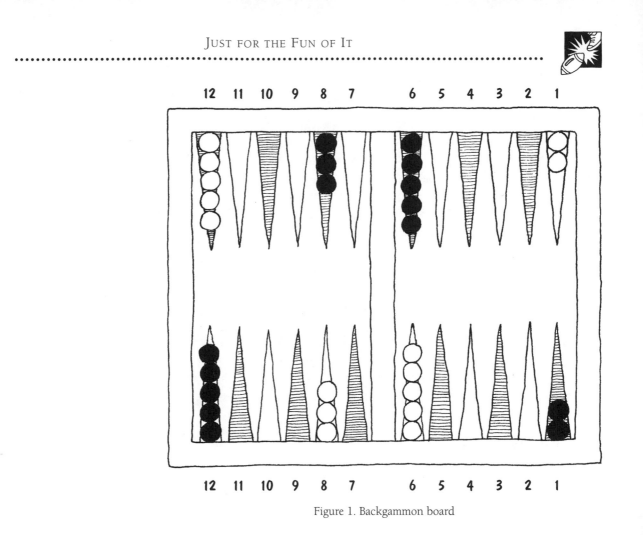

12 11 10 9 8 7 6 5 4 3 2 1

12 11 10 9 8 7 6 5 4 3 2 1

Figure 1. Backgammon board

Ride a Bicycle

Bicycles are a wonderful environment-friendly mode of transportation. Riding bikes allows us to exercise aerobically, tone up our legs, save gas, and have a lot of fun. In good weather, breezing down a road under your own power can be a real treat. Bicycle riding is popular too: in 1991, 53,972,000 Americans rode their bicycles at least once.

Before you do begin biking, familiarize yourself with traffic regulations. Even if a special lane is set aside for cyclists, you will still need to follow the rules set for automobiles. Remember to keep an eye out for pedestrians, joggers, and other bicycle riders as well. Help prevent accidents by wearing reflectors on your clothing (your back and heels are good spots), especially in the evening. Make sure your bike is equipped with front and rear reflectors. Always wear a helmet;

255

it can save you from serious head trauma. Unless you plan to compete in races, casual clothing like jeans, shorts, and sneakers are fine for bike riding.

Children usually learn to ride a bicycle by starting out on a tricycle, then graduating to a bicycle with training wheels, which are eventually removed. Adults, however, should have enough balance to learn to ride without assistance.

Choose a bicycle appropriate to the type of riding you plan to do. A ten-speed bicycle is useful for riding hilly terrain, going long distances, or racing. If you plan to use the bike mainly for transportation across flat land, a three-speed bike or one with no gears will be fine. Like a car, a bicycle needs to switch gears in order to gain better resistance when going uphill. Mountain bikes are hearty vehicles for off-road riding. If you intend to carry such items as books or groceries with you, be sure to install a basket or a "trap," a metal contraption that attaches behind the seat and secures books and other small items in its jaws. Water bottles that attach to the bike frame are useful for long rides, and city dwellers will need sturdy locks.

When you do ride, find a rate of speed that feels comfortable for you. Even if you are riding over long distances for exercise, you should breathe comfortably enough to speak normally or sing to yourself. Pedal steadily, and stand up carefully on the pedals when riding uphill. Rest when you have to.

In-Line Skating

Blading, or in-line skating, has become so popular that it is being considered as an exhibition sport for the Summer Olympics. Millions of people are enjoying the benefits of this excellent low-impact sport for cardiovascular fitness and muscle toning. Besides, it is a great way to get around!

Choosing Skates and Gear

Beginners should choose skates with an outer boot firm enough to give proper ankle support yet still be comfortable. More expensive skates have foam liners that fit to your foot's shape and offer the best protection from blisters and sprains. For jumping or racing, choose skates with a strong frame that doesn't twist or bend. Larger wheels give better speed but less stability. The best skates have high-quality ball bearings. Choose five-wheeled in-lines for efficient push-offs and stability at high speeds; four-wheeled skates maneuver better for fast turns and are probably better for the new skater. Most importantly, don't buy skates that hurt when you try them on in the store—hard-molded plastic doesn't "break in!" Look for a pair of skates that offers the best quality and the best fit (Figure 1). Rotating the wheels, lubricating the bearings, and replacing the brakes as necessary will keep your skates in good, and safe, condition.

Always wear a helmet, wrist guards, and knee and elbow protectors, and carry reflective decals for after-dark outings.

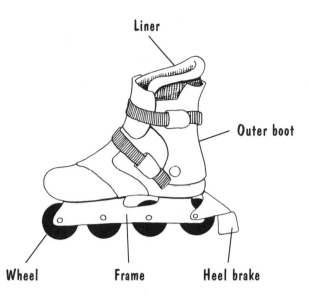

Figure 1. In-line skate

Blader Tips for Beginners

1. Stand with your hands on your knees for added balance as you learn to find your body center. If you feel you are going to fall, lower your center of gravity and return to this position.

2. With your nose, knees, feet aligned in the basic in-line stance and your skates hip distance apart, practice bringing your feet together by shifting your weight and placing toe to toe, heel to toe, and heel to heel. Actually tap the boots together to gain comfort in the motion. The foot tap increases the efficiency of your strides.

3. Everyone falls. Try to fall forward whenever possible, and keep your torso, arms, and legs relaxed. Practice falling to get used to the sensation. Avoid falling backward; rearward falls can damage the spine and create the most serious accidents.

4. If you are out of balance, don't panic and try to correct the situation by using your heel brake. Concentrate on what is happening, lower your center of gravity, and try to skate through it. A planned fall is better than braking without thinking.

5. Keep your balance. Never try a new movement without it.

6. Focus your gaze out ahead of you, not down at the ground.

7. For a solid push-off, bend at the waist and put your hands on your knees.

8. Stay low and keep your arms closer to your torso to get better speed and control down hills.

9. Learn to jump in place or "catch some air." Focus on achieving a flat-footed exit and reentry. Take off with your arms extended to either side and your skates parallel, hip distance apart. When landing, bend your knees and ankles slightly and bend forward from the waist.

10. If you use your in-line skates for transportation, always carry basic tools for repairs and an extra bearing. Bring a water bottle, and store your belongings in an easy-to-manage backpack. And don't forget bandages.

Fly a Kite

Where to Fly

While large open fields are a good bet, the breeze on the water makes the beach a great place for kites if you can get to one. Avoid places that are very crowded, and stay away from large buildings, electrical wires, and traffic.

Which String to Use

The string should be neither too heavy nor too thin. For most purposes, a medium twine will work well. Waxing the string makes it more resistant to wetness but is not necessary. Avoid using wire that will conduct electricity (unless you're Ben Franklin!).

Wind Conditions

A modest wind is always good to get the kite up and flying, but too strong a wind can destroy a kite. Judge whether the wind is too strong for the design and quality of your kite, keeping in mind that heavier kites can handle stronger winds. Light kites are better able to fly when the wind is very mild; some designs will have more trouble taking off and climbing without a stiff breeze.

Launching

Stand with your back to the wind, and hold the kite in your arms so the back of the kite faces you. Do not drag the kite on the ground. As a gust of wind blows by, throw the kite into the air. Release only as much string as is necessary for the kite to lift off and pull the string taut. Release more string as the kite climbs. If the kite begins to fall, step away from it to keep the string stretched, and reel some string in if necessary. Running with the kite can help raise the altitude.

Flying

For the kite to fly properly, find a balance between keeping the string taut and allowing the kite to fly freely. If the kite reaches a certain altitude and won't go higher, it may have reached an area of calm wind. If so, pulling down on the string and then releasing it may give the kite enough momentum to climb out of the calm area. How well the kit flies overall depends in part on its size, strength, weight, and material. If you have problems getting the kite to fly, the bridle, tow line, or tail may need adjusting. Too long a tail will make the kite slow to rise. An improperly set tow line and bridle will throw the kite off balance. A well-balanced kite will fly at about a 45-degree angle. Experiment with different lengths until you find one that works.

Winding In

To bring the kite down, slowly reel in the string. Don't worry if the kite dips suddenly at high altitudes, but be careful to keep the kite from crashing into the ground when it gets low. Keep the string taut for as long as you can so the kite gets pulled in rather than falling. When the kite lands, remove the flying string from the tow line and roll up the tail. Store the kite in a safe place.

Drive a Motor Boat

The safe handling of a small motor boat requires an understanding of the physical relationship of a solid object to an extremely flexible and ever-changing surface. Driving a car and piloting a motor boat are not the same! Their individual functions are not only unrelated but sometimes completely contradictory. There are, in fact, more differences between driving a car and boat handling than there are similarities. If you are considering the purchase of a motor boat, take lessons from the Coast Guard or local boating association.

The characteristics of a boat that affect its safe handling are its design, power, propeller action, and rudder action. The exterior forces that affect its maneuverability are wind, currents, waves, and sometimes depth. The operator of a small motor boat, whether an outboard or inboard, must take these complex conditions and forces into account when doing what can be relatively simple with an automobile: steering, stopping, avoiding potential colliders, parking, and handling a breakdown.

Most beginners have problems with steering and getting accustomed to the rudder. Turning the wheel to the right moves the rudder to the right and forces the stern (back end) to the left when the boat is in motion. But when the engine is put into reverse during this rudder position, the stern swings to the right. It takes practice to become accustomed to the wheel-rudder actions, especially when using forward and backward motions to dock the boat in a narrow space. For this reason, beginners should practice repeatedly in open water, and then carefully, and slowly, alongside a dock with plenty of space for mistakes.

Here are some important points to keep in mind when handling a small motor boat:

1. Always check your gas supply before starting out. Many boats, especially outboards, have gauges only on the tank itself. Attendants at a dock pump will know what type your boat uses and whether engine oil must be added to it.

2. Make sure there is an approved life jacket for each person in the boat, and of proper sizes for the wearers. Be confident of your passenger's abilities to swim

and take this into account when starting on your trip—don't motor into areas that are dangerous for the survival of passengers if something goes wrong.

3. Pump out all excess water that accumulates in the bilge (the lowest part of the boat), since this can greatly affect the efficiency and safe handling of the boat.

4. If the motor is the inboard type, lift its cover or run the air exhaust to get rid of gasoline fumes, which can be explosive when concentrated.

5. Unless you are very familiar with the waters over which you will cruise, have a chart handy to show the location of shallows, underwater obstacles, dockage facilities, navigation buoys, strong currents, and anything else that might affect your safe passage.

6. Pay vigilant attention to currents and tides that could carry the boat off course.

7. Have an emergency plan of action in the event the motor should die at any time. Chart your course so that in such an unlucky event, the wind would push the boat toward shore instead of into deeper waters. If wind conditions do not permit this precaution, carry an anchor and plenty of line.

8. Make sure the boat is equipped with at least two paddles, fenders for use when coming alongside a dock or another boat, a fire extinguisher, and a horn that works. A ship-to-shore radio is recommended for boats operating far from shore in deep waters.

9. If you plan to be out after dark, check your running lights and carry an emergency flashlight. It goes without saying that you should be familiar enough with the local waters to find your way home at night.

10. Start the engine and let it idle for a few minutes before leaving the dock. Check both forward and reverse settings. Have the engine serviced annually.

11. After you have untied the boat and are ready to leave, coil the lines neatly so they cannot be tripped over and so none can trail and tangle with the propeller.

12. Know who has the right of way when you sight other boats that may be approaching or passing. A sailboat *always* has the right of way over a power boat of any size in *any* situation.

Throw a Curveball and a Change-Up

The curveball is one of the hardest pitches to hit in baseball. A great curve will move out and down over the plate, dropping a couple of feet just as it crosses in front of the batter. Throwing a curve without a properly trained arm can cause wrist or shoulder damage, so exercise caution. Only after you have developed a good, strong fastball should you attempt to throw a curve. And for those who are ready to learn, have patience; learning to throw the pitch correctly and effectively can take years. Use the same stance, windup, and delivery as with the fastball, but follow these added instructions for your release.

Curveball Grip

Hold the ball with your throwing hand. Wrap your index and middle finger around the ball so that the pads of your fingers lay across the seam of the ball. Bend your thumb underneath slightly so that the inside edge of your thumb is holding the ball. Grip the ball with the pressure on the middle finger and thumb (Figure 1).

Figure 1. The curveball grip   Figure 2. The release

Release

To give the ball time to break, do not throw a curveball as hard as a fastball. As you bring your arm around in motion, try to bring your elbow above your shoulder to create an arc and downward momentum for the ball. You want to release the ball up and over your index finger, from the side of your hand. To do this, you may want to fold your wrist forward so your fingers go in front of the ball before release. As you release, use your thumb to twist the ball clockwise and up (for a right-hander) and snap your wrist as the ball leaves your hand. For best results, release the ball a split second later than usual so the ball stays low (Figure 2).

While the curveball can be difficult and potentially dangerous for a young pitcher to learn, the change-up is an important weapon every hurler can and should have in store. It is relatively easy to learn and safe to throw. A well-executed change-up will look just like a fastball but will cross the plate much more slowly. The effect is to throw the batter's timing off so the swing either comes too early and misses, or is weak from hesitation.

Change-Up Grip

Hold the ball deep in the palm of your hand, with your index and middle fingers lying across the top. Your thumb should be wrapped around the side of the ball to give it as little spin as possible. If it helps, you can actually touch your thumb to your index finger to form an OK sign. Do not use your fingertips when throwing; the grip should be loose (Figure 3).

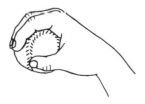

Figure 3. The change-up grip

The Motion

Because the effectiveness of the change-up depends on how much it looks like a fastball, the windup should be exactly like the fastball windup. The trick is to throw the ball without power while looking as though you are throwing hard. To help yourself do this, try to lead with your elbow as you bring your arm around (as opposed to your wrist in a fastball). Instead of putting your entire arm into the throw, try to use only your forearm for force. You'll get even less power if you avoid pushing off with your back foot as you bring your arm forward. As you release, simply open your palm and let the ball go. It may take some practice to do this with control, but release time is important. Again, don't ever make it look as though you are holding back or throwing sluggishly; it will give the pitch away.

Throw and Kick a Football

Throwing and kicking are the two most basic and important skills needed in football. Ball handling can be complicated and requires special attention because of the peculiar elongated shape of the ball. Once you get into the sport, you'll move way beyond these fundamental skills to learn the subtleties of strategy and technique. For the beginner, here's where to start for proper throwing and kicking form:

Throwing

Grip. To get the best hold of the football, spread the tops of your fingers comfortably across the laces and toward the back of the ball, with your thumb gripping the other side. How far back you hold the ball depends on the size of your hand—the smaller the hand, the farther back you should hold it. Some people even like to put their index finger on the point of the ball. Hold the ball firmly but do not squeeze it, and do not rest the ball on the palm of your hand. You may use your opposite hand to help hold the ball before the pass, but remove it when you are ready to throw.

Raise. When ready to pass, line your body up so the side opposite your throwing arm faces your target. Cock the ball back directly behind your head, with your upper arm parallel to the ground and your elbow bent. Your weight should be on your back leg. Use your front arm for balance.

Release. Step in the direction of the target with your front foot while you shift your weight completely forward, pushing off your back foot. At the same time, fling the ball forward in a smooth motion close to your head, and let the ball roll off your fingers as you extend your elbow. The ball should be pointed toward the object as you release it.

Follow through. Your throwing arm should continue down to a natural stop, with your shoulder and torso facing the target and your back leg resting in line with, or slightly behind, your front leg.

Kicking

Placekicking occurs during field goals and kickoffs, with the ball held on the ground by another player's finger or with a kicking tee.

Place the ball. The ball should rest 5 to 10 yards in front of your starting position, tilted slightly back with the laces facing forward.

Approach. Stride toward the ball with even steps, making sure the last step before kicking leaves your opposite foot about 18" behind the ball (and a few inches to the side so you can kick straight) (Figure 1).

Figure 1. The approach

Kick. The soccer-style kick is the one preferred by professional players. Bend your knee as you begin the kick, straightening it as you follow through. Kick the ball with the full instep of your foot (Figure 2).

Figure 2. The kick

Follow through. Straighten your leg and bring it up to chest level as you send the ball straight out and up (Figure 3).

Figure 3. The follow-through

In punting, the kicker receives the ball from the center, then kicks the ball as it drops from the kicker's hands.

Receive the pass. The center's pass should be a fast spiral to the waist.

Step and drop. With arms outstretched, hold the ball laces up and pointing forward, between your hands. Take a small step with your kicking foot, then a full step with your opposite foot, and release the ball as your second step hits the ground. Do not spin the ball.

Kick. Bring your kicking leg forward, bent at the knee. Extend the leg and connect with the ball around knee level. Lock your knee and ankle as you make contact, and be sure that you kick the ball with the entire top surface of your foot.

Follow through. Continue swinging your leg forward, and bring it naturally to a stop around head level.

Juggle

Juggling is an ancient art that dates back over 4000 years to the Egyptians. The word comes from the Latin word for "joke," and a juggler is a performer whose tricks fool the eye. Balance and coordination are the essence of juggling.

Palm a Yardstick

Develop hand-eye coordination by balancing a yardstick on your palm. Focus on the top of the stick; your hand will compensate naturally. When you gain confidence, try balancing the yardstick on your nose or elbow.

The Basic Toss with Two Balls

Hold a ball in each hand. Toss the left ball gently upward. When the left ball reaches its peak, toss the right ball. Catch the left ball with the right hand, and the right ball with the left hand. Practice, practice, practice.

The Three-Ball Toss

Toss right. Toss left. Catch left. Toss right. Catch right. Catch left. Repeat. Hold two balls in the right hand and one in the left. Beginning with the right, alternate tosses and catches. Throw the balls to the same spot, and work to develop a smooth delivery and rhythm. Practice with soft beanbags, which don't bounce or roll, or scarves, which float slowly, until your hand-eye coordination reaches the juggling zone.

Get Tickets for TV Talk Shows

For some of the best free live entertainment you can find, get tickets to the taping of one of the many television talk shows. Tickets can usually be obtained by writing a request to the show. Shows are taped during the day (even late-night shows are taped in the late afternoon), and most are filmed in New York or Los Angeles. If you want laughter and big stars, go to a late night show like the *Tonight Show* or the *Late Show*; if you want sensational real-life stories and heated arguments, go for daytime talk shows such as *Oprah* or *Geraldo*. Call the network or station that broadcasts your favorite show to find out precisely how to ask for tickets.

Donahue

Send a postcard specifying you would like to attend, with the date and number of tickets you want, to

NBC Tickets
30 Rockefeller Plaza
New York, NY 10112

You must be at least 16 to attend, and the show does not guarantee you will get the tickets you requested. There is about a three-month wait for tickets, so write far in advance. For more information, call 212-664-3056.

Geraldo

Send a self-addressed stamped envelope requesting the date and number of tickets to

Geraldo Tickets
CBS TV
524 West 57th Street
New York, NY 10019

For more information, call 212-265-8520.

Late Night with Conan O'Brien

Send a postcard specifying the show you would like to attend, the date, and the number of tickets to

NBC Tickets
30 Rockefeller Plaza
New York, NY 10112

You must be 16 or older to attend, and the show does not guarantee you will get the tickets you requested. There is about a one-month wait, and large groups can call to reserve seats in advance. Standby tickets are available on the day of the show; go to the NBC lobby at 30 Rockefeller Plaza at 9 A.M. on the day of the show. One ticket per person will be given as they are available. For more information, call 212-664-3056.

The Late Show with David Letterman

For a pair of tickets to the show, send a postcard with your name and address to

Tickets: The Late Show with David Letterman
Ed Sullivan Theater
1697 Broadway
New York, NY 10019

You must be 16 or older to attend, and tickets are usually given out six to eight months in advance. For standby tickets, go to the box office at the Ed Sullivan Theater at noon on the day of the show; tickets will be given on a first come/first serve basis, and you will not be guaranteed a seat. For more information, call CBS at 212-975-4321.

Live with Regis and Kathie Lee

Send a postcard with your name, address, telephone number, and the number of tickets to

Live Tickets
Ansonia Station
P.O. Box 777
New York, NY 10023

You must be at least 18 to attend, and there is a limit of four tickets per request. There is currently an eight- to ten-month wait for tickets. To get same-day standby seats, go to the offices of ABC Television at 67th Street and Columbus Avenue in New York City at 8 A.M. to get a number; tickets will be given on a first come/first serve basis. For more information, call 212-456-7777.

Oprah

To request tickets and reserve seats for the show, call 312-591-9222. You may request a specific date, and there is a limit of four tickets per caller. You must be 18 or older to attend. *Oprah* is taped in Chicago.

Sally Jessy Raphael

Send a postcard or letter with your name, address, and the number of tickets to

Sally Jessy Raphael Tickets
P.O. Box 1400
Radio City Station
New York, NY 10101
For more information, call 212-582-1722.

The Tonight Show with Jay Leno

Send a self-addressed stamped envelope, indicating the date and number of tickets you are requesting, and send it to

NBC Tickets
3000 W. Alameda Avenue
Burbank, CA 91523

You must be at least 16 years old (14 for some shows) to attend. Make your request at least one month in advance. To pick up tickets in person, go to the ticket office at the Burbank studio (off California Street) between 8 A.M. and 5 P.M. Tickets are given on a first come/first serve basis, and you will not be guaranteed a seat. For more information, call 818-840-2222.

Perform 2 Simple Magic Tricks

Who doesn't love a well-executed magic trick? It entertains and ignites the imagination. If you know a few magic tricks you can perform at any time and with no preparation, you'll mystify your friends and delight children.

Card Trick

In this trick, you will identify a card picked by a member of the audience and replaced in a deck. The selected card will magically appear as the only face-up card in a deck of face-down cards.

1. Hold the deck in your hand face down, with the cards spread so a member of your audience can pick a card. The card should be shown to everyone in the audience except you.

2. Square up the deck.

3. Explain to the audience that the card will be replaced in the deck, at which time you will put the deck behind your back and magically find the selected card.

4. Act out the steps as you talk to the audience, putting the deck behind your back as you speak.

5. With the deck behind your back, quickly and imperceptibly turn the bottom card in the deck face up and turn the deck over. Now the top card should be face down while all the other cards below it are face up.

6. Bring the deck back in front of you. To the audience the deck should look just as when they saw it last—face down.

7. Ask the audience member to replace the card anywhere in the deck. Keep the deck squared tight and be careful that when the card is slid back into the deck the other cards are not revealed to be face up. Once the card has been replaced, square the deck to lose the selected card.

8. Put the deck behind your back, just as you've already explained you'd do. Tell the audience that you will find the card without having to look at it, through your special powers.

9. With the deck behind your back, turn the top card back over. Now all the cards in the deck should be face up, except the audience member's card.

10. Turn the deck over so the cards are face down and it looks the same as always. Bring the deck back in front of you.

11. Turn the deck over again so that the audience can see the cards face up. Go through the deck, looking at each card and discarding them on the table. To add to the suspense, you may want to stop at one or two of the cards and touch them as if you are about to select them.

12. Continue discarding the cards until you reach the face down card. With a look of surprise say something like, "Oh, what's this card doing face down?" Flip it over to reveal the selected card as the audience applauds your magical abilities.

Coin Trick

In this trick you make a coin disappear by rubbing it on your elbow. Use your own coin; don't borrow one from your audience—you won't be able to give it back right away!

1. With the coin in your right hand, bend your left elbow and place your left hand on the back of your neck (Figure 1). Your left elbow should be sticking out toward the audience in front of you.

Figure 1. Rub the coin into your elbow.

2. Rub the coin into your elbow with your right hand. After a few seconds, let the coin drop to the floor. Retrieve the coin with your *left* hand and move it to your right.

3. Repeat Step 1.

4. Again, retrieve the coin with your *left* hand—only this time, just *pretend* to place the coin in the right hand. Be as nonchalant about the "transfer" of the coin from one hand to another as possible. Your audience must believe the coin has moved back to your right hand.

5. Repeat Step 1. This time, keep your right hand's fingers tightly shut as they rub the elbow. Drop the coin, still in your left hand, down your collar (Figure 2). The coin has disappeared!

Figure 1. Drop the coin down your collar to make it disappear.

Dance the Waltz

The waltz was considered a scandalous dance when first introduced in 18th-century Europe, because it allowed partners to hold each other tightly. Today, the waltz is one of our most elegant dances, usually reserved for a ballroom or formal party. The waltz is designed for two people: a leader and a follower. Traditionally, the man is the partner who leads (moves forward and guides the direction of the dance) while the woman follows. Reverse roles if it better suits you and your partner.

Stance

The partners face each other and stand with good posture. The leader puts a right arm around the waist of the partner with the right hand on the partner's lower back. Then, the leader bends the left arm and holds up the left hand, slightly above shoulder height. The partner places a left hand on the leader's shoulder and a right hand in the leader's left hand.

Steps

The waltz is danced in 3/4 time, meaning that there be three beats in the measure, with the accent on the first beat, counted off as: **1**-2-3, **1**-2-3. Waltz steps begin on the first beat, with the first step always on the left foot for the leader and the right foot for the partner (Figure 1). In the box step, the basic waltz move, the dancers return to their starting space after two measures of music, or six steps. Step gracefully on the balls of the feet, pivoting when necessary, and watch out for others on the dance floor. Above all, don't look down and be ready to whirl and twirl. Replay that famous scene from *The King and I* for inspiration—or how about Scarlett and Rhett in *Gone With the Wind*?

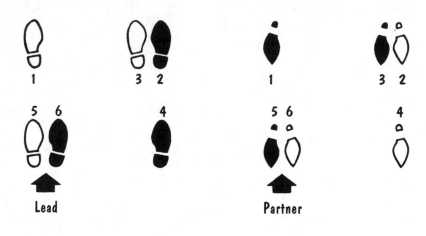

Figure 1. The waltz box step

Keep Score in Bowling

Bowling scores seem complicated but are actually very simple. What confuses many people is that when you bowl strikes and spares, the points will overlap—that is, the pins you knock down in one roll will count as points in more than one frame. To understand this, consider that a perfect game consists of only 12 strikes but 300 points. Read the following to better understand how to add points in frames and complete a score sheet. These are the basic concepts of scoring.

Score Sheet

The score sheet looks like a grid, with a space for the players' names in the left-hand column and a row of 10 boxes at the right. Each box represents one frame, with one or two (the 10th frame has three) smaller boxes inside for recording individual rolls and marks.

Recording Rolls

In each of the two small boxes within the frame box, record the pins dropped in one of the two rolls (if the sheet has only one small box per frame, record the first roll next to the small box and the second inside the box). Record the total score below in the large area of the frame box. For the bowler's next turn, record each roll in the small boxes as before, but in the main area write the total score so far (the total score from the previous frame added to the total score of the current frame) (Figure 1).

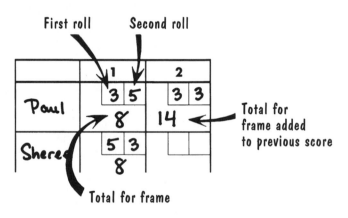

Figure 1. How to record scores

Strikes

If a bowler knocks down all the pins on the first roll, put an X in the first small box to denote a strike. Leave the main area of the frame box blank. The player receives 10 points for the strike plus the points from the next two rolls. Since the player will not bowl again until the next frame, a total for the frame cannot yet be determined. When the player gets to bowl again, record the scores for the rolls in the small boxes of the next frame as usual, then add the frame's score to the 10 points from the strike to complete the total score of the previous (strike) frame. Add the current frame's score again to the total from the strike frame to get the total score for the current frame. If another strike has been thrown in the current frame, put an X in the small box as before, and leave the current frame blank until a third ball is bowled in the next frame (Figure 2).

Frame 1   **Frame 2**

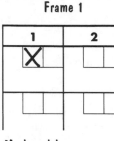 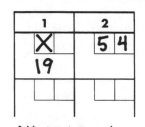 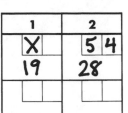

Mark and leave   Add 10 points to the   Then add total for
score blank.   total of the next two   Frame 2 to previous
                        rolls to get Frame 1 score. score as usual.

Figure 2. How to record a strike

Spares

If a bowler knocks down all the pins using both rolls, put a slash, /, in the second small box to denote a spare, and leave the main area of the frame blank. The player receives 10 points for the spare plus the points from the next roll. Again, the total cannot be determined until the bowler's next turn. Follow the same procedure as with a strike, but remember that only the points of one more roll are added to the spare's 10 points (Figure 3).

Frame 1   **Frame 2**

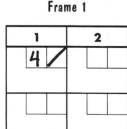  

Score for first roll.   Add first roll to ten   Then add total for
Mark and leave score   (from spare) to get   Frame 2 as usual.
blank.   Frame 1 total.

Figure 3. How to record a spare

Tenth Frame

If a strike is thrown on the final frame, the player takes two extra balls (that's why there are three small boxes on the score sheet). If a spare is thrown, the player takes one extra ball (Figure 4).

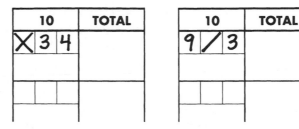

Figure 4. Scoring the tenth frame

Other Notations

✓ *Miss:* If a player does not hit any pins on a roll, mark a dash, –, in the small box corresponding to the roll.
✓ *Split:* If a player has created a split (leaving pins on both sides of the lane that cannot be hit by a single ball), note this by drawing a circle around the score of the roll.
✓ *Foul:* If a player has committed a foul by crossing the foul line, put an F in the small box corresponding to the roll; the player receives no points for the pins knocked down in that roll.

Basic Tennis Swings

Many tennis players, from rank beginners to amateur competitors, mistakenly believe that all they have to do is perfect their strokes and timing to end up winners. Pros give this advice.

Keep Your Eye on the Ball

✓ Keep your feet and body in constant motion; establish a pace of movement.
✓ Shift your weight forward on each stroke so that at impact, your weight is completely on the front foot.
✓ Anticipate what the opponent is going to do next.
✓ Concentrate squarely on the course of the ball after it has left the opponent's racquet and is about to be hit back.

✓ Be consistent, with a solid, steady stroke in play; resist the urge to use bad form to make a great point—you may win it, but you won't improve your game.

✓ Play one point at a time. Don't let go of your competitive urge each time a point is lost or an error made.

10 Tips for a Better Swing

1. After you hit the ball, whether on a serve or on a return, get your racquet back immediately and completely. Be ready for the next swing.

2. Hit the ball steadily down the middle, and deep. Let your opponent be the one to try fancy shots and make costly errors.

3. Perfect the most consistent swing you can. Stifle the urge to try risky sideline shots.

4. Position your feet solidly to hit your most consistent shot a high percentage of the time, and use all the strength your body has to offer.

5. Swing low, and quickly, when returning serves.

6. Have a tennis pro check your racquet to make sure it is properly strung and the right weight for your type of swing.

7. Let your stroke flow through its course without interruption or jerky motions.

8. Concentrate on each stroke. It is better to miss with a correct stroke than to hit the ball with an incorrect stroke.

9. Practice your grip so you can vary it quickly and correctly when switching from forehand strokes to backhand, or the reverse.

10. Time your swing for a three-motion sequence: racquet back, step, hit.

Forehand

As you move the racquet back, simultaneously transfer your weight back as well. Shift forward as your arm straightens to meet the ball (Figure 1).

Figure 1. Forehand

Backhand

See "Throw a Frisbee" for hints about developing a strong backhand. Turn your whole body and use the power of your strong back muscles to add force to your stroke (Figure 2).

Figure 2. Backhand

Service

Work on throwing the ball up consistently to the same spot. Move the racquet forward from behind the head once the ball reaches its highest point (Figure 3).

Figure 3. Service

275

Lob

Fake out your opponent by making the lob shot look like a normal forehand or backhand stroke (Figure 4).

Figure 4. Lob

Ski Basics

There are two types of snow skiing: cross-country and downhill.

Cross-country skiers travel over relatively flat land (as opposed to a slope) and require skis with bindings that allow the heels to lift up off the skis. In this type of skiing, you propel yourself using the forward motion of your arms and legs. Cross-country skiing can be done almost anywhere there is open land and snow. Even a golf course can serve as cross-country ski terrain.

Downhill skiers participate in their sport on mountain slopes with lifts to carry them up to the top of the trail so that they can ski down.

Certain equipment is absolutely necessary for skiing: skis, ski boots, and poles. These three items differ greatly for downhill and cross-country skiing, so be sure to specify which type of skiing you do. Most ski areas have ski stores on their premises where you can either purchase or lease equipment. For beginning skiers, or for young skiers whose feet can grow within a single season, renting may be a better option.

For both downhill and cross-country skiing, it is highly recommended that you wear a ski suit to keep you warm and protect you from the snow. You will want heavy mittens or gloves, a hat, and heavy ski socks to wear over ordinary socks. Goggles or sunglasses are also a big help in protecting your eyes. Even on hazy days, there can be a great deal of glare on snowy slopes. Particularly on the east coast of the United States, where winter temperatures can reach brutal lows, take precautions for avoiding frostbite. Dress warmly and comfortably in layers that will trap air in between them. Should you feel any tingling or numbness in your extremities, get to the lodge and allow yourself to warm up.

The importance of skiing lessons cannot be stressed enough for the beginning skier. Reading a book is in no way a substitute for on-site training. Any reputable mountain of a certain size will provide both group lessons (including those for adults) through a ski school and/or private tutoring. Many also have cross-country trails and offer cross-country lessons.

In cross-country ski lessons, you can expect to learn the correct technique for gliding across snow. Cross-country ski bindings hold the toes in place and allow the heels to lift up (Figure 1). Poles are used for further forward propulsion. Students also learn to navigate small hills and how to create tracks in freshly fallen snow. A half day of lessons should give you enough foundation in basic cross-country techniques for you to free ski with a buddy afterwards.

Figure 1. Cross country bindings allow your heels to lift up off of the skis.

Here is what you can expect to learn about downhill skiing.

1. Lift-riding. You may ascend the mountain on a rope-tow (a moving rope that you grip), a T-bar or J-bar (a metal bar you lean on), a chair lift (a seat), or, for more advanced skiers, a gondola.

2. Snowplowing. This is the basic V-shaped position for beginning skiers. With knees bent, the tips of the skis are kept together while the rear ends point outwards (Figure 2). This will keep your speed down until you learn to cross the mountain in a parallel position and to execute parallel turns.

Figure 2. The snowplow position will help keep your speed under control when you first begin to downhill ski.

3. Stopping. At first, widening the snowplow position will be enough to bring you to a halt, but eventually you will be able to stop by drawing your skis up parallel and sideways.

4. Keeping safe. Simple mountain etiquette will keep you from hurting yourself. Although hot-dogging (wild show-off skiing) is unusual on the beginning slopes (known as the bunny slopes), you will learn to avoid out-of-control skiers and snow machinery as well as how to signal to ski patrol personnel that you require assistance.

After a lesson or two, with caution and careful attention to the international skill-level symbols on the slopes, you may want to venture out on your own. Green circles indicate beginning slopes; blue squares, intermediate; and black diamonds, advanced. A good full-day schedule allows for a lesson in the morning and free skiing in the afternoon.

Like all physical exercise, downhill and cross-country skiing demand a certain level of physical fitness and flexibility. Both types place stress on knees. However, skiing is also a highly individual sport, which allows novices to pace themselves and take breaks whenever necessary.

Shoot Pool

The rules of the many types of pool games and the shots involved in skilled playing are too intricate and numerous to detail in a short space. For the particulars, consult a rule book or manual on the sport. Here, however, are the basics for good pool form and some easy tips on shooting.

Cue. The cue is the stick with which you hit the white cueball. Sticks come in a variety of weights and lengths. Choice is a matter of personal taste, but pick a cue that is comfortable to hold and easy to handle.

Chalk. The leather tip of the cuestick needs chalk to ensure a smooth, clean shot. Chalk the top often, perhaps before every shot. Make sure the chalk completely covers the leather. Also, chalk the area between your thumb and index finger to help the cue glide more easily.

Hand bridge. In order to line up your shot on the table, you need to use your opposite hand (left hand for right-handers) to hold the stick in place. Use your thumb and forefinger to hold the cue, and spread your other three fingers on the table for support. Make sure your hand is steady and the cue glides smoothly between your fingers. For high shots, where another ball or the edge of the pool table impedes your shot, rest the cue on the base of your thumb while raising the other support fingers up (Figures 1a and 1b).

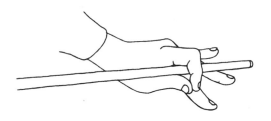

Figure 1a. The standard hand bridge

Figure 1b. Hand bridge for high shots

Grip. How you hold the cue depends on what is comfortable, but whatever method you use, be consistent. Grip the cue firmly, but not too tightly, with your thumb, index, and middle fingers.

Stance. When you shoot, be sure you are at a comfortable distance from the ball. Keep your back leg straight, your front leg slightly bent, and your weight evenly distributed. Bend forward at the hips. Extend your front arm and form the bridge with that hand while your back hand grips the stick. Line up your eyes with the stick to view the direction of your shot, and keep your head low.

Stroke. Use your forearm as a pendulum, swinging evenly from your elbow. Follow through on your stroke, letting the cue come to a stop naturally. Don't pull back after a shot unless you do so on purpose.

Aim. How you aim at a ball is a matter of physics. With the cueball, you must hit the point on a ball that is on the exact opposite side of the direction you want the ball to go (Figure 2). When banking a shot, remember that the angle of incidence equals the angle of reflection (Figure 3).

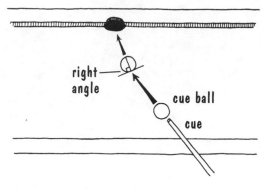

Figure 2. Proper aim

English. The way you spin the cueball, or put english on it, will have a great effect on your pool game. This skill takes time to master; the basic techniques are these:

1. Hit the bottom of the cueball in a downward motion to create a backspin, and the ball will either stop or roll backward when it hits another ball.

2. Hit the top of the cueball upward to make the ball continue rolling forward after it hits another ball

3. Hit the cueball on a side to make it spin in that direction when it hits another ball.

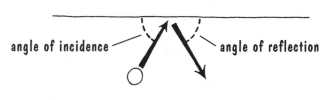

Figure 3. The bank shot

Game for Starters. The most common pool game for two people is called 8-ball. To start, arrange the balls (numbered 1 through 15) on the foot spot as shown, alternating striped with solid all around, and using a triangular rack (Figure 4). The cueball can be placed anywhere behind the head spot. One player hits the cueball into the racked balls to begin the game; this is called the break. The first player to get a ball into a pocket chooses to shoot for either solid colored balls (numbered 1 through 7) or striped balls (9 through 15); the other player must shoot for whichever set is not chosen. The players take turns hitting in their balls until all have been hit into pockets. On each turn, the player may continue shooting as long as he or she is successfully sinking balls (getting them into pockets). Once a player misses, the other player shoots. When a player has sunk all seven balls, he or she must then try to hit in the 8-ball. When shooting the 8-ball, a player must call which pocket the ball will fall into before taking the shot. If the ball falls into the wrong pocket, or if the cueball falls into a pocket (called a scratch), the player loses. The player who successfully sinks the 8-ball wins.

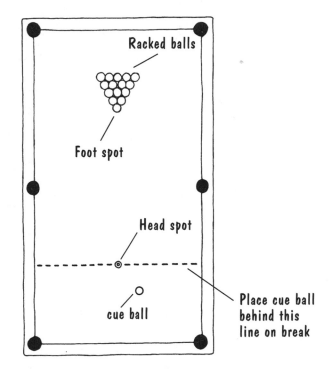

Figure 4. Pool table setup

Square Dance Steps

Square dancing requires you to interact with seven other members in your dancing group, or set. The form the dance takes depends on the caller, who announces in a very colorful rap the steps the dancers are to perform. The key to successful square dancing is knowing the steps well enough to keep up with your partner and the other members of your set, and also keep pace with the caller. Here are the basic square dancing steps. Have fun!

Starting Position

The starting position of a set consists of four couples arranged in a square formation, with each couple standing on a side, facing into the square (man on left, woman on right). The head couple begins the dance and stands at "home base," the side closest to the band and caller. The person closest to you on the other side of your partner (also of the opposite sex) is your "corner."

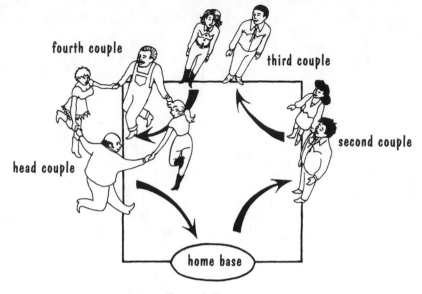

Figure 1. Progress

Honor Your Partner

To honor means to bow to your partner. To do this, turn and face your partner. The man bends slightly at the waist while the woman curtsies (a slight step forward, placing one step in front of the other, then bending slightly at the knees).

Swing Your Partner

This step is done with your partner only. To do it, stay in position and dance by turning clockwise in place with your partner.

Position. Partners face each other, but stand almost next to one another so their right sides are adjacent. They stand with feet slightly apart and weight shifted forward onto the right feet. The man's right arm goes around the woman's waist, while his left hand holds the woman's right hand. Arms extend out in a curve just below shoulder level. The woman's left hand is placed on the man's right shoulder.

Step. Step forward on the ball of the left foot, then raise the right heel and pivot right on the ball of the right foot. Lower the right heel then repeat so you and your partner move in a small circle. Lean away slightly as you turn to keep balance.

Promenade

To promenade is to walk arm in arm with your partner around the circle. Stand side by side with the man on the inside and arms crossed so right hand holds right, and left hand holds left. Walk counterclockwise once around the set.

Progress

To progress means that one couple goes to dance in a small circle with another couple. When a progress is called, the head couple begins to travel counterclockwise around the square, visiting each couple for a dance, then returning to home base. The second couple (to the head couple's right) then does the same thing and returns to its original position. The third and fourth couples follow and progress around the square (Figure 1).

Figure 2. Grand right/Grand left

Eight Hands Around, Back the Other Way

For this step, all the participants join hands to form a circle, then dance around the circle turning clockwise. Back the other way simply directs the dancers to change direction and dance in the circle turning counterclockwise.

Grand Right/Grand Left

For this step, partners face each other, clasp right hands, then walk past each other (men counterclockwise, women clockwise) toward the next person approaching from the adjacent couple. Clasp left hands with this person (of opposite sex) and continue moving around the circle, switching hands for each succeeding person until you return to your starting point (Figure 2).

Allemande Left

This dance is performed with corners. When this step is called, the man turns left to face his corner as she turns right to face him. They then join left hands. Holding hands, they walk counterclockwise in a complete circle and back to the starting point.

Hit a Baseball

Learning to hit a baseball is a challenging skill. It requires a high level of hand-eye coordination and timing, plus quick reflexes. While the only way to truly learn to hit a baseball is to practice long and hard, the following will give you some pointers on how to go about it the right way:

1. Choose the right bat. To get the best opportunity to hit, use a bat you are comfortable with. Consider the length, weight, and feel of a bat. A good test of how well suited a bat is to your body is to hold the end of the bat level with an outstretched arm. If you have trouble keeping the bat level, it is probably too long and heavy.

2. Grip the bat. Hold the bat firmly at the base without squeezing it too tightly. If you are right-handed, hold the bat with your right hand on top (left on top for lefties) and the middle knuckles of both hands in line. Sliding your hands a few inches up the bat (choking up) may give you more control.

3. Set your stance. *At the plate:* Stand close enough to the plate so the thick of the bat can cover all areas of the strike zone (see Step 4) but not so close that your hands enter the strike zone during your swing. Your front foot should line up with the middle of the plate.

   Legs: Legs should be firmly planted in the dirt, parallel to the plate and about 12" apart. Stand slightly pigeon-toed for balance, and distribute your weight more onto your back leg. Bend your knees slightly.

   Arms: When the bat is cocked, both upper arms should be parallel to the ground. Hold the bat at shoulder level, tilted at about a 45-degree angle to your body.

4. Wait for the pitch. Keep your eyes on the pitcher. Watch the ball the whole way as it comes to you. Swing only at pitches in the strike zone. The sides of the zone are determined by the plate, the top by the level of your armpits, and the bottom by the tops of your knees (Figure 1).

5. Swing. Your swing should be a fluid motion followed through completely. If it could be broken down, it would look like this:

   ✓ Step toward the pitcher with your front leg, approximately 6" to 12".
   ✓ Plant your front foot firmly on the ground and shift your weight onto your front leg as you begin your swing (Figure 2).
   ✓ Pivot your back foot as you thrust your hip forward and begin turning your torso toward the pitcher.

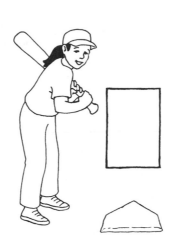

Figure 1. The strike zone

Figure 2. Beginning of the swing

Figure 3. A level swing

Figure 4. Proper follow-through

✓ Swing the bat around, with both power and control, parallel to the ground. Pivot your front foot on the heel and your back foot on the toes. Your eyes should remain on the ball, and your swing should be timed to meet the ball just as it crosses the plate (Figure 3).

✓ Follow through even after contact with the ball has been made. The swing should not stop until the bat is on the other side of your body and your torso is facing the pitcher. Your feet should remain on the ground, pointed at or turned past the pitcher (Figure 4).

Swing a Golf Club

These instructions will take you through the elements of a proper golf swing, one that maximizes swinging strength for straight shooting. Perfecting a golf swing takes a lot of practice. Don't get discouraged if this form doesn't work for you at first. Just keep at it, and soon enough you'll be swinging like a pro.

1. **Choose a club.** Depending on the type of shot you are making, you will need to decide whether to use a wood, an iron, a chipper, or a putter. Woods are used to hit long distances, irons for height and accuracy, chippers (or wedges) for high and short shots such as in sand or high grass. Putters are used only on the green, to roll the ball into the hole. For the purposes of the shot described here, a driving shot, you would want to use a wood.

2. **Line up your shot.** Stand behind the ball so you can see your target line— the direction you want the ball to go in.

3. **Grip the club.** (*Note:* These instructions are designed for right-handers; left-handers should reverse all hand and foot references). Grab the club with your left hand, about ½" from the end of the club. Wrap your fingers around the club firmly so that your left thumb is pointing down in line with the club head. Place your right hand on the club below your left hand, with your right pinky on top of your left index finger and your right ring finger touching your left thumb. The thumb and index finger of your right hand should form a V on the club in line with the club head.

4. **Line up your stance.** Stand with feet together and the ball lined up between them. Adjust your stance by spreading your legs out to a comfortable distance, parallel to the ball, and keeping the ball in line with the space between your feet. The ball should be centered between your feet or slightly closer to your front leg.

5. **Set your stance.** Bend at your knees and hips slightly while keeping your back straight. You should be well balanced, with the weight on your heels, and your arms should hang down comfortably (Figure 1).

6. **Waggle.** Line up your club behind the ball and go through the starting motion of the shot slowly a few times without actually hitting the ball.

7. **Begin your backswing.** When you are ready, pull the club straight back from its position behind the ball. Keeping your left arm as straight as possible, pull back and up as far as your arm will go. At this point the club should be over your head and nearly parallel to the ground, your torso should be twisted back, your left leg should be bent inward with weight on your right leg, and your left arm should be pointing down at the ball from the shoulder (Figure 2). Try practicing your backswing by using your left arm only. The left arm should carry the weight of the club; the right arm is mainly for balance. This takes strength. Resist the temptation to pull the club up and back with the right arm.

8. **Start your downswing.** As you begin your swing, keep your eyes on the ball the whole time. Begin by shifting your weight forward onto your left leg for

Figure 1. The stance from the side

Figure 2. The backswing

Figure 3. The downswing

Fig 4. The follow-through

momentum, reversing the motion you made on the backswing. As you move your legs back into place, start the swing by bringing your arms straight down toward your right knee. The downswing should be closer to the body than the backswing, which was straight back (Figure 3).

9. **Impact with the ball.** As you continue the swing, guide the club with your left arm while you give power with your right. As you hit the ball, your left arm should be straight and extended and your right index finger should be pointing at the ball.

10. **Follow through on the swing.** After impact with the ball, try to bring the club up and over your head as quickly as possible. Extend your right arm around and bring the swing to a finish behind your back, with the club perpendicular to the ground. Your weight should be shifted forward onto the left leg while the right leg ends up bent and turned forward with toes to the ground (Figure 4).

Throw a Frisbee

A Frisbee is a plastic disc toy that can be thrown with control and accuracy for long distances. It is used as the "ball" in some games, such as the soccer-like Ultimate Frisbee, or simply to play catch. While an advanced player may know many techniques for throwing a Frisbee, one need know only the basic toss to have fun with it. Here's how to throw.

The Grip and The Stance

Hold the side of the Frisbee so your thumb is on top, your index finger lines the rim, and the rest of your fingers support the Frisbee from the bottom. The grip should be fairly loose to allow a smooth throw (Figure 1). Stand with your feet about one foot apart, with the Frisbee in your throwing hand and your opposite arm slightly extended for balance. Your body should be loose and in line with your target, with your throwing arm in front.

The Backhand Throw

The entire motion should be smooth and easy.

1. Assume the Frisbee stance: hold the Frisbee out in front of you in line with the target. Bring your throwing arm back toward the opposite side of your body, twisting your torso away from the target. Allow your wrist and forearm to curl, as much as is comfortable, around the Frisbee rim as you draw back.

2. When you have drawn back as far as you can, bring your arm around in the opposite direction, toward the target. As you straighten your torso and begin to swing your arm around, uncurl your forearm and wrist.

3. As your arm comes around to the front, in line with your target, completely straighten your wrist with a quick flick. Release the Frisbee tilted slightly up, and allow it to roll off your index finger, which should end up pointing at the target (Figure 2).

For Greater Distance

✓ Follow through on your throw.
✓ Get a running start.
✓ Throw in the direction the wind is blowing.
✓ Increase the arc of your release (make a large circle when uncurling your arm).

Figure 1. Proper Frisbee grip and stance

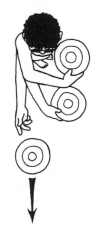

Figure 2. Curling arm and wrist and arm position at release

Play Charades

A vibrant game of charades may look like chaos to the unpracticed eye, but this traditional parlor game does have its own set of rules and customs.

The point of charades is for one player to convey a word or phrase without props and without speaking to the members of its team. The game requires at least four players, but the more there are, the more animated the session will be. The first player thinks of a word or phrase or is supplied one by an opposing team member. He or she must then act it out until another player guesses it correctly. Some players use a timer and set a time limit for each player's turn.

In the modern form of charades, the words and phrases are usually songs, books, TV shows, or movie titles. Many common gestures are used.

To indicate

✓ song, stand with a wide-open mouth as though singing.
✓ book, stand with your hands open in front of you as though reading.
✓ movie, rotate a fist next to your head as though running an old-fashioned movie camera.
✓ TV show, use your pointer fingers to mimic antennas above your head.

Once other players have grasped the category, indicate how many words there are in the title by holding up the appropriate number of fingers.

To show that you will now act out the first word in the title, hold up one finger. If you intend to act out the second word, hold up two fingers, and so on. Then, hold up fingers showing how many syllables there are in the word. Each time someone guesses what you have indicated, quickly nod yes and point at them so they know they're right.

If you wish to break up a long word and act out the syllables individually, hold up a finger again indicating the order of the syllable. For example, to show you will act out the first syllable of a four-syllable word hold up four fingers, and then one. The word *experiment* could be broken up into signs for *ex, pear,* and *mint,* while indicating there is a fourth penultimate syllable.

If the word is a short one such as *the, an, and,* or *if,* hold up an index finger and thumb very close together to indicate something small.

Tugging on your ear and then acting something out indicates to players that the correct word "sounds like" the word you are now acting out, so that you can point to your hand when the actual word is *land.*

It is acceptable and useful to use homonyms to act out a clue conceptually. For example, for Dickens' *A Tale of Two Cities,* you would first hold your hands out palms up to indicate it is a book, then hold up five fingers to show that there are five words in the title. You might then act out *tale* by holding up two fingers to show that it is the second word in the title, then one finger to show it has a single syllable. (The other players should be following along by saying "book," "five words," "second word," and "one syllable" as you go.) Then, use hand motions to mime having a "tail" in order to prompt the correct response.

Whether or not you are being timed, choose a method that conveys clues as quickly and efficiently as possible.

Be creative and inventive. Charades is a great game for loosening inhibitions and experimenting with natural gesture as a form of communication. You may be surprised at how easy it is to convey seemingly complicated words and phrases. The team or player who guesses the most clues correctly wins.

Contact a Celebrity

Depending on who the celebrity is, getting in touch will range from very easy to virtually impossible. Most celebrities, however, are fairly approachable if you have a good reason for contacting them. They are often glad to speak to you for an interview, for business purposes, or simply for a good cause. But just like you, they don't want to be bothered by strangers for no good reason, and they build defenses against unsolicited requests.

Nearly all well-known celebrities, from actors to athletes to rock stars, have agents or managers who handle their business affairs. An industry sourcebook (movies, music, television) may give you a list of agents, managers, and their clients. In addition to agents, celebrities sometimes have public relations people who can help you. Fan clubs sometimes have connections to celebrities as well. If you have no idea where to go to find any of these sources, start with what you do know: a network, a movie studio, a record company, a television station, a sports team. Even if they can't help you, they'll probably be able to start you in the right direction. As a last resort, you may want to try Celebrity Service, a company that will provide you with a celebrity agent's phone and address. This service is mainly for businesses with accounts, and the hefty $50 one-time fee discourages most fans from calling. The number in New York City is 212-757-7979. Here are some other useful phone numbers:

Agencies
William Morris Agency: 212-586-5100, 310-859-4000
Creative Artists Agency: 213-277-4545
International Creative Management: 212-556-5600, 310-550-4000

Networks
ABC: 212-456-7777, 310-557-7777
NBC: 212-664-4444, 818-840-4444
CBS: 212-975-4321, 213-852-2345
Fox: 212-556-2400, 310-277-2211

Record Companies
Warner Brothers: 212-275-4500, 818-846-9090
Sony Music (Columbia, Epic): 212-833-8000, 310-449-2100
Polygram Records: 212-333-8000, 310-996-7200

Sports Leagues
National Basketball Association: 212-826-7000
National Football League: 212-758-1500
Major League Baseball: 212-339-7800
Also consult individual teams

Movie Studios

Warner Brothers Pictures: 212-636-5000, 818-954-6000
Sony Pictures (Columbia, TriStar): 212-751-4400, 818-972-7000
Twentieth Century Fox: 212-556-2400, 310-277-2211
Disney: 212-593-8900, 818-560-1000

Professional Organizations

Academy of Motion Picture Arts and Sciences: 310-247-3000
American Society of Composers, Authors, and Publishers (ASCAP):
212-621-6000, 213-883-1000
Screen Actor's Guild: 212-944-1030, 213-954-1600

Throw a Boomerang

Boomerangs are long, curved sticks, usually made of wood, originally used by the aborigines of Australia. Though some boomerangs were used for hunting and warfare, the most well-known type is simply a toy. This type is interesting because, when thrown correctly, it will circle in the air and return to the thrower. The procedure for throwing a returning boomerang is rather simple, though actually developing the exact touch needed to make the boomerang return may be much harder than it looks. Have patience, and be careful where you throw.

A returning boomerang can be distinguished from other types because it will be uniformly (hyperbolically) curved, have arms twisted in relation to one another (like the propellers of an airplane), and have one surface that is more curved than the other (like the wing of an airplane). To throw the boomerang:

Figure 1. Boomerang grip and throwing motion

1. Grip the tip of the boomerang so it rests flat in the palm of your hand. The boomerang should curve so the top wing points forward (Figure 1).
2. Tilt the boomerang slightly outward, at about 65 to 70 degrees to the horizon.
3. Throw the boomerang straight out with a vigorous overhand motion, releasing it with a snap of the wrist.

The returning boomerang will take either of two possible paths (Figure 2).

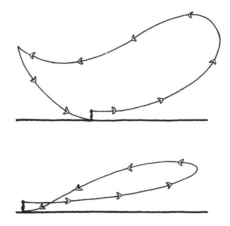

Figure 2. Possible boomerang return paths (ground-level view)

Basic Drawing Techniques

Despite what you may think, anyone can draw. While it is certainly possible to spend years learning and perfecting such drawing techniques as line, texture, composition, and perspective, most of us must first learn to overcome our insecurities and thus demystify the artistic process. The best way to do this is to learn how to access the right hemisphere of the brain. Much evidence indicates that the right brain controls creativity and the altered state of awareness that many artists report experiencing during the creative process. Here are some basic techniques to unlock the door to the artist within:

Draw Upside Down

Drawing a subject upside down forces us to perceive it in a different way. Our preconceived notions of how an eye or a nose looks in a portrait affects how we see and therefore how we draw. Upside down, we are forced to see the features as a series of lines and shapes. Our hands are freed to portray what we see rather than inadvertently impose our own rigid preconceptions.

Find a line drawing in a book—that is, a drawing mostly described by lines, one that does not have too much shading. Pen-and-ink drawings of a person or a

293

landscape are good subjects. Turn the drawing upside down. Using ordinary paper and a sharp pencil, begin to draw. Don't try to figure out whether your subject is a hand or a tree. Don't name the objects; just relax and draw the lines you see. You will feel yourself letting go of your anxiety over your ability to copy the drawing. You will become unaware of the passage of time—absorbed in the task, yet aware. This is right-brain consciousness. When you have finished your drawing, turn both your drawing and the subject right side up. You'll be amazed by the results. Practice this several times with various subjects.

Contour Drawing

This process produces a continuous line drawing in which you do not look at the paper, and during which your hand never breaks the line you draw. Although it sounds difficult, it is quite liberating. Draw your own hand, your foot, a flower, or any convenient subject. Don't worry if the result doesn't look exactly like the subject. The object is to get you to see in a different way, and to practice your hand-eye coordination.

Tape the drawing paper to a flat surface so it doesn't move. If you are drawing your hand, for instance, keep the hand you are drawing, and your head, in the same position throughout the drawing process. You want to portray only one point of view of the subject. Literally turn your head away from the paper to avoid the temptation to look at it. Fix your eyes on any contour, or edge, of the subject. Using a sharp pencil, draw the edge. As your eyes very slowly move along the contours of the subject, move your pencil at the same pace, never lifting it from the paper. Look and draw from edge to adjacent edge, drawing the inner and outer contours, ½" at a time. Imagine that your pencil is actually moving over the subject. This is called blind contour drawing. Practice the following variations on contour drawing:

Slow Contour

Allow yourself an occasional glance at the paper, but only to check hand position or the relationship of one shape to another. Remember that 90 percent of the time you should not be looking at the paper.

Quick Contour Drawing

Draw much faster; look more often at the paper. Try to capture the essence and feeling of the subject's movement rather than focusing on small details. Use a large piece of paper to allow you to make broader strokes.

Cross-Contour Drawing

Work at a slow speed, with an emphasis on the inner spatial relationships of the subject as well as the outer edges. Imagine the subject is made up of crosswise lines that describe the space it occupies, like a topographical map made up of lines. Draw the depth and dimension of the subject using these lines. Drapery and fabric are perfect subjects.

Texture, Shadow, and Light

Add depth and dimension to a slow contour drawing. Allow yourself to experiment with different drawing implements: an ordinary no. 2 pencil, Conté crayons or pastels, pen and ink, or professional drawing pencils of varying hardness. Visit a local art supply store and ask questions. Try different types of paper as well to achieve a variety of textural effects (Figure 1).

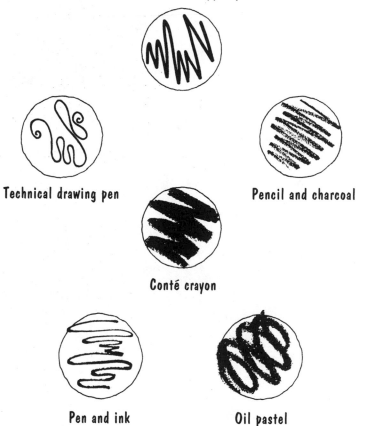

Figure 1. Marks made with various media

Look at the paper as often as you like. Gaze at your subject, focusing attention on the light and dark areas. Find the darkest part of the shadow, and see how it gets lighter and lighter until it disappears. Let your eyes perceive how the subject feels to the touch (Figure 2). Texture and shading can be added to a drawing by hatching, cross-hatching, squiggly lines, tiny lines, rubbing, erasing, using the edge of crayons, and smudging (Figure 3). An eraser may be used as an actual drawing implement to bring out light areas from a dark background. If you feel yourself becoming too judgmental of the work, try drawing the negative as opposed to the positive space—that is, the areas between objects rather than the objects themselves. This process helps break old visual patterns that center on the subject alone and do not consider the entire set of relationships in the field of view.

Figure 2. Examine objects to see how light and shadows fall and vary in intensity.

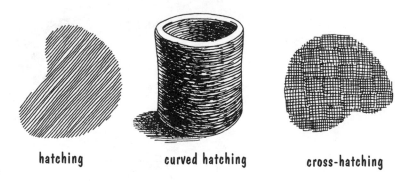

hatching   curved hatching   cross-hatching

Figure 3. Hatchings to create texture and shading

Blending to Emphasize Tone

After making a line drawing, contour or otherwise, use the edges of drawing implements, your finger, or an eraser or tissue to create light, shadows, and textures. Blur the outer edges by smudging the shadows and contrasting colors. Experiment with this technique to create a seamless effect. One shape blends into another; the only boundaries are tones and textures.

Drawing Without Defining Lines

Study a subject for its textures, lights, and shadows. Using the techniques listed for Slow Contour and Quick Contour Drawing, draw only the shadows, dark areas, light areas, and textures, without creating outer lines and edges to be "filled in." Like the Impressionists, experiment with the notion of color as perspective. Use contrasting color or tone to make objects advance or recede on the picture plane.

By practicing these exercises, you will make a quantum leap not only in your artistic confidence but also in your pure enjoyment of drawing and the sophistication of your visual perceptions.

Paint with Acrylics

Acrylics are a clean, quick-drying, easy-to-use and easy-to-clean-up medium that makes learning to paint fun and productive without the mess, smell, and long drying time of traditional oil paints.

Paintbox and Materials

Palette

Start with at least these basic colors:

- ✓ black
- ✓ titantium white
- ✓ cadmium red
- ✓ thalo crimson
- ✓ cadmium orange
- ✓ cadmium yellow
- ✓ yellow ochre
- ✓ permanent green light
- ✓ thalo green
- ✓ ultramarine blue
- ✓ cobalt blue
- ✓ purple
- ✓ burnt sienna
- ✓ burnt umber

Buy larger size tubes of black and white. Supplement your palette with other color variations in tone and intensity that strike your eye.

Brushes

Choose shapes and sizes that feel comfortable to your hand. This basic selection works well for all purpose use:

- ✓ ¾" bright soft flat
- ✓ ⅜" soft flat
- ✓ ³⁄₁₆" bright soft flat
- ✓ fine-point liner
- ✓ ¼" bristle flat

Drawing and Painting Tools

✓ art gum eraser
✓ painting knife
✓ paper towels or sponge
✓ no. 2 pencil or drawing pencil
✓ wax paper or palette paper
✓ water bottles
✓ hair dryer
✓ acrylic gloss medium

Canvas

Use prestretched canvases or canvas board. Or try stretching your own canvases with premade stretchers and unprimed sailcloth. Secure canvas to stretcher with a staple gun and coat it with a thin application of primer. Don't glob the primer onto the canvas; allow the cloth to breathe. Let the primed canvas dry completely before you begin to paint.

Acrylic Techniques

1. Sketch the base drawing on the canvas in pencil.

2. Acrylic dries quickly, so don't agonize over mixing just the right shade on the palette. Unlike oils, acrylics on your palette won't stay wet for hours. Mix your paints with a slightly damp brush and apply them to the canvas as quickly as possible.

3. Use water applied with a clean brush to keep your canvas workable, much as in water color painting. If the surface becomes too wet, use a hair dryer for quick drying.

4. Always clean your brush each time you change colors. Keep two water bottles, one with clear water for working paint on the canvas and one for cleaning purposes.

5. Lay out acrylic washes over the broad areas of the base drawing to form a surface color blueprint. Let the washes dry completely. Then begin to work specific areas of the painting for texture and detail. Use a layering technique to build the painted surface, allowing each layer to dry before another is applied. Add water to soften the edges when necessary. For a hard edge, let the paint dry completely, then paint in the desired edge with a small detail brush.

6. Experiment with palette knives, finger-painting, sponges, and other textured techniques. Van Gogh often squeezed paints directly from the tube onto the canvas.

7. Never leave brushes out in the air; keep them in the water bottle reserved for cleaning purposes. Paint will dry on brushes in a matter of minutes.

8. Clean up with mild soap and water. Store the brushes tip up in a used coffee can.

See also "Paint with Watercolors" and "Basic Drawing Techniques."

Paint with Watercolors

Many people who want to develop their artistic talents start with watercolor in the mistaken belief that it is easier than working with oils or acrylics. They quickly become discouraged when they find that they cannot make the colors go where they want or paint over their mistakes, as they could with other media. For the beginner, there are four basic techniques.

English Method

Light washes of various colors are superimposed over each other, and each is allowed to dry before the next coat is applied. This is the method usually described in how-to books on watercolor.

Sewing-Up Method

A somewhat wet brush is used, and narrow rims of white paper are left between brush strokes to prevent their running together. Hard edges between strokes are filled in after the color dries. Various degrees of blending can be achieved by waiting only until the strokes are partially dry.

Smooth-Paper Method

A more subtle blending and difference in tone uses combinations of hard lines and blending. This method, which builds upon the first two, requires a smooth paper and much practice to achieve the desired control.

Dry-brush Method

So little water in the brush is used that accidental pools and blendings are avoided. More wetness is used for large areas of wash, less wetness where the artist wants to obtain more distinct separations of colors and lines.

The following tips on equipment will help you begin as a watercolor painter:

1. Buy a heavy grade of medium rough paper in block (pad) form, in a size between 9" × 12" and 14" × 18." Don't be timid about asking for advice from the art supply dealer, and describing the extent of your experience, if any.

2. Buy paints in tubes, not pans, and select a simplified range of colors. Blending colors on the paper is the essence of watercolor technique. You will learn more quickly through experimentation.

3. For brushes, start with a sign painter's lettering brush, flat, ¾" wide, which can achieve any width stroke from its maximum to a pencil edge; a medium-sized watercolor brush that is round and comes to a sharp point when wet; and a line brush, which is thin and has all the hairs the same length.

4. Use a watercolor palette, which has small dishes for mixing colors. Test colors as you prepare them by squeezing out tiny amounts and mixing them with water. Then, apply the color to a piece of paper of the same type you intend to use for your painting.

5. Fancy water bottles are available, but you really need nothing more elegant than an empty jar with a wide neck to dip the brushes into, and a small jug of fresh water.

6. Useful accessories include a paint box, a square of cheesecloth, cotton, a small sponge, soft and medium-hard pencils, art gum, and a stool for use when sketching outdoors.

Before painting, use your soft pencil to make light sketches of the composition you have in mind. Number the color areas, starting with the lightest, as numbers 1, 2, and 3, working up in intensity. This determines the order in which you will paint. When your painting is dry, erase the pencil with art gum.

Unlike oils or acrylics, for which you can use an easel, watercolors must be applied on a horizontal surface to avoid dripping and runaway streaks. When you are painting in forest or field, a small folding table is handy.

Practice mixing colors right on your painting, blotting and/or adding wetness with the cheesecloth or cotton as needed. As long as the area is still wet, you can make adjustments in the color. But no other color can be put over the first one until it is dry to the touch.

Don't be afraid to experiment. Try mixing in different ways, using your brushes at varying angles and even applying the paint with something other than a brush. A small sponge produces an interesting effect, as can other materials that you blot or run across the paper to produce lines and streaks. Be patient, and remember that with watercolor, less is often more.

Learn to Swim

Swimming provides one of the best total-body workouts for heart, lungs, toning, and conditioning. A capable swimmer enters a whole world of water sports, such as sailing, water skiing, water polo, rafting, diving, and surfing. Part of learning to swim is understanding how to be safe in the water, and how to protect the safety of others as well. Wear goggles to protect your eyes from harsh chemicals in swimming pools; they should be snug enough to keep water out without being tight and uncomfortable.

Basic Swim Strokes
✓ Freestyle or Australian crawl (Figure 1)
✓ Backstroke (Figure 2)
✓ Breaststroke (Figure 3)
✓ Butterfly stroke (Figure 4)

Figure 1. Freestyle or Austrailian crawl

Figure 2. Backstroke

Figure 3. Breaststroke

Figure 4. Butterfly stroke

Swim Basics for Beginners

1. Never force a reluctant swimmer to put his or her face or head in or under the water. Let the beginner start by splashing water on the face, with a towel at poolside if necessary. Work up to retrieving an object from the bottom of the pool or touching the toes under water.

2. Remember to breathe. Standing in waist-high water and leaning over, practice inhaling in the air above the water and exhaling out by blowing bubbles under the water. Alternate exhaling through the nose and mouth to determine which is most comfortable. Practice breathing by making the arm and head movements of the freestyle stroke while walking across the shallow end of the pool. Breathe in and out on alternate strokes. For the more confident beginner, bob up and down in water that is one or two feet deeper than your height. Inhale above water and blow out all the air on the way down as your feet touch the bottom and as you rise back to the surface. Repeat the action until you establish a comfortable breathing pattern under water. Try not to

301

hold your breath while swimming—it wastes energy and throws off your natural rhythm of movement.

3. Float first. The key to balance in floating is to stretch gently and relax your body. Practice floating on your back and stomach. Then add the arm and leg motions of the freestyle or backstroke.

4. For the freestyle, keep shoulders level to avoid rolling from side to side. When kicking, move legs from the hip with slightly bent knees in a flutter motion; don't bicycle pump. Push off by floating first, then kick, and add the stroke last.

5. For the backstroke, begin by moving both arms together to get the feel of the proper stroke form before using alternating strokes. When kicking, keep your toes together and your heels a few inches apart. As with the freestyle, the backstroke push-off is float, kick, stroke.

For Advanced Swimmers

1. Learn to "ride high" by pushing your body up and out of the water to gain speed. Keep your shoulders high without allowing your legs to sink and produce drag. This reduces resistance, as bodies move faster through air than through water.

2. Streamline your motions to produce the least amount of disturbance in the water. Stretch for good leg and arm extension, and work on remaining steady, without rolling at the shoulders or hips.

3. If you are racing, gain speed by wearing a swim cap and by shaving body hair. The tiny air bubbles that form under water on our body hair contribute to drag and reduce swimming speed.

Water Safety

1. Don't push people into or under the water, especially in a shallow pool. Never hold a person's head under water.

2. Don't run on slippery poolside surfaces. Keep decks clear of clutter and small objects that can be tripped over.

3. Dive only where it is clearly marked safe to do so.

4. When swimming at the oceanside, remember that tides and undertows can be surprisingly powerful and even fatal. Swim only where there is a lifeguard, and follow all local safety regulations.

Points of Sail

Points of sail, determined by a sailboat's orientation on the water to the wind, are running, reaching, and tacking (Figure 1). Sailors choose the most efficient point of sail to reach their destination after carefully considering the water current, wind conditions, and relevant factors such as desired course or proximity to other boats, jetties, markers, rocks, or other obstacles. Luffing occurs when the sail loses the wind and simply flaps, slowing or stopping the sailboat altogether.

Running

In a run, the sailboat is moving dead before the wind with the wind coming over the stern of the boat. The sail is full with the boom to either side.

Reaching

Reaching gives the greatest speed, with the sailboat moving across the wind. A reach is considered broad, beam, or close. A broad reach occurs when the wind is moving over the boat's quarter from the stern. A beam reach occurs when the wind is blowing at a right angle to the course steered. If the wind is forward of broadside but still far enough back for the boat to steer a straight course, the point of sail is a close reach. A close reach is the most efficient point of sail.

Tacking

When a sailboat can no longer keep the sails full and steer a straight course but must trim sails close and make a series of close-hauled zig-zag movements to reach its destination, the boat is tacking, also called beating. Tacking requires much skill and determination and is the slowest point of sail.

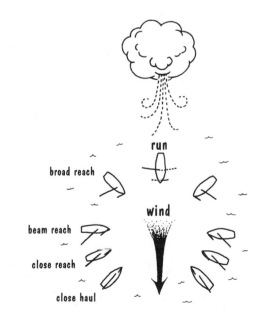

Figure 1. Points of sail

11. Legal

Find a Good Lawyer

The best way to find a good lawyer is to get a recommendation from a trusted friend, relative, or associate. Since you will probably need a lawyer for a specific reason—purchasing a home, writing out a will, or getting a divorce—seek out neighbors or co-workers who have had a similiar experience recently and ask if they were satisfied with their attorney. If so, request a name and phone number; then arrange a meeting.

If the above scenario does not produce any viable prospects, try asking a lawyer who specializes in another field for a recommendation. If you have used a real estate attorney to buy your home and now need an expert in immigration law, call up your real estate lawyer. He or she may be able to refer you.

State bar associations run legal referral services that can also help match up possible clients with qualified attorneys. Call the bar association office in your area, or the American Bar Association in Chicago at 312-988-5000. If you have a low income, you may be eligible for a pro bono (unpaid) lawyer. Contact Legal Aid or Legal Services in your area for assistance. Whatever you do, do not choose a lawyer from the phone book or television advertising. There is no guarantee such lawyers are qualified or that their claims are true.

However you first contact a lawyer, there are several things that can help you determine his or her suitability. First, pay attention to your gut instinct. The attorney-client relationship is intensely personal. Even in a seemingly straightforward business transaction, such as a real estate purchase, you will want to feel comfortable asking questions. Follow your instincts. Your attorney does not need to be your best friend, but the two of you must be able to communicate, and you must understand and endorse your attorney's plan of action.

Ask your attorney how long she or he has been in practice and how much of that practice centers on your area of interest. General attorneys often have little or no experience in personal injury or matrimonial law. You may want to hire a specialist. Also ask about education, how many years the lawyer has been out of law school, and whether or not any continuing education has been pursued in the field. An attorney who has not followed developments or taken a course in employment law since graduating from law school over 20 years ago is probably not up to date on that subject.

It might seem that asking about a lawyer's track record would provide an accurate assessment of performance, but that is not always true. Cases are very individual, and judgments are influenced by a wide variety of factors, including the judge involved, the opposing lawyer, personalities, and simple luck of the draw. Also, it is unrealistic to expect any attorney to have a certain percentage of "wins" and "losses." The legal arena is rarely so clear-cut.

The place to check out whether an attorney is in good standing (the legal equivalent of the Better Business Bureau) is the Office of Attorney Registration. This office is run through your local court system.

When you do decide on an attorney, you will be asked to sign a written agreement. Make sure that you read and understand it. If you do not, don't hesitate to ask questions. Fee arrangements vary widely from attorney to attorney. Generally, if you are being charged an hourly fee, that will include the time the lawyer or his or her staff spends talking with you on the phone and performing other duties. Contingency payment (wherein a lawyer is paid only after the case has been decided) is most common in the personal injury field, but even there it is far from the rule. Should you come across an attorney who does not ask you to sign a written agreement outlining the attorney's duties and fees for anything but the most uncomplicated of legal tasks, run, do not walk, out of that office. What kind of lawyer does not utilize a contract?

One final note: because locating an appropriate lawyer can be intimidating, people sometimes drag their feet about taking legal action. To do so can mean the end of your case. Statutes of limitations differ, but some are surprisingly short, so strike while the iron is hot.

File a Small Claims Court Suit

Before you decide to sue in Small Claims Court, consider the alternatives. First, make sure you have exhausted all efforts to settle the matter without involving a third party, through letters and phone calls. If your grievance is against a business unwilling to settle amicably, you can seek the aid of consumer action agencies, such as the Better Business Bureau, that are set up by private or government sources to protect consumers. These organizations may arrange arbitration, investigate your case, or file a complaint against the company. If you find no out-of-court action sufficient to settle your grievance, turn to the courts.

Determine the viability of your case. Arbitration and negotiations may have already started the process. Still, you must define the case clearly. Ask yourself these questions: Has there been a loss to you? What is that loss? Is the other party at fault?

Was a contract broken? Was negligence involved? Can you prove your charges? Unless you can provide clear answers to these questions, you may not have a case. Also, consider what you will likely win; it may not be worth the trouble.

Visit the court clerk's office. Because each state's court system works differently, it is important to know exactly what the local procedures are for filing a small claims suit. Go to the court where you plan to file the suit, usually in the district where the grievance occurred (not necessarily the district you live in). Ask the clerk's office for a brochure that explains how to go about filing a court suit; read it carefully. While you may ask a clerk procedural questions, the office is not allowed to provide legal advice.

File the suit. Filing a suit generally consists of filling out a form in the clerk's office and paying the required fee, which is usually a small one. Though the form will vary depending on your state, it will usually ask the following information: your name and address (plaintiff), the name and address of the person or party you are suing (defendant), the amount you are suing for (claim), and why you are suing (explanation).

As the *plaintiff*, list your name and all other coplaintiffs; if you are a business, write the name of the business. The *defendant* is the person or entity you wish to sue. If you are suing a corporation, write in the name of the corporation as defendant. If you are suing an unincorporated business, write in the name of the owner. Other special cases: if the case involves an auto accident, you must sue the driver and the owner of the vehicle (if different). If you sue a minor, you must list both the minor and a parent or guardian (laws restrict your ability to sue minors at all). If you sue a government official acting for the government, you must sue the government. Note that you cannot file claims against the Federal Government in Small Claims Court. When filing a suit against a local or state agency, first contact the Small Claims Court clerk for the proper procedure to follow—act quickly or you may lose your right to sue. Claims are usually filed directly with the offending government entity. If your claim is denied, the case moves to Small Claims Court.

Your *claims* for financial (or other) compensation should amount to as much as you can justify, though not more than is allowed by the Small Claims Court (larger amounts may need to go to regular Civil Court). This could include the value of property lost or damaged, the cost of repair to property, the value set out in a contract (plus interest), or medical costs and charges for pain and suffering if you sustained an injury. In some special cases, such as a landlord-tenant dispute, the plaintiff may be entitled to punitive damages above the actual cost of the contract. If a money value cannot be placed on property, you may be able to ask for "equitable relief" for an actual return of the property or some specific non-monetary reward.

Your *explanation* should be brief and to the point. Do not feel you must argue your case in the space allowed; simply point out the legal principle that has been violated.

Serve notice to the defendant. You will be required to inform the person you are suing of the upcoming hearing. There are strictly defined laws that govern how you do this (again, procedures vary from state to state). Generally, you must arrange for the defendant to be presented with an official court summons in person and within a specified period of time. The summons may be served by a law officer or by a professional server, both of whom will charge you a fee (though it can be reimbursed if you win the case). Or, you can have any disinterested adult serve the summons provided he or she fills out a Proof of Service form. Mailing a summons, even if by registered mail, is usually not allowed and is always unadvisable.

Await the defendant's answer. In an official statement filed with the court, the defendant will either challenge the amount of the suit, deny liability, file counter claims against you, or offer to settle out of court. Unless you can settle, expect to receive notice from the court of when to appear for a hearing.

Prepare your case. All that is left now is to build a strong case to support your claims and to show up at court on time. To prepare, collect all pertinent evidence (receipts, letters, pictures) and, if applicable, subpoena witnesses (a subpoena is a mandatory call for a witness to appear in court to testify). You do not need to hire a lawyer to represent you, but you may want to seek legal advice beforehand. The lawyer fees to appear in court would only reduce your award, and the judge will not be influenced one way or the other by the presence of counsel in the courtroom.

Make a Simple Binding Contract

In a world crowded with lawyers looking to stay busy, the practice of drawing up contracts has become overly complicated and unnecessarily exhaustive. Despite what you may have experienced, contracts are meant to be agreements and nothing more. Anyone can make them. In fact, the clearer and simpler a contract is, the better chance it has of being enforceable. If you wish to draw up a basic contract without professional legal help, you'll need to be acquainted with its necessary elements. A word of caution, though: writing a contract without professional help can be dangerous. A good lawyer may be able to pick apart and invalidate a contract written by a novice. Get help if you can afford it and if the contract means a lot to you. Otherwise, be careful and follow these guidelines.

1. Make sure both parties agree to the terms before you write a contract. Agreements should be finalized before they are put in writing to avoid rewrites or amendments afterward.

2. Write as clearly as possible. Leave the "legalese" for the lawyers. Explain the terms of the contract in the kind of language you would like to see in an explanation to you.

3. Avoid excessive wordiness. Be concise without sacrificing clarity. Refer back to past sections and shorten names to avoid repeating the same information, but make sure all names and terms are clear when first used.

4. Be complete, and include all aspects of the agreement. While there is no need to spell out all the possibilities and implications of an agreement, everything that has been specifically discussed and agreed upon should be explained.

5. Identify the parties involved. The names of the principal parties to the agreement, plus any other secondary parties, should be written in complete form. For people, include given names and names commonly used (if different), and addresses. For companies, include the full name of the business and the address, plus the full name of any person acting on behalf of the company.

6. Specify the consideration of both sides. All enforceable contracts need to have a mutual consideration. That is, both parties should get something as a result of the agreement. Be sure this is clear in the contract.

7. Outline the terms of the agreement and the obligations of both parties. Spell out completely what each party agrees to. This may include a service rendered, the sale of a property, or a giving of money. If applicable, specify when, where, and how the terms will be met.

8. Have both parties sign the contract. A contract cannot be official and effective until both parties sign it. If a company is a party to the agreement, be certain the person signing the agreement is authorized to act on its behalf. Have the person or company include a proper social security or employers identification number (EIN).

9. Sign every page and all changes in the agreement. Though it is not required by law, have both parties sign every page of the contract to ensure nothing is added to the agreement after it is signed. For the same reason, sign or initial any changes made to the original wording of the agreement.

10. Have a witness to the signing. An impartial third party should be present to confirm the making of an agreement. In some cases, a notary public must witness a signing and stamp the document to establish its authenticity (though other kinds of seals are rarely necessary).

11. Be sure the contract is properly delivered. A contract not only must be signed by both parties but must be released willingly. In other words, a contract signed but held by a party for some reason cannot go into effect.

12. Specify a means of settling disagreements or breaches in the contract. In case a problem arises, include a provision for settlement so you can avoid the cost and trouble of court. You may want to agree to a binding arbitration and specify the damages involved.

13. Specify which state's laws apply, particularly if the contract is entered into by parties from different states, to avoid confusion and problems in the event of a dispute.

14. Keep a copy of the contract in a safe place. Always hold on to an official, original copy of the signed agreement for the duration of the contract and for some time afterward. Store it in a place you won't forget—in a safe or locked cabinet if you fear it may be stolen.

See also "Read a Contract" and "Read a Lease."

Read a Contract

It is necessary to know how to read a contract agreement completely and to understand the difficult, often misleading technical language lawyers commonly use. Prevent other parties from taking advantage of you by making sure any questionable terms are defined within the contract—and don't be afraid to ask if you don't understand a term. If you can, change the wording of the contract to make it clearer and less technical. Here are the definitions of commonly misunderstood contract terms.

Acceptance. Agreeing to an offer in exchange for an item in question.

Agreement. The contract; an understanding between parties.

Arbitration. An unofficial means of reaching a settlement on a disputed issue; it may or may not be binding.

As is. A disclaimer of liability, usually referring to the condition of a property.

Bill of sale. A receipt.

Boiler plate. Standard provisions used in many contracts.

Bona fide. In good faith.

Bond. A written promise to pay a sum if a party does not perform the duties specified in a contract.

Breach. Violation of part or all of a contract.

By-laws. Rules governing a corporation.

Consideration. Something of value exchanged to justify a contract.

Contingency. A condition in a contract not certain of being fulfilled.

Co-signers. A third party who assumes equal financial responsibility with a party in an agreement.

DBA. Abbreviation for "doing business as," indicating an assumed name or company name used by a party in the contract.

Ipso facto. By the fact itself.

Liability. Legal responsibility for a debt owed.

Lien. A legal right to hold a claim on property as a security for the repayment of a debt.

Mechanical warranty. A guarantee that a property will perform properly for a specified period of time or else be repaired.

Offset. A counterclaim that can be deducted from a claim.

Power of attorney. Authorization for one to act on another's behalf in legal matters.

Premises. Matters already stated (can also refer to a piece of real estate).

Prima facie. At first sight; evidence adequate to establish a fact.

Pro rata. Proportionately.

Progress payments. Payments made in parts as services are rendered.

Proprietary. Dealing with ownership or a proprietor.

Retainer. A fee paid in advance (as with a lawyer's fee).

Settlement. The closing of a matter, when all agreements have been signed and money paid.

Subcontractor. One who contracts to do work fulfilling someone else's work contract.

Survival of terms. Provisions that stay in effect after the agreement expires.

Trust. A holding of property by one party in order to use or administer it for another.

Vested interest. A right to handle a property even though actual ownership is postponed.

Warranty. A guarantee.

See also "Make a Simple Binding Contract" and "Read a Lease."

Read a Lease

A lease is a contract for the renting of property. While it can also apply to equipment, the most common types of leases are for real estate—renting a house, apartment, or business space. Be certain you understand all the language and conditions of a lease and have worked out any problems before you sign it. Get legal assistance, if necessary. Leases vary greatly depending on the type of real estate and the specifics of the site, but here are some basic elements to look for when reading leases.

Rental space. The address, floor, apartment or suite number, and square footage of a rented space.

Landlord and renter. The full legal names and addresses of the landlord and the renter entering into the lease agreement.

Term. The exact dates the lease will start and end, and what happens if the space is not available on time or is overstayed.

Price. The cost per year and/or the monthly rent, or the cost per square foot of the space, plus any extra costs such as insurance, utilities, taxes, and future increases.

Security deposit. The amount of money, usually the equivalent of one month's rent, provided in case the renter fails to pay rent or fails to repair damaged property. This money should be held by the landlord for the duration of the lease and returned, minus the cost for repairs and owed rent, at the end of the lease period.

Renewal. The terms for extending a lease after the initial term has expired, including the renegotiation period and price increase, or necessary notice for vacating.

Maintenance. Which fixtures, equipment, and supplies the landlord will take responsibility for keeping up, and which ones the renter will be expected to maintain.

Obligations of lessor. Other requirements of the landlord (lessor) such as providing a livable/workable space, arranging for garbage pickup, or handling pest control.

Obligations of lessee. Other rules and requirements for the renter (lessee) such as honoring fire codes and keeping down noise levels, or the procedure for lodging complaints and repair requests.

Environmental protection. Guarantees made by the landlord to keep down the noise of other tenants, provide the use of an elevator, provide parking, or (for a business) restrict the renting of other space to competition.

Prior rights. Provisions for the continuance of the lease agreement in the event that ownership of the building changes hands by sale, bankruptcy, or default on the mortgage.

Termination. Under what conditions the landlord has the right to evict tenants, and how long tenants have to remedy a violation of the lease.

Responsibility for damage to property. Who must bear the financial and administrative burden for repairing and replacing damaged property.

Inventory of fixtures and equipment. List of the materials present in the rented space at the start of the lease and the conditions they are in.

Responsibility and rights for remodeling. Outline of what permission is required from the landlord prior to the renter initiating any changes in the rented space, and what kind of remodeling is acceptable.

Cleaning and use of public areas. What rights of access the renter has to public areas of the building (hallways, stairways, elevators, yard), and what provisions will be made for the maintenance of the public space.

Sublet allowances. Whether the renter may sublet the space and, if so, the conditions for such an arrangement.

See also "Make a Simple Binding Contract," "Read a Contract," "Lease Office Equipment," "Buy a New Car," "Buy a Used Car," and "Lease a New Car."

Track Down Missing Persons

Missing persons fall into two categories: children and adults who have recently disappeared, and relatives, friends, or associates you have lost track of over time and wish to contact. For the first, immediately contact the local police to fill out a missing persons report. Turn to a private investigator only as a last resort because of the cost. Contact national missing persons organizations like the Adam Walsh Child Resource Center or the International Sounder Reunion Registry for assistance in conducting your search.

In our mobile society, where people change jobs, addresses, and even names relatively easily, searching for someone can be frustrating. The search can be particularly difficult if the person you are looking for does not necessarily desire to be found—as with birth parents or an adopted child, or a former spouse eluding child support or alimony payments, or a runaway teen. To keep up your motivation over time, set weekly deadlines for yourself, and establish a reasonable deadline for locating the person.

Stay organized. Buy a notebook and keep careful notes of every source checked out. Take notes while you are on the phone. Write down the names of people you speak to, telephone numbers, and any information or leads you gather. Write down all information, whether it seems immediately relevant or not. As various pieces of information come together, the answer may, indeed, turn out to be stored in your notebook.

Draw up a written profile of the person to disseminate in your search. Mark down all physical characteristics you know, such as gender, height, weight, age, hair color, and clothing. Also draw up a list of personal characteristics: name and possible aliases, marital status, military service, date of birth, and any other vital statistics. Small details may be important later on, so be sure to list everything you can think of. A driver's license number can make someone immeasurably easier to locate.

Make a verbal composite of the last known sighting of this person. What was his or her mood? What did he or she speak of at that time? Where was this last sighting? Record all such information in your notebook.

Whenever you request information from a government body, whether it be the Department of Motor Vehicles or the Social Security Administration, be as complete as possible. Your request will need to identify the person you seek by name, succinctly explain why you are seeking him or her, and give your relationship to the person and all other information you know, particularly full name, last known address, date of birth, and, if possible, Social Security number. You may be required to make your request in writing. Do not neglect to include your own name, address, and phone number so that you can be contacted easily. Depending on the size of the city where the person was last seen and how common his or her surname is, you may have success simply by sending letters to the County Records Office and the Police Department. Driver's license regulations vary from state to state, but the Department of Motor Vehicles can often tell you whether or not someone is registered and when their registration expired. Do not overlook the telephone book or directory assistance. Again, the more unusual the person's name, the more likely you are to have success with these initial methods.

Next, contact the person's acquaintances. Be careful to diplomatically state your purpose in attempting to locate someone. Relationships can often be sensitive and complicated. Use your instincts to gauge a source's reaction and helpfulness. Take notes regarding someone's eagerness, hostility, or indifference to your search. You may also want to try running an advertisement in a local newspaper, contacting organizations the person may have belonged to in the community or professionally, and/or making up posters with the person's likeness to hang on telephone poles. (Be sure to indicate that the person is not being sought for any wrongdoing.) Of course, if the person you are seeking has not been seen in the area for ten years or more, this is less likely to help. However, these steps will usually turn up at least one lead for you to follow up on, and you will find that the trail takes on a certain shape from there. One person will lead you to another. Sooner or later, this chain of individuals may match you up with the long-lost subject of your search.

Copyright Your Work

A copyright officially registers your original creations and protects them against unauthorized performance, reproduction, distribution and adaptation by others. Literary, musical, dramatic, and artistic expressions, as well as certain intellectual works, can be copyrighted. Facts, ideas, and methods cannot. In addition, works in the public domain cannot be copyrighted. Public domain refers either to works created before copyright laws existed (such as ancient plays), or works whose copyrights have expired or been forfeited.

All works, whether published or not, are eligible for copyright registration with the Library of Congress. Publishers will frequently take care of copyrighting and register works on behalf of the author in the author's name. Registration is not necessary for a work to be considered copyrighted, though. A work is copyrighted as soon as it is created, and registration merely establishes a formal record of your creation. Still, you may be entitled to infringement damages only if your work has been registered correctly.

Formally copyrighting a work is quick and simple if you know exactly how to go about it. Here's how to register.

Ask for and fill out the proper forms. There are several different forms to choose from when registering a copyright. The proper form depends on the nature of the work to be registered. Pick the appropriate form:

- ✓ Form PA   for performing arts (plays, choreography)
- ✓ Form VA   for visual arts (paintings, sculpture)
- ✓ Form S   for sound recordings
- ✓ Form SE   for serials (a written work that appears in separate parts, such as a continuing magazine piece)

To receive the proper form, call the Copyright Office at 202-707-9100, or write to Copyright Office, Publications Section LM-455, Library of Congress, Washington, DC 20559. If you have further questions about forms or other matters, you can call the Copyright Information Line at 202-707-3000.

When you receive the correct form, fill out all necessary information by typing or printing legibly in black pen. Along with the form, you will need to send in a copy of your work and the fee.

Deposit a copy of your work. For published material, send in two copies of your work after it has been published. For unpublished works, send in only one copy. For works too large to send in, such as a large sculpture, send in identifying material like a photograph of the work and sample pages. The Library of Congress will keep a copy of your work on file as proof of your authorship.

Pay the registration fee. Copyright applications cost $20 to file. Make out a check or money order to the Register of Copyrights. Mail the check along with the proper form and copies of your work to

> Copyright Office
> Library of Congress
> Washington, DC 20559

Allow from one to three months for the copyright office to process your application, although registration becomes effective as soon as it is received. You will be sent a formal certificate of registration for your records.

Copyrights for new works created after 1978, remain in effect for the life of the author plus 50 years and do not need to be renewed. Works published before 1978 have a copyright that lasts 75 years. If the work was published before 1964, the copyright needs to be renewed by the author or the author's estate when the first copyright term (28 years) expires; after 1964, renewal is automatic.

Special Copyrights

✓ **Works for hire.** A piece of writing is deemed work for hire if the entity commissioning it owns all title and copyright to the text; for example, when a publishing company or journal buys text or illustrations directly from a writer or artist. Work-for-hire copyrights remain in effect for 75 years after publication or 100 years from creation, whichever is shorter.

✓ **Journal articles.** Usually, the owner of the journal publication will control the copyright. The author is granted the right to reprint the article without permission, as long as a proper credit line also appears.

✓ **Magazine articles.** Usually, the magazine will copyright the entire contents of an issue but the author will retain copyright to his or her specific work.

✓ **Revised editions.** Any new materials added to a work must be copyrighted. Compilations of public domain text, such as anthologies of 17th-century poetry, are copyrightable with respect to their organization and contents, though the source text itself cannot be registered and remains in the public domain.

✓ **Electronic formats.** If you are authoring a text that may go on-line, protect your rights to copyright. As new electronic database and CD-ROM outlets for printed materials expand, authors must be vigilant in safeguarding their proprietary rights to reproduced texts.

Trademark a Name

A trademark is an effective legal means of establishing your right to use a name for commercial purposes and to protect yourself from others using the name for financial gain. Company names like Coca-Cola and McDonalds are trademarked, as are product names like Coke and Big Mac. Since the establishment of trademark legislation in 1905, over one million trademarks have been granted, though only three out of four applicants are accepted as legitimate. To be registered, a trademark must be either a name, a symbol, or a device used to identify goods and must qualify for registration. While a mark need not be registered to be used, registration is beneficial because it establishes the date you first used the mark and gives you a basis upon which to sue for trademark infringement.

Determine Whether a Trademark Is Possible

Make sure your name, symbol, or device qualifies to be trademarked. There are eight basic instances in which a trademark would be denied:

✓ It is not a name but rather a slogan or long written material.
✓ It too closely resembles another registered trademark.
✓ It contains a national, state, or municipal flag or coat of arms.
✓ It is considered immoral, disparaging of other people or institutions, or suggests a connection to other people or institutions.
✓ It includes the name, signature, or likeness of a living person without the person's consent.
✓ It is misrepresentational.
✓ It is merely a surname.
✓ It is merely descriptive or generic.

In the last two cases, the name may instead go on the Supplemental Register.

Conduct a Trademark Search

Check to make sure the name, symbol, or device you wish to trademark has not already been trademarked. Hire a law firm to do a professional trademark search or perform the search yourself. You will need to go to the Trademark Office in Arlington, Virginia, or to a Patent and Trademark Depository Library located in many major cities.

Apply

If you have determined that a trademark does not already exist to prohibit your name, symbol, or device from being trademarked, begin the application process. The elements of the application are these:

✓ **Form.** Call the Commissioner of Patents and Trademarks at 703-557-5249 for the appropriate forms.

✓ **Drawing.** Drawings are necessary only for symbols and devices, not unde-signed names. Drawings should be rendered in black ink on letter-sized bond paper. Any specific colorings should be represented by linings or shadings, with a color key on the same page.

✓ **Specimens.** Five instances where the mark is used, such as on a package label or in advertising, should be included with the application. Duplicates are acceptable if the mark is attached to a three-dimensional object.

✓ **Fee.** The current fee for a trademark registration is $200. Write out a check or money order to the Commissioner of Patents and Trademarks.

Send In the Application Materials

Mail the application, fee, drawings, and specimens to

Patent and Trademark Office
Commissioner of Patents and Trademarks
Washington, DC 20231

The process may take over a year to complete. If accepted, the trademark registra-tion will last indefinitely if it remains in use, or ten years with a ten-year renewal if not. Your rights to use the trademark exclusively are established only through use and not solely through registration, though you may also apply for an intent-to-use registration.

Get a Patent

Up to 100,000 patents are issued every year for new inventions or improved devices. A patent is essentially a deed of property that protects inventors from having their ideas stolen or used without permission, and most last for 17 years if maintained. But while patents exclude others from laying claim to an invention, they do not necessarily give an inventor the right to make, use, or sell the invention.

Only the inventor can apply for a patent, which can take anywhere from one to three years to obtain (although there are ways to expedite the process if you qual-ify), and can cost as much as $2000 or more from start to finish. To be granted a patent, an invention must satisfy four basic requirements.

1. It must be either a process, a machine, a manufactured product, a composition of matter, or a new form or use of any of these.

2. It must have utility.

3. It must be in some way different from anything before it.

4. It must not be something obvious to others working in the field.

If an invention qualifies, here's how to apply for a patent:

Patent Search

To save yourself the time and money of applying only to find out that someone has already patented your invention—or has found a better way to accomplish the same result—it is advisable to conduct a patent search. A patent search can also give you tips on how to present your invention and possibly tell you if your invention can be improved by other methods. Also, a presearched application will get priority in the Patent and Trademark Office (PTO). There are four ways to go about doing a patent search: hire a lawyer to do it, get a professional patent search agent or firm to do it, get an amateur researcher to do it, or do it yourself. Lawyers will likely just go out and subcontract a search agent or firm and therefore charge more, but they may know the best agents to get the job done. Search firms alone will charge either a flat fee or about $50 per hour, while amateurs cost less but are less reliable. (Beware: You may find companies that offer to help you with the development and promotion of your patent for a large fee. These companies are often scams. If you wish to hire someone qualified to help you through the patent process, a good patent attorney is your best bet.) Doing the search yourself will require a lot of research time, and your lack of experience could make the search difficult and incomplete. If you do decide to do it yourself, though, you have more than one option. At no charge, you could go to the Patent Public Search Room in Arlington, Virginia or to a Patent Depository Library located in most states. For a charge, you could use a computer patent search service.

Disclosure Document Program

If you have invented something but do not want to go through the patent process right away, you can file the invention with the Disclosure Document Program at the U.S. Patent Office. This merely registers the invention, inventor, and date in case you need to prove it in the future. The disclosure document lasts two years and costs $10, much less than the patent application fee. Remember, however, that a disclosure document cannot substitute for a patent application.

Application

When you decide to begin the application process, it will be important to get all the necessary forms and specifications. Call or write the Commissioner of Patents and Trademarks at the Patent and Trademark Office, Washington, D.C. 20231. You will need to obtain a government publication entitled *General Information Concerning Patents* (Govt. Printing Office stock no. 003-004-006-617). This will give you all the information you need to complete the application, including sample applications to guide you and the necessary forms you'll need to fill out. In general, the application will require these six parts:

Oath or declaration. This document states that you are the original inventor. The declaration is an official form, and an oath is a personal statement that must be notarized. Either is adequate.

Description of invention. This includes the title (keep it short and exact), summary, and detailed explanation of what the invention is and does, and your claims about what's new about it. It should also include any background or related information and address the significance and advantages of the invention. This is the heart of the application; it should be as long as necessary to describe your invention adequately. Be clear, thorough, and concise.

Drawings, if applicable. The PTO sets up definite specifications for drawings. They should be in black ink and on 8 ½" × 14" (or 13") thick erasable bond paper or board with a 2" top margin. Above all, the drawings should be clear, or they won't pass the PTO's standards; provide views from different sides if necessary, and explain all parts and symbols. Hire a draftsman if you need to, but if you do, make sure you get a guarantee from the draftsman that the drawing will be acceptable to the PTO in case you need to have the invention redrawn or recover the draftsman's fee.

Fee. There are many fees, and the amounts vary; contact the PTO for exact fees. Fees include an initial application fee, an issue fee, and three maintenance fees, the total of which can be reduced if you are an independent inventor, a nonprofit organization, or a small business.

Self-addressed receipt card. The PTO will mail this back to you when your application has entered the processing stage. Expect it in about a month.

Transmittal letter. Include a cover letter with your name, address, title of invention, and the number of pages and drawings in the application, as a record of what your package contains.

First Office Action

Any time from six months to two years after submission, the PTO will notify you of any problems in your application, objections to your case, or a rejection on specified grounds.

Response

You'll be given a period (probably three months) to make amendments to your application or point out errors in the PTO's review. Send it back for reassessment.

Final Office Action

The PTO will reassess your application and either accept or reject your patent request. This is supposedly the end of the line if your request is rejected, though it's likely you will be able to appeal a rejection to the examiner of your application. If your invention has been approved for a patent, you will be sent a note of allowance.

Note of Allowance

This tells you that you've been granted a patent and that you should send in your issue fee.

Official Patent Deed

When the issue fee is paid, the PTO will send your official deed, putting your patent formally into effect. Remember to pay maintenance fees promptly to keep your patent active. Check with the PTO for the exact schedule of payment; maintenance fees are due about every five years.

Get Your Birth Certificate

It's not as difficult as you might think to obtain a copy of your birth certificate, even if the hospital where you were born no longer exists. The state or county in which you were born has an agency that will provide you a copy.

Birth records are usually archived in state or county agencies often named something like the Bureau or Department of Vital Statistics or Vital Records. This department is sometimes a subdivision of the state's Department of Public Health. You can obtain the telephone number of the state government agency by looking it up in the government section of the telephone white pages directory or by dialing the area code for the state capital, plus 555-1212 for directory assistance. (If you do not know the area code of the state capital, local information will be able to help you.)

Call the appropriate state or county agency and ask for the request form you will need to fill out, as well as the amount of the fee you must pay to obtain a copy of your birth certificate. In 1988, the time of publication of *Vital Records Handbook*, a directory of state agencies from which birth, death, and marriage certificates may be obtained, fees ranged anywhere from about $5 to $11. When you receive the request form, fill it out completely and enclose the appropriate fee. Unless your information is erroneous or is not complete enough to facilitate a proper search for your records, you should have no problem obtaining a copy of your birth certificate. Make sure you ask the state agency how long it takes to receive your copy. If you are planning a trip abroad and need your birth certificate to obtain a passport, time may be an important factor.

If you urgently need a copy of your birth certificate, some states will allow you to make your request by telephone and charge the fee to a credit card. There is generally an additional fee for this service. You can also save time by visiting the reference section of your local public library to consult the *Vital Records Handbook*. It has state-by-state listings of appropriate agencies and fees, as well as sample request forms that may be photocopied and used.

Typically, the copy of the birth certificate you receive from your state agency will be embossed as evidence of its legitimacy. Photocopies of the certificate that do not carry the embossed seal of the state bureau will not be considered as valid proof of birth or identity.

What To Do When Someone Dies

When someone close to you passes away you may feel too overcome with grief to think of anything but your loss. While business may be the last thing on your mind, there are several important matters to take care of if you are left in charge of funeral arrangements or the deceased's personal affairs. When tending to these matters, keep in mind the wishes of the deceased. He or she may have specified a type of funeral and burial, a donation of organs, or some other final request. Whatever they may be, it is important to grant and honor these final wishes. Start first by taking time to collect yourself as best you can. Once you feel ready, these are the steps to take.

1. If your loved one has died at home, your doctor or hospice nurse should be informed immediately to confirm that death has occurred and to establish cause and time of death. If your loved one dies in a hospital or nursing home, you have most likely been informed by their medical staff and you will not need to contact other medical authorities.

2. Call family members. Begin with the deceased's closest relatives and friends. From there, word will spread on its own.

3. Notify the funeral home. Funeral arrangements have sometimes already been arranged, other times not. Either way, you must call as soon as possible so the funeral director can begin making preparations. The funeral director will guide you through setting a date for the burial and memorial service, choosing a casket and tombstone (if they have not already been chosen) or arranging for a cremation, setting up transportation to the house of worship and the cemetery, and composing a proper obituary notice.

4. Inform the clergy or appropiate spiritual counselor. The deceased's spiritual counselor, minister, priest, or rabbi, or whoever is to conduct the ceremony, should be informed of the death as soon as possible so he or she can make arrangements to perform religious rites, conduct services and prepare a eulogy. For those who did not practice a religion in life, consult the deceased's will for information on any desired burial services.

5. Provide information for the obituary. The funeral director will take care of contacting the newspaper, but you will need to provide information about the deceased to go into the obituary.

6. Get a death certificate. The funeral director will create the death certificate, and you will need to get notarized copies of it. The death certificate is a necessary legal document when you are handling the deceased's business affairs.

7. Notify business contacts. Call the deceased's boss or associates, landlord or mortgage holder, and banks and credit card companies. Also call Social Security to inform them of the death and to get a death benefit check for the deceased's heirs.

8. Notify the lawyer, who will need to begin executing the deceased's will.

9. Make arrangements for a wake or shiva house. You may need to arrange for food and drink if mourners will be gathering at a house. Shiva houses require special preparations, so ask your rabbi for details if necessary.

Most importantly, allow yourself the time and space to feel and acknowledge your grief. Let family and friends help you with the arrangements. Don't overlook your responsibility to maintain your own health and well-being during this confusing, stressful period of loss.

Make Your Own Will

If you feel that having your will made is bad luck or indicates a morbid preoccupation with death, consider this: although you may not like to think about your own mortality, the fact is that having your will made, which need not be costly or complicated, allows you, not the state, to decide who gets your property after you die. If you die without a will, you have given up the right to choose.

It is possible to have an attorney prepare your will for no more than about $100 to $300. If you prefer, you can draft the will yourself. Although you may feel that such an important legal document mandates hiring an attorney, there are do-it-yourself books and computer software on the market that contain samples of proper format and guidelines to follow. Some states offer a preprinted legal form called a statutory will, but they are very limited in terms of the number and type of provisions allowable and are therefore not the best choice for most people. If you'd prefer to make your own will, make sure the book or software you obtain is clear and easy to understand and that it has been written by an attorney. Although a do-it-yourself book can help you draft a fairly complex will, it might not be able to address all your concerns. In this case, hiring an attorney is certainly advisable.

Hire a lawyer if you have reason to believe someone will contest your will. A trained legal professional is better equipped than a lay person to guard against potential loopholes. Also, if you are extremely ill and your illness either prevents you from drafting your will or may put its validity in question, seek out the services of a lawyer.

Whether you do it yourself or hire an attorney, the first thing you should do is make an inventory list of your estate. This list should include not only your personal possessions, such as furniture, jewelry, artwork, and personal papers such as letters and diaries, but also financial assets such as bank accounts, IRAs, CDs, stocks, money market accounts, life and health insurance policies, safe deposit boxes, and real estate holdings. Include on your list the names, addresses, and account numbers of the financial institutions, and copies of deeds. Your inventory list should also include a list of your debts. In short, gather together all documentation of your assets as well as your liabilities. This will make your job, or your attorney's, shorter, easier, and less costly in the long run. Your assets will also be easier to locate after you die. Most importantly, setting down everything on paper will allow you to clearly see what you own and what you wish to pass on to your loved ones. It will make your task seem less overwhelming.

For your will to be legal, it must be typewritten or computer printed. Many states do not recognize handwritten, or holographic wills. If your state does allow holographic wills, it must be written entirely in your own handwriting, including the date and signature. A word of caution is in order here: even in the states where handwritten wills are recognized, they are often legally challenged.

A legal will must also have at least one essential provision, usually that you are leaving property to someone, who is called a legatee. Although not legally essential, it is certainly a good idea to designate a successor legatee for each of your legatees. The successor legatee is the person who will inherit that particular portion of your estate if the legatee should predecease you.

You must also appoint an executor, who is the person or bank that will carry out the terms of your will. Choose this person carefully, considering whether or not he or she has the time, inclination, and level of competency to do the job properly. The executor of your will may also be one of your legatees. Again, although not essential, it is advisable to designate a successor executor, in case your first choice dies before he or she can complete the job.

For your will to be legal, you must be a legal adult, according to your state's age requirements, and you must also be "of sound mind." You must sign and date the will in the presence of two to three witnesses, depending upon your state's requirements. To be on the safe side, it's a good idea to have one more witness than the minimum requirement. Legally acceptable witnesses must be legal adults, also of sound mind. They must watch you and the other witnesses sign the will, and know that the document they are witnessing is a will. They do not need, however, to be told what the will actually says. Note that witnesses cannot also be legatees of your will. If an attorney prepares your will, witnesses are generally provided by the attorney.

Your witnesses should sign the will, then print their names and addresses beneath their signatures. Although the will itself does not have to be notarized, some states also require an affidavit of the witnesses, which is basically a notarized document signed by the witnesses stating what they witnessed. Even if your state does not require an affidavit of the witnesses, you might consider having one anyway. Such a document will avoid the necessity of having to find witnesses to prove their validity, as this may occur years after the will is signed and when memories may have faded.

Once you decide who your legatees are and what each of them is to receive, and have clearly designated your wishes in your will, it is also a good idea to include what is known as a residuary clause. Such a clause will leave everything else not otherwise mentioned in the will to a particular person, known as the residuary legatee. Because it's possible that the value of your estate could substantially increase from the time your will is written to the time of your death, the residuary legatee is usually the person you wish to receive the largest portion of your estate.

You may also wish to include instructions in your will about any preferences you have regarding burial, cremation, and funeral arrangements.

These basic guidelines should give you an idea of what is entailed in having your will made and should put you on the right track to completing this most essential task.

Living Wills and Durable Powers of Attorney

Living wills and durable powers of attorney for health care are the best legal means U.S. citizens have to safeguard their health care treatment choices. As medical technology makes end-of-life care more complicated, living wills allow people to specify their preferences and desires in care and treatment if they should experience a medical emergency or situation that does not allow them to speak for themselves. These directives must be followed by health care providers. A durable power of attorney for health care is a document you can use to appoint a specific person as your legal health care spokesperson to further ensure that your wishes are carried out.

Most states have standard living will forms you can fill out on your own; a lawyer is not necessary. Contact your state department of health. Most local attorneys, however, can give you insight on state laws and practices regarding living wills. After completing your living will, have it notarized and witnessed. Give photocopies to your doctor(s) and to family members or friends who may be involved in decisions regarding your care. Keep the signed originals in a safe deposit box; initial and date the originals periodically to update the document and show that the living will is still current.

How to Complete a Living Will

Cardiopulmonary resuscitation (CPR), mechanical ventilation, dialysis, surgical techniques, antibiotic drugs, and artificially supplied nutrition and hydration through tube feeding are all ways that medical technology can use to sustain life and aid in the cure of serious diseases. These techniques can also, often cruelly, prolong the dying process. Living wills allow individuals to state specific wishes about end-of-life medical treatment: which treatments to accept or refuse and under what circumstances to do so. If you are not sure exactly how to word your directive, consult your family doctor and ask questions about treatments and procedures. If you have a serious or debilitating illness, it may be wise to question your doctor or representatives of any health care facility such as a hospital, hospice, or nursing home for their policies regarding end-of-life treatment; don't assume that they match your own.

Having a living will and appointing a legal durable power of attorney for health care ensures that your medical care will conform to your own wishes and not those of an institution or third party, needlessly prolonging a terminal illness merely because the technology exists to do so.

12. The Mind

Psych Up

We all face moments in our lives when we must mentally psych ourselves up to accomplish a particular task. Whether that task is something you dread or something you really want to achieve, use one or a combination of the following tips to psych yourself up.

✓ Make a list of your strengths, good qualities, and things that you like about yourself. How do they apply to the situation or problem at hand?

✓ Set clear and realistic goals. If the goal is a large or long-term one, like painting the inside of your house, approach it through a series of smaller goals, like painting the living room first and the bedroom second.

✓ Compose and follow checklists and schedules to keep you on track and give you a sense of accomplishment.

✓ Reward yourself for completing a difficult task. Rewards, no matter how big or small, increase your motivation to accomplish your goals.

✓ Before you tackle a task, imagine yourself doing it. Sit in a quiet place, close your eyes, and practice deep breathing. Imagine yourself performing your task, noting possible snags and hitches and how to avoid or solve them. Accomplish your goal in your mind, and note how good it feels.

✓ Ask others to help you reach your goal—don't be afraid to ask for help.

✓ Prepare to meet your challenge by dressing comfortably, wearing a piece of "good luck" clothing, or carrying a good luck charm.

✓ Be aware of procrastination, which will no doubt try to stop you from achieving a difficult task. Be aware of the things that sidetrack you, and avoid them.

✓ Listen to a favorite piece of music, or read an inspirational poem or piece of literature.

✓ Treat yourself. Do something special to psych yourself up for the task at hand and to reward yourself once you've accomplished it.

Meditate

Transcendental meditation can be an effective way of relaxing, relieving stress, and staying focused throughout the day. To gain the most benefit, meditate twice a day, in the morning and early evening, for 20 minutes each time. It is not important exactly when you meditate, but setting a time beforehand may help you stick to it. The actual method of meditation is different for everyone, so it cannot be taught precisely. What's most important is finding what works best for you. Here is a general framework for beginning a meditation practice.

1. Find a good setting. While it's best to find a quiet, secluded area, it is not essential if you are able to block out noise. You should be removed, though, from ringing phones and any factors that will break your concentration. Some people find that meditating outdoors in a natural setting adds to the experience.

2. Find the position that's best for you. Many meditators sit cross-legged on the floor or on a pillow, but you can sit in a chair if that's more comfortable. Don't lie down, though, and don't try to meditate in bed—you may fall asleep. Keep your back straight but relaxed, and fold your hands in your lap. Relax all your muscles and close your eyes. Loose clothing will make you more comfortable. Depending on the temperature, you may want to wrap a blanket loosely around yourself.

3. Breathe in deeply through your nose, extending your diaphragm. Don't force the air; let it flow in and out naturally. Breathe only to a comfortable level.

4. Concentrate on your breathing as you exhale slowly and completely. Focus on the air as it leaves and enters just below your nostrils. Return to this focus whenever you're aware of being distracted.

5. Repeat Steps 3 and 4, breathing in and out. Feel the movement of the breath through your body as it relaxes. You may count the number of times you exhale if it helps you to focus on your breathing, but don't worry too much about the numbers. If your thoughts wander let them go; observe them but don't become judgmental. Return to thinking about your breathing. Also, be aware of how you are feeling. If a particular muscle or joint feels uncomfortable, breathe into that spot. Meditation is not a process that leads to relaxation; meditation is relaxation. Accept the way your body feels at this moment.

6. When you feel ready to end your meditation, gradually open your eyes. Stay in position for a moment while you notice how your body feels and what emotions come to you. When you are finished, go back to your day in a refreshed and healthy frame of mind.

Remember Names

Say the Name When Introduced

Repeating a name shows you are interested in the person and also embeds the name in your memory. If you do not understand how to say a name, ask the person to repeat it or to spell it out.

Associate the Name

Focus on the name or on the person. Associate the name with a word it rhymes with or sounds like. Associate a person with a name by mentally tying a characteristic or feature of the person to his or her name. Form a mental picture of the association and think it through. You may also be able to associate the person with someone else you know.

Use the Name

Using a person's name from time to time in conversation is polite and will make the person feel good. It also reinforces the name in your mind. As the saying goes, "use it or lose it."

Make Decisions on Complicated Matters

Decision making—from buying a house or car to choosing an entree at a restaurant to making a marriage proposal—can seem daunting. In reality, it is merely a matter of lining up alternatives and determining which factors are most important and in what order. Your first step: make a relaxed evaluation of the major decisions you face today and which will affect you, and your loved ones, tomorrow. Take the following steps in order, at the start of each week or month:

1. List all the important decisions you know you will have to make during a particular time period.
2. Sort them chronologically, from earliest to latest.
3. Sort them in order of significance, from most important to least.
4. Make alternative lists of other decisions that might have to be made and should be kept in mind.
5. After each entry, list sources of data or opinions that might help you in reaching your decisions, including people, documents, reports, and other pertinent facts. When the solution to a problem can be arrived at with outside assistance, take advantage of the help available. Make a list of questions you are unable to answer yourself, and how you might best obtain solutions.
6. List the people who will be affected by your decision. Consider whether your goals are compatible with those of others, and if this is important to you. Make a list of friends, relatives, and co-workers who may try to influence your decisions for good or bad, and why this is so.

As you face each decision, take the time to weigh carefully each factor and essential. Choose an uninterrupted period to concentrate in a relaxed manner. Allow sufficient time. When in doubt, don't rush a decision; hasty decisions are usually flawed. As you consider all the components that bear on the matter at hand, jot them down on paper. List your alternatives and the consequences:

✓ What will happen if course A is chosen?
✓ What will happen if you take course B?
✓ Is it possible to combine your electives?
✓ What are the alternatives?
✓ Will others be affected by this decision? Should they be consulted?
✓ What if you postpone the decision until future events occur that may have a bearing upon it?
✓ What if you do nothing?

Take whatever time you need or is available to you—but don't wait for the problem to solve itself. Procrastination not only prolongs the process but often allows a small problem to grow. Once you've reached a decision, follow through.

Everyone makes choices—good, bad, or indifferent. Don't panic if you make a poor decision. Take the optimistic position that the next one will be better.

Relieve Stress

When you experience debilitating stress, it is crucial to confront its sources immediately. Ignoring the signs of stress can only lead to deepening mental and physical ailments that could become quite serious. Try to identify both the factors causing the stress and the physical and emotional effects of that stress on your body and mind. Below are some techniques for stress management. No one treatment works for everyone, so find the methods that suit you best.

Therapy

Seek out help from a psychologist or psychiatrist to begin psychotherapy. This can be a costly but effective way to manage stress. Gear your therapy toward learning to understand the way you react to stress and the factors underlying it. Explore new coping techniques to combat these factors. Be prepared, though, to spend a long time in therapy if you want to make significant long-term changes in your ability to manage stress, particularly if the stress is severe. If you are opposed to spending a lengthy period in therapy, arrange for a set number of sessions that will take you through the stressful event and help you to understand it and move on.

Support Groups

Join together with other people who have similar problems. This is a less costly and potentially very effective means of coping with stress. It often helps just to know there are other people who understand and relate to your problems. Contact a hospital or community center for more information on local support groups, or consider starting your own.

Family and Friends

Many people who experience intensive feelings of stress or depression find comfort in being around people who love them. Whether or not members of your family can relate to your problems, just knowing you are among people who care about you can be helpful.

Exercise

Physical activity can reduce stress in two ways. First, a healthy body is less susceptible to the physical effects of stress, such as sore muscles and fatigue. Second, a healthy body leads to a healthy mind, and a sense of well-being is important to your mind's ability to minimize the effects of stress. Avoid medications that promise temporary relief.

Eat Well

This is not the time to stop eating, start bingeing, or take refuge in empty calories. Try pasta for quick energy and plenty of fruit for vitamin C and natural sugars. Eat regular meals every day.

Relaxation

To reduce stress on a day-to-day basis, many people practice meditation (see "Meditate") or yoga (see "Simple Yoga Exercises to Do at Work") and other muscle relaxation techniques. Try to recognize the physical signs of stress (fast heartbeat, stiff muscles) and condition your body to consciously recognize and respond to them. Get enough rest, eat well, and allow yourself to have a good time.

Management

Lessen stress by learning to better manage your workload, activities, or problems. Take large, stress-inducing issues and deal with them in more manageable parts. Organize your time better, or cut down on your activities. Talk to your supervisor about unrealistic workloads. Get family and friends to assist you in sorting out your responsibilities, help you fulfill them, and get to a more peaceful time.

Optimism

Dwelling on the factors that cause you stress will only intensify the feeling. Treat problems as they arise, but stay in good spirits and look forward to a time when you will feel more free from stress. Concentrate on what gives you pleasure and relaxes you.

Open-Mindedness

Sometimes stress can be magnified from within. Let yourself solve problems effectively. Be open to any possible solutions to your problems, and don't give up on the healing process before it has a chance to be successful. If it is possible to remove yourself from the situation, person, or problem contributing to your stress—for even a short time—do so. You may be able to regain some much-needed perspective.

12 Ways to Improve Listening Skills

1. Look directly at the speaker, whether that person is next to you or at a distance. Look into his or her eyes, if possible.

2. Clear your mind of all other subjects.

3. Show your interest, but be as relaxed as possible.

4. Don't interrupt the speaker's train of thought. If something is unclear or you have questions, withhold them until an appropriate moment.

5. Don't be diverted by insignificant distractions, such as noises outside the room, other people's conversations near by, jiggling keys or change, or the actions of others who may also be listening. If the noise is too much, ask the speaker to stop briefly, or move to a better location for privacy and effective communication.

6. When possible, learn something about the subject beforehand, so you can make better judgments and ask better questions about what is being said.

7. Make mental notes of the key points made. Jot them down in a small notebook.

8. Pay attention to voice and body language: actions of the speaker that may modify the meaning or impact of what is being said, such as tone of voice and intensity of speech; gestures with the head, hands, or body; the speaker's dress and carriage.

9. Don't let your mind wander. If you're bored, anticipate the next point.

10. Emphasize your own reactions to what is being said, not by interruptions but by smiling, nodding, or leaning your head toward the speaker.

11. Try to put yourself in the position of the speaker and to understand more fully the viewpoints expressed.

12. Repeat the main thrust of the speaker's argument to him or her without embellishing or adding your own reactions and insights. Have the speaker confirm that you have accurately recounted the thoughts spoken.

Accelerate Learning

In our fast-paced, information-overloaded society, we often need to learn and remember new tasks and process unfamiliar subjects with lightning speed. Here are some mnemonic skills to accelerate the learning process.

While we usually define studying as poring over books, you can train your mind to study even as you go about your daily routine. The subconscious mind takes in vast quantities of information while you focus on another project. For example, watch a video on refinishing techniques while you do housework. Reinforce what you've heard by reading an article or book on the subject later in the evening.

Record information and play it back. To improve your vocabulary, make a tape of yourself reading words and their definitions. You can also buy tapes to help you learn anything from how to play bridge to repairing a carburetor. If you are taking a formal class, bring a tape recorder with you to tape lectures; play them back to yourself later on. If you walk long distances or exercise in a gym, a portable cassette player can do more than just play music. Use that time as an opportunity to build mental fitness and flexibility as well.

Keep a notebook and write down things you want to remember. If you need to remember ten new products for a business presentation, for example, write each one in your notebook ten times. The very action of forming the letters of the words help. Write sentences using the product names as you will in your presentation.

Have you ever noticed that you forget important dates like birthdays and anniversaries but somehow remember the lyrics to hundreds of different songs? Making up a poem, a song, or even just a brief sentence can be a good way to retain this kind of information. All of us can recite the verse that tells us how many days are in each month of the year. If you want to learn a new skill rapidly, read how it is done, watch how it is done, and imagine yourself doing the skill successfully before actually trying it.

Go a step further and write down information you want to memorize—say, the names of U.S. presidents and their terms of office—on Post-it notes, and distribute them around your home in places where you look every day: the bathroom mirror, the clothes closet, and over the kitchen sink, for example. After four or five days, take them down and replace them with a new subject. You can also make flashcards and use them in a more traditional way.

Immersion is an excellent technique. It forces you to grasp knowledge quickly, if not completely. Seek out situations where the information you want to learn will surround you, whether they are restaurants where a particular cuisine is served or conferences on technical information. Do not feel you need to participate fully. People who have studied oil painting do not spontaneously paint masterpieces, but they do find they have the ability to render simple forms. In other words, immersing yourself will not make you an expert, but it will familiarize you as you learn by absorbing your environment.

Prepare yourself so that when you do study your mind is clear. Daily physical exercise and short periods of meditation can improve your concentration dramatically.

13. Money, Math, Finance

How Much To Tip

This guide indicates what is generally a fair and acceptable tip for good service. It is by no means inflexible, though. If your service has been especially good, feel free to tip more. If you've received bad service, you don't have to tip as much—or tip at all.

Place	Person	Amount
Airport	flight personnel	none
	skycap	$1 or more for all baggage on a cart
Barbershop	haircutter	15% of cost, at least $1
Beauty shop	manicurist	15% of cost, at least $1
	stylist or cutter	15% of bill
	shampooist	$1 to $2
Car/parking	car wash attendant	$1 to $2
	valet parking attendant	50¢ to $1
Cruise ship	cabin, dining room steward	2.5% to 4% of total fare
	cabin person, wine/bar steward	5% to 7% of total fare divided among them at end of cruise
Hotel	bellhop	$1 per bag carried
	cleaning person	$1 to $2 a night per person or $5 to $10 a week for longer stays
	concierge, lobby attendant, desk clerk	none, unless special service is given, then $5 to $10
	room-service waiter	15% of bill (make sure tip is not already included in bill)

Place	Person	Amount
Movers	moving person	$10 to $20 per person for a full load
Restaurant	waiter	15% of bill
	bus person	none
	headwaiter/maitre d'	none unless special service is provided, then about $5
	wine steward	15% of wine bill
	bartender	10% to 15% of bar bill
	coat check attendant	$1 for one or two coats
	restroom attendant	50¢
Sports arena	usher	50¢ or $1 if shown to seat
Taxi	driver	15% of fare, at least 50¢
Train	bartender, waiter	15% of bill
	redcap	$1 per bag (or the posted rate)

Other service people you deal with regularly, such as building superintendents, doormen, and mail carriers, should be tipped when they provide a special service; anything from $1 to $5 is appropriate. It is also proper (though not absolutely necessary) to give these people a larger tip, perhaps $10 to $25, or a small gift at the holiday season.

Note: You can quickly approximate a 15 percent tip by using the amount of tax on a bill, provided you know the tax rate for the service purchased in the state or country you are in. If the tax is 8 percent, simply double it for the tip. If it is 5 percent, triple it. Otherwise, determine 10 percent by moving the decimal point one place, and add half of the result to determine 15 percent.

Balance a Checkbook

Although balancing a checkbook may seem like a daunting task, these simple instructions should help to take the anxiety out of opening your monthly bank statement. You'll never have to worry that you made a grievous error in your checkbook, because a thorough balancing will uncover any mistakes you or your bank might have made.

The basic principle of balancing (also known as reconciling) is as follows: Compare the bank's ending balance with the checkbook ending balance, then add and subtract appropriate sums from the bank balance until the two balances are the same.

The bank statement's ending balance is what the bank shows you have in your account as of a particular date. This balance includes only those checks cleared or paid by the bank as of that date, and only those deposits you made as of that date. The balance in your checkbook, however, includes all checks you have written, whether they have cleared the bank or not, and all deposits you have made, whether the bank has recorded them or not.

If you've let a few months worth of statements pile up, balance them all at once, using the instructions below. When you reach Step 4, use the ending balance of your most recent bank statement. It helps to use a calculator with a printing tape.

How to Balance Your Checkbook

1. Compare the list of cleared checks and withdrawals (including automatic teller machine or ATM withdrawals) on the bank statement with the entries in your checkbook. Put a check mark next to each check or withdrawal listed on the bank statement, and a corresponding check mark next to each matching entry in your checkbook. If you find you have forgotten to record a check or withdrawal in your checkbook, do so now and adjust your checkbook balance accordingly.

   Note regarding Step 1: If cleared checks are not listed in check number order on your bank statement, you may wish to assemble the actual cleared checks that have come with the statement in numerical order. It's always faster and easier to compare the check register and the statement when both are in numerical order. If your bank does not routinely send the actual checks with your monthly statement, you may request them; your bank may charge a fee for this service.

2. Note any miscellaneous charges listed on your bank statement, such as check printing charges, monthly service charges, or charges for using ATMs not owned by your bank. Make sure you note these charges in your checkbook and subtract them from your checkbook balance. Check off these charges in your checkbook and on the bank statement.

3. Compare the list of deposits on the bank statement with the entries in your checkbook. Again, check off the deposits on the bank statement and put corresponding check marks next to the matching entries in your checkbook. If you find you have forgotten to record a deposit in your checkbook, do so now and adjust your checkbook balance accordingly. If the bank statement indicates any automatic deposits, interest paid, or wire transfers, be sure to record them in your checkbook and add them to your checkbook balance.

4. On the top of a blank piece of paper (plain lined paper or accounting columnar paper), write down the bank statement ending balance. The reverse side of the bank statement usually provides a preprinted form for this purpose; however, there sometimes isn't enough space on it for a list of all outstanding checks.

5. Now, on the same piece of paper, write down the date and amount of each outstanding deposit (deposits that have not yet been recorded or credited by the bank) you find in your checkbook. These should be easy to spot; they're the ones that do not have check marks next to them. Add up the total outstanding deposits, and write down the sum. Add this sum to the bank statement ending balance, and write down the subtotal.

6. Write down the check number and amount of each outstanding check (checks that have not yet cleared the bank) that you find in your checkbook. Again, these checkbook entries will not have check marks next to them. Add up the outstanding checks and write down the total. Subtract the total outstanding checks from the subtotal reached in Step 5, and write down the result. This new total should agree with your checkbook balance. If it doesn't, don't panic.

What to Do If Your Checkbook Doesn't Balance

1. Compare the total reached in Step 6 above with your checkbook balance. How far off are you? This number may be easily spotted in your checkbook as a check cleared by the bank but not checked off in your checkbook. Dividing the number in half may indicate a deposit subtracted instead of added. Here's another tip: if you are off by an amount that is divisible by nine, then you may have transposed two numbers somewhere.

2. Double-check the addition and subtraction in your checkbook and on the balance sheet. You may find the error there.

3. Carefully compare the amount of each check and deposit listed on the bank statement with the amounts listed in your checkbook. Did you record something incorrectly? One wrong number, a misplaced decimal point, two transposed digits, or an extra zero can throw you way off.

4. Make sure you have listed all outstanding checks and deposits in your checkbook on your sheet of paper.

5. If you still haven't found the error, repeat Steps 1 through 6 under "How to Balance Your Checkbook."

6. If all else fails, and you are convinced that either the bank has made an error or you're about to take a plunge off the nearest bridge, call the customer service department of your bank and ask for assistance.

Establish and Maintain Good Credit

Contrary to widespread belief, credit cards are not magic pieces of plastic that allow you to buy things without paying for them. Rather, credit cards simply enable consumers to make purchases and pay for them later, or pay for them gradually with interest. Credit card companies make money from the high interest rates consumers pay.

If you buy something with a credit card and do not make the payments on time, or do not make them at all, you will be charged a hefty late penalty and your account will continue to accrue interest. Worse, you will develop what is called bad credit. Having bad credit can stop you from qualifying to borrow money from a bank, because the bank will always do a credit check on your card accounts; it's one of the ways they judge how reliable you are in repaying your debts. If you have bad credit you'll be unable to get loans, and without a bank loan you'll probably be unable to buy a car, a house, or any other expensive item. That is why it is important to maintain good credit.

Establish Credit

Getting a credit card early is a good idea, but only once you understand how a credit card works. Companies often offer to open accounts for college students, even if they are without assets, in the hope of reaching customers early. Also, young people often buy impulsively and end up paying the most in interest. If you can get a card as a student, do so, but use it sparingly. Once you are out of school, you will usually be required to have a minimum salary to qualify for a card. If you do not qualify on your own, though, you may still be able to get a card with the help of a cosigner with established credit, most likely one or both of your parents, who promises to pay your debts if you don't.

When deciding which card to apply for, consider these factors: availability, annual percentage rate (APR), service charge, and other benefits. As for availability, some credit cards are accepted nearly anywhere you'd want to buy; others can be used only at selected places. Next, look for a card with the lowest possible APR, which is the interest rate and other fees on paying back charges; they'll vary according to which bank or organization issues the card. Some banks offer low competitive interest rates for specific introductory periods; after that, the interest rate goes up. Read the fine print. Don't apply for a card with a rate over 16 percent! It's too high in today's market. Find out if the card has an annual fee or other charges for such things as spending over your credit limit or making late payments. Most cards will have an annual fee of about $20 a year, although it shouldn't be difficult to find cards without any charge at all. Sometimes banks will waive annual or late fees if you challenge them about it. This is more likely to happen if you already have a good credit rating and the bank wants your business. Finally, look into what else a card will offer. Some cards entitle you to discounts, frequent flyer miles, or other bonuses, such as transferring balances between cards to get a lower interest rate. Weigh all these factors when deciding which card to apply for.

Note: Cards like Visa and Mastercard are issued by many different banks and organizations. Each company has different rules and policies for their card.

Maintain Good Credit

The only way to maintain good credit is to pay your bills on time. This refers not only to credit card bills but to car payments, mortgage payments, and even phone and utility bills. To ensure that you pay monthly bills regularly and on time, keep a record of payments and mark a certain day each month as the day to pay bills.

Don't buy anything on a credit card that you don't have the money currently in the bank to pay back. Try to pay bills off completely each month—not only will you avoid interest payments, but your credit ranking will improve. If you cannot pay off balances initially, pay as much as you can, and pay the full amount as soon as you are able.

Make sure your credit record is in good standing and the information in it is correct by requesting to see your report every few years, or just before you expect to have it examined by a lending institution, insurance company, or some other interested party. Credit reports can be obtained by calling credit bureaus in your area (look in the Yellow Pages under Credit). There may be a service fee to have your report sent to you. Negative information usually stays on a credit report for seven years, though incorrect information can be deleted.

Save with Coupons

Clipping coupons from newspaper circulars can yield significant savings on your grocery bills, but it can also be a costly waste of time if you are not organized and practical. Some small specialty stores refuse coupons altogether. Your best bet for saving with coupons is to shop at large supermarkets that carry a wide variety of brands.

Manufacturers offer coupons to convince you to buy a product you normally would not consider purchasing. Keep this in mind to save you from several of the usual coupon pitfalls.

Each time you get a circular, leaf through it and clip coupons only for products you use regularly. Changing brands to save a small amount of money can actually cost money when you end up discarding the product because it does not satisfy you. Do not save coupons for items you try to steer away from—snack foods, for example. Discard them immediately.

As you clip the coupons, use a highlighter pen to mark their expiration dates. (Cashiers love this because it helps them move checkout lines more quickly.) Divide the coupons into two groups: perishable products such as orange juice or cookies, and nonperishable ones like coffee filters and kitty litter.

In a drawer or folder, organize the two groups of coupons by expiration date, with the coupons closest to expiring on top. Each time you open the drawer or file, discard any coupons that have passed their expiration date. Since you only buy perishable items for immediate use, look through these coupons whenever you make out a shopping list and match them to what you need. Beware, however, of buying certain products just because you have coupons. Always stick to your weekly menu or budget. Consider the coupons to be secondary.

Also browse through the coupons for nonperishable items when you make up your shopping list. Try to use up any of the coupons on the verge of expiring. The more space you have at home, the more easily you can stockpile nonperishables while racking up savings. Of course, if you run out of paper towels and do not have a coupon, you will purchase them anyway. If you do not have a desperate need for a nonperishable item, and you have a coupon that does not expire for quite some time, hold onto it.

The biggest savings come from combining coupons with store discounts for the same brand. Check your grocery store's circular when it comes out. If your super-market allows you to purchase only a certain number of sale items, and you have several coupons for that item, it may be worth your while to make a few trips to the grocery store that week. If you have a coupon for a product that is on sale but the store has run out of stock, be sure to get a rain check from the manager. This allows you to purchase the item at the sale price once the shelf is full again.

Although fewer and fewer stores offer double and triple coupon values, they do still exist. Watch carefully for announcements. Always use your biggest coupons for nonperishable items on those days, as well as any other coupons you may have for your regular shopping needs.

Manage a Budget and Pay Bills Effectively

No matter how much money you make, budgeting can be a formidable task. It's probably easiest to figure out and work with a monthly budget. First you must calculate your real yearly income:

Add

Wage earnings _____

Interest and dividends _____

Rents and royalties _____

Profits from business _____

Pension/annuity/disability _____

Social security _____

Other _____

Total: _____

Deduct from total

State/federal/local taxes _____

Social security taxes _____

Payroll deductions _____

Spendable income: _____

Divide this income by
   12 to get a monthly figure: _____

337

Compose a Budget Chart

1. Divide a sheet into four columns. Use a separate sheet for each month.

2. In the first column list all of your fixed monthly expenses and variable monthly expenses.

3. In the second column record your estimate of the amount you should spend monthly for each item. The total of this column should not exceed your monthly income.

4. In the third column list the actual amount you spend for each item.

5. At the end of the month, total the third column and see how it compares with your projected costs and monthly income. If it exceeds your monthly income, examine where you can cut back expenditures, and record the amount to reduce each item in the fourth column. If the total falls short of your monthly income, consider yourself lucky and begin to save for a rainy day!

6. To factor nonmonthly bills, divide the yearly cost by 12 and budget that amount each month. If necessary, keep money for these bills in a separate account to make sure that you don't spend it.

7. Do the same for predictable medical and dental expenses: estimate the amount you will spend during the year and place this money in a separate account to be used for this purpose.

Sample Budget Chart

Fixed Expenses	Estimated Cost	Actual Cost	Cut Costs
Mortgage/rent	_____	_____	_____
Gas	_____	_____	_____
Electric	_____	_____	_____
Oil	_____	_____	_____
Gasoline	_____	_____	_____
Phone	_____	_____	_____
Water	_____	_____	_____
Garbage	_____	_____	_____
Insurance	_____	_____	_____
Installment payments	_____	_____	_____
Interest on notes	_____	_____	_____
Loan repayments	_____	_____	_____
School/college	_____	_____	_____
Dues	_____	_____	_____
Children's allowances	_____	_____	_____
Parent's allowance	_____	_____	_____
Food	_____	_____	_____
Child care/household help	_____	_____	_____
Other	_____	_____	_____

Variable Expenses	Estimated Cost	Actual Cost	Cut Costs
Savings deposit	_____	_____	_____
Clothing	_____	_____	_____
Doctor	_____	_____	_____
Dentist	_____	_____	_____
Pharmacy	_____	_____	_____
Entertainment	_____	_____	_____
Books/magazines	_____	_____	_____
Home repairs	_____	_____	_____
Car repairs	_____	_____	_____
Cleaning/personal care	_____	_____	_____
Church/charities	_____	_____	_____
Furniture/appliances	_____	_____	_____
Household supplies	_____	_____	_____
Gifts/holidays	_____	_____	_____
Hobbies	_____	_____	_____
Vacation	_____	_____	_____
Other	_____	_____	_____
Totals:	_____	_____	_____

Pay Bills Effectively

1. Calculate fixed bills (gasoline, phone, utilities, etc.) into your monthly budget.
2. Note at what times during the month you receive each bill, and budget your monthly income on a weekly basis to cover all bills.
3. If you must use credit cards, try to pay them immediately rather than carry balances that draw finance charges.
4. Pay off credit card bills with the highest finance charges first.
5. Ask your utility companies if you can get on a budget plan, in which you pay a set monthly rate throughout the year.

Make Lists Work for You

Grocery Shopping List

1. Brainstorm a preliminary list of all the items you buy.
2. For your master list, categorize the items into groups: dairy, frozen foods, meat, bread/cereal/pasta, canned fruits/vegetables/fish, snacks, fresh fruits/vegetables, toiletries, household/cleaning supplies, paper goods, bakery, deli.

3. When you write your master list, place a box or line before each item so that you can check them off (or you can circle the items you need).

4. If you're a conscientious coupon-user, leave space below or beside each item to indicate whether you have a coupon for that item and for what brand—this will make your shopping more efficient.

5. Make several copies of your list. Be sure to save the master list for making future copies.

"To Do" List

1. Jot down all the tasks you wish to accomplish and then reorder them by priority.

2. Next to each task, write
   - ✓ Supplies and tools you'll need
   - ✓ The time it will take to complete it
   - ✓ Steps to accomplish the task efficiently

3. Looking at the time needed to complete each task, organize your list day by day. Try not to overestimate what you can do in one day. Be realistic and reasonable about your goals.

4. Cross off each task from your list as you finish it. This will give you a real sense of accomplishment.

Vacation Packing List

1. Depending on how many people are going on the vacation, divide a sheet of paper into boxes or use a separate sheet for each person.

2. For each list, make categories for shirts, pants/shorts, underwear, socks, bathing suit, shoes/sneakers/boots, sweaters/sweat suits, jackets/hat/gloves, belts/accessories, toiletries.

3. Fill in the number of items for each category, or list the specific items to bring.

4. If you plan to pack food, make a shopping list and check off each item as you pack it in a cooler or bags.

5. Make a list of miscellaneous items: bicycles, rafts/surfboard/floats, fishing gear, camping gear, snow/ski equipment, boating gear, skates/snowboards/skateboards, lawn/beach chairs, golf clubs, tennis racquets/balls, etc.

Vacation "To Do" List

When planning a vacation, compose a "to do" list to make sure that everything gets done. Your list should include the following:

✓ Make reservations for travel and confirm them before leaving.
✓ Make accommodation reservations and confirm them before leaving.
✓ Plan budget and buy traveler's checks.

✓ Stop mail and newspaper delivery.
✓ Arrange for pet and plant care.
✓ Compose packing lists.
✓ Tell someone where you can be reached in case of emergency.

Using Lists Effectively

✓ Use your lists to keep track of things—don't just compose a list and then toss it aside.
✓ Keep lists handy—in your purse or briefcase—or post them visibly—on the refrigerator or a bulletin board, for example.
✓ Have a pen or pencil near your list for marking things down or crossing things off.
✓ Whenever you compose a new master list or chart, store the original in a safe place for making future copies.

Set Up a Garage Sale

✓ Gather the items you want to sell and make sure they are reasonably clean and in working order.
✓ Organize your garage sale items by category: sporting goods, games, books, kitchen gadgets, clothes, furniture, etc. This makes it easier for shoppers to browse and find what they want.
✓ Apply masking tape or stickers as price labels, or attach tags with string to each item showing the price.
✓ Before you open for business, stock up on coins and bills for change. Keep a cash box (in a safe place) or wear a money belt during the sale.
✓ Post signs listing the location and hours of the sale throughout your town and the neighboring area.
✓ For greater exposure, advertise your garage sale in the local newspaper.
✓ Make sure parking places and the sale area are both easily accessible.

Tips for a Successful Garage Sale

✓ Price items reasonably—people are looking for bargains!
✓ Be willing to negotiate to sell your stuff quickly.
✓ Ask your neighbors if they'd like to join you—you can pool your items or hold individual sales on the same day.
✓ Try to hold your sale over at least two consecutive days, preferably on the weekend. Word-of-mouth advertising will bring more visitors.

Buy at Auctions

One of the most enjoyable—and potentially cheapest—ways to buy antiques, collectibles, or other high-priced items is at auction and estate sales. Because the price goes only as high as the highest bid, you can almost be guaranteed to pay a lower price. Many people frequent auctions to learn about collectibles or as an exciting form of entertainment. Observe a few auctions before jumping in. Auctioneers will make you pay for your mistakes—make sure you understand the rules of the house!

Determine What You Want to Buy

Know what you are looking for. If you are starting a collection, focus on things that interest you as pieces of art or history. Eclectically focused collections from passionate collectors bring more pleasure and attention than those assembled only with hopes of financial gain.

Get Auction Catalogues

Call local auction houses to see whether they deal in your collectibles. If so, request a catalogue of merchandise. Catalogues cost about $10 for a single auction or $50 for an entire year's subscription to merchandise catalogues in your interest area. Each catalogue features a list of items offered for auction, including a picture (if applicable) and the estimated price.

Visit the Auction House

In the days before the auction, the house will display pieces up for bidding. Anyone can come to inspect the merchandise, and it is important that you do so if you are serious about buying. While visiting, ask a representative to assist you by providing background information. Find out about an item's age, authenticity, style, desirability, and likely price; ask whether there are any flaws in the object. Examine the piece carefully with your own eyes and take any relevant measurements.

Research

Good collectors go beyond the information supplied by auction houses. Go to the library to research the period. Visit other dealers to compare prices of similar items or of reproductions (particularly if you are looking for furniture to use in your house). The more research you do, the better you'll get at recognizing valuable items and estimating fair market prices.

Arrive Early at the Auction House

Come about half an hour early on the day of the auction if your item will go up for bidding early (if you know your item will not come up for over an hour, you may decide to arrive late). If you don't know when your item will be presented, check the chronological listing. Arriving early lets the auctioneer see you are serious about buying; he or she will recognize you more readily when the bidding starts.

Bid

1. If you cannot attend the auction but feel comfortable about the item you are bidding for and the price you are willing to pay, place a bid in advance. Attend the auction if you can—you never know how the bidding will go.

2. Private collectors have an advantage over dealers because they do not have to worry about resale profit; be willing to go a little higher than a dealer would.

3. When you bid, be clear and confident. If you look too eager, other bidders will raise the ante without worry. If you look as though you're ready to go all out, real competitors may continue bidding in the hope you will drop out. Put on your best poker face. Don't open the bidding if you can avoid it.

4. Above all, don't make a mistake! Auction houses don't give refunds and don't want to hear about how you got confused and bid on the wrong item. Stay alert and follow the auctioneer's rules.

Pay

When you purchase an item, you must pay immediately with cash or a personal check. The auction house adds a 10 percent commission to the payment; figure that in when you bid.

Appraise and Set Prices on Antiques

All antiques and collectibles you sell need to be appraised. While it may not be worth paying for a formal appraisal on lower-value items, it will still be necessary to determine a fair price for your merchandise.

Sources for Appraisals

Price Books. These books list prices of antiques; some are more reliable than others, and some are easier to use than others.

Antiques publications. Magazines provide information on prices and offer a wide variety of antiques for sale. Compare the prices of similar items.

Other collectors and dealers. Visit shops, shows, and auctions to find out how much an item is going for. Talk to experienced dealers and collectors to get current prices. Keep in mind, though, that any one "expert" can be completely wrong; go to more than one source for your information.

Formal appraisals. Avoid the expense of a professional appraiser unless you have items of great value that you expect will recoup the cost of appraisal. Don't hire an appraiser if you plan to put the items up for auction; auction houses appraise items themselves. Professional appraisers are listed in the Yellow Pages and in antiques magazines. Some auction houses occasionally will offer a day for free appraisals to drum up business; look for these ads. If you pay, expect the appraiser to charge $100 an hour or more.

Factors Increasing the Price of an Antique

✓ Mint (untouched) condition
✓ Original box or container
✓ Brand names or labels still intact
✓ Manual, information booklet, or accessories included
✓ Previously owned by someone famous (proof is required)
✓ Connected to important historical event, such as documents or souvenirs of a political campaign
✓ Complete series, as with plates or figurines
✓ Miniatures
✓ Manufacturer or artist who designed the item
✓ Rarity of the item

Setting the Price

When determining the price of antiques for sale, keep in mind the following factors:

Demand for the item. This may change over time and depend on the area (state, region), so keep up on the current levels of interest.

Condition. The item must be in good condition to be worth any significant price. Original condition is best. Be careful when repairing antiques; while repairs can sometimes raise the value of a piece, they can also make it worthless. Do research before attempting restorations.

Who is the buyer? Private collectors pay a higher price than dealers because dealers must resell the item for a profit. An inexperienced or uninformed buyer may also be willing to pay a higher price.

Price of the item sold new. Check the price of a similar item that is new. Depending on the item and its condition, the antique's price should be relative to the price of the new item.

Desire to sell. The higher the price you set, the harder it may be to make a sale. If you are anxious to get rid of an item, consider lowering the price to spur interest.

Figure Your Net Worth

To determine your total net worth, fill out this form as completely and as accurately as possible. Any significant financial asset or liability that does not fall into a category listed below should be identified and placed in the space marked "Other."

Assets

Liquid assets

    Bank account   _____

    Value of life insurance   _____

    Value of U.S. bonds   _____

    Pension funds   _____

    Brokerage funds   _____

    Money market funds   _____

    Trusts   _____

    Other assets_____   _____

    Debts owed to you   _____

    TOTAL   _____

Investments

    Real estate   _____

    Stocks   _____

    Corporate bonds   _____

    Business investments   _____

    Mutual funds   _____

    Certificates of deposit   _____

    IRAs   _____

    Other investments_____   _____

    TOTAL   _____

Personal Holdings

    Home(s)   _____

    Car(s), boat(s)   _____

    Major appliances   _____

    Computer and hardware   _____

    Art   _____

    Antiques and collectibles   _____

    Jewelry and fine clothing   _____

    Other holdings_____   _____

    TOTAL   _____

Total Assets: _____

Liabilities

Remaining loans   _____

Remaining mortgage   _____

Credit card debts   _____

Other bills due_____   _____

Taxes due   _____

Stock margin accounts payable   _____

Other debts_____   _____

Total Liabilities: _____

Net Worth

Total assets: _____

minus

Total liabilities: _____

TOTAL NET WORTH: _____

Buy Insurance

The principle of insurance is easy enough: you pay a company a premium or annual fee, and they agree to reimburse any loss you may have according to the terms of the policy. Finding affordable insurance that offers adequate coverage—whether car, life, health, homeowner's, disability, or liability—is much more difficult. Shop around, ask questions, determine exactly what kind of coverage you really need, and follow these basic guidelines.

Where to Look for Insurance

Ask friends, relatives, and business associates. You can get a lot of helpful information from people who have already been through the process of shopping for insurance. Ask people you trust for advice and potential agents and companies. Your family or employer may have used an insurance agent for many years.

Consult government agencies. State governments have offices that regulate the insurance industry. By calling them you can get helpful consumer guides. Later on in the process, you can use these agencies to check into past complaints filed against specific companies.

Call agents and companies. When buying insurance, you can either buy directly from a company, if it is a direct writer, or through an insurance agent, if the company is an agency company. To look into direct writers, call the company office in your area. To find an agent, you can either look in the Yellow Pages under "Insurance agents" or call an association for insurance agents for referrals to area agents.

These organizations include the Independent Insurance Agents of America (phone number 800-221-7917) and the National Association of Professional Insurance Agents (phone number 703-836-9340). If you are interested in buying insurance from a specific agency company, you can call the company and ask for the names and phone numbers of independent agents representing that company in your area.

What to Look For in an Insurance Policy

✓ Consult hospitals. More health maintenance organizations and consortiums of doctors are forming in this age of managed health care. Good, affordable alternatives may be available through local hospitals.

✓ Consult professional associations. Health and life insurance are often offered to members of organizations. Make some calls and compare. These policies are often much cheaper than insurance you obtain on your own, and group plans are administered by the organization.

✓ Make sure you truly need it. Before you even start shopping for insurance, assess your requirements. Otherwise, you may be convinced to buy insurance you don't really need.

✓ Make sure it is affordable. While even skimpy insurance coverage will rarely seem inexpensive, it is definitely worth paying more for a better policy. Consider cost at all stages, and factor in insurance costs when buying something you need to insure such as a car or house. Figure out whether you can afford to pay the premiums. Also, consider the deductible, which is the amount you will have to cover on your own loss before coverage begins. Make sure you can afford it.

✓ Make sure the coverage is comprehensive. Whatever you pay for insurance, make sure you are satisfied with the amount of coverage you receive.

How to Decide On a Policy

✓ Decide whether to use an agent or buy directly. Buying directly may be cheaper because you avoid the agent's commission. On the other hand, an agent may have more at stake in finding you the best possible deal. It's likely, though, that you can get a good policy either way.

✓ Compare many different policies from different companies and with a variety of agents.

✓ Read the entire policy and make sure you understand it completely.

✓ Make sure the company you are buying from is reputable, stable, and trustworthy. To check, call state insurance agencies or consult books (*Best's Insurance Reports* rates companies) and magazines (*Consumer Reports*, *Forbes*, *Money*, and other publications cover the insurance industry).

✓ If you use an agent, be certain you feel confident about the agent's reliability.

✓ Continue to check regularly for better prices even after you buy your insurance. Don't give up insurance, particularly if you are ill or elderly, until you have determined—without a doubt—that you do not need it. Once a policy is canceled, it might not be easy to replace.

Tips for Keeping Costs Down

✓ Pay the entire premium at once; it is cheaper than paying in installments.

✓ Watch out for extras, riders, and endorsements that raise the premium but may not be worth while for you.

✓ Insurance packages that cover a variety of areas can be cheaper than buying coverage for each area separately; the more insurance you buy the cheaper it is, relatively.

✓ Do the math to figure out how much you must pay for premiums and deductibles before benefits will accrue. This is particularly important for health insurance. It may actually be cheaper to choose a lower deductible and a slightly higher premium than to opt for lower monthly payments but a hefty out-of-pocket expense.

✓ Ask about discounts for nonsmokers, the physically fit (health and life insurance), senior-citizen drivers, and drivers with clean records (car insurance), security systems (home insurance), and other "good client" incentives.

✓ Avoid limited specialty coverage such as cancer insurance or personal accident insurance; these perils should be covered in a larger comprehensive plan.

✓ Avoid duplicating coverage on more than one policy; know exactly what is already covered before you buy more.

Set Up an IRA

Individual Retirement Accounts (IRAs) are designed to encourage workers—particularly self-employed workers not covered by a company pension plan—to save for retirement. Two types of tax incentives are provided to people who set aside a part of their yearly salary for a retirement fund. First, the money invested is tax deductible if you are self-employed or earn less than a specified amount. Second, the money is tax deferred, meaning that you do not have to pay income taxes on it until you withdraw it far in the future. These incentives offer great advantages: a tax-deferred investment will appreciate over decades into many times the amount of an equal, non–tax-deferred investment, and the tax deduction helps lower your yearly income tax payment.

An IRA does not refer to any specific type of investment. You may create IRAs out of stock portfolios, mutual funds, savings accounts, real estate, or other investments. There are limits, though, to how much you can invest per year into an IRA, and you will be penalized heavily if you withdraw the money early. But if you can afford to set aside funds regularly and commit to keeping the money invested, there's no better way to invest than with an IRA or similar tax-incentived retirement plan. Here are some important details about IRAs and some tips on investing.

Requirements

While anyone can open an IRA and enjoy the benefits of tax deferment, not everyone can deduct IRA contributions from their taxable income. Contributions are fully tax deductible if you or your spouse is not in a company-sponsored pension plan, or you are in a pension plan but your adjusted gross income is less than $25,000 ($40,000 if married) a year. If your adjusted gross income is between $25,000 and $35,000 ($40,000 and $50,000 if you are married) you are entitled to a lesser tax deduction.

Age

At age 59½ you can begin to withdraw money from an IRA account without penalty. You will, though, have to pay income tax on the money at this time (it is likely your tax bracket will be lower in retirement than when the contributions were made). You must begin to withdraw from your IRA by age 71½, at which point you can no longer make contributions.

Types

The type of investment you choose for your IRA should be judged according to the current economic environment, the risk factor, and your age and income. Certain investments cannot be made into IRAs. They include commodities, margined stocks, mortgaged real estate, leveraged investments (made with borrowed money), and collectibles (art, antiques, and jewelry; coins are acceptable if held by a custodian). If you plan to contribute regularly, open a **contributory IRA,** which allows you to invest up to $2000 a year. If you wish to invest a lump sum, you can open a **rollover IRA,** which allows you to make tax-free transfers of assets between plans.

Rules and Fees

If you plan to open an IRA, it is essential that you read up on the rules that apply; they will vary. You may open more than one IRA, but you cannot invest more than the $2000 limit per year into all your IRAs combined (you may also have a required minimum yearly contribution). Excess money invested in an IRA will be taxed highly as a penalty. Also, you will be charged a maintenance fee for each account, so you may want to limit the number of IRAs you open. All money invested into an IRA must be earned income—not social security payments, interest or dividend earnings, or money from rent.

Advice

1. The sooner you start, the better. Remember the Rule of 72, an arithmetical certainty: take the rate of interest earned, say 10 percent, and divide by 72 to get the number of years it will take to double your investment. Time really is on your side.

2. IRA contributions should be managed, not set aside and forgotten about. You want to create the best return for your investment.

3. Diversify your investments: put some money into safe and steady earners and some into more risky investments with higher payoffs.

4. The closer you get to retirement, the less risk you should take with your investments.

5. It's still worth keeping an IRA even if you don't qualify for the tax deduction on contributions.

See also "Research a Stock," "Research a Mutual Fund," and "Prepare for Retirement."

10 Tips for Bargaining Effectively

1. **Know what you want.** If you want to buy something, be sure it is really the item or service you want; otherwise, both the buyer's and the seller's time is wasted. Comparison-shop and do research until you are sure. If this is a business deal, explore all your alternatives.

2. **Know what price you are willing to pay.** Before you even start bargaining, know your maximum limit. This will ensure that you aren't led to buy something you can't afford, and it will save both parties the time of bargaining if the price is completely incompatible with what you want to pay. Keep in mind, though, that you can never be too sure how far the seller may be willing to drop a price. Be prepared to walk away if the terms aren't right, and let the seller know it.

3. **Know about the object or service for sale.** You can't truly bargain for a lower price unless you have an idea of its worth in the marketplace or you can give a reason why the price should be lowered. For example, if you're buying a used car, know the flaws in the car so you can back up your argument for a lower price. Try to know why something is being sold, recognize the cyclical seasons of supply and demand, and understand the other party's motives for selling at a certain price.

4. **Be willing to compromise.** Face the facts—you're not going to get something for nothing. Be ready to give a little if the other party is also willing. That's the only way an agreement will be reached.

5. **Be fair and realistic.** When you make an offer, don't insult the seller by making it ridiculously low.

6. **Be firm in your offer.** Any offer you make initially should be lower than what you are actually willing to pay; keep in mind that you are willing to compromise. How much lower your initial offering should be depends on the maximum you're willing to pay, what the asking price is, and how much you think the other party will budge. While your first offer need not be final, present it seriously and without hesitation, and don't budge until you see that the other party is inflexible. Again, remember that no deal can sometimes be better than a bad one.

7. **Sell your offer.** Even if you're the one buying, you are still selling. Sell the seller on your price. Make people feel you are honestly interested in buying, that you have made a good offer, and that they need your money as much as you need the item.

8. **Don't be intimidated.** Just as it would not be right for you to bully your way to a better price, it's not right for the other party to try to intimidate you to accept a price you don't want. Ultimately, you are the one with the power to make a deal or not. You can't lose by passing on a bad offer. The seller, however, has inventory to think about.

9. **Don't be overly emotional.** Surely there should be a human element in everything you do. Don't be cold-hearted, particularly if you are in a position to exploit a weakness in someone. On the other hand, don't let others exploit you by appealing to your emotions; it will often be merely a trick. It's best to keep emotions out of a commercial transaction altogether if possible. Sellers who know you want a particular item will make every effort to play upon your desire and foster a sense of desperation and urgency. Don't fall into this trap.

10. **Present yourself well.** Don't look ill-kept if you are trying to impress upon someone that you are a professional. Speak clearly and directly, and make eye contact to convey the message that you are confident. Honor any agreements you make, and insist that the seller do the same. Finally, always be courteous; getting mean and ugly will only hinder the bargaining process.

Barter

Bartering can be an effective method of trading goods and/or services for individuals and business people who may have a surplus to unload or a deficit to make up. Make sure the trade is an equal one. If possible, inspect all bartered goods before the exchange to ensure you don't make an honest trade for a lemon. When exchanging goods for services, try to have the service performed first. If this isn't possible, build in some kind of guarantee, such as a delivery date or time frame, for the service to be fulfilled. Remember that transfers of goods and services are likely subject to sales taxes and are subject to income tax; consult your accountant about the tax implications of barter exchanges.

Get or Refinance a Mortgage

A mortgage is a loan from a bank to let you buy a house or property, for which the bank holds the property deed until you have paid back the loan in full with interest. Unless you have the money to pay for a house on your own, you'll have to get a mortgage in order to buy one. There are many types of mortgages suited to an array of financial needs.

Get a Mortgage

Find a House or Property

You can't apply for a mortgage loan until you find a particular house you want to buy. That's because you need to know how much money you want to borrow, and the bank needs to be able to determine whether you can afford to pay back a loan of that amount. If you are unsure how high a mortgage a bank would approve for you, ask for a preliminary consultation with a bank loan officer to determine a safe range for your level of financial buying power before you begin your house search. This will avoid unnecessary time and disappointment later.

Research Banks

Different banks offer different conditions for lending money. To find out what these conditions are, call local banks and inquire. The newspaper usually lists information once a week on all area lending establishments. You may also want to consult a mortgage broker. If you do, make sure the broker is a reputable one. Banks consider three elements in granting a mortgage loan: interest rate, points, and down payment.

1. The interest rate is the percent of the total loan that you will have to pay in addition to the principal cost of the loan, as a charge for borrowing money. Obviously, you want to find the lowest interest rate available. To do this, keep in mind the prime rate; this is the rate at which the government lends money to banks. Look for interest rates that are closest to the prime rate (though they will always be a little higher). Also, remember that interest rates go up and down periodically. You'll want to borrow money when interest rates are lowest.

   Mortgages generally fall into two types: fixed-rate and adjustable-rate (ARMs). Fixed-rate mortgages are preferable in times of low interest rates and usually cover a 15-, 20-, or 30-year period. ARMs feature rates that rise or fall over the life of the loan, based on a nationally published index. ARMs often boast low initial rates for a fixed period of years, after which the rate will vary. Your bank loan officer will help you understand the advantages and disadvantages of each type of loan. Make sure to find out which mortgage alternatives have renegotiable terms.

2. Points are the percent of the total cost of the house that you will have to pay the bank up front. They are usually only one or two (1 percent or 2 percent of the cost of the house), though even that amount can add up to a lot of money. Unless you have the money to pay immediately, look for the bank that will ask for the lowest number of points. Sometimes the seller will pay the buyer's points to close the deal in a difficult market. Ask.

3. The down payment is the percent of the total cost of the house that you will have to pay to the seller initially. The bank will require this as an assurance that you do have the money to pay back your mortgage loan, and it lessens the amount that the bank will have to lend to you. Down payments vary

greatly, from about 5 percent to as much as 30 percent, so determine how much you can afford to pay up front.

Weigh these factors in deciding which bank to apply to for a mortgage loan. Not all lending institutions will offer all types of mortgages. Get as much information as you can about the bank and the kinds of mortgages available, then decide which type of mortgage is best for you.

Apply to a Bank

Go to the bank you wish to borrow from. Speak to the appropriate representative, who will ask you a few preliminary questions to determine whether you qualify for a loan and then provide you with the application forms to fill out. You will need to outline and prove your salary (provide copies of recent tax returns), your assets (other property, cars), and your bank and credit accounts.

Response from Bank

Because the seller will be waiting for an answer from you, the bank tends to respond to mortgage loan requests quickly. Expect an answer in less than a week. During the waiting period, the bank will verify all the information you have supplied and run a credit check to determine how responsible you are about paying debts. Here's where good credit will help you (see also "Establish and Maintain Good Credit"). If you are turned down by the bank because of poor credit, you may apply to another bank, though you're likely to encounter the same problems. Your best bet is to straighten out your credit problems before reapplying for a mortgage loan.

Mortgage Commitment

If the bank approves your request for a mortgage loan, it will notify you (probably both by phone and officially in a letter). It will outline the final terms of the loan and tell you how long the offer holds. This will give you a period of time (usually 30 or 60 days) to buy the house and reach a settlement. The bank will help with the settlement, though it will charge you additional fees to pay for municipal taxes, lawyer's fees and closing costs.

Begin Payments

About a month or two after settlement, you will start to receive monthly bills for paying back your mortgage. If the bank lowers its interest rate before you have begun making payments, you should ask that the lower rate be applied to you (make this part of the agreement initially). If interest rates come down significantly while you are making mortgage payments, you should consider refinancing your mortgage. Make sure there are no penalties for paying off your mortgage early!

Refinance a Mortgage

In refinancing a mortgage, you sell the mortgaged property back to yourself and get a new mortgage at a lower interest rate that pays off the original mortgage. Refinancing can potentially save you thousands of dollars in house payments.

Determine the Potential Savings

It is generally recommended that you refinance your mortgage only if the interest rates have fallen more than 3 percentage points below the level you currently pay. That's because when you refinance you have to pay settlement costs, as you did when you originally got a mortgage, plus other new fees (such as appraisal fee and prepayment penalty) that may run in the thousands of dollars. Unless the savings you get from a lower interest rate can significantly beat these supplementary costs, don't bother refinancing. Consider also how much you have paid on the principal of your mortgage loan. If you don't have much longer to go in making payments, it probably won't be worth it to pay all the costs of refinancing. Finally, consider whether you are willing to go through the trouble and paperwork involved—it may not be worth the hassle if savings are not substantial.

Reapply at Bank

If you decide to refinance, go back to the bank that gave you your mortgage originally. While the bank stands to lose money on the deal, it won't try to stop you from refinancing because it knows you can always go to another bank for refinancing. In fact, if you find you can get an even better interest rate from another bank, go there. The only advantage to using your old bank is that it is familiar with your mortgage and can deal with the paperwork more easily.

To refinance, you'll have to go through much the same procedure you went through for your original mortgage (see also "Get a Mortgage"). It will be quicker, though, because you won't need the time to close the deal on the property.

Reschedule Payments

Some people refinance in order to have cheaper monthly mortgage payments. Other people refinance so they can shorten the length of the loan repayment at the same monthly cost. Consider what works best for your finances when you decide whether to reschedule or not.

Buying and Selling with Classified Ads

There is a subtle art to classified advertisements. Buyers and sellers alike enter a world of creative descriptors designed to catch the eye and the wallet. Here's how to get the best deal.

Advertise in the best place. The local newspaper is always good for a wide variety of sale items, but also consider publications that specialize in what you are selling—one you know is read by people likely to be interested in your item. If you are selling a computer, consider a computer publication; if a car, then an auto magazine. Take into account how often an issue comes out; a monthly publication will take longer to print your ad but will stay on the newsstands longer than a weekly. Also consider new electronic bulletin boards available through computer on-line services. These can be widely read, and ads are inexpensive to post. If you are looking to buy, also hunt for sources off the beaten track like newsletters and trade publications where information and services are often exchanged. The best ads and leads often appear there.

Determine the section or category to place the ad under. Most times this is apparent—apartment rentals go in the real estate section; employment offers go in the help wanted section. Nevertheless, selecting a category is crucial to getting your ad seen by the right people. If you are looking to buy, read any category that may be connected to the item or service you want— don't narrow your focus, or you might miss out on a good deal.

Find out the cost. Publications often charge for classified ads by the amount of space used, and measure it by the number of characters (letters, spaces, punctuation marks), words, or lines in the ad. The charge should specify how often the ad will appear (once, every day for one week, once a week for two weeks). If you are buying, or applying for a job, look to see whether the ad is repeated or run only once for clues to the seller or employer's success in placing the item or hiring for the position.

Write out the ad. If you are charged by the character, write economically. Use abbreviations suggested by the publication running the ad. Read other ads to get ideas on how to position your ad competitively. Include all relevant contact information. Some publications offer mail boxes for responses so you don't have to give out personal information.

Turn in the ad. Mail, phone or fax your ad to get the quickest insertion date. Consider when you'd like the ad to run, and for how long.

Reading classified ads. Know the lingo. Whether you are looking to adopt a pet, rent an apartment, or buy a bicycle, determine the "code" of ad-speak. Read between the lines to get a working idea of what is *really* being offered. The more ads you study, the better you'll get at cracking the code.

Negotiate. Always arrange to see the item offered. Have it inspected or appraised by a third party, if appropriate. Make your own offer—don't rely on the ad's asking price. Use common sense; don't give out personal information over the phone, and never go to someone's home alone. Avoid being scammed; keep your radar up.

If you are responding to an ad for employment or looking for a service, don't hesitate to compare your needs, schedule, and skills with those of the employer or provider. Explore criteria for the most advantageous situation for both parties.

Happy hunting!

Research a Stock

Playing the stock market is a gamble. There's no sure-fire way to invest money that will guarantee you a profit. But while deciding which stocks are best to buy is ultimately a guess, there are strategies that can allow you to make it at least an educated guess. Here are several things you can do to mitigate some of the risk.

What to Look For

Consider growth industries. Some industries will become more important in years to come, and others less important. Think of the new technologies and materials needed to make these products. A company in a growing industry is more likely to gain in profitability, whereas companies in obsolete industries will diminish in profits.

Look for companies that are growing through mergers and diversification. Companies can also grow and become more profitable by gaining interests in new industries or by acquiring other companies. But watch out for companies that seem erratic or reckless in their growth.

Consider long-term profitability. While some companies may make moves to gain a quick growth spurt, others with slow but steady growth will often prove more gratifying—that is, unless you want to make a quick buck and get out fast. But again, you also risk losing more that way.

Where to Get Information

Newspapers. Most major newspapers have a business section that will give you news and list the previous day's stock market activity. Some newspapers are geared mostly toward business, like the *Wall Street Journal*. If you're watching a particular company, keep track of its stocks over an extended period to determine the direction in which the company is heading. Also, be creative. You may read a story in the entertainment section about a great new film and decide to invest in the film's production company—don't limit yourselves to business news. The best foretellers of growing stocks are the people who spot trends first.

Print media and on-line services. Books such as *How to Buy Stocks* (Little, Brown and Co.) by Louis Engel and Henry R. Hecht offer in-depth advice on playing the stock market; most large bookstores will have that and other helpful books in their business section. You can also subscribe to an on-line computer service such as Reuters, Dow Jones, or Knight-Ridder that will give you up-to-the-minute business news and database information on past news. These services can be costly, but they offer the most accurate, complete, and current information available. General on-line services such as America Online and Compuserve also provide information on the stock market.

Annual reports. All major corporations publish an annual report and will be more than happy to send you one. The reports outline the company's products, profits, expenses, and objectives for the coming year. Remember, though, that these reports are written by company executives and may tend to over-accentuate the positive.

Financial analysts and stock brokers. Unless you buy stocks directly from a company, you will need a broker to handle your purchase. In addition, they will give helpful advice based on their experience, research, and business contacts. Though these financial services can be costly, a good broker can make a significant difference in the amount of money you make in the stock market.

Research a Mutual Fund

As an alternative to speculating directly in the stock market, you may want to consider investing your money in a mutual fund. Mutual funds behave like companies whose assets consist entirely of stocks (and/or bonds) bought with the money of its investors, from which it manages and pays dividends. The advantage to mutual funds over stocks bought directly is safety: where one stock may fail, many stocks in a well-diversified portfolio are not likely to fail at once. Also, investors benefit from the experience and resources of the fund managers. The disadvantage of a mutual fund, though, is that the potential for profit is smaller and slower than with a single hot stock because a booming stock in a mutual fund portfolio will be counterbalanced by other lagging stocks, keeping profits even. Still, a good mutual fund should be able to double your initial investment in five to ten years with relative ease. There are thousands of mutual funds in existence, and choosing the best one for you can be difficult. Before you invest, be sure you know as much as possible about the fund.

Evaluate Your Goals and Strategies

Before you invest, have a clear idea of what you want in an investment: extra money? a retirement fund? a college fund? This will help you decide whether or not you will invest money regularly, how much money you will invest, and whether you will take dividends or reinvest profits.

Decide on Load or No-Load

There are two ways to invest into a mutual fund: through a broker or directly. If you use a broker, you will be charged a commission, called a sales load, that can be as high as 8.5 percent of your total investment. Don't buy into a load fund if you plan only a short-term investment—you won't even make back the commission cost. No-load funds charge no commission and are generally just as safe an investment as funds with loads. Most have a toll-free number and must be called directly. Beware: some no-load funds are actually low-load (2 percent to 3 percent) or charge extra administrative fees.

Get a Prospectus

When you call a mutual fund's 800 number, ask for a brochure, or prospectus, that provides detailed information on the fund. Read the prospectus to learn about a fund's rules, objectives, investment strategy and philosophy, and fees and expenses; the diversification of its portfolio; and most importantly its track record over the last decade.

Consult Other Sources

Forbes magazine rates funds in August, *Barron's* issues a quarterly guide, and publications like *Money*, *Kiplinger's*, and *Morningstar* track funds in every issue. Also, the American Association of Individual Investors puts out a guide to no-load funds, and daily newspapers usually provide some mutual fund coverage.

In your research, pay attention to these issues:

Philosophy. Find out whether a fund looks for stocks with potentials for quick income, steady growth, or a combination of both, and whether the fund has a specialty (such as foreign companies, technologies, metals, or environmentally safe companies).

Close-ended/open-ended. Close-ended funds have a fixed capitalization, and so are closed to new investors. Open-ended funds have no limit, so its shares are always fluctuating.

Performance. Check the performance figures of the fund over one, three, five, and ten years to see whether it has grown steadily and has remained stable in a down market. Look at the change in share price, or net asset value (NAV), and the total return on investment, which also takes into consideration reinvestment and capital gains.

Fees. Besides the traditional load, there are a number of other charges that may arise. A *back-end load* is a charge for selling shares of a fund. A *deferred load* is sometimes charged if you sell before a specified time, while a *reinvestment load* is a commission charge for reinvesting. *Hidden loads* cover the advertising and marketing fees of the fund, and *management fees* take between 0.5 percent and 1 percent to pay for the fund manager.

Size. A big fund is advantageous because of the lower administrative costs per investor, but it may miss out on small investments that pay off big. A small fund, though, may be a sign of a lack of success.

Prospects. If the fund specializes in one area, such as health care, consider the future of that business.

Management. If a fund has been successful in the past, see that the same manager is still with the fund. Keep in mind that larger and more prestigious parent companies tend to attract the best managers.

Family of funds. Some funds are part of a group of funds an investor can switch back and forth between. This is beneficial, particularly if each fund has a different specialty.

Turnover. A high turnover of assets can mean the manager is looking for fast gains or that the manager is scurrying to cover mistakes. High turnover rates will also mean high commissions and higher capital gains taxes for you.

Volatility. Risk is measured by the difference between the beta values of the fund and stock market. The market's beta value is always 1.0. If a fund has a beta value of 1.5, it will be 50 percent more volatile than the market; if 1.25, then 25 percent more.

See also "Research a Stock" and "Set Up an IRA."

Prepare Tax Returns for the IRS

April 15 comes all too soon every year for most of us. Avoid the pain of the last-minute rush by advance planning. File an extension if you must—but remember that if you owe taxes, you'll be paying an interest charge on the amount owed for late filing. Use these strategies to make filing easier.

✓ Investigate the many computerized programs available for preparing tax returns. The most valuable feature of such a program is its interview function. Programs use your answers to figure out which schedules or deductions you may be able to rely upon and flags appropriate entries in the tax return itself. Programs also supply relevant definitions and offer advice. This advice does not, however, take the place of an accountant's expert consultation.

✓ Keep good records during the year. Avoid a day-long scramble to find records and analyze them.

✓ If you know you will receive a refund, file early. If you know you'll have to pay, file in April.

✓ Plan for quarterly estimated payments by opening a special savings account devoted only to tax payments and social security withholding. Never dip into these funds for other purposes.

✓ Electronic filing can speed up refunds by as much as two to three weeks.

✓ Consult an accountant about any special deductions you may qualify for, such as moving expenses, owning a home, rent credits, and deduction for dependents.

✓ Open an IRA. This deduction can save you taxes every year and allow you to build for your retirement as well.

✓ Don't be afraid to call the IRS directly for advice. Conversations are confidential and won't increase your chances of an audit.

✓ Make sure all information is entered correctly and legibly. Mistakes can affect the processing of your return and may become a red flag for an audit.

✓ Remember that any regular employee of your household, such as a nanny or a housekeeper, must be reported to the IRS by both employer and employee.

To Avoid or Prepare for an Audit

✓ Save all receipts, especially for unusual deductions or large purchases.

✓ Keep logs for income not covered by a paycheck, such as tip logs for waitpersons.

✓ Keep logs for travel and entertainment expenses, complete with person, company, date, and reason for the meeting. Keep mileage logs if you use your car for business purposes.

✓ Check with your accountant regarding red-flag line items for an audit. Don't ask to be audited by filing in a high-risk category, such as deducting for home office space when you have a full-time job away from home.

Simple Mathematical Formulas

Circumference

Circle: diameter × π (approximately 3.1416, or 22/7)

Polygon: add the lengths of all sides

Area

Circle: radius squared × π

Triangle: ½ × base × height

Rectangle (square also): length × width

Trapezoid: base × height

Regular pentagon (all sides same length): length of side × 1.720

Regular hexagon: length of side × 2.598

Regular octagon: length of side × 4.828

Cube: length of side squared × 6

Surface of a solid: length × width of each side added together

Cylinder: height × circumference of base + radius of base squared × π

Sphere: diameter squared × π

Ellipse: long diameter × short diameter × .7854

Volume

Rectangular solid (cube also): length × width × height

Pyramid: area of base × height × ⅓

Cylinder: radius of base squared × height × π

Cone: radius of base squared × height × π × ⅓

Sphere: radius cubed × π × ⅘

Other

Pythagorean theorem: the hypotenuse squared equals sum of the square of the other two sides

Einstein's mass/energy equation: $E = MC^2$

Rate of motion: distance × time

Percentages: $\% = \frac{x}{100}$

Logarithms: log(ab) = log a + log b

Imaginary numbers: $i = \sqrt{-1}$

Zeno's equation: $\frac{1}{2} + \frac{1}{4} + \frac{1}{8} + \ldots = 1$

Tell the Worth of a Diamond

The best way to judge a diamond's worth is to understand what makes it desirable. Four main criteria determine a diamond's quality and value.

Weight

Carats and points. A carat is a measure of a diamond's weight (not to be confused with karat, the measure of gold's purity). One carat equals 200 milligrams. Points are more specific measures of diamond weight; there are 100 points in one carat.

Approximating weight by size. Carats are often approximated by size, on a diamond template. The logic is that two diamonds of the same size will be about the same weight. This is fine for general measurements but may not be accurate. Sometimes a bigger diamond actually weighs less. For exact weight, make sure you use a diamond scale.

Judging by carat. The heavier diamond is not necessarily better. For instance, a diamond can lose half its weight in cutting, but the cut will make it more valuable. In truth, while carat may be the first thing you hear about a diamond, weight may be the least important consideration in determining a diamond's worth. Still, recognize that in general, the heavier the diamond, the more it will be worth.

Color

Importance of color. With most diamonds, the less color the better. A completely colorless diamond is the most valuable; most diamonds are yellowish in varying degrees.

Color scales. Judging color is always somewhat subjective, so be careful. There are many systems for grading color; the most widely used was created by the Gemological Institute of America (GIA). According to this system, a D grade is the best (completely colorless), followed by E, F, and so on to Z, which is worst (clearly a yellow tint).

Fancy stones. Besides diamonds that are white and yellowish, some rare diamonds are red, orange, green, blue, pink, or other colors. If a diamond is clearly and naturally colored it can be very valuable (the Hope diamond, one of the most valuable diamonds in the world, is blue). Diamonds can also be artificially colored. While this is legitimate for decorative purposes and may raise the price slightly, do not confuse true fancy stones for false ones. Artificially colored diamonds will not be worth nearly as much as true fancy stones.

Judging color. To help judge color, the GIA sells master sets, which contain examples of each common grade letter (E through I). Master sets are expensive, but some dealers have them. Other dealers use a color set of fake diamonds; these are less expensive but also slightly less reliable. When viewing a diamond for color, make sure you have a good, clean light source. To get the best view, look through the bottom of the diamond (it should not be set in jewelry) against a white background and next to a master set.

What to buy. The best color of diamond to buy depends on you. D grades are best for investment purposes, but they are also the most expensive. For wearing, you may decide you don't like colorless diamonds or that they are not worth the price. Anything lower than K grade is probably not a good buy. Never buy a diamond solely because of its color, no matter what the grade.

Clarity

Importance of clarity. Imperfections in the clarity of a diamond always make the diamond less valuable because they affect the way light is reflected in the stone. Perfect clarity and brilliance are the ideal.

Types of imperfections. The main types of imperfections are inclusions and blemishes. Inclusions can be cloudy spots, small cracks inside the diamond called feathers, small white dots called pinpoints, or crystals that either stick out of the diamond surface or are trapped inside called knots. Blemishes include scratches, pits (indentations on the surface), abrasions (chips on the edges), and percussion marks (bruises).

Judging clarity. Just about every diamond has some sort of imperfection, though some flaws are more noticeable than others. How much an imperfection reduces the value depends on how big the flaw is, how many flaws there are, and how the flaws affect the brilliance. Very noticeable flaws should be avoided. If a diamond has no visible imperfections when viewed under 10 × magnification it is said to be perfect. Truly perfect diamonds are very rare and quite expensive.

Clarity scale. The most widely used system for judging clarity was devised by the GIA and uses these letters: IF, internally flawless; VVS1 and VVS2, very very slightly imperfect; VS1 and VS2, very slightly imperfect; SI1 and SI2, slightly imperfect; I1, I2, or I3, imperfect. Diamonds graded past VS2 are probably not a good investment, though they may still make nice jewelry.

Cut

What it means. Cut refers to the shape, the size of facets, and the geometric proportions of the diamond. The work of the diamond cutter determines the "make." Because craftsmanship often determines a diamond's brilliance and attractiveness, much of a diamond's value depends on its cut. But while cut is the most important consideration, it is also the most difficult for a novice to judge.

The brilliant cut. The most common diamond cut is the brilliant cut, which looks like a flattened pyramid on top of an inverted pyramid. The ideal brilliant cut is designed to bring out the maximum brilliance of the stone. But not all diamonds are cut according to the ideal, partially because not everyone agrees it is actually the best cut, and partially because some cutters opt for a larger stone over a better proportioned one.

Other cuts. Diamonds can be found in other shapes, including the emerald cut (rectangular), the princess cut (squarish), and pear shape, oval, heart shape, or marquise (long and rounded).

Judging cut. When viewing for cut, look for a well-balanced diamond that captures the most light. Watch out for diamonds that have been repolished to hide imperfections; unless each facet has been polished equally, repolishing will throw off the balance of the stone. Look for diamonds that are not too deep or too shallow, or that have too wide a girdle (the thin side edge); these characteristics will all negatively affect light reflection.

When Shopping

✓ Watch out for fakes, such as cubic zirconia or pyrite. Ultimately, only an expert can tell a real from a fake, so go only to reputable dealers.

✓ Check on a dealer by calling the Better Business Bureau or the Securities and Exchange Commission.

✓ Look for the AGS certification on the windows of reputable dealers.

✓ When buying a diamond as an investment, ask to see the diamond's GIA certificate. The certificate will give reliable grades for color and clarity, plus the weight and dimensions of the diamond (it will not tell the price, though). Keep in mind, that not all diamonds have certificates, and a diamond that is certified is not necessarily better than one that isn't. For $50 to $100 you can have the diamond certified by a GIA-recognized gemologist.

✓ When buying a diamond, ask the dealer to give you a guarantee (either a money-back guarantee or some other assurance) that the diamond is worth what you are paying for it. Remember, that diamond prices will vary tremendously depending on where you buy it. Jewelry stores, for instance, may be a little more expensive than a private dealer because of store rent and employee salaries.

Quickly Compute Sales Tax

Know how to figure out the sales tax on an item before you pay. Sales tax varies from state to state.

Multiply the price of the item by the percent sales tax and move the decimal point two places to the left.

6 percent sales tax on $10: 6 × $10 = $60; move decimal point two places to the left; sales tax is .60, or 60 cents.

Figuring 5 Percent Sales Tax

Cut the price in half and move decimal point one place to the left.

5 percent sales tax on $15: Half of $15 is $7.50; move decimal one place to the left; sales tax is .75, or 75 cents.

Approximating 7 Percent and 8 Percent Sales Tax

Figure out 5 percent sales tax (above) and add half of that to itself. This will give you 7.5 percent, from which you can approximate 7 percent or 8 percent.

7 percent sales tax on $15. From the above calculations, we know the 5 percent sales tax is 75 cents. Half of that is about 37 cents, added to 75 cents gives us $1.12. This is slightly more than the actual 7 percent, which is $1.05.

Figuring 10 Percent Sales Tax

Move the decimal point of total cost one place to the left.

Ten percent sales tax on $14: Move decimal place on $14 to get sales tax, or $1.40.

See also "Simple Mathematical Formulas."

Compute Simple Interest

When you borrow money, it is important to know whether the interest is simple or compound. Depending on the size of the loan, the difference can amount to a lot of money. Simple interest is a set percentage of the total loan, whereas compound interest accrues at a higher rate over time because interest is charged on the interest of the unpaid money. For the borrower, simple interest is not only kinder to the wallet, but easier on the brain. Here's how to calculate simple interest, and a quick reference chart for figuring the simple interest on $1,000.

1. Multiply the principal (the original amount of the loan) by the annual interest rate. Remember, when you multiply percentages you must convert the number into a decimal; for instance, 5 percent becomes .05; 25 percent becomes .25. The number you come up with will be the amount of interest you pay on the loan per year.

2. Multiply the interest per year from Step 1 by the time period to repay the loan. Time should be calculated in terms of years; for instance, 6 months is .5 years, and 24 months is 2 years. The number you get will be the total amount of interest owed beyond the repayment of the principal.

Simple interest on $1,000:

	5%	6%	7%	8%	9%	10%	15%	20%
6 months	$25	$30	$35	$40	$45	$50	$75	$100
1 year	50	60	70	80	90	100	150	200
2 years	100	120	140	160	180	200	300	400
5 years	250	300	350	400	450	500	750	1,000

Compute Compound Interest

Unlike simple interest, compound interest requires you to pay interest on the interest already accrued and compounded regularly. The longer the loan is outstanding, the higher the annual interest becomes.

Calculating Compound Interest

Because compound interest is cumulative, you must know the interest on the previous period to figure it out for the current period. We'll assume the interest period is one year (compounded annually), though interest can be compounded quarterly (every three months) or over some other period.

For the first year, compound interest has not yet had time to accumulate, so it will be identical to simple interest.

To figure out compound interest for subsequent years, first add the interest from the previous year to the principal (the original amount), then multiply the sum by the interest rate. Next, add that product to the interest from the previous year to get the new compounded interest.

Compound Interest on $1,000 Compounded Annually

	5%	7%	9%	10%	15%
1 year	$50.00	$70.00	$90.00	$100.00	$150.00
2 years	102.50	144.90	188.10	210.00	322.50
5 years	276.30	402.60	538.60	610.50	1,011.36

Compare the interest on $1,000 after 25 years at 15 percent:

Simple interest: $3,750

Compound interest (compounded annually): $ 31,918.91

14. Outdoors

Make a Stone Wall

What You Need
- ✓ Heavy-duty work gloves
- ✓ Goggles (to wear if you chisel rocks)
- ✓ Wheelbarrow
- ✓ Sledge hammer
- ✓ Cold-tempered chisel
- ✓ Shovel
- ✓ Powdered chalk or twine and stakes
- ✓ Crushed rock or stones (for base layer)
- ✓ Rocks (for wall)

Prepare the Site
1. Separate the wall rocks into piles:
   - ✓ The squarest, flattest, most regular
   - ✓ The rounder, irregular stones that may need cutting
   - ✓ Small, wedge-shaped stones to use as shims
2. Mark the length and placement of the wall with twine or powdered chalk.
3. Dig a flat trench approximately one foot below the soil level along the site line.

Build the Wall
1. Fill the trench approximately 6" deep with crushed rocks or stones and tamp down. This provides drainage and stability.
2. The bottom of the wall should be 4" to 6" wider than the top for stability. Lay the largest stones on the tamped gravel in the trench. Dig the trench deeper to accommodate larger stones and to keep the top as level and straight as possible.

3. For greater stability with successive layers of stone, use a two-over-one and one-over-two technique: place stones over the joints in the layer below (Figure 1).

4. Place a cross-bond stone—one that is as long as the width of the wall—every few feet to prevent separation of back and front facing stones (Figure 2).

5. Place riser stones—ones that are twice as thick as the other stones—every few feet to help knit the wall together (Figure 3).

Figure 1. One-over-two method

Figure 2. Cross-bond stones

Figure 3. Riser stones

6. Each stone should sit solidly on the stones below it. If it wobbles, try turning it around, use a different stone, or use a small stone shim to secure the stone, placing it toward the inside of the wall so it doesn't pop out.

7. If your wall will have a corner, use stones with three or more flat sides for the corner. Make sure all joints overlap and interlock for stability.

8. Use flat, heavy stones that are as wide as the wall for capstones—the top layer. Fit them together snugly so that they do not dislodge from movement, frost, or ice.

Where Do You Get Stones?

✓ Your backyard
✓ A construction site
✓ Near an old wall or foundation, stream or lake shore, empty fields
✓ From an excavation or landscape contractor
✓ Sources listed under "Stone" in the Yellow Pages

Note: If you collect stones from a place other than your own yard, be sure to ask permission from the person who owns the property!

How to Cut a Stone

1. Use a cold-tempered chisel and sledgehammer, and wear goggles.

2. Score a groove ½" deep along the grain of the stone if possible.

3. Cut by one of these methods:
   ✓ Lift one end and strike the groove with a sledgehammer.
   ✓ Lay the stone on a bed of sand and strike the groove with a sledgehammer.
   ✓ Place an angle iron beneath the stone and strike it from the top with a sledgehammer.

Trim a Hedge

✓ Use hedge shears to clip small-leaved shrubs, or pruning shears for long-leaved shrubs.
✓ Power trimmers work best on young short shoots; make sure your trimmer is powerful enough to cut woody branches cleanly.
✓ Stretch a line between two stakes to mark the height you wish to trim your hedge.
✓ To encourage a thick base, taper the sides of the hedge toward the top.

Informal Hedges

✓ Clip back newly planted hedges by one-third.
✓ If the hedge blooms on the previous season's shoots, trim the hedge after it flowers; if it blooms on the current season's shoots, trim it in the spring.

Formal Hedges

✓ Trim the hedge by one-third after planting to encourage thick growth.

✓ Trim by one-half to one-third of the new growth each year until the hedge reaches the desired height.

✓ Maintain the desired height by trimming back new growth each year.

✓ If the hedge grows rapidly, trim it two or three times each year in the spring and summer.

Consider These Hedge Plants . . .

. . . but first check for their hardiness in your locale and find out whether they thrive in sun or shade.

Deciduous Plants	Evergreen Plants	Flowering Plants
Barberry	Arborvitae	Camellia
Beech	Boxwood	Cherry laurel
Buckthorn	Bush cherry	Forsythia
Forsythia	Cotoneaster	Fuschia
Fuchsia	Fire thorn	Flowering quince
Hawthorne	Hebe	Flowering plum
Hornbeam	Hemlock	Lilac
Mock orange	Holly	Mock orange
Privet	Honeysuckle	Peegee hydrangea
Quince	Leyland cypress	Rose
Rose	Oleander	Rose-of-Sharon
Willow	Yew	Spireas

Make a Garden Plan

Before you begin planting, take a close look at your home and yard, and think about how you would like your landscape to look. Landscaping is an investment, one that will grow and change over time, so it's important to consider not only how it will look now but what it will look like years from now.

1. Examine your yard from the outside, as well as the views from the windows of your home.

2. Photograph your property and use the pictures to make notes and plan your design.

3. Using graph paper, draw an outline of your home and property to scale (e.g., 1 inch = 10 feet). Mark the location of your home's doors, windows, water spigots, electrical outlets, utility boxes, air conditioners, and roof overhangs. Add the driveway, walkways, patio, fences, and the location of above- and below-ground utilities.

4. Overlay the drawing with tissue paper on which to draw your landscape plans and make notes.

5. Begin planning your garden by thinking about what you want your garden to accomplish and how you want it to look. Do you want lots of flowering plants? Do you prefer evergreens to leaf-bearing trees? Do you want a vegetable or herb garden? Do you envision a seasonal garden or one in constant bloom?

6. Do you want a formal or informal garden? Formal gardens are symmetrical, with straight edges, neatly trimmed hedges and plants, and carefully maintained beds. They clearly show the control you or your landscaper has over the garden, and they require much maintenance to keep them looking manicured. In contrast, informal gardens are asymmetrical, with curving lines and natural instead of trimmed, controlled growth.

7. Decide how to use trees and shrubs to separate areas, create borders, and hide elements you don't want to be visible.

8. Be sure to plan for nonliving elements: fences; pools; brooks or fountains; bird baths, houses, and feeders; walkways, benches, a gazebo, and so on.

Labor-Saving Tips

✓ Use a solid 6" to 8" border such as concrete, bricks, or railroad ties around your lawn for easy trimming and a neat look.
✓ Keep hedges low so they are more convenient to trim.
✓ Plant beds that are narrow enough to reach in for weeding.
✓ Border your beds for neatness.
✓ Create paths in your garden. They will make it easier for you to roll a garden cart or wheelbarrow through and to get around your garden for weeding and planting.
✓ Remember that rock gardens and perennial borders require greater maintenance.
✓ Install an underground sprinkler system for convenient watering.

Tips for Choosing Plants

✓ Mark the plants you want to use in various areas on your garden plan graph.
✓ Make a chart of your plant choices, then research them for appropriateness to your location, maintenance, size and growth rate, color and blooming times, and pest resistance and whether they are poisonous. (This is important if you have pets!)
✓ Make sure your selections fit your climate, the amount of sun and shade in the area where you wish to plant them, the amount of water they need, and the type and pH balance of your soil.
✓ Consider the appearance and care of your plants throughout the seasons, particularly in areas where there are marked seasonal changes in climate.

See also "Keep Flowers Longer," "Arrange Flowers," and "Care for Houseplants."

Keep Squirrels Off the Bird Feeder

✓ Position your bird feeder at least 10 feet from branches or a fence to prevent squirrels from jumping onto it.

✓ Hang your bird feeder from wire stretched between two poles or trees.

✓ Use a squirrel guard: before you fasten your tray feeder to a person-height metal pole, slide a metal cone, 18" in diameter, midway on the pole facing downward.

The Predator Slide

1. Before you fasten the feeder to a pole, slip on a piece of PVC overlay pipe 18" in length. The inside diameter of the pipe should be at least ¼" larger than the pole to fit properly.

2. Fasten a screw eye at the top edge of the pipe.

3. Attach a pulley to a nearby tree or another pole that is the same height as the feeder pole.

4. Run wire or monofilament through the screw eye and pulley. The wire should be long enough to allow the overlay pipe to slide down the pole to the ground.

5. Attach the wire to a counterweight that weighs 1 to 2 ounces more than the overlay pipe.

6. When a squirrel reaches the overlay pipe, its weight will cause the pipe to slide down toward the ground. When the squirrel jumps off the pipe, the counterweight will pull the overlay pipe back into position on the pole (Figure 1).

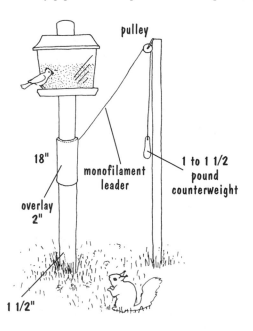

Figure 1. The Predator Slide

Identify Trees

Like birdwatching, identifying trees is a fun, educational activity you can enjoy outdoors, especially for those who hike for recreation and exercise. While over 750 different kinds of trees can be found in North America, identifying them is not as difficult as it may seem once you become familiar with common tree types and learn some basic facts about trees. A good guide book will help to start you off.

When to Go

Nearly any time of year is suitable for tree identification outings. In spring, you witness the often beautiful opening of buds and flowers. In summer, trees are in full bloom and you can study the fully grown leaves and flowers. In autumn, fruits mature and the leaves of some trees change colors and fall. In winter, many trees are bare; this is a good time to observe bark and twigs.

Where to Go

Though certain areas of the country are more heavily populated with trees than others, it's likely that no matter where you are, you are close to many trees. State and national parks are often good for hiking, but nearly any wooded area with marked paths is suitable.

How to Look

Once you become familiar with trees, you'll be able to identify common types simply at a glance, based on their form and shape. For other trees, you must get closer to observe their characteristics more precisely. When examining a tree, collect as much information as possible. Note the size, shape, and type (evergreen or deciduous, broadleaf or conifer) of the tree. Get samples of twigs, leaves, flowers, fruits, or bark to help in identification. Consult a tree guide.

What to Look For

Trees can be distinguished from a bush or shrub because they have only a single trunk and grow over 15 feet tall. The most common types of trees found in the United States are broadleaves (or hardwoods) and conifers. Examine each part of the tree, including the following:

Leaves. There are several basic leaf shapes; observe the size, shape, texture, and color of many leaves on the tree, and note how they are arranged on the branchlet. Conifers are usually evergreen (leaves stay on the tree year round) and their leaves tend to be either sharp and needlelike or scaly. Broadleaves can be either evergreen or deciduous (leaves fall in autumn); the leaves vary widely in shape but are usually flat and veined (Figure 1).

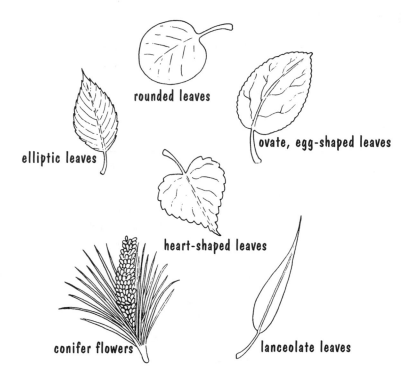

Figure 1. Common leaf shapes

Flowers. Many flowers are made up of petals, stigmas, and anthers, but they vary greatly in size and shape. Conifer flowers do not have petals and are either male (releasing powdery pollen) or female (colorful and ornate); broadleaf flowers are usually bisexual (having male and female parts in each flower) and have petals. Note where the flowers are located; they will often be small and high up.

Fruits. Fruits develop from flowers and come in many forms, including pines, acorns, nuts, berries, and pods as well as the familiar fruits we eat. Most conifers have scaly cones for fruits or a seed with a berrylike coating; broadleaves have a variety of fruits, including the edible fruits. Fruits may be high up on the tree and out of reach; look also on the ground for fruits that have fallen.

Bark. Trees develop bark patterns as they grow, so look only at mature trees when examining the bark. Young trees will not have fully developed bark patterns. Bark may be rough or smooth, ridged or scaly, and with horizontal or vertical lines.

Twigs and branches. These are good for examining in winter, when leaves, flowers, and fruits may be absent. Leaves and buds leave distinct scars on branches, twigs, and shoots that can help you identify the tree.

See also "Birdwatch."

Pitch a Tent

Readymade tents come in many different shapes and sizes designed to accommodate your particular needs. Like all tents, they are made of a waterproof tarp for shelter and have poles and stakes to the support the structure. Most readymade tents will come with instructions for how to erect them. While these tents are easy to use and are sure to provide adequate shelter, you may not always have access to one when you need it. When a makeshift tent is required, it is possible to construct a basic shelter structure on your own with only a few materials. Here's how to do it.

Materials

You will need a piece of strong, waterproof tarp, the size of the tarp depending on how large you want to make your tent. For a one-person tent you will need at least a 8' × 9' piece for the roof, front, and back, while a two-person tent should be at least 12' × 12' (Figure 1). Try to find tarp that has rope holes—or better yet, ropes already attached—along the edges so you can tie the tarp to the ground. In addition, you may want another piece of tarp (about 3' × 6' for one person, 5' × 6' for two) to function as a floor, though this is not absolutely necessary if you are really roughing it. Instead, you can use a blanket or sleeping bag as a floor covering. Finally, you will need stakes to secure the tent to the ground and a good deal of strong rope for various uses.

Tools

If you have to, you can probably get away with no tools at all. But if you can arrange it, bring a hammer for driving stakes and a strong knife for cutting rope and the tarp.

Procedure

1. Cut slits in the tarp (Figure 1). If possible, do this before you leave.

2. Tie the support rope. Find two trees within 15 feet together, that have flat, dry ground between them. Tie a line of rope between the trees so the rope is pulled tightly about 3 to 4 feet above the ground. If possible, tie the rope above a branch or knot in the tree to prevent it from slipping down.

3. Drape the tarp over the rope. Lay the tarp so it is suspended by the rope through the line where you cut the slits. Both sides of the tarp should hang down and touch the ground. If the rope is not completely straight, the tarp will sag in the middle; in this case you may want to tie a pole to the rope (or run the rope through a hollow pole) and drape the tarp over the pole.

4. Tie down the tarp. Stretch out the sides of the tarp to form a triangle with the ground as the base. Then, nail the stakes into the ground a few inches outside the corners of the triangle, and use rope to tie the edges of the tarp to the stakes.

5. Form the front and back. Fold the flaps created by the slits in the tarp over each other to close up the back of the tent, then tie them with rope to seal them. Leave the front open so you can enter the tent, though you may want to tie the flaps shut at night.

6. Lay the floor tarp. Once the roof is secure, you can spread out the second tarp (if you have one) on the ground inside. Lay the tarp out flat and curl up the sides if they run into the walls; this will help keep the inside dry and sealed from bugs.

7. Ditch the outside of the tent. If you expect a lot of rain to fall during the night, it may be a good idea to ditch the perimeter of the tent. This entails digging a ditch a few inches wide around the sides of the tent so that rain can run down into the ditch from the tent walls. If you are on a slight incline, also ditch whichever side is lower, the front or back.

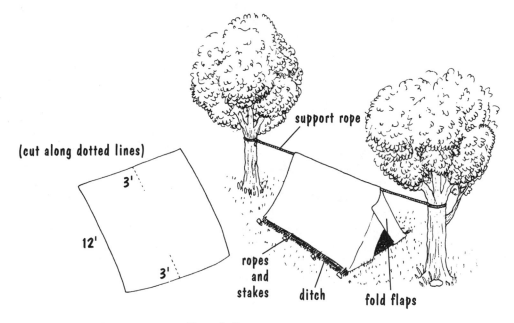

Figure 1. Two-person tent tarp

Pack for a Camping Trip

Camp smart and prepared. While it's usually better to be safe than sorry when packing, don't overload yourself with supplies. Think about the activities you'll be doing, about the weather and terrain where you are going, and about the length of the trip. Also, consider what could go wrong, and pack materials for any emergency. Here is a complete outline of the supplies you may need.

✓ Clothing. For warm weather, bring plenty of underwear, socks, cotton shirts, pants, shorts, bathing suits, light water-resistant shoes, and a light water-resistant jacket. If the weather will be cold, pack a hooded sweatshirt, sweaters, thick shirts and pants, long underwear, gloves, scarves, a wool hat, wool socks, warm boots, and a thick coat.

✓ First-aid kit (see also "Ingredients of a Good First-Aid Kit")

✓ Insect repellent

✓ Hot water bottle, and containers of fresh cold water

✓ Toiletries, towels, and wash cloths

✓ Sun glasses, sun screen, and suntan lotion

✓ Drinks such as juice or soda

✓ Canned and dried foods

✓ Cooking supplies. Plates, cups, pots, pans, utensils, can opener, cooler, foil, grill, charcoal, fire starter, matches, cutting board, detergent/disinfectant, garbage bags, paper towels/napkins

✓ Tent, with ground liner, ropes, and pegs

✓ Carrying bags, knapsacks

✓ Sleeping bags, blankets, pillows, portable air mattresses

✓ Flashlight

✓ Compass and maps

✓ Pocket knife and hatchet

✓ Canteen/thermos

✓ Duct tape

✓ Basic tool set

✓ Tire pump and spare tire

✓ Alarm clock

✓ Spare batteries

✓ Binoculars

✓ Camera/video equipment, film

✓ Radio/walkman, tapes

✓ Games, books, magazines, and writing supplies

✓ Sporting equipment for fishing, skiing, biking, canoeing

✓ Life jackets and life preservers

✓ Fire extinguisher

✓ Extra fuel for lanterns and stoves

Catch a Fish

As many a die-hard sportsperson will tell you, fishing can be both an enjoyable way to spend time outdoors and a good source of food. Few fish taste more satisfying than the ones you caught yourself. As with all outdoor sporting activities, safety is a major concern. Obey all local and state boating regulations and fish-and-game laws, as well as some common-sense rules of conduct. Watch for others if you are casting a line; don't fish where a lot of people are already fishing;

keep sharp hooks in a safe place when you are not using them. And, as ever, be kind to the environment and do not litter or exploit natural resources.

Go at the Right Time

Generally, the best times to fish are just before dawn and right after dusk, when the fish are feeding. Other occasional instances, such as during a full moon or just before a storm, can also be good times for fishing.

Go to the Right Place

If you plan to fish in a lake or river, go to shallow areas near the bank. If the weather is warm, though, fish will often stay in deeper areas or in shaded areas where the water is cool.

Know About the Fish

The more you know about the fish, the better chance you'll have of catching them. Find out what types of fish are present in a body of water, what the fish feed on, where they feed, and how deep they usually swim. Find out *before* you start.

Use the Correct Bait

Different fish prefer different types of bait, so learn the best bait for the fish you'll be trying to catch. One way to find out is to cut open a fish and check its stomach. A better bet is to just ask someone who knows. Popular baits include bugs, insects, worms, small fish, crab eggs, crayfish, cheese, and hot dogs. You may want to use an artificial look-alike bait.

Employ the Correct Style of Fishing

There are many different ways to fish. The method you choose depends on how much experience you have fishing and which type of fish you are trying to catch. Still-fishing is the simple, by-default style that requires you to stand with rod in hand and line under water waiting for a fish to bite. Other more advanced types of fishing include spin-casting, bait-casting, and fly-fishing.

Have the Proper Materials

Your method of fishing will determine the equipment you need. At its most simple, fishing requires only a line and hook, or even just a net, but to be successful you should come better prepared. Bring at least a set of hooks (various sizes), a telescoping rod, a spinning reel, and strong fishing lines, with lures, weights, and nets included as necessary. If you need a license to fish, be sure to bring it with you.

Ask Locals

The best advice about fishing in a given area will probably come from the locals. Ask the employees of the area bait-and-tackle shop, or even a friendly fellow fisherman or fisherwoman, about what to expect from the fish or the area. You'll be able to get reliable information on bait, techniques, and the best areas and times. Don't be afraid to ask; others are usually more than happy to impart their knowledge to a willing listener.

Tie 6 Knots

Knowing how to tie basic knots is essential to outdoor sports and camping. A good knot comes in handy nearly any time you don't have fastening tools—whether to tie a present, bundle firewood, or fasten a bandage. Here are drawings and descriptions of some of the most common and most useful knots.

Half hitch. A basic knot, the half hitch is used for tying one rope around an object. It is not the strongest knot, so bind the end to prevent the knot from coming undone (Figure 1).

Square knot. This knot is used for joining two ropes together or fastening objects. It is also known as a reef knot (Figure 2).

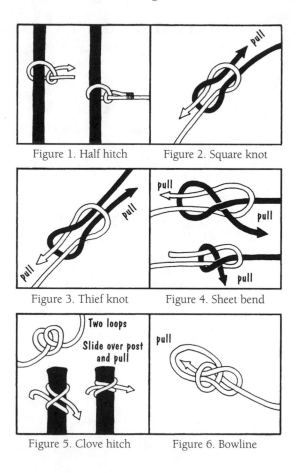

Figure 1. Half hitch Figure 2. Square knot

Figure 3. Thief knot Figure 4. Sheet bend

Figure 5. Clove hitch Figure 6. Bowline

Thief knot. This knot is the same as the square knot except that the ends of the two ropes come out on opposite sides. Because it looks so much like the square knot, sailors used this knot in the eighteenth century as a trick when tying their bags. Thieves on board would retie the bag with a square knot and thus give themselves away (Figure 3).

Sheet bend. This is another variation on the square knot, except that one rope (black) goes under itself and over the other rope. This knot is good for attaching a thick rope (white) to a thinner rope (black) (Figure 4).

Clove hitch. To attach the end of a rope to a post, two loops are made with the rope, one overhand and one underhand (Figure 5).

Bowline. To haul and lift objects with one rope, make the big loop large enough to wrap around the object, and pull the end to tighten (Figure 6).

Recognize Poison Ivy and Poison Oak

Poison ivy is the scourge of many a camping trip. This plant, which goes by the Latin name *Rhus radicans,* is a vine or shrub causing an itchy, red rash in sensitive people. Some who are extremely allergic can get the rash without actually touching the plant; they need only pet an animal that has rubbed against it or come into contact with it in some other secondhand way. Others report contracting poison ivy when it is mistakenly burned with other leaves in the fall; merely the smoke resulting from such fires can cause a flareup in the most sensitive. The rash has even been found inside the throat and on the stomach lining. Poison ivy's cousin, the shrub, poison oak (*Rhus diversiloba* or *Rhus toxicodendron*) has a similar effect, as does poison sumac (*Rhus vernix*).

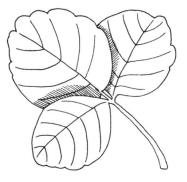

Figure 1. Poison oak

Poison ivy and poison oak are most easily recognized by their leaves, which fall off each year and are replaced by a new set (Figure 1). The leaves grow in groups of three, generally with a larger leaf in the middle and two smaller ones on either side; each have a few jagged edges, or teeth on either side. The leaves appear shiny green in spring and summer and color in the fall. Sometimes poison ivy plants will produce flowers or small gray berries.

The substance in poison ivy and poison oak that causes this uncomfortable rash is an oily compound known as urushiol. It is present in the entire plant, including the stems and roots, so beware when you are weeding. Spray the offending plant with an environment-safe herbicide to remove it from garden areas.

As with any rash, keep a poison ivy or poison oak rash as clean as possible. Sponge it clean with alcohol. Calamine lotion or another topical ointment, lotion, or salve may relieve some of the itching. Avoid contact with a rash on another person's skin, and above all, do not scratch since this only spreads the rash. In the event of severe reactions, consult your primary care physician, who may prescribe a corticosteroid drug.

When walking in the woods, keep your eyes open and your hands in your pockets. If possible, wear long pants, or at least high socks and sturdy shoes. Wear gloves if you are gardening and suspect these plants may be present.

Young children often contract the rash by running their hands through the underbrush. Stay alert!

Birdwatch

Birdwatching is an educational exercise, a healthy and environmentally conscious outdoor activity, and a challenging recreational game. The skill of finding and identifying birds in the wild is difficult to cultivate and can frustrate beginners, so don't let yourself become discouraged when you are starting out. By keeping your eyes open and your head attuned to the activity, you'll soon develop a wide knowledge of the birds in your area and evolve into an expert birdwatcher.

Tools

✓ Field guide. A dependable and easy-to-use guide to the birds in your area is the most important tool to have with you. A guide should be current and contain drawings of every bird species. Organize the book before you go by marking pages with birds found in the region, altitude, season, and habitat you are visiting. Personalize your guide book with notes and highlights.

✓ Notebook. Keep a log of all your birding excursions. Record the date, location, and habitat of the birds you identify and refer back to it for help. You may also want to take notes on a bird's characteristics and appearance, drawing a sketch if you can.

✓ Checklist. Guides often categorize birds according to family and provide information in graph or map form on the habitat and migration of birds. For guides that don't, a separate checklist will be useful as a supplementary source.

✓ Binoculars. If you plan to birdwatch regularly, invest in high-quality binoculars that are strong enough to allow long-range visibility but not so high-powered that they are difficult to handle. Look for binoculars that allow in lots of light and focus quickly and easily.

✓ Clothes. Dress appropriately according to where you are birding. Wear hiking shoes and clothes to protect you from the sun or the cold as needed.

Procedure

1. Prepare sources beforehand. Try to know something about each bird family you are likely to find. Learning a lot about one species will often tell you about other species in that bird's family.

2. Come prepared. Bring the proper tools, clothes, food, and drink.

3. Locate birds. Train your eyes to see birds far away and camouflaged by trees. When you locate a bird, study all aspects of its appearance and behavior to identify the species (Figure 1).

4. Narrow down the possibilities to identify the bird. You can eliminate 90 percent of the 700 species of birds before you even start by considering only those birds known to be present in the location, elevation, habitat, and season you are currently in. Narrow down a bird's family by inspecting such characteristics as shape, size, general behavior, and appearance of the bill, tail, and legs (for specific bird anatomy, refer to the guidebook illustration). **Family** tests are often easy, as just about anyone can tell the difference between an owl and a duck. **Species** tests, on the other hand, can be more difficult. Distinguish species by coloring, design pattern, specific behaviors, and voice. Appearance clues can be slight and difficult to see—look for eye rings, stripes, tail bands, breast streaks, and wing bars. Behavior characteristics such as flight patterns, posture, and feeding motions also reveal species. A bird's vocalization can sometimes be the best (or only) clue to its species.

5. Record your findings. Annotate your birding notebook.

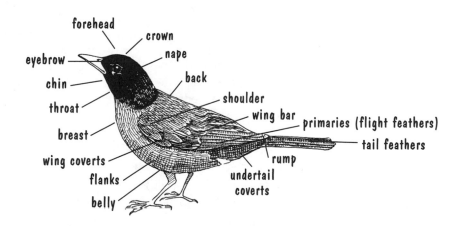

Figure 1. Anatomy of a bird

15. Parenting

Breast-Feed Your Baby

In the first few months after a baby is born, breast-feeding is one of most important things a mother can do to help in her child's development. The advantages over bottle-feeding are many, and the possible problems are few. Breast milk has been shown to reduce the chance of infection, illness, allergy, and crib death. It not only provides all the food nutrients a baby needs but also helps to build the bond between mother and child that lasts for life.

When to Breast-Feed

Begin breast-feeding almost immediately after giving birth, but wait at least until the baby is awake and alert so it will know what is going on. In general, the baby is most receptive to feeding when it is relaxed and well rested. Breast-feed the baby for about 15 minutes every two to four hours; you may vary this if you find you are over- or underfeeding the baby (if you are feeding the right amount you should have to change the baby's diapers five or six times a day). Begin feeding your baby solid food after six months, though you may want to continue breast-feeding beyond that point.

Breast-Feeding Procedure

1. Sit in a comfortable position.
2. Hold the baby in your lap, facing your breasts (Figure 1). You may want to wrap the baby so its arms are tucked in and won't get in the way.
3. Support your breast by holding it with your fingers around the areola—the darker area around the nipple.
4. Touch the nipple to the corner of your baby's mouth or cheek; this triggers a reflex that opens the baby's mouth.
5. Put the nipple into your baby's mouth so the lips wrap completely around the nipple and touch the areola.

6. Allow the baby to feed itself by sucking on the nipple, but make sure the baby's nose is free to inhale.

7. Don't allow your baby to chew on your nipple; it will cause soreness. Use a pacifier to help lessen chewing.

8. To end nursing, touch the corner of your baby's mouth with your finger; this will break the suction.

9. Do not wipe off your nipple; let it dry naturally (wiping will cause soreness).

10. Burp the baby by holding it on your shoulder and patting gently on its back until you hear one or two burps.

Figure 1. Breast-feeding position

Alternative Methods for Breast-Feeding

If for some reason you cannot breast-feed (if you will be away from your baby, for example) but you still wish to give your baby your breast milk, use a breast pump to extract milk and store it for bottle-feeding. Breast pumps are simple suction devices that draw out milk from the breast. Breast milk will keep about two days in a refrigerator, and many months if frozen. Any cooled milk should be allowed to thaw to room temperature (do not heat) before feeding. Breasts will continue to produce milk as long as you are feeding, so if you must temporarily stop breast-feeding but wish to resume, you must squeeze out milk regularly. Always have formula available in case problems occur.

Diet and Health While Breast-Feeding

To provide healthy milk for your baby, you must be healthy as well. Stay away from alcohol, drugs, and cigarettes while breast-feeding (as during pregnancy), and consult a doctor before taking any medications. Try to be relaxed and well rested, as difficult as that may be when you are caring for a newborn. Eat well, increasing your intake of calories and protein. Drink more water and milk than usual. Incidentally, some food flavors show up in breast milk a few hours after eating. If your baby displays a distaste for a particular flavor, you may want to stop eating that food.

Possible Breast-Feeding Problems

Women do not usually encounter serious problems with breast-feeding, but occasionally difficulties arise. Nipple soreness is common for the first few days but will usually go away.

If your breasts become red and tender and you feel as though you have the flu, you may have a breast infection. While this is not likely to be serious, see your doctor immediately for treatment.

If your breasts hurt and feel swollen, they may be too full; this could be a sign that you need to nurse more or else just squeeze some milk out.

A nursing bra is helpful for support while you are breast-feeding; a pad set in the bra will absorb leaks from the nipples.

Inadequate milk production may mean that you need to supplement feeding with formula.

Some babies experience breast milk jaundice, a yellowish discoloration of the skin and eyes, and may need to stop breast-feeding though perhaps only temporarily. Infants with a cleft palate or lip may also experience difficulty breast-feeding.

A change from breast milk to formula is not a sign of failure. Don't feel guilty about it, and do continue to nurture and bond with your baby.

For Further Information

To start with questions about breast-feeding, ask friends and relatives who have been through the experience. For more technical information, consult your doctor or La Leche, an organization dedicated to providing information on breast-feeding and related issues.

> La Leche International
> 9616 Minneapolis
> P.O. Box 1209
> Franklin Park, IL 60131
> 312-455-7730

Pack a Hospital Bag for Childbirth

Before the final weeks of your pregnancy, pack a bag of items to bring to the hospital with you when you go into labor. Bring objects that may come in handy before, during, and after you give birth. While many of these things are available at the hospital, you will appreciate the convenience of not having to ask nurses and friends to fetch simple items that will add to your comfort. Keep the bag near the door or in your car to make sure you don't forget it when the time comes.

✓ Food, particularly for your partner or friends who may be waiting at your side for a long time. Bottled water and crackers are a good idea.
✓ Manual for childbirth, if you have used one
✓ Travel pillow for extra comfort
✓ Towels to keep you cool and dry
✓ Talcum powder for rashes
✓ Ice pack, heating pad, and/or tennis balls (as massagers) for back pain
✓ Small ice cubes, a clean sponge, and/or lemon slices to suck on in case of a dry mouth
✓ Lip balm or petroleum jelly to keep lips moist
✓ Portable room fan to keep you cool
✓ Socks and extra blankets to keep you warm
✓ Small paper bag in case of hyperventilation
✓ Comforting object, such as a teddy bear or a favorite picture to focus on during labor pains
✓ Music with a tape recorder to soothe you during labor
✓ Camera and film to take pictures of the baby
✓ Nightgown or pajamas for your hospital stay
✓ Comfortable shoes, slippers, or sneakers, for walking during labor
✓ Toiletries for your stay
✓ Change of clothing for leaving the hospital
✓ Baby clothes for the baby's first ride home
✓ Car seat to hold the baby during the ride

Diaper a Baby

As any mother will tell you, putting a diaper on a baby is the easy part—it's cleaning up beforehand that's a challenge. Still, for whatever unpleasantness there may be, you don't need to be a genius to change a diaper. Just remember to be as gentle as possible, and follow these directions.

Cloth Diapers

Before the invention of disposable diapers, cloth diapers were the only diapers. While they are fairly uncommon today, they are currently experiencing a comeback of sorts because cloth diapers are reusable and therefore kinder to the environment—not to mention more economical. Check to see whether a diaper service is available in your area for washing and supplying clean diapers. Here's how to use cloth diapers:

1. Remove the panties and soiled diaper. Lay the baby on its back on a towel or blanket. Take off the plastic panties that usually cover cloth diapers, then undo the safety pin that holds the diaper together, and remove the diaper from the baby.

2. Wash the baby. With a soft and wet cloth rag or disposable baby wipe, clean the soiled area by wiping from front to back. Do not wipe too hard—you will irritate the baby's skin.

3. Treat the baby's skin. Wash the baby's bottom again with warm water and pat dry with a towel. You may want to apply lotion or baby powder to the baby's bottom to prevent irritation.

4. Prepare the new diaper. Cloth diapers are generally square. Fold the diaper to form a right triangle, and place the baby's bottom on the triangle so that the right angle is between the baby's legs and pointing to its feet.

5. Wrap and secure the diaper. Pull the point of the diaper up between the baby's legs and rest it on the baby's tummy. Wrap the other points (to the sides) around the baby's waist and use a safety pin in the center by the navel to attach all three points securely, but not too tightly, together. Use a special diaper safety pin, which has no sharp edges and is harder to undo.

6. Replace the panties. Unless the panties were also soiled, you may put the same panties back on.

7. Prepare the soiled diaper for washing. Flush any solid waste down the toilet. Rinse the soiled diaper under a faucet to get it as clean as possible. Place the diaper with other soiled diapers in a covered bucket, and wash them together when they've accumulated.

Disposable Diapers

Most people agree that disposable diapers are easier and more pleasant to use than cloth. You can buy them in the store in large packages, throw them away as they are soiled, and buy more when you run out. They are, though, both more wasteful and more expensive. The following explains how to use disposable diapers.

1. Remove the diaper. Undo the tape that secures the diaper, and remove the diaper. Place the baby on a towel or blanket.

2. Wash the baby. See Steps 2 and 3 above.

3. Place the baby on a new diaper. The disposable diaper is already fitted to wrap around the baby. Just make sure you have the correct size diaper for your baby's age. Place the baby so that the tape side of the diaper is in back.

4. Pull the diaper up between baby's legs. The diaper should now be completely wrapped around the baby.

5. Attach tape to the front. Firmly stick the tape to the smooth tape surface on the front part of the diaper, making sure that the diaper is centered on the baby's body. Be sure not to get lotion or powder on the tape, or it may lose its adhesiveness.

6. Dispose of the soiled diaper. Place the soiled diaper in a plastic bag and seal it shut. Do not flush it; rather, throw the diaper in the trash immediately.

Put a Baby to Sleep

Facts About Baby Sleep
✓ Babies' sleep cycles are shorter and have more light than deep sleep, making babies more likely to wake up.
✓ Babies enter deep sleep through a light sleep period of about 20 minutes. During deep sleep they are hard to awaken.
✓ Sleeping "through the night" really means about five hours.
✓ Sleep habits are connected more to the baby's personality than to parenting techniques.
✓ Your baby will outgrow the frequent waking stage!

Helping Baby to Sleep
✓ Create a secure environment: quiet, dimly lit, not too warm or chilly.
✓ Keep a night light in your baby's room. Some babies don't like complete darkness, and it will help you find your way around too!
✓ Try feeding on demand during the day in order to satiate the baby for the night.
✓ Breast- or bottle-feed your baby to sleep.
✓ Newborns like to sleep swaddled, while older babies prefer a loose covering.
✓ Try to keep your baby's day as calm as possible to minimize anxiety.
✓ Keep bedtime consistent, especially for older babies.
✓ Hold, rock, or stroll your baby around the house, or go for a drive—this often does the trick!
✓ If your baby likes a bath, give a warm one before bed.
✓ Gently massage or rub your baby to sleep.
✓ Dress your baby in comfortable sleepwear.
✓ Use disposable diapers at night because they are super-absorbent, or two or three cloth diapers to decrease the sensation of wetness.
✓ Certain sounds can lull a baby to sleep: a loud-ticking clock; mellow classical music; a recording of a waterfall, rain, or the ocean; a lullaby tape–either store-bought or with your own voice singing.
✓ Lie down with your baby until he or she is completely asleep.
✓ For older babies, make it a point to say goodnight with hugs and kisses, and put your baby's favorite soft toy or stuffed animal in the crib.

Potty Train a Child

Potty training is not something you can program into your child systematically. Special care should be paid to the individual needs of your child so you do not make the mistake of starting to train too soon. Keep in mind that before children are ready, they need to reach a certain degree of mental and physical development. They must be able to recognize the signs indicating a need to urinate or excrete, and they must understand potty training and be able to communicate their needs to you. Physically, children must develop enough muscle control to hold waste in for a time (developed at around 1½ to 2 years), and their bladder and bowels must grow large enough to store waste (at around 2½ to 3 years). Eventually you will detect signs that your child is ready. Only then should the process begin.

How Children Let You Know They Are Ready for Potty Training

✓ They show interest in the bathroom and may imitate others going into the bathroom.
✓ They ask to be changed.
✓ They have more regular bowel movements and keep dry for hours at a time.
✓ They may want to relieve themselves in private, leaving the room before they urinate or excrete.

Techniques for Potty Training

✓ Get a portable potty chair and/or put a seat insert into the toilet for your child to use.
✓ Show your child how to use the toilet. Children may be afraid of the toilet initially, so show them it is a friendly and useful part of the bathroom.
✓ Encourage children to let you know when they have to use the toilet. Communication is the crucial element in this process.
✓ Dress the child in clothes that are easy to undo, such as Velcro-fastened garments or training pants.
✓ Be consistent with your training. Coordinate between both parents and the baby-sitter or nanny if you have one. The language and techniques you use with the child must be uniform and steadily reinforced. Update each other on the progress the child makes.
✓ Allow children to see how you use the toilet, so they can imitate you. The most common way children learn at that age is through imitation.
✓ Spend a few full days with the child at first to get him or her accustomed to the potty process. Be available if the child needs help or reassurance.

Other Tips

✓ Be positive and supportive. Treat potty training like a fun, natural part of growing up—something the child should look forward to. Give lots of positive reinforcement, and don't show your displeasure if the child fails. That will only add to the pressure.

✓ Don't rush children; they will only grow frustrated and resentful of you.

✓ Don't potty train during a time you know will be full of other changes, such as when you are moving or when a new baby has just arrived. Outside distractions make training more difficult.

✓ Don't put the child in a position where there is no alternative to using the diaper. Avoid going on long trips without a potty seat—it will be a sign of inconsistency and set the child off track.

✓ If you do take the child out, know where the closest toilet is at all times, and go there immediately if the child asks.

Choose a School for Your Child

Things to Consider

✓ Do you want a public or a private school?

✓ Is the school in a safe, convenient location?

✓ Is there adequate security at the school?

✓ Is transportation to and from school available and convenient?

✓ Are you impressed by the appearance of the building, classrooms, and school-yard? Does the school have a comfortable atmosphere?

✓ What is the teacher-student ratio? (The primary grades should have no more than 20 to 25 students per class; the secondary grades should have no more than 30 to 35 students).

✓ Do large classes have teacher aides?

✓ How diverse is the student population regarding ethnic, religious, and socio-economic backgrounds?

✓ What is the school's track record on standardized tests?

✓ What are the average GPA and attrition rates?

✓ Does the school "track" students according to their academic abilities? Are you for or against this practice?

✓ What is the philosophy of education? Is it traditional, with homework every night, lectures, and standard textbooks, or does it take a more alternative approach, using cooperative learning and diverse curriculum materials?

✓ Are there special classes, like music and art?

✓ What extracurricular activities are offered?

✓ Are special-needs students mainstreamed in the school? Are there adequate facilities, instruction, teachers, and personal aides?

✓ How does the school handle disciplinary problems?

✓ Are parents actively involved in the school, and in what way?

✓ Are field trips an integral part of the learning experience?

Visit Schools—What Do You See?

✓ Are classrooms clean, well lit, and well ventilated?

✓ Are classrooms well stocked with books, computers, art supplies, puzzles, and games?

✓ Are the bathrooms clean and well ventilated?

✓ What condition are the hallways in?

✓ Do the children seem to be enjoying school?

✓ What is the library like? Is it well stocked and well organized?

✓ What kind of equipment is in the gym and on the playground? Does it appear safe and in good condition?

✓ Is the schoolyard clean and safe?

✓ What is the cafeteria like? Is it clean, well ventilated, and monitored by teachers?

✓ Are the hallways, cafeteria, and classrooms excessively noisy or extremely quiet? Either one might be a red flag.

✓ Does the school feel like an inviting, friendly place, with mutual respect between teachers and students?

✓ How do teachers interact with students? In general, do they have complete control over their classrooms, or do they allow for group work, discussion, and peer-teaching?

✓ Is there a good mix of active and quiet times?

✓ Do teachers seem enthusiastic and well prepared for their classes?

✓ Is the school a place you'd want to go to every day?

Hire a Baby-Sitter or Nanny

Arranging for the proper care of your child is a personal matter. The most important considerations are that you feel comfortable leaving your child with the baby-sitter or nanny and that your child feels comfortable being left with that person. Be cautious and insist on proof that the child caregiver is qualified and trustworthy, then let your instincts judge the rest.

Where to Go to Find a Baby-Sitter or Nanny

✓ Family members. Whenever possible, this is the best bet. There is often no one you can trust more than your immediate family, and you already know their qualifications. What's more, they'll likely be happy to look after the child, particularly if they are the grandparents.

✓ Referrals from friends and family. If you know others with young children, ask them to refer their baby-sitter or nanny to you, if they are willing to share.

✓ High school or college students. Place an advertisement on a high school bulletin board or in a college employment office.

✓ Community child care agency, baby-sitter, or nanny service. These offices will either refer you to childcare-givers or supply you with one. Be sure that any company you hire is reputable.

✓ Local hospital, gym, or elementary school. These are all places frequented by young mothers and are good sources for reliable referrals in the community.

What to Look For in Professional Childcare-Givers

✓ Interview impressions. Conduct an interview to get a feel for the applicant's viewpoints and personality. Try to determine how the applicant will interact with your child.

✓ Training and license. All professional childcare personnel should be trained in first-aid and parenting skills and should be licensed by the state. Do not hire anyone without proof of qualifications and a background check.

✓ References. Always follow up on the references an applicant gives you. Call and ask references about the applicant's qualifications and previous work experience.

✓ Compatible views on child care. To ensure your child is not confused by varying degrees of structure, discipline, teaching, and safety standards in his or her life, be certain the childcare-giver understands and agrees with your philosophies on raising your child and is consistent in dealing with your child.

✓ Ability to take and heed advice. Remember, this is your child. You have the final say on your child's care. Be certain the baby-sitter or nanny understands your wishes.

✓ Good rapport with child. For your child's sake, make sure the caregiver likes and gets along with your child.

✓ Healthy and disease-free. Ask about the applicant's medical history, and encourage baby-sitters and nannies to stay away when sick.

✓ Cost. Some sitters charge a set fee; others are negotiable. Baby-sitter agencies will be more expensive because of administration costs, but they may be more dependable. Set a price before the sitter begins.

✓ Availability. Make sure the baby-sitter or nanny is available at the necessary times. Set a schedule well in advance so no misunderstandings occur.

Other Considerations

✓ Reassess a baby-sitter's or nanny's performance regularly. Continue to watch a caregiver's performance even after hiring.

✓ Avoid changing baby-sitters or nannies often. While this may be necessary if you cannot find a caregiver who meets your needs, frequent changes will cause disruption and confusion in the child's life.

✓ Remember that any steady employee of your household must be included on your tax return and you must pay taxes for the employee (this applies even if you are *not* considering running for public office . . .).

10 Things to Tell the Baby-Sitter

Leaving your child with a baby-sitter can cause a lot of anxiety at first. Make sure the sitter can handle any situation that may occur while you are away. Most importantly, make sure both you and your child are comfortable with the sitter. Once you have decided on the right person, feel free to give the baby-sitter as much information and as many instructions as you feel are necessary. Here is some of the most fundamental information a baby-sitter should have:

1. The child's bedtime

2. The house rules for the child (no ball-playing, no food outside the kitchen, no TV after 8 P.M., share toys and games, be polite)

3. What the baby-sitter is expected to do with and for the child (cook, feed, bathe, tutor, entertain)

4. What the baby-sitter can and cannot do in the house (use the TV, VCR, computer, telephone, have guests)

5. The telephone number and location where you will be, and when you will be returning

6. The telephone numbers of relatives, neighbors, and friends to call if you cannot be reached

7. Emergency telephone numbers (911, your pediatrician, poison hotline, relatives, neighbors)

8. The child's favorite activities, foods, books, records, and other habits and preferences

9. Any medical problems your child may have and how to handle them (medicines, treatments)

10. Any psychological information you can supply about your child that will help the baby-sitter understand her or him

Set an Allowance

Once children begin to exhibit a certain degree of independence, as early as 5 or 6, it's time to consider setting an allowance for them. A regular allowance can be a useful tool for teaching a child the value of money and how to manage it. While there's no correct amount to give a child as a weekly or biweekly allowance, there are several factors to keep in mind when you are setting one.

What You Can Afford

While a young child's allowance of a few dollars a week probably won't set you back too far, don't give your child more money than you can afford.

Age of Child

As children grow up, their needs expand. A 10-year-old will have less need for money than a 16-year-old, so set and raise allowances accordingly.

Need of Child

Some children, regardless of age, have a greater need for money than other children. How much money a child will need often depends on what the child is expected to pay for with the allowance. Make it clear whether the child should use the allowance to pay for things like lunch at school or gas for the car (if they drive), or whether those costs will be paid for separately.

Extent of Chores

A good way for a child to learn the value of money is to earn it. If you give your child a weekly allowance, it's a good idea to require a weekly chore in return. A simple chore like vacuuming the house or cutting the grass, in addition to keeping their room clean, will give children a sense of having worked for their money without keeping them from more important things like school and friends.

Responsibility of Child

Don't give your children more money than they can handle or really need. Some children are just not ready to deal with their own finances, while others will surprise you with their sense of responsibility. You know your children and should be able to judge what they can handle.

The Child's Future

Consider making a savings plan a condition of your child's allowance. Open a joint savings account in the child's name and encourage the child to save a portion of the allowance each week or each month. Help the child set long-term goals for the savings, such as a bicycle, special gift for a family member, or college tuition. Develop early *savings* habits as well as *spending* habits.

Other Income

Once the child reaches the legal working age, you may want to encourage him or her to get a part-time job. This will further develop the child's sense of independence and responsibility. If your child does work and earns money separate from the allowance, it may be time to discontinue or adjust the allowance.

Childproof Your Home

The addition of a small child to a household changes everything. It not only reshapes the new parents' life in very obvious ways, it should also significantly alter the look of the house the child will live in. Houses with small children need to be free from things that may seem safe to an adult but can potentially cause injury to a child. It is important to remember that children are very curious; don't give children the chance to play with something that might hurt them. Here is a list of some of the ways to protect your child in the house. How long these measures remain in place depends upon how quickly the child develops a sense of independence and an understanding of the dangers in the house. While you don't want to make the child feel dependent on you to unlock cabinets for longer than necessary, don't be in a rush to ease these safety measures. They can promote safety even in a house without small children.

✓ Keep the windows locked. Any window the child could potentially fall through, get stuck in, or run into should be kept shut and locked whenever possible. Consider placing stickers low on glass doors, like sliding porch doors, to keep the child from walking into or breaking them. Use window guards.

✓ Lock restricted rooms. Any rooms you do not want your child going into unsupervised, such as a tool workshop, should be kept locked.

✓ Lock cabinets with poisonous substances. Cabinets underneath sinks often store hazardous cleaning supplies.

✓ Keep glassware out of reach. Store breakable glass and china in overhead cabinets that are too high for a child to get to.

✓ Store knives and utensils out of reach. Sharp kitchen implements should be stored either overhead or in a locked drawer.

✓ Lock the medicine cabinet. Pills and other medicines can be mistaken for candy by children if they get a chance to explore the cabinet. Make sure child-proof caps are securely fastened.

✓ Tape or remove sharp edges. While it is nearly impossible to rid your house of all edges, be aware of the sharper and more prominently exposed edges on your furniture and hardware, particularly those at the child's height level. Crawl around the house on your hands and knees to detect sharp edges at child height. If you cannot remove dangerous edges, putting masking or electrical tape on them will help to blunt corners. Run Styrofoam around the sides of glass-top tables.

✓ Hide electrical wires. Don't leave wires exposed on walls or floors where a child can play with them.

✓ Cap unused electrical outlets. Any open outlets should be plugged with plastic safety caps to prevent children from sticking their fingers into the sockets. Plugs are available at hardware or electronics stores.

✓ Keep appliances away from the child. All heavy appliances such as a television or computer should be secure and unmovable. Lighter appliances, particularly kitchen appliances that get hot or that cut food, should be kept out of a child's reach altogether.

✓ Tape rugs to the floor. Rugs that can shift or be lifted should be secured to the floor so the child can neither slip on nor crawl underneath them. Use either heavy tape or adhesive strips.

✓ Keep a gate at the top of staircases. If the child is upstairs, a gate should be drawn to prevent the child from falling down the stairs. Stair gates are available at hardware and department stores.

✓ Buy a safe crib. If your baby's crib has bars on it, be sure the baby's head cannot fit between the bars.

✓ Move small objects out of reach. Any knickknack or small item can become a toy if the child can reach it. Scrutinize your home for any items that are easily within a child's grasp but may prove dangerous. Don't leave coffee cups or other items unattended. Little hands move quickly.

Your Child's Height and Weight

Children's growth rates are as individual as their personalities. The following charts show the average range of height and weight for girls and boys from 1 to 12 years. If your child falls within the shaded area, you can assume that the growth rate is normal. If your child falls above or below the solid lines and you believe that he or she is gaining weight too quickly or too slowly, discuss your concerns with your doctor.

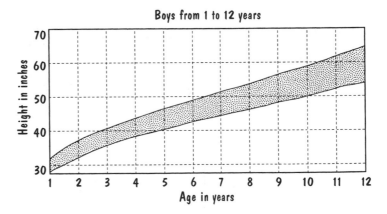

Boys from 1 to 12 years

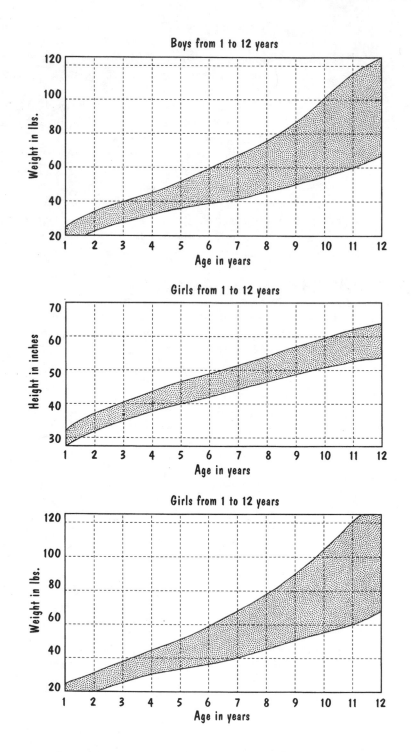

16. Personal

Make Braids and French Braids

To Make a Braid

1. Divide hair into three even sections.
2. Bring the right section over the middle and pull the original middle section under it to the right.
3. Bring the left section over the middle, and pull the middle to the left.
4. Repeat this right-over-middle, left-over-middle process until you reach the end of the hair (or the point at which you want the braid to end).
5. Use an elasticized hair band to tie the end securely. Cover this with a scrunchie or ribbon if you wish.

Note: Pulling the middle sections snugly to the sides as you go will make a tighter braid.

To Make a French Braid

1. Starting at your temples, draw your thumbs in a straight line to the middle back of your head. Gather and smooth this hair to use to begin your braid.
2. Divide this hair into three even sections.
3. Begin by making a regular braid for two or three crossovers.
4. On the third or fourth crossover, begin to add in small sections of hair to each section as you cross it over the middle section.
5. To gather the added-in hair, hold the three main sections of the braid with one hand while you use your opposite thumb to draw from the scalp line straight back (as in Step 1). Making sure that the strands are smooth, add the hair to the section of the braid that will cross over the middle section.
6. Continue until all of the hair is used, and then continue making a regular braid until you reach the end.

7. Tie off with an elasticized hair band.

Note: French braiding takes a lot of practice before you get the hang of it. Practice making French braids loose or tight, adding thin sections of hair or thicker sections, and starting the braid at different points on your head.

Give Yourself a Manicure and Pedicure

Give Yourself a Manicure

1. Use cotton balls and nail polish remover to remove old polish.
2. Soak your finger tips in bowls of warm soapy water. This will soften your cuticles.
3. Dry your hands, and smooth on a moisturizing hand lotion.
4. Use an orange stick (a component of a manicure set) to gently push back your cuticles. If you don't have an orange stick, the dull rounded end of a nail file can work—but be gentle!
5. Use small, sharp manicure scissors to trim off hangnails and loose skin around the cuticles and nails.
6. If you want to shorten your nails significantly, use a nail clipper or manicure scissors to cut them.
7. Use an emery board to file your nails (see tips below).
8. For long-lasting polish, apply a base coat, one or two coats of polish, and a top coat. Make sure each coat is dry before applying the next one.
9. Use a nail polish fixative (in a spray can), or a drying unit, or allow your nails to dry naturally.
10. Use a cotton swab dipped in nail polish remover to carefully clean the skin around your nails of polish.

Nail Filing Tips

✓ Use a file not to shorten your nails, but just to shape them. Too much filing will weaken your nails.

✓ The strongest shape for nails is round or square, not pointed.

✓ Do not file straight into the sides of your fingertip. Allow for natural growth of the nail on your finger.

✓ Use gentle even strokes in one direction. Don't saw back and forth.

Give Yourself a Pedicure

1. Do a pedicure after bathing, since your nails and cuticles will be softened then, or begin your pedicure with a warm, soapy foot bath.

2. Use a pumice stone to gently rub the tough, calloused parts of your feet: the heels, balls, and Achilles (back) tendon of your ankles. Using a pumice stone regularly will soften the rough and tough spots.

3. Wash your feet, pat dry, and apply a moisturizer. Be sure to include your entire foot and ankle.

4. Use a sharp nail clipper or manicure scissors to trim your nails. Do not cut them too short, as this could cause the tip of your toe to become irritated. Cut your nails **straight** across, not in a round shape, which can cause ingrown nails to develop.

5. Use an emery board to smooth snags, filing straight across the nail.

6. For long-lasting polish, apply a base coat, one or two coats of polish, and a top coat. Allow each coat to dry before applying the next.

Give Yourself a Facial

Facial treatments (or simply, facials) clean pores, discourage wrinkles and blemishes, and generally enliven the skin. What kind of facial is best for you depends on what type of skin you have and what makes you feel good. A facial is as much for your relaxation and enjoyment as for skin care.

Exfoliation

The first part of your facial, called exfoliation, involves washing away dead skin cells to give your face a deep cleaning and to leave your skin softer and smoother.

Facial scrubs are creams that contain an abrasive element to scrape away dead skin. You can buy facial scrubs that contain bits of apricot seed or nutshells to act as abrasives, or make your own at home, using oatmeal (mixed with almond oil into a paste) or a small amount of salt (mixed with ordinary face cream). To apply, first wet your skin, then rub the cream over your face and neck (be careful to keep it out of your eyes and mouth). After about ten minutes, rinse with warm water.

Abrasive sponges, with face cream or soap lather, can be used to gently rub your face for a few minutes. Don't scrub too hard, or you may irritate the skin.

Exfoliating masks, because they don't require rubbing in, are recommended for sensitive skin. Simply apply the mask, leave it to dry for 15 or 20 minutes (or whatever is recommended by the brand), then either peel or wash it off with water. Masks both clean and treat the skin.

Facial Masks

Once your skin is cleansed and free of dead cells, revitalize and nourish your skin type with a restorative mask. If you use homemade masks, experiment with the ingredients below to find a mask that feels and works best for you. Don't use any ingredients you are allergic to.

Dry skin (feels tight, flakes, makeup cakes) requires a moisturizing mask. Buy a cream-based product. For a homemade mask, mash together a banana and some strawberries, or an avocado with a beaten egg.

Oily skin (large pores, blackheads and pimples, greasy, makeup discolors or fades) needs a mask to remove oil and tighten pores. Buy a mud- or clay-based mask, or make a mask at home: (1) yogurt, ground almonds, and lemon juice, (2) oatmeal and orange juice, or (3) beaten egg whites and honey. Mix ingredients to an even, pasty consistency.

Combination skin (dry and oily skin in different areas) may require different masks for different areas of your face. With combination skin, usually the forehead and nose are oily, and the cheeks are dry. For a homemade mask, (1) blend an egg with a splash of apricot oil and lemon juice or (2) mix oatmeal and milk with a mashed cucumber.

Other masks can benefit a variety of special skin types. Mineral masks nourish old and tired skin; gel masks make the skin tingle and the blood circulate.

To apply masks, wipe a thin coat smoothly and evenly on your face. Lie down on your back and keep your face still so the mask can dry and turn stiff. Relax for 15 to 20 minutes, or whatever amount of time is suggested by the mask manufacturer (gels usually require only three to five minutes), while the ingredients sink in. When the time is up, wash or peel the mask off completely, depending on the material, and use moisturizer to finish.

Face Massage

End a good facial with a face massage to release tension and improve circulation. Before you begin, make sure your face and hands are clean.

1. Apply massage oil or skin cream over your face with your fingers (avoid eyes and mouth) in a light circular motion.
2. Massage slowly across your forehead in an up-and-down motion, using the pads of your fingers.
3. Massage lightly around your eyes, on your brow, and across your cheekbones.
4. Massage slowly with your fingers, from your cheek down to your chin, then back to your jaw.
5. Massage your neck deeply, using your fingers and the palm of your hand.
6. Repeat for ten minutes, then wash off the oil or cream with warm water or a damp cloth.

Tie a Necktie

The modern necktie came into existence around the end of the 19th century. While it is only one of many types of neckwear (including the bow tie and the ascot), the necktie has become the standard for business and semiformal occasions. Three techniques are commonly used; each forms a slight difference in shape. The most complex is the Windsor knot, named for the fashionable Duke of Windsor (Edward VIII). Next is the simpler half-Windsor knot and finally, the common four-in-hand knot. The following explains how to tie each of the three knots. In the directions, "right" and "left" refer to your right-hand side and left-hand side, respectively. The diagrams present a mirror image of how the tie should look.

Beginning Position for All Knots

Start with the tie draped around your neck so the wide end hangs down on the right, narrow end on left. The wide end should hang lower than the narrow end. How much lower, though, depends on the length of the tie and which knot you are tying. In general, the more material required to tie the knot, the lower the wide end should hang. The Windsor knot requires more material to tie than the half-Windsor; the four-in-hand requires the least.

The Windsor Knot

1. Cross the wide end over the narrow, then wrap it behind and up through the loop created, leaving it off the left.

2. Wrap the wide end around the left side and behind the knot to the right side.

3. Bring the wide end up and through the loop, then down to the left side.

4. Wrap the wide end around the front of the knot to the right side.

5. Bring the wide end behind and up through the loop.

6. Slide the wide end down through the knot, and straighten without pulling down too tightly. Use the narrow end to tighten the knot around your neck, and adjust as necessary (Figure 1).

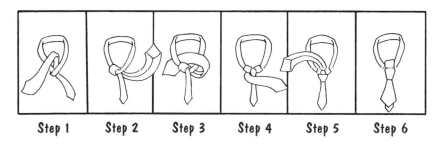

Step 1   Step 2   Step 3   Step 4   Step 5   Step 6

Figure 1. Windsor knot

The Half-Windsor Knot

1. Cross the wide end over the narrow, then wrap it behind and off to the right.
2. Bring the wide end around front, then down through the loop created and off to the left.
3. Wrap the wide end around the front of the knot, and off to the right.
4. Wrap the wide end around the back and up through the loop.
5. Slide the wide end down through the knot, and straighten without pulling down too tightly. Use the narrow end to tighten the knot around your neck, and adjust as necessary (Figure 2).

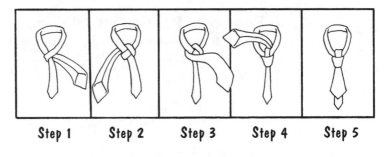

Figure 2. The half-Windsor knot

The Four-in-Hand Knot

1. Cross the wide end over the narrow, then wrap it behind and off to the right.
2. Wrap the wide end around the front and off to the left.
3. Wrap the wide end behind the knot and up through the loop.
4. Slide the wide end down through the knot, and straighten. Use the narrow end to tighten the knot around your neck, and adjust as necessary (Figure 3).

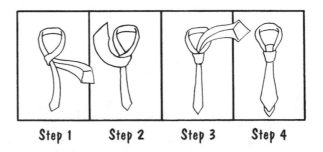

Figure 3. Four-in-hand knot

5 Folds for Scarves

The Square Knot

1. Fold a large square scarf in half to make a triangle.
2. Wrap the scarf around your back so the points fall over your shoulders and cross in front, with the end pointing to the right on top of the end pointing left.
3. Wrap the right behind the left and up through the loop created.
4. Bring the right around and behind the left to create another loop.
5. Pull the right end through the loop so it once again falls on the right side. Tighten to form the square knot (Figure 1).

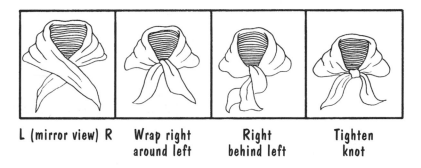

L (mirror view) R   Wrap right around left   Right behind left   Tighten knot

Figure 1. Square knot

The Ascot

1. Wrap a long rectangular scarf around your neck so the ends fall in front.
2. Bring the end on your left over the end on your right.
3. Wrap the end on top around and up through the loop at your neck.
4. Tuck the ends into your shirt, and fluff out the scarf material (Figure 2).

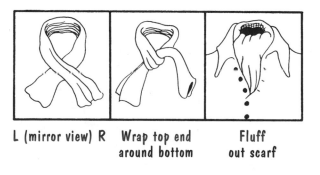

L (mirror view) R   Wrap top end around bottom   Fluff out scarf

Figure 2. The Ascot

The Bib Wrap

1. Fold a large square scarf into a triangle.

2. Lay the scarf on your chest and wrap the points behind and around your neck. The wide point should be in front, pointing down.

3. Cross the points behind you and bring them around the front of your neck.

4. Tie the ends in a square knot (see Figure 1).

5. Optional step: Pull the front point up and tuck it into your neckline to cover up the knot (Figure 3).

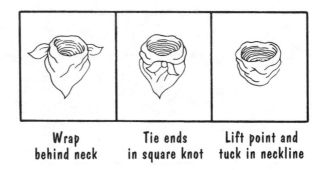

Wrap behind neck   **Tie ends in square knot**   **Lift point and tuck in neckline**

Figure 3. The bib wrap

The Bow

1. Tie a loose knot in the middle of a long, thin scarf.

2. With the knot in the front center, tie the ends of the scarf around the back of your neck and around to the front. You may need to wrap it more than once so that only a few inches of each end remain.

3. Slide both ends through the knot, and let the ends hang (Figure 4).

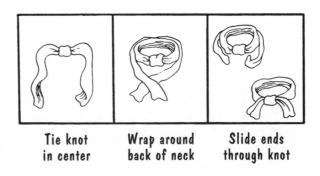

Tie knot in center   **Wrap around back of neck**   **Slide ends through knot**

Figure 4. The bow

The Hacking Knot

1. Fold a long, thin scarf in half so that the two ends meet.

2. Wrap the folded scarf around the back of your neck and over your shoulders to your front, so that one end is formed by the fold and the other end is formed by both ends of the scarf.

3. Stick the two loose ends through the loop created by the fold.

4. Optional step: Make a bow out of the remaining material on the ends (Figure 5).

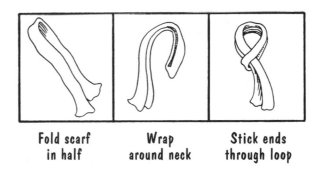

**Fold scarf
in half**　　**Wrap
around neck**　　**Stick ends
through loop**

Figure 5. The hacking knot

Spit Shine Shoes

Spit shining may sound disgusting, but it really works. You can use your own saliva to give leather shoes an extra-glossy, patent leather shine. To do it, you first need to shine your shoes with polish regularly, then apply the spit. Here's the complete procedure (which we recommend you do in private).

1. Brush off the dirt. With a brush, wipe off any dirt or dust from the shoe. If you need to use water to clean off the dirt, use only a small amount.

2. Dab the polish with a rag. Scoop a little bit of shoe polish onto the rag. The polish should match your shoe's color.

3. Rub the polish evenly into the shoe. Make sure the polish covers all areas of the shoe, but do not rub it in too vigorously.

4. Buff the shoe. With a brush, rapidly rub the polish into the shoe until the polish shines evenly. When you have finished buffing with the brush, you may want to buff again with a clean rag. This is not necessary, but it may create a brighter shine.

5. Spit on the shoe. Apply saliva to the top of the shoe. How you get it there is up to you.

6. Dab the polish with the rag. You don't need as much polish this time because there's already polish on the shoe.

7. Rub the rag into the spit. Mix the polish with the saliva, and rub over the entire shoe. Add more saliva if necessary, and continue rubbing until the shoe shines to your satisfaction. You do not need to buff again.

Ask for a Date

Regardless of gender or age, dating etiquette calls for politeness, respect, and courtesy. Whether you already have a friendship with someone, such as another student at your university, a co-worker, or colleague, or whether you have just met the person at a party, professional conference, or chance meeting, the same etiquette applies. Here are some strategies for working up the courage to ask for that first date.

✓ If you are acquainted with the person, suggest an activity you know that person enjoys, such as tennis, movies, or dining out. If you've just met, ask the person what he or she likes to do. This is a great way to discover common interests and hobbies.

✓ Choose a private setting to make your invitation. Don't surprise or embarrass someone by asking for a date in front of co-workers or friends where he or she may feel uncomfortable.

✓ If you have friends in common, suggest a double date. This can reduce the awkwardness of a first date and give you a context for getting to know your dating partner in a social environment.

✓ Suggest taking a class together, jogging together, or studying together. This allows you to see a person regularly and get to know him or her over time while enjoying a shared experience.

✓ Avoid cleverness or cuteness. The straightforward approach is usually the best one.

✓ If someone refuses, don't push. Let him or her know a change of heart would be welcome, but accept and respect the boundaries set for the relationship. Who knows—you might meet someone else!

Research Your Family Tree

The secret to conducting a genealogical search is thoroughness and organization. Keep precise records of where you've searched and what information you've found so you can verify sources. Compile your facts into a family record. Consider printing your findings. Your family history is an invaluable document for your relatives, both immediate and distant, and will also help other genealogists in their own searches. This is a great family project to teach children research techniques and the value of preserving their family's heritage and traditions. Knowing your family's medical history can help in prevention and early diagnosis of illnesses and conditions with genetic tendencies.

Family Members, Friends, and Other Primary Sources

Interview relatives. The best place to start a genealogical search is with older family members such as grandparents, great grandparents, or great aunts and uncles. Conduct interviews to learn as much as you can from your family's own oral history. Keep in mind that such information is not always accurate. Contact relatives by mail first if you do not know them personally, then go in person whenever possible to conduct the interviews. Audiotape or videotape them. Ask relatives simple questions and allow them to ramble—this technique brings out the most colorful and useful information. Share what one relative tells you with other relatives in the hope this will jar further memories.

Family documents. Ask relatives for permission to search their attics or closets for old pictures, diaries, birth certificates, or letters. Old family Bibles often contain records of the births, deaths, and marriages of family members.

Family associations. Some old and well-established families have associations that include all the people descended from a single ancestor. These groups may have archives of family records.

Small-Town Libraries

Visit local libraries and historical societies in the towns where your ancestors lived. There you may find some of the following:

- ✓ County or town histories.
- ✓ City directories or old telephone books.
- ✓ Town reports and records, including information on the town's founders, residents, taxpayers, new residents, town meetings, and elections.
- ✓ Institutional histories, documenting local businesses, banks, churches, charity groups, fraternal societies, or militias.
- ✓ Newspapers. Old local publications will likely feature birth, marriage, and death notices.

Local Courts and Town Clerks

Many of the most valuable records are found in the archives of local governments. These may include the following:

- ✓ Vital records—documents of a person's birth, death, and marriage. You may need to prove your family relation before gaining access. If you write to request copies of vital records, be specific. Provide your ancestor's name, address, and date of death, and include the appropriate fee.
- ✓ Probate records, such as wills, property inventories, and letters of administration and guardianship. These court documents will contain the names of relatives and provide clues to family relations, religious affiliations, property, and wealth.
- ✓ Land records. Besides basic property deeds, these include land patents that document the transfer of frontier land from the government to private citizens, and bounty land warrants recording land given in exchange for military service.

Church and Cemetery Records

Churches and synagogues can sometimes provide dates of births, baptisms, marriages, burials, circumcisions, bar mitzvahs, bat mitzvahs, and confirmations. Cemeteries will, of course, provide you with a gravestone. Be wary, though, old gravestones can be inaccurate.

Genealogical Libraries

Many cities have libraries with special sections for genealogical information. Here you may find bibliographies and indexes that outline the types of documents available to you and where to find them. In addition, you may find such documents as these:

✓ Census records. These are widely available on microfilm and provide a lot of very reliable family information. Keep in mind, though, that until the 1850 census only the head of the household was identified, and only after 1880 were relationships of family members provided.

✓ Military records. To search records of service you must know when and where your ancestor served. Veteran pension and bounty records are arranged alphabetically and will provide this information. Muster rolls give very specific information on a soldier's occupation, home town, and even his personal appearance. Pension and widow pension applications tell about a soldier and his family after military service. *Note*: Colonial army records are held in state archives, Civil War records do not document volunteers, and recent military records (the last 75 years) are restricted and require special permission to inspect.

✓ Publications. Genealogical magazines provide useful information and contacts for your search; ask at the library.

For Immigrants

Finding detailed information on immigrant families can be a problem. Until recently, many counties kept few or no records of their citizens, and many immigrants changed their names upon arriving in the United States. Some sources, though, are helpful in tracing the lives of new immigrant families:

✓ Passenger lists. Ship records may provide the name, age, occupation, race, and national origin of passengers, and the name of the ship and date of its voyage. Many records can be found at the National Archives in Washington.

✓ Naturalization records. These may be difficult to track down; they are located at the court where your ancestor was made a citizen.

✓ Ethnic newspapers. These may provide birth, marriage, and death notices, as well as other community news and information concerning immigrant families.

Give a Great Massage

Holistic massage, as opposed to the solely muscular massage you might get from a physical therapist, affects many levels of your body and mind. It starts with the skin and moves deeper to work the muscles and bones, improve circulation, release tension, and rid the body of toxins and impurities. Your level of relaxation and your overall mental state improve. To be truly effective, though, both the giver and receiver should be in the right frame of mind: tranquil and meditative. The following is a massage routine that covers the entire body in a flowing and unified progression. Feel free to change the routine as you see fit to better suit yourself or your partner.

Basic Strokes

Effleurage involves light and gliding strokes applied with the entire flat surface of the hand at the beginning and the very end of the massage. These strokes are not aimed at any specific muscles but rather cover large areas when you spread oil or connect parts of the body.

Medium strokes include kneading (squeezing and releasing flesh), pulling, and wringing. They are done in rhythm on fleshy areas and are designed to relax muscles.

Petrissage involves deep strokes done with the fingers or heels of the hand. These strokes work specific muscles to release tension. Apply a good amount of pressure, particularly to reach deeper muscles but not to the point of causing pain.

Tapotement involves laying hands on a fleshy area and vibrating the fingers to shake and loosen muscles.

Percussion strokes are designed not to relax but to stimulate. They include beating with the fists, plucking with the fingers, and cupping and chopping with the hands. They are performed in a fast, rhythmic motion. Percussion should be done after other strokes over the entire body to reinvigorate, improve circulation, and tone flabby areas, but they are not always necessary or appropriate.

Using Oil

Oil is recommended because it allows for smooth movement of the hands on the body; it can also be good for the skin. Heat the oil slightly before using, then pour it into your hand and spread it out evenly. Apply the oil sparingly on only one part of the body at a time as you go. Use ready-made massage oil or vegetable, almond, coconut, or baby oil (you may want to scent these oils with lemon or perfume).

Sequence for a Full Body Massage

The key to the full body massage is unity. Work all areas of the body in a logical progression, then connect all body parts together. Work slowly and deliberately, and perform as many of the strokes on each area as apply. Here is a good sequence to follow:

1. Back and buttocks. Have the person lie on his or her back. Cover the area generally, then work specific parts.

2. Back of the legs and feet. Do one leg at a time, gliding up from the ankle to the thigh, then kneading back down to end up at the foot. Massage the bottom and sides of the feet and wiggle each toe.

3. Shoulders and neck. Begin kneading one shoulder at a time, then work the neck deeply.

4. Head and face. Turn the person over to the front to work through the scalp and hair, then move down to the face. Massage the face muscles, moving outward from the forehead to the chin. Concentrate especially on eyes, nose, ears, and jaws.

5. Chest and belly. Move from the upper chest down to the ribs, abdomen, and sides. Finish by gliding back up toward the chest. By massaging the chest, abdomen, right arm, and right side of the face and neck, you will be helping the lymphatic system to drain the whole body of toxins and debris. Professional athletes use massage as a way to release wastes built up during exercise.

6. Arms and hands. Work on each arm separately, as with the legs, working up from the wrist, then back down to the hand. Massage the hand, wrist, and fingers.

7. Front of the legs. Repeat Step 2 for the front of the legs.

8. Connecting strokes. Finish off the massage with long gliding strokes along the entire body. Touch all parts and connect them to create a sense of the body's unity.

See also "Relieve Stress."

Plan a Wedding

You shouldn't be surprised to learn that the biggest event you will ever organize (unless you plan to be a professional event coordinator) is likely to be your wedding. From the engagement to the wedding announcements, here's a guide for all aspects of a wedding that require planning.

Initial Planning

Make a budget. Determine how much can be spent on the wedding. Traditionally, the bride's parents foot the bill, but this is no longer necessarily the case.

Decide on the size and tone of the wedding. Will it be grand or intimate? Formal or informal?

Set the date. Choose a month or season for the wedding. Be flexible—everything and everyone you hire must be available on the date.

Make an invitation list. If your wedding is large, you may wish to invite certain people only to the ceremony and others to the ceremony and reception.

Order invitations. Invitations are printed by small specialty shops or directly through printing presses. Visit a few stores to get samples of different design options and texts before you decide on your own. Be precise about the dates and spellings printed on your invitations. Read the completed invitation carefully to make sure it is correct before you accept the order and mail the invitations out. Invitations should be mailed about eight weeks in advance, to give guests a few weeks to respond and still allow you at least a month to solidify the guest list.

Get rings. You may already have selected an engagement ring and wedding bands. If not, search until you find a pair you love—don't settle for anything less. Buy the bands a few weeks before the wedding, at the latest, to give you enough time to have them fitted. Consider having a local jeweler design rings for you.

The Ceremony

Reserve the church, synagogue, or hall. Make sure the venue is available and set the date. The sooner you do this the better—some places require a reservation up to a year in advance because of the many people who wish to use them.

Retain a priest, rabbi, other clergyperson, or justice of the peace. If you have the wedding in a house of worship, the clergy attached to it will officiate at the ceremony. Make sure they too are available on your date. A justice of the peace must be hired separately.

Arrange for a florist. Find a florist that is reasonable in price and dependable. Choose the arrangements yourself.

Arrange for transportation. Some weddings use limousines to transport the principals to and from the ceremony and reception. While this is expensive and not necessary, you may decide you want to do it. If so, choose the limousine company according to price and service.

Choose the attendants. Large weddings include bridesmaids and ushers in addition to a maid of honor, best man, ring bearer, and flower girl. Choose attendants from your close friends and relatives.

Choose a wedding gown and gowns for bridesmaids. It is no longer ever too late to wear white, the color of celebration. If you have bridesmaids you may want to coordinate their dresses. Allow enough time for alterations.

Arrange for tuxedo rentals, if necessary. If the groom, best man, and ushers plan to wear tuxedos, you will need to rent them. This will require each attendant to go for a fitting.

Hire photographer and/or videographer. Choose a photographer based on cost, reputation, and how well you get along and by viewing samples of previous work. Make sure the photographer knows exactly what you want and gets pictures of everyone involved in the wedding.

Have a rehearsal. A few days before the wedding, or the day before, have a rehearsal at the venue to go through the procedure of the ceremony. Make sure everyone involved is present. You may want to arrange a simple meal afterwards—the traditional rehearsal dinner.

The Reception

Reserve a hall. If the reception will be in a different place from the ceremony, reserve a hall far in advance. Find out what the hall offers: some will handle flowers, cake, and catering. Taste samples of the food and shop around for prices before you decide.

Hire a band or D.J. Decide on what style of music you want: contemporary music, jazz, classical, or a combination. Hear the band or D.J. perform before hiring and compare prices.

Find a caterer. If the hall does not take care of catering, hire an outside company. Compare prices and menus to find the caterer that best suits you and your reception.

Choose the cake. If the catering does not include the wedding cake, find a baker that makes and delivers wedding cakes. Decide on the look and type of cake you want. Compare prices and presentation before deciding.

After the Wedding

Newspaper announcements. Contact your local paper to find out when and how to go about announcing your wedding.

Thank-you cards. As soon as you've returned from your honeymoon and have had a chance to organize all your gifts, it is important to send out thank-you cards. Write the cards by hand, and specifically mention the gift given. If possible, include details as to how you will use the gift and comments about your relationship to the giver.

Make Sure You Are Never Late

Some people are just born to be late. If you are among the habitually tardy, here are some suggestions to help get you there on time.

✓ Set an alarm. Set alarms during the day to remind you of important appointments or other responsibilities. Alarms on wristwatches or other portable clocks are ideal.

✓ Set your clock or watch forward. It won't fool you, but it may help you be aware of the current time earlier than usual and get you moving sooner.

✓ Get enough sleep. The chance of oversleeping is lessened if you are well rested. For an early morning appointment, plan to get enough sleep the night before. Tiredness causes sluggishness during the day and may lead to further lateness.

✓ Plan. Arrange enough time to do everything. Don't overbook your schedule, or you are bound to fall behind. Write down everything you need to do, and keep a calendar so you don't forget important tasks or meetings.

✓ Allow yourself more than enough time to travel. Add 15 minutes to half an hour to travel time to account for unexpected delays. It's better to be early than risk being late.

✓ Be aware of conditions that might cause you to be late. If you are traveling by car or bus, check traffic conditions before you leave. Call airports or train stations to check for delays. Always consider weather conditions. Call anyone who may be meeting you if you need to revise your plans.

✓ Don't allow yourself to get sidetracked. Don't start new business or make phone calls that may result in throwing you off schedule. Keep your mind on getting to your destination on time.

✓ Think about others. No matter how informal your appointment may be, keep in mind how much you inconvenience others by being late. Sometimes, just a little feeling of guilt can help to set you back on track.

✓ Call if you know you are running late. People understand a little lateness now and then and appreciate the honesty that allows them to adjust their own schedules.

Prepare for Retirement

A healthy retirement marks the beginning of a life stage where you can enjoy the luxury of travel, hobbies, learning, or anything else you may be interested in. Ensuring that your retirement is all you want it to be requires logistical and financial planning.

Considerations

Location. Will you stay where you currently live, or will you move? Florida, Arizona, Colorado, and Vermont are popular with retirees for the weather, climate, and scenery. Will you move to a retirement community for the social environment and convenience of services, or stay in a house? While moving offers many advantages and opportunities, some people prefer the comforts of a familiar environment.

Home. Will you keep your current house or move to a smaller apartment to better suit your daily living needs? Can your home be adapted for the needs of an older person—including wider halls, fewer stairs, accessible bathrooms, and a greater attention to security? If you are single, can you manage the rigors of independent living on your own, or would you enjoy the companionship offered by homesharing?

Health. As you get older, maintaining good health becomes a larger consideration. How will you provide the necessary exercise and nutrition your body needs to stay fit? Walking, swimming, tennis, golf, bicycling, and dancing are just some of the ways you can stay in shape. Make sure you receive regular medical exams. Seek out doctors experienced in geriatric care who can offer the best treatments to aging patients. Make out a living will, if you wish, and appoint a durable power of attorney for health care to be sure that your wishes are honored by medical professionals and family members.

Insurance. Make sure you have adequate health and life insurance. Understand the Medicare system and get a good "Medigap" policy to fill in Medicare's blanks.

Investigate long-term care policies that will protect you in the event your physical condition necessitates that you move to a care environment such as a nursing home.

Finances. Continue to build your savings as you approach the retirement years, through investments, bank savings, individual retirement accounts, pension accounts, social security, and other sources. Your retirement income should match or exceed your living expenses, which you can expect to be about 80 percent of what they were when you were working, depending on your own situation.

Activities. Staying active is the most important part of having a happy and productive retirement. Pursue interests you never had the chance to pursue: learn painting, start collecting, work in the garden, catch up on reading, take a class, teach a class. Your activities need not be expensive, and they need not be extremely demanding; try many things if you are not sure what you want to do. Many retirees find themselves working part-time. If you are financially secure, consider volunteering at a hospital, charity, school, nursing home, or library. Your knowledge and experience are always needed in these places, and the activity will provide you with companionship and fun.

How to Plan

✓ Keep a positive outlook about retirement.

✓ Set goals for what you want to accomplish in retirement, and plan how you will follow through on them.

✓ Discuss and coordinate your plans and desires with your spouse, and be sure you share similar attitudes toward retirement.

✓ Encourage the input and support of family and friends.

✓ Hire or retain professionals you trust to take care of your business concerns, including a lawyer, financial consultant, broker, and accountant.

✓ Before you retire, you must be psychologically ready for it. Until you really want to slow down and pursue leisure, you will not be able to get the most out of retirement.

See also "Living Wills and Durable Powers of Attorney" and "Make Your Own Will."

17. Pets and Animals

Bathe and Groom a Dog

Bathing and grooming your dog regularly will help it to live a long, healthy life. Don't worry about getting wet—wear old clothes or cut armholes into an oversize plastic garbage bag, and get the job done! Remember, bathing dogs too often will remove oils from the hair, causing their fur to dry out. In addition, never bathe small puppies or dogs that are sick or pregnant. Instead of bathing, groom the dog with a brush and damp washrag whenever possible.

Preparation

Get the dog ready. Prepare the dog for the bath by putting cotton in its ears and a dab of Vaseline in the corner of its eyes to keep soap out. If the dog has paint or tar stains on its coat, do not use paint remover or turpentine. Instead, soak the area with vegetable oil and leave overnight, then try to shampoo the stain out during the bath. If the stain does not come out, you may just want to cut out the small area of stained hair with scissors—it will grow back soon enough.

Get the proper materials. Bathe the dog in a sink or tub, or in a large basin outside. Wherever you do it, be sure the air is warm so the dog will not catch cold. If you put the dog in a tub, place a bath mat in the bottom for traction. A spray hose is preferable to a bucket of water or a shower head because it will give you more control of the water supply. Gather all materials you will need for the bath:

✓ Soap or shampoo: Do not use regular "people" soap or shampoo or household detergent. Special shampoo for pets is available at pet care stores. It should be tearless and antistatic; some may also enhance hair color or condition. If you use flea shampoo, follow the directions on the bottle carefully.

✓ Sponges and washcloths: Scrub the dog with materials that will not irritate or hurt it. Be especially careful when washing the dog's face.

✓ Towels: Have enough towels to dry the dog completely after the bath. You will probably need another towel for yourself.

Handling the Dog

Make the bath easy and comfortable for the dog by assuming a reassuring and positive tone while remaining firm. Avoid surprising or scaring the dog with sudden movements or hostility, and make sure the dog has relieved itself before you start. It may be helpful to have someone with you to hold the dog steady while you wash. Rest assured—dogs become more relaxed and compliant the more you bathe them.

Bathing Procedure

1. Allow a few inches of tepid water to accumulate in the tub.
2. Place the dog in the tub and keep the dog steady.
3. Wet the dog completely, beginning with the tail and working up to the head.
4. Shampoo the dog with your hands, also from tail to head. Massage the shampoo into the dog's skin, but don't rub too hard.
5. Wash the dog's underside and legs. These may be the dirtiest areas and may require scrubbing with a cloth or sponge.
6. Wash the dog's face lightly with a soft cloth or sponge, taking care not to get shampoo in its eyes. Clean its ears with the cloth, but do not go in too deep.
7. Rinse thoroughly. It is important that no shampoo is left on the dog. Dried shampoo can irritate the dog's skin, so rinse more than once.
8. Allow the dog to shake itself dry. Dogs have a natural way of drying themselves and should be allowed to shake before you towel-dry. Keep the dog in the tub and stand clear, or you're likely to get quite wet. Hold up a bath sheet to protect the room from the spray.
9. Take the dog out of the tub and rub its hair thoroughly with towels to get it as dry as possible. This is when the dog is most susceptible to catching a cold, so be sure to rub thoroughly.
10. Keep the dog in a warm area for a few hours until it is completely dry. You may want to use a hair drier to speed up the process.
11. Remove the cotton from the dog's ears and wipe the Vaseline from the corners of its eyes.
12. Once the dog is completely dry, brush it thoroughly to untangle hairs and groom the coat.

Alternatives to a Bath

To avoid the unpleasantness of getting your dog wet, you may want to consider a dry or no-rinse shampoo. Available at pet care stores, these products can be rubbed into the dog's hair without using water, then either brushed out or simply allowed to dry. Read all directions before using these shampoos. Rubbed-in baking soda is also said to soften, shine, and deodorize a dog's coat.

Maintain a regular grooming schedule for your dog.

✓ Brush once a day or once a week, depending on the breed. When the dog is shedding in spring or autumn, you may have to brush more. Always brush in the direction of the coat's nap. Choose a nylon brush for long-haired dogs, metal for medium-haired dogs, or either for short-haired dogs.

✓ Clean the dog's ears, eyes, and teeth. Every week, use a cotton ball to remove any discharge from the dog's ears. Use cotton soaked in sterile water to remove accumulations from the corners of the eyes. Rub the teeth, if your dog will let you, with a damp cloth soaked in baking soda or lemon.

✓ If your dog spends time outside on hard surfaces, its nails will wear down naturally. Otherwise, have the nails clipped during regular visits to the vet.

✓ Check the paws for debris and wash them daily. Soften them with petroleum jelly once a week, especially during winter or dry weather.

House-Train a Dog

Because dogs are pack animals and are willing to follow a leader, they are generally not very hard to house-train. Puppies are harder to train because their muscles are less developed. Certain breeds of dogs accept conditioning more easily. Whether you train your dog to go outside or in a designated papered area inside, there are a few important guidelines to help make the process as short and painless as possible—both for your sake and for your dog's.

✓ Give your dog an area to become familiar with before you let it roam freely around the house. It may be a crate (if your dog or your home is small) or a blocked-off area of the kitchen or laundry room. The dog naturally won't want to relieve itself there because it will understand that to be "home." Instead, the dog will wait for a chance to get out of the area, such as walk time or access to the papered area.

✓ Follow a consistent walking or papering schedule. The dog will adapt its own natural timetable to meet it. Keep the dog's needs in mind. It will need to be walked at least three times a day—more often for a puppy. Try to walk your dog about one hour after each feeding and once before you go to bed.

✓ Provide a nutritious diet, and establish consistent eating habits. Good food will make the dog less in need of relieving itself and will keep the dog generally healthy. Feeding at the same time every day means that the dog will have to go at the same time every day.

✓ Use positive reinforcement. Praise goes a long way with dogs. If they learn that when they do something they'll be made to feel good about it, naturally dogs continue doing it. Don't feel you need to give the dog a snack; "Good Dog!" and a friendly petting will suffice.

✓ When you need to correct the dog's actions, do so in the most effective way. When it comes to negative reinforcement, physical punishment is not the best or the most humane technique. Again, "Bad Dog!" will suffice if you are firm enough about it. If you catch the dog in the middle of relieving itself in the

417

house, try to distract it so the dog will stop before finishing. At that point take your pet outside; if the dog finishes there, give praise. If you catch the dog after the fact, don't rub its nose in it—that will make your pet feel dirty. Rather, reprimand the dog strongly while pointing to the offensive spot; your pet will understand what you mean.

✓ When you begin to recognize that the dog is getting onto a schedule, perhaps even within a week or two, you can ease up and let it roam freely. Try to stay as consistent with feeding and walking times as possible, though, to keep the dog on schedule.

Teach a Dog Basic Tricks

As a dog owner, you already know your pet responds best to only one type of stimulus: food. While some dogs can be weaned slowly off treats and are satisfied instead with the reward of your affection, it is best initially to keep a large supply of dog biscuits on hand. Never tease a dog by holding out a snack and then not delivering it, or pretending that you have one in your hand when it is empty. It is better to give a small piece of food for each correctly performed trick (and even the good tries). Never attempt to train an unfamiliar or unfriendly dog. You will be moving the dog about physically, and it could bite you quite easily.

The dog must know two basic positions before it graduates to performing tricks: sitting down and lying down. It is best to begin teaching these commands as soon as you acquire the dog and it feels comfortable with you. Teach sitting first. Stand a foot or two in front of the dog. Sharply command "Sit" in a medium to loud voice. (At first you may feel uncomfortable giving your dog commands, but do not make the mistake of speaking in a sweet voice. Dogs respond almost solely to tone, and you need not worry about insulting them, since they actually enjoy performing assigned tasks.) While repeating "Sit," gently push the dog's haunches down to the floor until it sits naturally. Praise the dog and give it physical attention, such as patting its head. Give it a treat. When the dog stands again, repeat the whole process. Practice sitting about ten times, then stop no matter how much progress you have made. Begin again the next day.

When your dog can sit, you are ready to teach it to lie down. First command the dog to take a sitting position. Then, while saying "Lie down," gently grasp its front paws and pull them forward until the animal is in a prone position. Praise the dog, feed it, and repeat this action about ten times.

On the third day, begin by practicing the "Sit" and "Lie down" actions. If the dog resists performing either one, or if it confuses the two, keep practicing. If it seems to grasp these movements, you are ready to move on to more complex maneuvers. The same basic process of training will always apply. It is a good idea to teach separate tricks on separate days, to keep from confusing the dog. Only you can judge how quickly your pet is ready to move along. Some breeds learn tricks quickly, whereas others are more resistant. Here is a list of simple tricks and how to teach them.

✓ Shake hands. With the dog in a sitting position, grasp one paw in your hand and lift it up and down a few times while commanding "Shake." Always choose the same paw and shake it with the same hand.

✓ Roll over. This is much easier with two people. With the dog in a "Lie down" position, one person gently rolls the dog over while the other rotates the treat in front of its face. The command is "Roll over."

✓ Speak. With the dog in "Sit" position, command it to "Speak," then immediately make a barking sound yourself. Continue repeating "Speak" and bark until the dog barks too. (The first few times this may happen out of frustration rather than comprehension.) When the dog begins barking after the first command, start saying "Speak" without barking yourself. Say "Speak" five or six times, and if the dog does not respond, bark again. Keep at it until the dog barks at the sound of the word rather than your "bark."

✓ Stay. Two people are helpful here, too. With the dog in "Sit" position, set a treat on the floor about two feet away. If the dog appears to want to approach the treat, gently but firmly hold it by the collar. Repeat the word "Stay" several times, then say "Okay" while simultaneously releasing the dog. Repeat the exercise until the dog stays in position until you give the "Okay." Try moving the treat to other spots and finally removing it altogether. Eventually the treat becomes a reward for executing the "Stay" behavior instead of a temptation to be overcome.

Keep a Pet Bird

Birds That Make Good Pets

Parrots

Parakeets

Canaries

Mynahs

Ducks and geese

Cockatoos and cockatiels

Love birds

Finches

Pigeons and doves

Choosing a Bird

When you buy a pet bird, look for these features:

✓ Sleek plumage

✓ Bright eyes

✓ Alertness

These are bad signs:

✓ The bird is fluffed up and sitting on the bottom of the cage.

✓ There is diarrhea in the cage.

✓ The bird constantly picks at its feathers and plucks them out.

Keeping Your Pet Bird

✓ Large birds should have enough room to stretch their wings and fly—consider building an aviary if you want to keep large birds as pets.

✓ Canaries, parakeets, and finches do well in indoor cages.

✓ Keep the bird cage in a sunny spot away from drafts.

✓ Set the bird cage in an area where you and others will interact with the bird.

✓ Cages should have a removable floor tray for easy cleaning, self-feeding seed and water holders, and perches.

✓ To prevent your bird from getting bored, put a swing, bells, a mirror, and fresh vegetation in the cage.

✓ Place grit on the cage floor—birds eat this to aid their digestion.

✓ Fasten a cuttle bone to the cage. This is a good source of calcium and keeps the bird's beak in good condition.

✓ Cover the cage at night to protect the bird from drafts and to give it a sense of security.

✓ Clean the bird cage regularly and often to prevent parasites, and give the bird fresh seed and water daily.

Photograph Your Pet

✓ Shoot in daylight, especially cloudy bright conditions, to avoid the "red eye/green eye" phenomenon of direct camera flashes. Outdoor lawn settings are perfect.

✓ Use zoom or telephoto lenses to catch good shots from a distance.

✓ Keep a loaded camera ready. Pets, like children, do the darndest things!

✓ For a portrait, brush and groom the pet before posing.

✓ If your pet does tricks or makes charming responses to familiar tones or commands, take advantage of that skill. Don't overdo, or your pet will lose interest.

✓ Keep the backgrounds simple and out of focus. Come down to your pet's level and look the pet in the eye. Put puppies, kittens, and other small animals on a table.

✓ Reward good behavior with a special treat.

✓ Take several pictures. The more you take, the more accustomed your pet will be to the process.

✓ Have a friend engage the animal so you can focus on setting up the shot.

✓ Be patient! Modeling isn't easy.

See also "Take a Great Picture."

Basic Cat Care

Indoor cats are remarkably independent animals and perform many self-grooming activities. Still, owners should pay close attention to a cat's coat, nails, ears, and teeth.

Coat Care

The indoor cat rarely needs to be bathed by an owner and will groom its own coat. Bathe a cat only when you suspect fleas or if a toxic substance, such as insecticide, wall paint, or polish, gets on the cat's coat and could make the cat sick if it tries to lick the toxin off while self-grooming.

If you do try to bathe your cat, never put the cat in a tub or sink while the water is running. This will most likely panic the animal and make a good bath impossible. Before bathing, put cotton in the cat's ears to protect them and a drop of mineral oil in each eye. Place your cat in a tub or sink with only an inch or two of warm water, wash from head to toe with a mild tearless shampoo, and rinse completely. Try putting some plastic mesh in the bottom of the tub for the cat to grip its claws into during the bath. When finished, wrap the pet in towels and pat dry thoroughly; keep the cat in a warm room to avoid chills.

You can help your indoor cat's self-grooming by brushing its coat regularly. House cats shed all year around. Use a plastic or rubber-bristled brush, never metal, and make strokes along the nap of the coat. Brushing regularly keeps cat hair off furniture and rugs and also helps prevent fur balls in the cat's stomach. A healthy-looking coat is a strong indication of your pet's well-being. If a cat stops grooming, or if the coat looks straggly or oily, loses its sheen, or sheds clumps of hair, take the pet to the vet immediately for a checkup.

Nails

A cat's natural instinct is to claw and scratch. If you have an indoor cat, protecting your furniture, clothes, and rugs can be a challenge. Teach your cat to use scratching posts and other designated areas for this necessary activity. If a cat persistently scratches where it shouldn't, keep a water bottle handy and spray the cat in the act. One or two bursts convey the message quite effectively.

Trim cat nails with special clippers available in pet care stores. Gently press the cat's toe to reveal a nail. Clip off only the sharp tip while aiming the clippers from above or below the nail, not across. Don't cut into the pink area of the nail; this will hurt your cat badly. You need only trim the front claws. Most cats struggle during this process; make it part of your cat's normal weekly routine and be consistent about where, when, and how the nails are clipped.

Declawing is a surgical procedure performed when cats are young. It can be a dangerous operation for an older cat and may cause psychological problems related to cats' strong instinct for clawing.

Ears

Delicate cat ears shouldn't be touched. Remember to protect them with cotton while bathing. If you suspect an ear infection or other problem, take your cat to the vet immediately. Indoor cats are far less prone to ear problems than outdoor cats. If the vet discovers that your cat has a problem with earwax buildup, clean ears with a cotton swab moistened with a drop or two of mineral oil. Move the swab gently over the ear's contours; don't poke or jab. Never clean the ears with soap and water.

Teeth

A healthy indoor cat with a good diet won't need much tooth care. Ask the vet about the best food for your cat's age, weight, and general health. Older cats with urinary or digestive difficulties will require a special diet.

You can help prevent tartar buildup on your cat's teeth by rubbing them twice a month with cotton or a child's toothbrush moistened with baking soda and water. Cats older than ten may benefit from professional oral hygiene from the vet to prevent gum disease and keep teeth healthy.

If your cat stops eating for a mysterious reason, always check inside its mouth for any problem that may be lurking there. See your vet.

House-Train a Cat

Unlike house-training a dog, teaching a cat to use the litter box requires little effort and very little time. Cats are naturally inclined to use a litter box, and a small amount of encouragement is often all a cat needs. Here are some tips on how to go about it.

Initial Litter-Training

Very often cats are already trained by the time you get them; they might have learned from their mother or from watching other cats. If the cat is already familiar with litter boxes, simply introduce the cat to its new box and keep an eye out for a few days to make sure the cat isn't experiencing any difficulties.

A good way to get a cat used to its litter box is to take the cat over to the box right after meals for the first few days. Put the cat into the box, then move its front paws in the litter. Because cats instinctively bury their waste, doing this should be enough to explain to the cat what the box is for.

To reinforce good behavior, praise the cat the first few times it uses the litter box. Also, be patient when teaching the cat, and don't be surprised if it has a relapse now and then in the beginning.

Possible Problems

If the cat has difficulty learning or is reluctant to use its litter box, the problem may be minor and easily solved. Some possible problems and solutions include these:

✓ The cat may be afraid of something near the box. Simply move the litter box to a place where your cat will be more comfortable.

✓ The cat may want a bit more privacy when using the litter box. If so, buy a kitty screen or cover for the box.

✓ The cat may be picky and not like the shape of the box or the type of litter you are using. Experiment with different shapes of boxes and different kinds of litter.

✓ The box may be dirty. Cats are very clean animals. The problem might be you—make sure you keep the litter box clean.

Corrective Techniques

With pets, it's always better to prevent than to correct. But if you continue to have difficulty getting your cat to use the litter box, you may have to resort to more drastic measures. Check with your vet to rule out medical problems. Here are some ideas:

✓ If there is an area where your cat continually soils, put its food there. A cat will never soil where it has to eat. After it has eaten, take the cat to its box.

✓ Take the soil and put it next to the cat, so it can smell it wherever it goes. This will send the message that what it did was bad, and that it cannot escape responsibility. Do this only for ten minutes or so. Never rub a cat's nose in it, or humiliate the cat.

✓ Confine the cat to a small area for a short time. Put only its litter box, food, and toys in the area. The cat will be forced to use the box because it won't want to soil its dining or play area.

Litter Maintenance

For most cats, any litter you use is fine. Clean the box often to prevent odors from developing and to keep it attractive to your cat (not to mention your guests). Every other day, empty the box of the cat's soilings and stir the remaining litter to refreshen it. Empty the box completely and wash it with soap (don't use other chemical cleaning products) about every two weeks.

Health Alert

If an adult cat stops using the litter box and cannot easily be persuaded to resume normal hygiene habits, it may be sick. Take the cat to the vet for a checkup. A common and dangerous ailment, most frequent in male cats, is a blocked urinary tract. If your cat is lethargic and you've noticed that he hasn't used the litter pan for a day or more, or if he returns to the litter pan every few minutes without being able to urinate, get him to your vet immediately.

Set Up an Aquarium

Not only is a home aquarium a place to keep your pet fish; a well-designed and healthy aquarium can also be a dramatic feature of any room.

Tank

Start with the tank. Purchase a tank that is leakproof and strong enough to support the water it will hold. Test the tank before you furnish it by putting it in a tub and filling it with water. Small leaks can usually be repaired. New tanks should not leak at all.

The appropriate size and shape of the tank depends on the number and size of its fish. The tank should be big enough to allow all fish enough room to move. More important than the volume is surface area. Because fish breathe air caught in the water, the surface, where outside air and water meet, must be large enough to trap a suitable amount of it. Generally, there should be about 25 square inches of surface for every 1 inch of fish. A tall, thin tank will hold fewer fish than a wide tank of smaller volume.

You'll also need a tank cover and stand. The cover keeps dust out of the tank and keeps the fish in, and it should fit the size of the tank. The stand is not necessary if you plan to rest the tank on a tabletop. Stands, preferably made of iron, should be strong enough to support the tank when it is full of water.

Place an aquarium tank where it will get some sunlight, though direct light may raise water temperature and harm the fish. Do not place the tank near heaters or air conditioners, or in any other spot susceptible to temperature changes. Avoid drafty areas. Remember to place the tank near an electrical outlet; you will need power for the filter, aerator, and heater.

Tank Equipment

Tank light. Because natural light is usually not sufficient for an aquarium inside a house, most tanks need some sort of artificial light to act as a "sun" for the fish and plants. Fluorescent light strips that fit onto the top of the tank work best and can be bought at an aquarium shop. The light need not be strong—about 20 watts for every 12 inches of depth in a tank is enough—and should be turned on about 12 hours a day—more if you have live plants.

Aerator (air pump). To make sure there is enough oxygen in the water, attach an air pump to your tank. An electrically powered aerator releases air bubbles in the tank, circulates the water to expose more of it to surface oxygen, and removes carbon dioxide.

Filter. The filter keeps the water clean and clear of contaminants such as fish waste, old food, dust, and dirt. With mechanical filters (electrically powered), water is drawn in and cleaned as it passes through—the filter often serves to aerate the water as well, making an aerator unnecessary.

Furnishing and Decorating the Tank

When decorating the tank, create a natural environment for the fish.

Gravel. Nearly all aquariums use small, coarse gravel as a base. It is not only decorative but serves to hold down plants and other fixtures. Wash gravel thoroughly before adding it to the tank, then lay it so it slopes down slightly from the back.

Stones and/or wood. Wash wood before adding it to the tank. Stones should be insoluble and boiled before using.

Plants. Because live plants require as much attention and upkeep as the fish, many beginners choose to put plastic, artificial plants in their aquarium. Live plants, though, can serve as food and as a nesting area for the fish. If you use live plants, make sure they are compatible with the type of fish in the tank, and make sure they are germ-free (avoid wild plants).

Toys. Other decorations such as treasure chests, deep-sea divers, and coral castles are common in aquariums, particularly those operated by children. Any toy you would like to add is fine as long as it won't harm the fish or the water. Too many toys, however, can take away from the natural look of the aquarium and deprive the fish of swimming space.

Water

Most tap water is initially unsuitable for fish because of its chlorine and other chemical content. To condition tap water, fill the tank and let it stand for a week before putting fish in. About a day before you add the fish, begin aerating and filtering the water to allow all chemicals to evaporate or settle. Use water treatment products to clean the water and protect the fish.

For fresh-water tropical fish, keep the water temperature close to 75° F. While some fish require higher temperatures, water that is too warm will become ripe for bacteria. Use an underwater thermometer to regulate temperature. To maintain proper temperature, get a heater with a thermostat for the tank; place the thermometer across the tank from the heater to get the most accurate reading. To ensure that the heater is strong enough to warm the entire tank, multiply the number of gallons in the tank by seven to get the approximate number of watts needed.

Regulate your aquarium's water for acidity. Use a pH test kit to regularly gauge the water; a normal pH reading falls somewhere between neutral (7.0) and slightly alkaline (7.5), though it is best to maintain the same pH level as was used in the store where you purchased the fish. Water that is overacidic can be neutralized by adding bottled water or with special chemicals available at your pet shop.

Change 25 percent of the water in the tank about every three weeks. Pretreat new water before adding, then siphon out old water and replace with new.

Adding the Fish

Once the tank is set up, decorated, and filled with healthy water, it is time to add the fish. Remember the surface area considerations and the full-grown sizes of fish when you decide how many fish to buy. Also, keep in mind compatibility: Some fish are not friendly to other species, while some fish are hostile to their own species. Some fish tend to stay near the surface; others swim near the bottom. Get some of both kinds so they will spread out. Of course, avoid fish that eat other fish. Consult a fish guide or ask the aquarium salesperson to help you make sure all the fish you buy will live happily together.

18. Safety and Emergencies

Perform the Heimlich Maneuver

Choking can be caused by food, drink, gum, or objects accidentally inhaled through the nose or mouth that block the airway to the lungs. If air is unable to reach the lungs, death may result. The Heimlich maneuver is one of the most effective ways to help a choking person (Figure 1).

1. Make sure the victim is choking. The victim will not be able to talk but will probably communicate through signs and actions, such as grabbing his or her throat. Get someone to call 911.

2. Stand behind the victim and put your arms around his or her upper abdomen.

3. Make a fist at the bottom of the victim's breastbone.

4. Push your fist upward into the victim's chest in a quick motion, putting pressure on the lungs. This will push air out of the lungs and into the windpipe, forcing the object to dislodge from the throat.

Push upward into chest

Figure 1. The Heimlich maneuver

5. Repeat the procedure. It may take many tries before you dislodge the object.

6. If the victim is pregnant or obese, pressure should be directed to the chest instead of the abdomen.

7. If the victim is unconscious, turn him or her onto the back. Put your hand against the victim's middle abdomen. Place your other hand on top, and push upward with a sharp thrust. Try to remove the obstruction with your fingers. If the victim stops breathing, begin artificial respiration.

8. If the victim is a child, put the heel of your hand above the navel and well below the rib cage. Cover it with the other hand and push down with a sharp upward movement. The child should be on his or her back.

9. If the victim is a baby, straddle the infant over your arm with its head lower than the torso. Hold the baby's jaw in your hand to support the head. Give four back blows between the shoulder blades to dislodge the foreign object.

Swallow a Big Pill

Swallowing pills, especially chalky tablets or large "horse" pills, can be enough to make anyone gag. Follow these tips to help the medicine go down smoothly.

1. If the pill is scored, use a sharp knife to break it in half, and swallow one half at a time.

2. Have a glass of water, juice, or milk ready; make sure that juice and milk are not contraindicated with your specific medication.

3. Place the pill as far back on your tongue as you can, then take a large enough swig of liquid to wash it down.

4. If you find the pill has not moved after you've swallowed, try placing it farther back on your tongue and tipping your head back as you swallow.

Bandage a Cut or Wound

Different types of wounds and their location on the body require different kinds of dressings and bandages. It is preferable to use sterile store-bought supplies, but in an emergency, any clean cloth or paper goods such as tissues or toilet paper can be used. To dress a wound, you will need these items:

✓ A dressing or compress, such as a gauze pad, handkerchief, napkin, or other fabric (avoid cotton balls, as the fibers will be difficult to remove from the wound).

✓ A bandage, such as gauze bandaging, elastic material bandages, triangle or square bandages, Bandaids, or in an emergency, a belt, tie, sock, stocking, towel, handkerchief, or other piece of fabric.

How to Apply the Dressing and Bandage

1. Use a dressing that covers the entire wound.

2. Hold the dressing over the wound and lower it into place.

3. Secure the dressing with bandages or tape, taking the ends around in opposite directions to encircle the area (wrist, arms, leg, chest, etc.); fasten with a clip, safety pin, tape, or by tying off.

4. The bandage used to secure the dressing should be snug but not too tight—this will inhibit circulation. Do not wrap the bandage completely around the wounded area in case swelling occurs.

5. When bandaging a leg, foot, arm, or hand, leave the toes and fingers exposed in order to check for swelling or change in color or temperature, which indicate a bandage is too tight.

6. Be especially careful not to wind too tightly when using an elastic bandage; do not use a wet gauze bandage because it may shrink as it dries and become too tight.

Bandages for Specific Body Parts

Fingers or Toes

1. Draw the bandage from the base of the finger over the tip to the base on the other side of the hand. Repeat for several turns.

2. Starting at the base, wrap circular turns of the bandage around the finger, gradually working up to the tip and back down to the base.

3. To secure the bandage, pull the bandage diagonally across the back of the hand to the wrist, circling the wrist one or two times; pull the bandage from the opposite side of the wrist back up to the finger; loop it around the finger and back to the wrist to tie off (Figure 1).

Figure 1. Fingers or toes

Ankle and Foot

1. Circle the bandage around the ball of the foot a few times.

2. Bring the bandage diagonally across the front of the foot, and wrap it around the ankle.

3. Bring the bandage diagonally down across the front of the foot and under the arch.

4. Repeat to cover the foot and ankle, and tie off at the ankle (Figure 2).

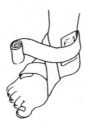

Figure 2. Ankle and foot

Hand and Wrist

1. Circle the bandage around the palm a few times to anchor it.

2. Bring the bandage diagonally across the back of the hand and around the wrist, then back diagonally across the back of the hand and back to the palm.

3. Repeat this figure-eight wrap several times, and tie off at the wrist (Figure 3).

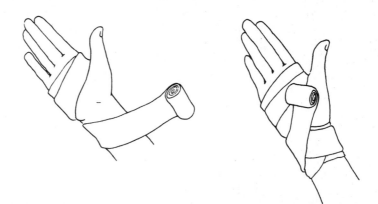

Figure 3. Hand and wrist

Arm and Leg

1. Place dressing on the wound and hold in place.

2. Anchor the bandage by wrapping it around the limb below the wound; make spiral turns up the limb to cover the dressing.

3. Secure the bandage above the wound by tying it off (Figure 4).

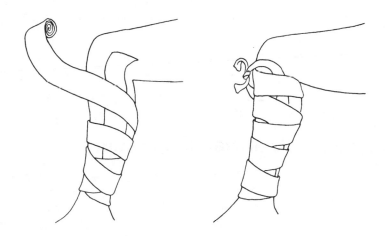

Figure 4. Arm and leg

Elbow or Knee

1. Hold the dressing on the wound and anchor the bandage above the joint by circling the limb several times.

2. Bring bandage diagonally across the dressing, circle the limb below the joint, then bring it back diagonally across the dressing.

3. Repeat this figure-eight wrap until the area is securely covered, then fasten above or below the joint (Figure 5).

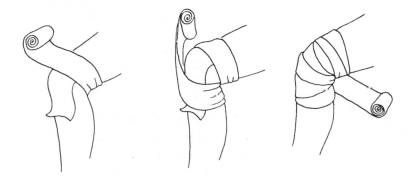

Figure 5. Elbow or knee

431

Remove a Splinter

1. Using soap and water or hydrogen peroxide, wash the area that contains the splinter and the hands that will remove it.

2. Use a tweezer, needle, or pin that has been sterilized with rubbing alcohol or by a flame.

3. Using the tweezer, pull the splinter out at the same angle it entered to avoid breaking it.

4. If the splinter is under the skin, use a needle or pin to gently open the wound enough to pull the splinter out.

5. After removal, cleanse the wound with soap and water or hydrogen peroxide.

Administer Artificial Respiration

Artificial respiration is vital first aid. It is relatively safe to administer and can be crucial in saving the life of someone who has stopped breathing. Begin artificial respiration immediately once you have determined the person has stopped breathing, if you can see that the face is gray or the lips and tongue have turned blue. Tell someone else to call 911, or do it quickly before giving mouth-to-mouth resuscitation (Figure 1). Remember, even six minutes without breathing can cause death. If there is no pulse in the wrist or neck, or no discernable heartbeat, cardiopulmonary resuscitation (CPR) must also be administered (see also "Perform CPR").

1. *Determine consciousness.* Ask "Are you okay?" If you get no response, or the person has no breathing or only weak, labored breathing, start treatment immediately.

2. *Put the person on his/her back,* face up and laid out flat.

3. *Clear the mouth of any obstructions.* Make sure the person's tongue is flat and has not fallen back into the throat.

4. *Open the air passage.* Tilt the person's head back so the chin points up. Do not tilt the head if the person has sustained neck or head injuries; simply open the mouth by pulling down on the jawbones. If it is a young child, do not tilt the head back as far as you normally would—a child's neck and airways are more fragile than an adult's.

5. *Bring your head close to the person's head.* With your ear over the mouth, take five seconds to listen for breathing. Also watch the chest to see if it expands. If there is no breathing, continue.

6. *Pinch the nostrils.* Resting your hand on the forehead, pinch the nostrils with your fingers. Support the neck with your other hand.

7. *Take a deep breath.* Fill your lungs with air, then place your mouth against the person's mouth to create an airtight seal.

8. *Breathe into the mouth.* Breathe until the person's chest inflates with air. If mouth-to-mouth breathing is not possible, breathe into the person's nose while keeping his or her mouth closed. For infants, place your mouth over both the mouth and the nose, and give less air. It may take several breaths to inflate the person's chest, so make sure the lungs do not deflate between breaths. If the chest does not rise, there could be an obstruction. In that case, you must attempt to dislodge whatever is blocking breathing (see also "Perform the Heimlich Maneuver" on page 401).

9. *Pull your mouth away.* When the person's chest is fully expanded (or you have blown four full breaths into the mouth), remove your mouth.

10. *Listen and watch for exhale.* Repeat Step 5.

11. *Repeat until breathing starts.* Redo Steps 6 through 10 every five seconds if the person is an adult, four seconds if a child, and three seconds if an infant.

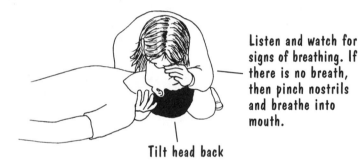

Listen and watch for signs of breathing. If there is no breath, then pinch nostrils and breathe into mouth.

Tilt head back

Figure 1. Administering artificial respiration

Perform CPR

Cardiopulmonary resuscitation (CPR) is initiated when someone is not breathing and it is likely that the heart has stopped beating. CPR cannot be learned in a crisis; contact your local hospital, Red Cross, or YMCA for information on training classes. If circulation is interrupted for more than three to four minutes, keeping oxygen-rich blood from reaching the brain, brain damage can occur. CPR is a vitally important medical emergency skill to have (Figure 1).

1. *Determine that cardiac arrest has occurred.* Make sure the victim has not merely fainted. When breathing is present, even if no pulse is felt, this usually means the heart is still beating. In cardiac arrest, the victim will have little or no discernable breathing, pale skin color, and blue-gray lips. No pulse will be felt in the wrist, in the neck, or by listening to the chest. Have someone call 911 or do it yourself quickly, if possible.

433

2. *Begin mouth-to-mouth resuscitation* (see also "Administer Artificial Respiration").

3. *If breathing does not restart, begin CPR.* Place one hand on the lower part of the victim's breastbone, well below the chest area. Cover with your other hand. Press with the heel of the lower hand. Give two breaths of mouth-to-mouth after every 15 compressions (80 compressions per minute). If two people administer CPR, one should give mouth-to-mouth resuscitation while the other presses—one breath every five compressions (60 compressions per minute). Rest about a second between each sequence.

If you do not have formal CPR training in a crisis, and other people are present, yell out. Ask if anyone knows CPR. Once your loved one has recovered, get yourself to a training class—and take a friend. There are special CPR procedures for children and infants. Learn these too!

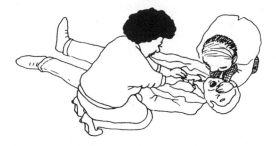

Figure 1. Performing CPR

Start a Fire Without a Match

Method 1

1. Find two stones, preferably flint.

2. Build a small mound of dry leaves and grass or finely shredded paper to use to start the fire.

3. Holding one stone steady, strike it in a flat, sharp, sweeping motion with the other stone, avoiding your fingers.

4. Do this repeatedly, holding the stones close to the mound of dry materials. The striking will produce a spark that will catch the dry materials.

5. Once the fire catches, add twigs and bark, then larger branches.

Method 2

1. Build a small mound of dry leaves, grass, or shredded paper.

2. Find two sturdy sticks. In one stick, hollow out a small groove that will fit the butt end of the other stick. Place this stick among the dried materials, groove side up.

3. Fit the end of the other stick in the groove, and hold the vertical stick between the palms of your hands.

4. Rub your palms together rapidly so that the stick is rolled between them. This movement will produce friction (and heat) at the contact between the two sticks, and the dried materials will gradually begin to smolder.

Tips for Building a Fire

1. Build a fire in a level area sheltered from high wind and cleared of leaves, grass, and other brush as well as fuel.

2. Build a mound of leaves and bark, then place twigs so that air can circulate.

3. Start the fire and add larger twigs and branches as the fire grows.

4. Keep the fire small and never leave it unattended. Extinguish it with water or by covering it with dirt. Do not leave until you are sure the fire is out.

Get Into a Locked Car

Newer cars are made tougher to break into; specialized tools are often required for particular vehicles. Although these tools are available for purchase, check with your local police department to find out whether they are legal to own. If you lock yourself out of your car, your best bet is to:

1. Call the local police department. They most likely will have the tools necessary to open the car door.

2. Call a local locksmith.

3. If you have a tool such as a Slim Jim, insert it between the window and door to pop the lock. Consider that a Slim Jim may damage power windows.

4. Try spreading the door with a wedge, then inserting the Slim Jim or another similar tool to pop the lock.

Thwart a Mugger

Avoid Trouble and Prepare Beforehand

✓ Be alert when walking on the street.
✓ Don't look scared; walk tall and relaxed.
✓ Walk among a group of people or with someone else you know.
✓ Don't walk through deserted parks or dark alleys alone.
✓ Cross the street if you see or suspect trouble ahead.
✓ Don't wait for buses alone.
✓ Sit near the driver on a bus or subway at night. Use the middle cars on the subway at night.

✓ Know where you are and where you are going. Confused pedestrians are easy targets.

✓ Know where police or fire stations are located in your neighborhood.

✓ Know which stores are open on a street, especially late at night, in case you have to duck in somewhere to avoid trouble.

✓ Walk close to the curb so you can see whether someone is hiding in a doorway or around a corner.

✓ Walk against traffic so a car cannot follow behind you.

✓ Don't carry valuable items if you can avoid it. Dress appropriately. Expensive suits stand out in depressed neighborhoods.

✓ Carry your purse securely under your arm, or your wallet in your front pocket. Consider carrying a backpack or other bag with your purse securely buried within it. Choose a purse with many zippers and flaps.

✓ Carry a whistle or aerosol spray for defense. Remember, though, that weapons you carry can be used against you.

Handle a Confrontation

✓ Cooperate if you truly fear the mugger will harm you otherwise.

✓ Don't fight back unless you have a clear advantage or a clear opportunity to disable the mugger. Be sure the mugger is not carrying any lethal weapons.

✓ Yell for help in anger; don't scream in fright.

✓ If you can run away, run toward help.

✓ Do not carry a dangerous weapon unless you know how to use it defensively, you can access it quickly, and you can be certain it will not fall into the hands of the mugger.

✓ Remain balanced if you see the mugger charging, and use his own momentum against him to throw him off balance.

✓ Attack the mugger's weak points: poke the eyes with your fingers, keys, or pen; jar the nose with the flat, reverse side of your fist; hand chop the throat; pull the hair; squeeze the neck; poke the chest; punch or kick the stomach; punch or kick or squeeze the groin; kick the shins; stomp the toes.

✓ Don't give the mugger any hint, such as a darting glance or a tensing of muscles, that you may attack; use the element of surprise.

✓ Use your body as a weapon: butt with your head, bite with your teeth (but do not break skin), strike with your elbow, poke or punch or scratch or pull with your hands and fingers, kick with your knee or foot.

✓ Learn specific self-defense moves by taking a class or consulting a book, and practice them.

✓ Get a good look at the mugger and where he or she runs off to; seek help immediately.

Stay Warm

With a temperature of 98.6°F, the human body needs a certain amount of warmth in order to survive. When you are exposed to cold, your blood retreats inward toward the core of your body to protect the vital organs. Extreme exposure of the extremities can lead to frostbite, while a drastic drop in your core body temperature will result in hypothermia.

Stay Warm Outdoors

✓ Dress in layers—you can always peel one off if you become too warm.
✓ Wear long thermal underwear, silk sock and glove liners, woolen socks, a turtleneck shirt and sweater, heavy pants.
✓ Always wear a hat—you lose most of your body heat through your head. Make sure that your hat covers your ears.
✓ Wear a scarf or neckband wide enough to cover your mouth and face, if necessary, as well as gloves or mittens.
✓ Wool sweaters are best; they are warm and will not trap moisture as cotton and acrylic will.
✓ Down-filled jackets offer the greatest warmth; try wearing ski pants too.
✓ Wear hiking boots or lined snow boots designed to protect in very cold temperatures.
✓ Wrap yourself in blankets, sleeping bags, or other similar items.
✓ If it is necessary and feasible, build a fire to stay near for warmth.
✓ Seek shelter from the wind in a cave or dense evergreen forest, or behind a mountain, boulder, building, or other structure, depending on your location.

Stay Warm in Cold Water

✓ Remove as much of your body from the water as you can by getting into a boat or onto a raft, log, buoy, or other floating object.
✓ Try to stay still. Swimming or treading water will cause your body to cool much faster.
✓ Since most heat is lost through the head, try to keep your head and neck above water.
✓ The torso and the groin are other areas of great heat loss, so try to float keeping your knees drawn up and your arms hugging yourself.
✓ If you are with other people, huddle close in a circle side by side to help preserve heat.

Remove a Tick

Method 1

1. Dab the tick with an alcohol-soaked cotton ball; the alcohol will cause the tick to loosen its hold.

2. Grasp the tick with tweezers or cotton, and rock it back and forth as you slowly pull it out.

3. Try not to break the tick but pull it out whole; if the mouth part remains lodged in the skin it could cause an infection.

4. After removal, wash the area with soap and water.

Method 2

1. Cover the tick with heavy oil, such as mineral, vegetable, or machine oil. This will close its pores and cause the tick to release its hold.

2. If the tick does not disengage within 30 minutes, use a sterilized tweezer as indicated in Method 1 to remove it. Be sure to get all of the parts.

3. After removal, wash the area with soap and water.

Note: If you have a fever or a red bulls-eye rash (signs of Lyme disease), seek medical treatment immediately.

Ingredients of a Good First-Aid Kit

One of the most important pieces of equipment you can have in your home, car, or office is a well-equipped first-aid kit. Ideally, you won't need to use it very often, but you'll be glad to have it with you in an emergency. A good first-aid kit will have the necessary materials to cover as many potential injuries and sicknesses as possible. Make sure you know how and when to use each ingredient of your kit. While no first-aid kit can cover every situation, one with the following materials will enable you to treat a wide variety of emergencies, or at least stabilize them until further medical help can be reached:

✓ Adhesive strip bandages, for small cuts
✓ Cotton balls
✓ Gauze pads. Should be sealed, sterile and of various sizes
✓ Bandages (a long, rolled strip, 1" or 2" (or both) wide) and safety pins
✓ Towels. Size depends on size of first-aid kit box, but have at least one or two clean hand towels
✓ Adhesive tape
✓ First-aid cream and Calamine lotion
✓ Antiseptic soap or cleansing agent
✓ Antiseptic wet wipes

✓ Simple medicines, for pain relief (aspirin or aspirin substitute), motion sickness (Dramamine), sore throat (drops), and allergies (antihistamine)

✓ Thermometer

✓ Syrup of ipecac

✓ Cups; should be reusable and made of unbreakable plastic

✓ Salt, baking soda, and iodine

✓ Wood sticks to use as splints. Have small tongue depressors for finger injuries, and foot-long pieces for arms and legs

✓ Scissors (preferably blunt-nosed), tweezers, and pliers

✓ Hydrogen peroxide or rubbing alcohol

✓ Flashlight and blanket

✓ Bottled water

✓ Any other tools or medicines that may apply specifically to you or your family, such as an extra inhaler for asthmatics, or insulin for diabetics

Contact the local Red Cross, YMCA, or community hospital for information on first-aid and CPR training classes. It never hurts to be prepared. Never attempt to move someone badly injured without trained help unless loss of life is an immediate factor—this is especially true for persons with suspected spinal injuries. In the event of any emergency, call 911 as quickly as you are able. Stay level-headed; use common sense.

Put Out a Fire

Some fires can easily be extinguished, but if you are unsure whether you can extinguish a fire, call the fire department before you do anything. Don't even attempt to fight a fire if there is a risk of being trapped. Just call the fire department and leave the area (or leave and then call, depending on the severity of the blaze).

Cooking Fires

✓ For a fire in the oven, turn off the heat and keep the door closed until the fire burns out (usually in a minute or two).

✓ For a pan fire on the stove top, shut off the heat and cover the pan with a lid or plate.

✓ For a toaster fire, pull the plug and use a fire extinguisher.

✓ For a deep-fat fryer or other grease fire, turn off the heat and cover the appliance with a metal lid. If it is flaming, use a fire extinguisher.

✓ Never use water on an electrical or grease fire. Use a fire extinguisher or smother the fire with a lid, plate, or baking soda.

Clothing Fires

1. If your clothing or someone else's clothing catches fire, do not run. The air will simply fan the flames and make them worse.

2. Immediately drop to the ground and roll repeatedly to smother the flames.

3. Wrap the person with a blanket, rug, drapery, towel, or coat to help smother the flames.

4. If outdoors, drop to the ground and roll, and use snow, dirt, or sand to smother the flames.

5. Try to remove the burned clothing, but do not pull it over the head. Seek medical attention immediately to treat burns.

Trash Fires

✓ A trash fire will spread quickly. If you get to it in time, extinguish it with water. If it has begun to spread, call the fire department before attempting to fight the fire.

✓ To prevent trash fires, keep rubbish, old clothing, toys, rags, and boxes to a minimum, and store them away from flammable chemicals and devices, such as the furnace or heater.

✓ Keep trash in metal garbage cans with lids.

✓ Keep wastebaskets and other garbage containers away from sources of heat such as the stove or a heater.

✓ Do spring, summer, autumn, and winter cleaning if necessary to keep your home, garage, and yard free from combustible debris.

✓ After painting and refinising projects, throw away oily rags immediately to avoid the hazards of spontaneous combustion. Don't store them.

Campfires

1. Drown the fire with water.

2. Stir the coals and soak them again.

Drive in Snow and Fog

Few things are as potentially dangerous as driving without proper care in bad weather. Not only is your life at risk, but the lives of other passengers, drivers, or pedestrians are placed at peril. That's why it is absolutely essential to be a cautious driver, no matter what the weather, but especially when the weather is bad. The two conditions that most commonly require special care on the road are snow (ice) and fog. Check weather reports for potentially dangerous driving conditions in your area before setting out on the road. If possible, stay off the road altogether during bad weather conditions. If you must drive, follow these tips for reducing the danger.

Snow (Ice)

✓ Reduce speed. The simplest and most important technique for driving on roads that are slippery is to slow down! It not only lengthens your reaction time if a problem should arise but also allows your car's tires to get a better grip on the road.

✓ Don't panic. Excessive worry and fear will only make matters worse. Be attentive to the road but not to the point that it makes you tense. Be level-headed at all times.

✓ Use proper tires. Have snow tires or all-season radial tires during the winter; many states even require them. Putting chains on your tires is also effective.

✓ Reduce air in tires. Letting a little bit of air out of each tire will increase traction by increasing the area of each tire that touches the ground. Do not let too much air out, though, or you'll risk damaging your car. Let a service station attendant do this for you.

✓ Drive a car that handles well. Generally, four-wheel-drive cars and front-wheel-drive cars handle best in snow and ice. If you have a choice, drive such a car.

✓ Clear windows and lights. Before you start driving, make sure all windows and outside lights (headlights, brake lights) are completely clear of ice and snow. It's important that you have complete visibility at all times, but especially when you are driving on slippery roads. It's also important for other cars to be able to see you coming. Use an ice scraper or snow brush to clean off your car.

✓ Fill up on windshield washer fluid. Windshield washer fluid is particularly helpful in snow driving for two reasons: It washes off the salt and slush from the road that accumulates on your windshield and makes visibility difficult, and it can help melt the ice that forms on your windshield.

✓ Carry emergency equipment. If your car is buried in snow, if it stalls, or if you are in an accident, it will be helpful to have the proper supplies to deal with a road emergency. You may want to have salt, cat litter, or sand with you in case your car is stuck and needs traction, or a shovel to dig your car out of a heavy snow. A first-aid kit will be useful in an accident (see also "Ingredients of a Good First-Aid Kit"), though be certain you know how to apply first-aid before you treat anyone. In case you stall, road flares will notify oncoming cars that you are stopped, and a blanket will keep you warm while you wait for help (but do not stay in a stalled car unless you are completely off the road). Finally, it's always good to have your trusted ice scraper with you at all times.

✓ Know how to handle a skid. To avoid skidding, pump your brakes when you must come to a sudden stop. Applying pressure on and off the brakes will make sure your brakes don't lock—never slam on the brakes. If you do skid, do not apply the brakes immediately. Instead, simply remove your foot from the gas, turn the steering wheel in the direction you are skidding, and allow your car to slow down. If you begin to fishtail, stay with it and continue steering into the skid. If you have front- or rear-wheel drive, gently pump the brakes once the car begins to slow to bring it to a stop. If you have anti-lock brakes, do not pump them; begin to apply the brakes slowly with a gentle even pressure. Remain calm. Pull over safely and collect yourself if need be; don't continue on if you are badly shaken by a rough skid.

✓ Keep away from other cars. In case you skid, staying as far away from other vehicles as possible will make a collision less likely and will increase your reaction time.

✓ Avoid hills. Find a route that doesn't require you to climb potentially icy slopes. Hills are frequent trouble spots.

✓ Use major roads. If possible, stick to the larger roads or highways; they are usually the ones that get plowed first.

✓ Keep your car in good shape. A snowstorm is no time to find out that your brakes need fixing. Prepare your car for winter before winter starts.

Fog

✓ Reduce speed. Whenever road conditions are treacherous, slow down.

✓ Drive with low beams. Do not put on your high beams (brights) in the hope of seeing farther; you'll only be blinded. Use fog lights if you have them.

✓ Open a window. Unless it's too cold outside, crack open a window slightly when you drive. This should prevent your windshield from fogging up. Otherwise, let vent air blow on the windshield to prevent fog.

✓ Allow for stopping distance. The distance it will take you to stop your car should not exceed your range of visibility. Figure your stopping distance and adjust your speed accordingly.

✓ Stay within clearly marked areas. Particularly if you are unfamiliar with the road, stay in your lane and carefully observe all visible signs and boundaries. This is not the time for risk-taking or fancy driving. Stop if you have to and as far away from moving traffic as possible—don't make yourself an unwitting target.

19. Travel

Get the Most Out of Trip Planning

Your trip is only as good as your planning. Plan well in advance of your departure, and devote plenty of time to the process. Consider these major elements.

Transportation

Unless the method of moving from here to there is already decreed, weigh the pros and cons of motoring, flying, hiking, cycling, going by boat, or combining two or more means of transportation. For most people, cost is the major factor. Look at all the options. Is it better to get to your destination at higher cost but enjoy more time there? Or do you prefer to save money on transportation and spend more on food, lodging, and recreation? Is the journey itself a means or an end?

Accommodations

Look for special hotel packages, as well as for the amenities. Find out whether basic charges include hidden benefits, such as free breakfasts, tours, or the use of sports and recreational facilities at no extra charge. Also look for hidden charges like surtaxes and additional fees for services.

Consider such offbeat ideas as living on a college campus for a week, joining an archaeological tour, or rafting the Amazon. Investigate relaxing spa resorts or invigorating activity-oriented retreats. Make a list of what you'd most like to experience from your accommodations, and look for that kind of setting.

Dining

Upgrade meals by going for "early bird" dinners or discovering little-known, out-of-the-way restaurants not frequented by tourists. Research street fairs with ethnic foods, church suppers, local markets, or small-town community barbecues that will save you money while you sample local flavor.

Participation

Pursue a new interest. The most satisfied travelers are often those who discover an activity they had never really thought about before, such as birdwatching, scuba diving, collecting shells or gemstones, museum going, or learning how to sail. Arrange in advance for lessons or tours. Read up on local specialties. Be sure to pack any special clothing or equipment you might need, or arrange to rent it at your destination.

En route

Pack all prescriptions and other medications, glasses, and other health necessities. If you are driving, take car registration, insurance data, maps, and driver's licenses. Include any personal security devices you may have for emergency use. Keep a list of phone numbers handy for all kinds of crisis situations.

Overseas Travel

Remember your passport. Make sure you meet all requirements for entry into any foreign country. Obtain a visa if necessary; check with the country's embassy if you are not sure. Purchase foreign language phrasebooks and maps; memorize basic questions and familiarize yourself with simple routes and landmarks. Study the currency used. If you can, obtain at least $20 worth of the host currency while still in this country; it may come in handy at the airport or when checking into your hotel.

Confirmations

Double-check all reservations and planned activities one week in advance of departure. Confirm transportation once more the day before departure. Make sure secure arrangements have been made for the care and maintenance of your home while you are away.

12 Things to Do Before You Leave On Vacation

1. Ask a neighbor or friend to watch the house. Having someone collect the mail, check the answering machine, water the plants, and perform other simple household chores makes it seem as if you are home. If you have a newspaper delivered every day, call and have the delivery temporarily discontinued.

2. If you are still worried about burglary, set lights or TVs on a timer to further create the impression you are home.

3. Secure the house. Check the fire alarms and burglar alarms, and make sure all windows and doors are completely locked. Alert your security company that you will be away and give instructions for who to contact in case of a problem or an emergency.

4. Supply a friend or relative with your vacation itinerary so you can be reached in an emergency.

5. Pack smart. Bring only what you will need, and don't forget things like road maps, plane tickets, passport, or foreign currency, if applicable.

6. Make sure you've paid all bills that will become overdue while you are away.

7. Throw out all perishable food in the refrigerator.

8. Make sure you haven't left any loose ends at work that may distract you and keep you from relaxing.

9. Have someone start your car occasionally if you will be away for a long time, especially during winter.

10. Confirm all reservations—flights, hotels, car, to name a few—the day before you leave.

11. Turn off the water in the house.

12. If you have a pet, arrange for its food and care. If you can't take it with you, have a friend familiar with the animal take it in, or board your pet at a good kennel until you return.

Get a Passport or Visa

Passport

The U.S. Department of State issues passports for two reasons: as identification for U.S. citizens and as a way to document their foreign travel. Your passport is one of the most important documents you have; keep it in a safe place. Always know where your passport is, especially if you are outside the United States. To apply for a passport, or to renew it if it has expired, do the following:

If You Have Never Been Issued a Passport

1. Go to an office that handles passport applications.

   ✓ Passport agency.
   ✓ Court. See the clerk of a federal, state, or designated probate court, or the judge of a probate court that accepts applications.
   ✓ U.S. post office.
   ✓ U.S. embassy or consulate. If you are outside the country, you may get passport assistance from a diplomatic or consular agent.

2. Fill out the application form DSP-11. You must appear in person if you are over the age of 13; parents or legal guardians may handle the applications of children under 13.

3. Present proof of citizenship. Valid documents include the following:

✓ For those born in the United States, a certified copy (not a photocopy) of your birth certificate is required. If a birth certificate is not available, you may be able to use another document; check with the State Department to find out which documents are acceptable.

✓ For a non–native-born citizen, bring your Certificate of Naturalization or Certificate of Citizenship.

✓ For a citizen born abroad (whose parents are U.S. citizens), a copy of your Certificate of Birth Abroad or Consular Report of Birth is required, plus proof of your parent's citizenship.

4. Present proof of identity. To prove you are the person whose name you've written on the application form, you must present an official picture ID card such as a current driver's license. Make sure the picture ID is a front-view head shot and closely resembles your current appearance. You may be required to bring a witness.

5. Supply photographs of yourself. Two identical photographs that are less than six months old must be turned in with the application: 2" × 2" front-view head shots on a white background, with your face no smaller than 1" and no larger than 1⅜."

6. Pay the fee. The passport fee is $55, plus a $10 fee for processing your application. For children under 18 the fee is $30 (plus the $10 execution fee).

If You Have Had a Passport Before: Two Alternatives

1. Apply in person. If your passport has expired and you no longer have it, or your passport is more than 12 years old, you must apply in person. Follow the procedure outlined above for new passports.

2. Apply by mail. If you are over 18 years old and your last passport was issued less than 12 years ago, you may apply by mail. To do so, get form DSP-82 from any of the appropriate offices listed above and fill it out completely. Mail the form with the expired passport, two recent photographs (fitting the proper size specifications) and a $55 fee (the $10 execution fee is not required) to the National Passport Center, P.O. Box 371971, Pittsburgh, PA 15250-7971.

To Report a Lost Passport

If your passport has been lost or stolen, report it immediately by calling Passport Services at 202-647-0518, or write to that office at 1425 K Street NW, Department of State, Washington, D.C. 20524.

Visa

A visa is a stamp put on your passport to signify you have been granted permission by a foreign government to enter its country. Usually given by representatives of the country's consulate or embassy in the United States, a visa lasts for a limited time. The procedures for getting a visa, and the restrictions on travel abroad, vary greatly from country to country. Generally, countries with strong diplomatic ties to the United States will not require a visa for short stays. Some consulates issue visas on the spot if you appear in person; others have a processing period. Ask what documents besides your passport and plane tickets you will need to bring with you. Immunizations may be required.

Always check a country's visa requirements long before you travel there. It is your responsibility to get a visa if necessary, and without one you will not be allowed to enter the country.

Write or call the State Department to request a brochure called "Visa Requirements of Foreign Countries." It provides complete information on visas. The address is Bureau of Consular Affairs, CA/PA Room 2807, Department of State, Washington, D.C. 20520 (include a self-addressed stamped envelope); the phone number is 202-647-9000.

For a fee, a visa service can handle all the details of getting your visa. These services often guarantee visa delivery within a few days if you are in a rush. Two such companies are International Visa Service (800-627-1112) and World Wide Visas (800-527-1861).

Partial List of Countries That Require Visas

Albania, Algeria, Australia, Bahrain, Brazil, Cameroon, Chad, China, Congo, Egypt, El Salvador, Ethiopia, Ghana, Guatemala, India, Jordan, Kenya, Kuwait, Laos, Lithuania, Mali, Mongolia, Mozambique, Nepal, Nigeria, Pakistan, Panama, Romania, Russia, Saudi Arabia, South Africa, Taiwan, Ukraine, Venezuela.

Packing List

- ✓ *Clothes.* Take only what you know you will wear—no more than one outfit per day. Pack items that can be mixed and matched or worn more than once. Avoid bulky clothing or easily wrinkled things. Your packing list should cover, as appropriate: underwear, socks, pants, shirts, sweaters, T-shirts, bathing suits, sweats, sleepwear, slippers, suits or dresses, ties or accessories, jewelry, belts, shoes, hats, robes, coats, scarves, and gloves.
- ✓ *Toiletries.* Carry them together in a case or bag and include the following if applicable: makeup, soap, shampoo and conditioner, toothbrush, toothpaste, dental floss, shaving supplies, comb, emery board, special hair care products, portable hair dryer, deodorant, contact lens supplies, perfume, feminine hygiene products, tissues, mouthwash, lotion, cotton swabs. If possible, bring mini- and sample-sized supplies.
- ✓ *Identification/currency.* Traveler's checks, driver's license, passport, credit cards, AAA card, frequent flyer card. Carry at least $20 of foreign currency with you when leaving the United States.
- ✓ *Travel documents.* Tickets, itinerary, maps, phrasebook.
- ✓ *Medicine.* Bring only what you know you'll need that is not otherwise available. Take written prescriptions from your doctor if you have reason to believe you'll need refills.

✓ *Extra bags.* Use for dirty clothes, shoes, or purchases that won't fit in your luggage on the way home.

✓ *Umbrella.* Make it compact, if possible.

✓ *Camera* or video recorder. Film.

✓ *Alarm clock.* It should be small and battery-operated.

✓ *Flashlight.* A small, battery-run light will come in handy when you least expect it.

✓ *Extra batteries.*

✓ *Electric converter* (if you are traveling to another country).

✓ *Phone/address book.* It should contain emergency information and phone numbers and addresses of family and friends.

✓ *Books/magazines.* Include a travel guide, if desired.

✓ *Walkman/tapes.*

✓ *Notebook computer* with fax/modem for business trips.

✓ *Food/bottled water.* Make sure food is nonperishable; bring it only if no food will be available while you travel.

✓ *Sports equipment* or clothing (unless you will be renting it at your destination).

✓ *Keys.*

✓ *Gifts* (if you are visiting relatives or friends you have not seen in a long time).

Pack a Bag

The goal when packing is to fit as many things as possible into as small a space as possible and have it all survive the trip intact. It's easier than it sounds. Here's how to do it.

What To Take

Before you can do anything else, you need to figure out what you're going to take with you. Think about where you are going—the general climate, the expected weather conditions, the time of year. Think about how long you are going to stay—a day, a week, several weeks—and about what you will be doing—business, vacation, or a little of both. See also "Packing List" for reminders on what you may need to bring with you.

Type of Bag

Choose an appropriate size to fit all your belongings, and also consider the structure of the bag. Soft bags like backpacks and duffel bags are lighter and easier to carry than suitcases and chests, but hard containers give more protection. Pick the bag that works best for the situation.

Packing

First Layer

In the bottom of the bag, pack hard, unbreakable, and bulky items like shoes or a hard toiletry case. If possible, take only one other pair of shoes besides the pair you plan to wear. To save space, pack socks, belts, small bottles, or other loose items inside the shoes. Put the shoes in a plastic bag, particularly if they are dirty or have shoe polish on them. Bring along two more plastic bags for your dirty and wet clothes. Fill the area around the bulky items with socks and underwear to make a flat level for the next layer of packing.

Second Layer

Pack pants, shirts, and sweaters here. While some would suggest folding the clothes and wrapping them with plastic to prevent wrinkling, a better technique is to roll up shirts, pants, and then sweaters. This prevents creases and saves space.

Third Layer

Fill the space in between and above the clothes with more socks and underwear. This is also the space to put breakable items like glass or china, wrapped to protect your clothing in case they do break. Keep vulnerable pieces in the middle of the bag, cushioned from all sides with clothing. If possible, avoid packing breakable items in luggage altogether.

Fourth Layer

The last articles of clothing you should put in your bag are those most susceptible to wrinkling. Lay jackets, suits, or skirts flat on top. If you must fold these items, wrap them in plastic or tissue paper. If possible, tuck the ends of jackets or skirts down the bag sides to avoid folding. Leave ample space so the bag can be zipped or closed with ease; overstuffing will lead to wrinkles. Try to distribute the weight of items evenly in your bag.

Get the Best Airfare

While the easiest way to book a flight is to call a travel agent and have them work out the details, calling airlines directly usually saves more. Airlines know about and will allow a number of legitimate "tricks" to get lower fares. If you find a low-priced ticket, put it on reserve, but don't buy it just yet; check several different airlines.

Watch for Fare Wars

You will often hear about airlines having fare wars—competitions between airlines to offer the best price on a specific destination—on the news or in the paper. You can also call airlines to ask if they are currently engaged in a fare war.

Know Airline Hub Cities

Each airline has one or more airports for its operations center, called hubs, and a large portion of an airline's flights will travel through this city. You can often get a bargain fare to a hub city based on the high volume of flights the airline has there.

Plan Ahead

Unless you are traveling on short notice, consider well in advance where you'd like to go. That way, if a fare war or specially priced flight should arise, you can act immediately. Except for on commuter flights, normal budget fares usually require at least a two-week advance purchase. The better the fare, the quicker tickets will sell out.

Check for Specially Priced Days or Times

Sometimes traveling at night or adjusting your travel plans by only one day can save you a lot of money. Ask the booking agent if there are certain days or times when it is cheaper to fly. It may also be that while all discount seats on your original flight are sold out, discount seats are available for the same flight on another day. If you can be flexible, it may get you a significantly better fare.

Set Up "Open-Jaw Tickets"

The concept of open-jaw tickets may sound a bit complicated and suspect, but it is an effective and legitimate technique for lowering airfares. In an open-jaw ticket, you use two round-trip tickets in conjunction to qualify for a discount rate. Often a discount plane ticket will require a Saturday-night stayover before your return flight. This is fine if it fits your travel plans, but not if you want to travel during the week. If the latter is the case, and the discount ticket is cheap enough to make it worthwhile, you can buy two round-trip discount tickets and use them in tandem. To clarify the concept of open-jaw tickets, here's a possible scenario:

You wish to fly from New York to Chicago on a Monday and return on a Thursday in October. In order to get the discount flight, though, you must stay over a Saturday. You know you will make the same trip (Monday to Thursday, New York to Chicago) again in November. You can make one of your flights a round trip that leaves New York on the Monday in October and returns from Chicago on the Thursday in November. The second flight will be a round trip leaving Chicago on the Thursday in October and returning to New York on the Monday in November. For your October flight, use the first part of each round-trip ticket, and in November use the remaining halves. Both flights stay over a Saturday night.

Call Other Airlines

Once you think you have found the best possible price for a flight, check with other airlines to see whether they can match it. If you present a booking agent with the price you've found, the agent either will tell you immediately that the airline cannot match your price or will offer you a price you did not know about.

Call a Travel Agent

For a final check, call one or more travel agents to see if they can find a better price for you. Travel agents should not charge fees to research flight prices, and you never know what they might find.

Sign Up for a Frequent Flyer Program

Airline frequent flyer miles are offered increasingly as incentives by hotels, phone companies, credit card companies, and car rental companies. Don't miss a chance to rack up miles by checking for deals that feature frequent flyer bonuses.

Get a Good Seat on an Airplane

Determine your seating preference or special needs. Window or aisle? First, business, or tourist class? In the front, middle, or rear of the plane?

Familiarize yourself with the layout of the plane. Ask at the airline desk for a diagram of your flight's seating plan. Seats commonly are arranged in pairs, triples, or more. You want to avoid being caught in a confining area, jammed against a bulkhead, or at the center of an annoying traffic pattern, especially if the flight is a long one. Make any special needs known at the time of reservation, such as a leg injury that makes it helpful to have an aisle seat, or travel with a small child or infant. If you are elderly, you will want easy access to rest rooms and flight attendants. Take into consideration the ease of getting in and out of your seat, view of the movie screen, or proximity to overhead storage space.

Make your seat selection as early as possible, preferably when confirming your flight reservation. Your travel agent will be familiar with the peculiarities of different plane interiors and can choose seating most advantageously.

If you are assigned to a seat you do not like once you have boarded the plane, ask to stand by for an alternative when reserved seats that have not been claimed are released by flight attendants, generally ten to 15 minutes before departure time.

When traveling solo, ask for an aisle or window seat where the seats are three across and one is already reserved by another single. Unless the flight is heavily booked, chances are that the middle seat will remain vacant.

If your seat is located at one of the plane's emergency exits, study the layout carefully and be prepared to assume responsibility for use of the exit. If you are unwilling or uncomfortable with this airline requirement, ask for another seat close to, but not directly adjoining, the emergency exit.

Exchange Foreign Currency

Traveling in a foreign country is exhilarating but can be very difficult. Not only must you contend with the language barrier and unfamiliar customs, you also have to figure out a new system of currency. To make things a little easier for yourself, do some research before you leave so you know the names and divisions of foreign currency and the value of the money in relation to U.S. dollars. In exchanging currency, the bottom line is, of course, getting the most out of your money. Spend wisely.

Use Traveler's Checks

If you travel with large amounts of cash, convert it into traveler's checks before you leave. Your bank will charge you a fee for traveler's checks, but the fee is well worth it. Should you get robbed or lose your money, traveler's checks can be replaced, whereas cash cannot. Still, bring along a small amount of cash in case you cannot immediately use your traveler's checks, and bring a credit card for large purchases.

Do Not Convert a Lot of Money Before You Leave

Exchange rates will be better once you arrive in the foreign country than in the United States. It's advisable, though, to convert a small amount—$20 to $50—before you leave to pay for a taxi or bus from the airport, for food, or for other immediate needs.

Exchange the Appropriate Amount

Because you are charged a fee every time you change money, it is best to do it as few times as possible. Do not exchange so much money, though, that you will be in trouble should the cash be lost or stolen. Also, don't leave yourself with amounts of foreign currency under $20—you may not be able to convert it back to dollars.

Compare Exchange Rates

The exchange rate is the ratio of foreign currency you will get per dollar exchanged, and it will vary depending on where you go. Look for the best exchange rate you can find.

Compare Commission Costs

This is usually a flat fee, though it may be a percentage of the amount you exchange. The exchange office may also charge a higher commission to change traveler's checks than to change cash, though that shouldn't deter you from carrying traveler's checks anyway. Look for the lowest commission charge you can find.

Find the Best Exchange Places

Exchange rates vary from day to day and from one exchange office to another. Banks generally give the best exchange rates but charge a moderate commission. You may also get decent rates at train stations, tourist offices, and exchange bureaus on the street, and these places may or may not charge a commission. Hotels will exchange money, but usually at a higher rate than most. Where you go to change your money will often depend on the amount you wish to change. For large amounts, take the better rate and service charge of a bank. For smaller amounts, it may pay to go with a lower rate but no service charge.

Don't Get Stuck Without Money

Banks and many exchange bureaus are closed on weekends. Make sure you have enough money on Friday to last the next few days. In an emergency, hotels will still change money, but you'll get a poor exchange rate.

Avoid the Black Market

You may meet people who will offer to exchange your money at a rate much better than you can get at a bank. Beware of this kind of black market operation; it is illegal. Also, you have no guarantee you will not be robbed or given counterfeit money. It's best to stay away from such operators—remember Lucy Ricardo in Paris!

Keep Your Money Secure

Every country has its criminals who prey on tourists. Don't let yourself be a victim. Don't carry a large amount of cash with you. Keep your wallet or purse shut and secured close to your body. Wear a fanny pack if you need to have freedom of movement without worry. Be alert for potential muggers and people who offer you unbelievably marvelous bargains.

Get Around in a Strange City

Unfamiliar places can be confusing, and the challenge of getting around is all the more intensified if there is a language barrier. There are ways to make traveling in a new city safer, cheaper, and easier.

Prepare

Read travel books before you arrive to learn what there is to see and do in the city. Take note of where the main attractions (museums, parks, monuments) are located, and use them as landmarks to orient yourself. Buy a phrasebook and memorize simple questions such as "How far?" or "Which direction?"

Get or Take a Map

The visitor information office in the train station or airport will probably give out free maps. Get one and inspect it carefully. Carry your map and phrasebook at all times.

Learn About the City's Transportation Systems

If you don't have the use of a car, you'll need to rely on public transportation. Get a map of bus or subway routes and chart your course in advance. Purchase an extended ticket or pass, good for a certain number of days or trips. These are usually a bargain and are available at hotels, newsstands, or stations.

Avoid Bad Neighborhoods

Certain areas of town may not be safe for tourists to walk through. Use common sense; be observant enough to recognize the universal signs of danger and stay away from them.

Walk, Don't Drive

While you can get lost just as well on foot, it's easier to get directions while walking and it's more difficult to stray far. It should not be necessary to rent a car in a foreign city, and it's probably not worth it. Gas is expensive, traffic is bad, streets are confusing, and a special driver's license may be necessary.

Be Wary of Cabs

If you take a cab ride in a foreign city, ask the driver for an estimate of the fare before you go. Also ask someone who would know (such as a hotel desk clerk) how much the fare should be. Depending on the city, tipping the driver may or may not be appropriate.

Rent Bikes or Mopeds

Two-wheel transportation is popular in many foreign cities. Find out where to go for rentals at a visitor information center or hotel. Remember to lock up bikes and mopeds when you leave them. Obey all traffic laws.

Don't Act Lost, Even If You Are

Criminals prey on unsuspecting tourists who lose their way. It's okay to have trouble finding your way around—just don't make it obvious to everyone else.

Ask for Directions

When you are lost, go into a store and ask the counter or sales person to direct you. If the person does not speak English, use your phrasebook to help you communicate. Always be courteous, and do not assume that everyone you meet should speak your language.

Embrace Your Spirit of Adventure

Explore, enjoy, and open yourself to the flavor of a city's movement and rhythm—from Los Angeles to Paris to Tangiers to Hong Kong. Enter the flow and experience the culture's unique approach to getting around.

See also "Read Foreign Language Menus," "Exchange Foreign Currency," "Develop a Sense of Direction," and "Read a Map."

Take a Great Picture

Know what your camera will and will not do and how you, as the photographer, can activate each of its functions. Even though most models today have built-in automatic features that simplify operation and improve results, no camera is fool-proof. Pictures can still come out fuzzy, too dark, overexposed, off target, or tilted.

Choose the right film for the environment. The higher the ISO/ASA number is, the more light-sensitive the film. In low or indoor light, use 400 ASA film. Use 200 ASA for outdoor shots. Generally, picture quality improves at lower sensitivities.

Follow these suggestions and techniques to take some really great shots.

✔ Study photography books that cover the kinds of subjects you might want to photograph—the mountains or seashore, for example, as well as people engaged in a variety of activities. Examine their composition and lighting. Always remember to rewind the film before opening up the back of a 35-mm camera. You may want several rolls of varying speeds and exposures if conditions will change rapidly. Anticipate your film needs.

✔ Experiment with scenes, settings, and subjects close to home. You may waste a roll or two, but you'll be sure not to miss that perfect shot when the moment arises.

✔ Avoid the urge to shoot everything in sight. Pick your subjects carefully.

✔ Avoid times and places where the light is glaring, too dark, or with harsh clashes of bright sun and dark shadows.

✔ Remember that most flashes only illuminate effectively to a range of 15 feet. Watch for surfaces that may reflect a flash and avoid them. Midday sun gives the most natural color.

✔ If you are in situations where the light conditions clash, stick to subjects that are close by and more manageable to illuminate.

✔ Plan a varied selection of distances—closeup, intermediate, and far away—to avoid the monotony of too many exposures that look alike.

✔ If you are unsure of your lighting conditions or the way you want to frame your picture, shoot two or three alternatives.

✔ Vary the position and angle from which you take your pictures. Don't always stand up straight; stoop, kneel, lie down, or hold the camera high over your head.

✔ When taking shots in the distance, include something close up on one side of the viewer, such as a tree, to give depth and proportion to the picture.

✔ When taking pictures of people, capture them in an interesting and meaning-ful activity, not just standing and posing.

✔ Avoid "red-eye" by having subjects turn their heads slightly from the camera. Many new models come with features that minimize the red-eye effect.

Read a Map

Think of a map as a sketch made from a satellite photograph, looking straight down at the earth and covering the defined area on a sheet of paper. Most maps, especially those used for highway driving, are realistic, detailed, and accurate in their proportions or distances. But unless they are relief or topographical maps, they cannot show you heights and depths except by the use of imprinted figures for extremes of altitude.

Maps are created with the following elements. Learning more about them will enhance your ability to read and follow complicated maps, gaining access to the maximum amount of information presented within them.

✓ **Projection.** The transfer of the features of the earth onto a flat surface.

✓ **Scale.** The relationship between distances on a map and distances on the ground, such as one inch to one mile. A large-scale map is one that shows great detail, such as the street map of a town. A small-scale map, such as a road map, is one that covers much more distance, and on which a town might be no more than a pinpoint.

✓ **Compass position.** The direction in which the map is oriented. Most maps show the arrow pointing north, toward the top. Compasses are good tools to supplement map research; keep one handy at all times.

✓ **Landmark.** Any point on the map specifically identified in print or with a symbol, such as mountain peaks, historical sites, or dams.

✓ **Grid.** A reference system consisting of straight lines running from top to bottom and left to right, which intersect to help you determine the position of places on the map. One set of lines is marked alphabetically, the other numerically. Each entry in the list of points on the map is followed by a letter and a number. Thus, if you are looking for the town of Plainville and it is identified by "7D," you look for it in the grid formed by the intersection of lines 7 and D.

✓ **Index.** The list of counties, towns, recreational parks, lakes, and other features on the map. On a traditional road map, these are listed alphabetically by states. Generally, population figures are printed under towns and cities of more than 1000 people.

✓ **Legend or key.** The panel or box prominently placed on a map to help you identify data. Usually included are the date; the publisher; the scale; the various lines used to indicate different types of roads and highways; symbols for principal recreation areas, campgrounds, airports, bridges, ferries and other points of interest; and the ways in which cities and towns are distinguished by size.

✓ **Distances.** These are marked with mileage numbers, usually in red, between two points marked by stars. Many maps also have a chart you can use to calculate the mileage between major cities in the total area covered on the map, or in the country as a whole.

✓ **Altitude.** This is shown in figures (usually black) next to the name of a mountain range or peak.

✓ **Points of interest.** Many road maps today list points of interest, providing locations and brief descriptions. These include historical sites, museums, battlefields, churches, restorations, natural wonders, monuments, castles, forts, scenic drives, antique railroads, sports centers, major galleries, craft guilds, military facilities, dams, lakes, beaches, botanical gardens, zoos, aquariums, plantations, educational centers, and memorials, among many other features.

✓ **Recreational charts.** It is commonplace for maps in locations that are known for recreational popularity to contain charts of state and national forests, campgrounds, seashores, mountain trails, fishing grounds, caverns, beaches, hunting preserves, aerial tramways, and marinas. These charts provide specific data about such matters as seasons and hours of availability, license and reservation requirements, boat ramps, facilities for recreational vehicles, and lodgings.

Here are some tips for using road and travel maps more effectively.

✓ Don't leave the map at home! Take it with you.

✓ When planning a long car trip, use a highlight marking pen to chart the routes you want to take, without smearing names and numbers underneath.

✓ If you belong to AAA or another motor club, request maps with route markings and information about construction and other traffic problems.

✓ Write to individual state tourist offices for specific maps, scenic route suggestions, and current traffic delay information.

✓ If you are visiting a new city or one in a foreign country, carry a bus and/or subway map with you at all times. Mark the map at the place where you are staying, and notice your orientation to that spot at all times.

✓ Practice folding maps for easy reference to specific areas. Don't wait until you are en route and have to cope with a floppy mass of paper as you also try to drive a car.

✓ On family trips, appoint your spouse, other adult, or older child to serve as the navigator, leaving you free to drive safely.

✓ Before leaving home, make a list of emergency numbers you can phone to get reliable information about routes and locations, in the event you get lost or want to try back roads to avoid unexpected traffic crunches.

✓ Review your map beforehand and judge distances and driving times so you avoid cities during commuter hours and other traffic peaks.

✓ Use loops around major cities, such as Richmond, Virginia, or Washington, D.C. These are designated by three-digit figures starting with an even number.

Read Foreign Language Menus

One of the most delightful, savory experiences in your travels to another country is enjoying the unique culinary specialties of the region. If you don't have the time to take intensive Italian courses prior to your trip to Rome, never fear. A compact phrasebook or travel guide is an essential, easily obtainable tool that will enable you to read a menu and order with confidence.

A multilingual dictionary can help you to recognize and understand the names of some basic foods and terms in several languages. To fully prepare your traveling taste buds, however, you should obtain a separate phrasebook or travel guide for each country you plan on visiting. You can easily locate a selection of these inexpensive books in the travel or foreign language section of your local bookstore. Some of these books are pocket-sized and quite convenient to carry with you to restaurant outings.

If you are traveling to Italy, for example, a traveler's phrasebook can provide you with English-to-Italian translations (complete with a pronunciation guide) for the basic foods found on an Italian menu, as well as phrases for ordering and asking questions in a restaurant. Make sure the book you select provides such helpful information as the components of a typical Italian meal, how to select wines, tipping practices, and an overview of the various categories of eating establishments one usually finds in Italy. Traveler's phrasebooks can also tell you about national and regional specialties you may wish to try, as well as how much you should expect to pay for a moderate to an expensive meal.

Unlike the United States, where the 24-hour restaurant chain is the norm, many countries have customary dining hours with few or no restaurants open at other times. Your phrasebook can acquaint you with the country's usual hours of restaurant operation. Many countries include service charges in the bill, to which you may or may not be expected to add an additional gratuity. This, too, varies from country to country. Although the policy is often stated on the menu, don't hesitate to ask if you are unsure. Your phrasebook will tell you how.

With a phrasebook at your fingertips, you can transform a foreign language menu from an unintelligible enigma to an exciting puzzle whose solution is, at the very least, a new eating adventure. If you are truly brave, leave the menu behind and ask the waitperson or proprietor to serve you the specialties of the house, characterisitic of the region you are visiting. There is no better way to immerse yourself in the culinary customs and traditions of another culture.

Make the Most of Frequent Flyer Miles

✓ Plan ahead. Calculate how many frequent flyer miles you will accrue from trips you are planning. Know how many miles are required to fly free to a destination of your choice.

✓ Get a frequent flyer voucher early. When you acquire enough miles for a free flight and plan to redeem them within the year, call or write the airline for a voucher. You will need it when making a flight reservation.

✓ Build miles from subsidiary sources. Many car rentals, hotels, credit cards, and phone companies, offer miles as incentives. Over time they add up substantially.

✓ Keep track of miles. When you check in at the airport, make sure to ask the airline personnel to credit your frequent flyer account with the flight you are about to take. If you forget, send in your ticket stubs to get credit.

✓ Book nondirect flights. Often, nondirect flights get you twice as many frequent flyer miles as direct flights.

✓ Ask employers about frequent flyer policies. Many companies allow employees to keep or share the frequent flyer miles they earn on business trips.

See also "Get the Best Airfare" and "Get a Good Seat on an Airplane."

20. Writing

Put Together an Effective Resume

Along with a cover letter, your resume represents you to prospective employers in the initial stages of a job search, giving them an all-important first impression.

Heading

Place your full name, address, and phone number (plus fax number and e-mail address if you have them), at the top of the resume. Design the type to be eye-catching but not flashy or difficult to read.

Body of Resume

There are many effective resume styles.

Chronological Resume

This common, all-purpose style lists all relevant employment from most recent to oldest. Include the name of the company, the date (month and year) you started and ended, your title, a description of your duties, and a brief explanation of some of your projects and accomplishments.

Skills Resume

More unusual, this resume is designed to highlight your abilities instead of your work history. List skills, accomplishments, and special knowledge in a cohesive order; refer to specific jobs as necessary. Skills resumes work well when you are planning a career change or reentering the work force because they mask any gaps that would be evident in a chronological resume and emphasize your strengths.

Goal Resume

This resume style works best if you know exactly what kind of job you are looking for and have experience in the field. Here you state a career objective or goal below the heading and list past job experiences that relate directly to it in chronological form. The goal should not be too general, vague, flowery, unrealistic, or inappropriate; rather, it should be sharp, focused, specific, and doable.

Education

If you are a recent college graduate you may want to put educational history at the top of the resume, before skills or experience. Otherwise, put it below. Be sure to include, from most recent to oldest, the name of each school, the years you attended, the degree you received, your grade point average (if recent and particularly impressive), and any honors or awards. Also list relevant courses, clubs, or associations. Include high schools only if you are still in college or if you attended a prestigious and well-known school.

What to Leave Off Your Resume

Under most circumstances, do not include a photograph of yourself or state salary requirements or history. Highlight interests and hobbies only if they relate directly to your experience or are particularly fascinating. You need not include your age, marital status, family information, or reasons for leaving past jobs on your resume. Do add the line "References available upon request" to the end of the resume. Prepare a separate page listing references that can be submitted if a potential employer asks for it.

Design

Your resume should cover only one page. Fit in as much information about yourself as possible without cluttering the page or making the print too small to read. Make sure the design of the page is well organized, neat, and readable. Keep the white spaces pleasingly balanced on the page. Use bold, underlined, and italic print to highlight important information or to organize a parallel structure—for example, put jobs in bold type and job titles in italic type.

Slant

The information on your resume should of course be true and accurate, but by no means should you be modest or objective. Boost yourself up and make yourself look as good as possible. Use varied, accurate nouns and action-oriented verbs. Be concise and clear.

Write a Follow-Up Letter

Follow-up letters are used as friendly reminders. Leave an appropriate amount of time for the recipient to respond to your original letter, application, or interview before you send a follow-up. Two or three weeks is a safe period to wait after a contact that you initiated. A follow-up thank-you note should be sent immediately after a job interview.

1. Use good-quality paper with your own letterhead, if possible. Follow business letter format. Address your letter to the appropriate person or company representative. If your original request or letter was not sent to a specific person, try to get the name of the appropriate person to address. Be sensitive to hierarchies and chains of command—don't go over someone's head unless it is proper or absolutely necessary as a last resort.

2. Remind the recipient why you are writing. Mention specifics about the company to display your interest and initiative. Include a new fact or piece of information that can assist the recipient or pique his or her interest. Mention the names of all people who attended a relevant meeting or contributed to your project. Send copies of the letter to each person, as appropriate. If you are writing because your initial letter received no response, don't demand a reason. Always be courteous. Assume the recipient's response is assured by the tone of your prose.

3. If you are following up an application letter or an interview, reiterate the points you made originally concerning your experience, your skills and potential value to the company, and your reasons for seeking employment. Address any questions or concerns raised by the interviewer. Emphasize what you can contribute to the company.

4. Be formal in your writing unless you know the recipient appreciates informality. Don't use overblown and unfamiliar language or terminology that may alienate the reader.

5. In your closing, indicate that you will call the recipient in the near future; leave your phone number (if it is not already in your letterhead) in case the recipient wants to call you first.

6. Resend your resume (when following up an employment application) or any other related documents (contract, offer) with the letter.

   See also "Write Without Bias."

Write a Thank-you Letter

A thank-you letter can be both a gracious note of personal appreciation and a shrewd business tool for cementing relationships. A courteous gesture can go a long way. Make it a habit to write notes of thanks for gifts, special favors, attendance at special events, or important business meetings or contracts. Always write thank-you notes immediately after formal interviews for employment.

✓ Personal thanks should be handwritten on note stationery. Professional thanks should appear in business letter format.

✓ Thank the person immediately in the first paragraph of your letter.

✓ If you are responding to a gift, mention the gift in the note and describe how you will use it. Mention the event, such as a wedding, anniversary, or birthday, that occasioned the gift.

✓ If you are responding to an event or invitation, refer to the nature of the event and some of those who attended. Mention what attendance meant to you and how the experience affected you.

✓ In responding to a meeting or business affair, repeat the function of the event and summarize the points of action discussed or agreed upon. Outline strategies for further action, and give a schedule for future discussions. Let the other party know how valuable the business relationship is to you and your company, and make it clear that the relationship will be honored and respected.

✓ In response to an interview, summarize what the interviewer is looking for and how your qualifications fit the requirements. Send any materials not on your resume—samples, demos, press clips—that may give the interviewer a more complete idea of your talents and accomplishments.

✓ In either a personal or professional thank-you letter, do not use colloquialisms unless you are sure they will be appreciated. Avoid demonstrating bias toward gender, ethnicity, religion, or race in your prose. Avoid being overly saccharine, but do foster a tone of respect and grateful consideration. Thank-you notes are, after all, about building relationships.

See also "Write Without Bias."

Write a Letter of Complaint

To formally complain in writing about bad service or a bad product is tedious and time-consuming, and most people would rather avoid it. Unfortunately, though, complaint letters are often the most effective means—sometimes the only means—of correcting a consumer problem. The secret to being an effective complainer is to be firm, straightforward, and serious without coming across as angry, illogical, and belligerent. Rubbing someone the wrong way will never help you get anything accomplished, and the person who deals with your letter probably had nothing to do with the experience you are complaining about. Exactly what you write in a complaint letter depends, of course, upon the nature of your distress. Here are a few things every complaint letter should contain.

1. Determine the best person to write to. Address the Consumer Service Manager if there is one; if not, try writing to the president or a senior executive. It is usually most effective to select a person of authority.

2. Include your name, company (if applicable), address, phone number, and the name, company, and address of the person to whom you are complaining. Type your letter on letter-sized paper. If you cannot type, write neatly with a dark-colored pen.

3. Be direct and concise. Include the following information:

   ✓ Date and place of purchase or service
   ✓ Description of the product or service (give the model or serial number if available)

✓ Explanation and/or history of the problem you have with the product or service

✓ How you would like the person or company to remedy the problem

✓ A reasonable length of time you will wait to have the problem addressed before you take further action

4. With your letter, send copies—not originals—of all receipts and documents you have relating to the product and your problem. Keep a copy of the letter for your records.

5. If you want to have proof, for legal purposes, that the person you are sending the letter to has received it, send the letter by certified mail, restricted delivery, return receipt requested. The person must sign for your letter, and you will receive a receipt with the person's signature for your records.

6. You may want to register your complaint with the Better Business Bureau or another consumer advocacy agency associated with your product or service. These groups and agencies can provide useful information, assistance, and advice regarding your complaint. If necessary, consider small claims court or consult an attorney about the best course of action.

Write Effective Letters of Recommendation

Most of us are asked to write letters of recommendation at some time or another, usually for a former employee during a job search, a prospective student seeking an advanced degree, a volunteer, or someone providing a specific service or product. Your letter of recommendation will leave one of two impressions: you are interested honestly in matching the very best candidate to the most favorable environment, or you are trying to do someone a favor. It should highlight information by following these directives.

✓ Use positive, pertinent words and phrases that show your familiarity with the requirements of the person or organization to whom the letter is addressed. For example, "The Botanic Garden's publications require attention to detail and flawless research for accuracy."

✓ Describe the person you are recommending in a way that indicates your familiarity with his or her experience and qualifications for the desired position. "John's painstaking focus and carefulness suit a researcher's temperament and goals."

✓ Provide enough information about yourself, without being presumptuous or boastful, so that the addressee feels you speak with authority and intelligence. "As copy chief for an academic publisher, where accuracy is also of paramount concern, I found that John's talents proved invaluable to the research process."

Your letter has to reflect a team awareness; you are a matchmaker with a vested interest in the outcome. Don't write a letter of recommendation if you feel at all uncomfortable about the request or if you are not convinced that the situation is a good one for both parties. Ask the following questions of those who ask you to give recommendations. Make sure their answers are valid and earnest.

✓ What are the details and duties of the position, program, product, service, or project? Why does the applicant want to be involved?

✓ To whom will the letter be addressed? How much personal contact has the requester had with the person or organization to receive the letter?

✓ In order of priority, what areas of past and current experience are likely to make the best impression?

✓ Name at least three qualifications that should be touched on in the letter. Are any forms or supplementary information necessary?

✓ What is the best date and time for the letter of recommendation to reach the addressee?

Some colleges and programs have cutoff dates that may affect a person's acceptance or eligibility. Be respectful and prompt. If the letter must be mailed overnight or by certified mail, arrange to give the letter to the person for whom you've written it in a presealed envelope for mailing. If you mail the letter yourself, let its subject know the task has been completed.

How formal should letters of recommendation be? That depends on the kind of position that is open, the personality of the addressee insofar as you can determine it, whether you are known to the recipient, and the impression or attitude you want to convey. Under no circumstances should your letter use inappropriate colloquialisms, colors, or inserts simply to attract attention. Convey sincerity, enthusiasm, and concern.

Write a News or Press Release

Even if you are not in public relations, it is helpful to know how to write a news or press release when you are engaged in self-promotion or in publicizing your business. Here's how to create one.

1. *Letterhead.* When publicizing a company, put the first page of a release on that company's letterhead. Put subsequent pages on good-quality plain paper.

2. *Opening.* Many releases begin with the phrase "For Immediate Release," flush left (often underlined and in all capital letters) to signify the information is new. A date is advisable only when it is relevant; otherwise leave it off so the release appears current for an extended time.

3. *Headline.* Write a headline. Center it and put it in boldface capital letters. As in a newspaper headline, give the reader a quick idea what the release is about. The person, company, or event you are publicizing should appear in the headline.

4. *Bylines and datelines.* Bylines indicating the writer of the release are not necessary. Datelines that name the city where the event takes place are common but optional.

5. *Lead paragraph.* In a straight news release, the first paragraph, or lead, should answer the four Ws: Who, What, Where, and When. A more creative feature lead can set a scene or provide background, with the four Ws coming within the next few paragraphs. When the release is connected with your business, remember to highlight your particular interest; for example, a benefit should not be written of as simply an event but rather as an event you attended.

6. *Body of release.* The fifth W is Why? The release should read like an article; make it clear and concise, and include appropriate quotes. When deciding who and what to quote, keep in mind that these quotes may be picked up by journalists. Do not feel you need to present both sides of the story—tell only your perspective. The release should generally progress from the most important or memorable information to the least important; this is called the inverted pyramid style.

7. *Slugs, More lines, and Ends.* If your release reaches the bottom of a page and must continue to another, write the word more and center it on the last line of the page. It may be written -more-, (more), or MORE. The top line of every page except the first should have a slug at the left margin. A slug is a one-word or two-word description of the story (such as "Gala" or "Charity benefit") followed by a comma and the page number of the release. Skip a few lines before continuing the body text. When you reach the end of the release, signify this by typing either END or ###, centered a few lines below the final text line.

8. *Contact.* A press release should always include the name, address (if not listed on the letterhead itself), phone/fax number, and e-mail address of the person to be contacted for more information. This appears at the end of the release with the words "For more information contact:" or it may be placed above the headline on the first page.

9. *Other materials.* Photographs, sample product, interviews, and giveaways can all accompany a press release as part of a promotional press kit package. Consider what the media can use to get the word out about your report and include it in your press kit to make fast, accurate reporting easier and more probable.

Write an Effective Letter to the Editor

Hundreds—sometimes thousands—of indignant readers (or irate or disbelieving ones) write letters to the editor after reading a feature article or editorial in a newspaper or magazine. Very few of these letters end up in print. The following suggestions, from working editors and publishers themselves, will increase the chances that the letter you submit will be chosen for publication.

1. Address your envelope and letter to a specific editor on the publication's masthead—either the managing editor or the department editor in the subject area discussed, such as sports, entertainment, local news, or foreign affairs.

2. Make sure you have the right address if the publication has more than one office.

3. Send your letter as soon as possible after the publication date of the periodical in which the story you are citing appeared. Fax or modem it, if this technology is available.

4. Identify the specific issue, date, and location of the story that motivates your letter.

5. If the subject is controversial, make it clear in the first sentence what side you are on.

6. Stick to the point. Suppress any urge to ramble or overstate your case.

7. Be as brief as possible. Newspapers and magazines have space constraints. A powerful short letter will win out over the most articulate and considered of tomes.

8. Proofread your letter carefully to avoid errors and typos or otherwise give the impression that your comments were written too hastily or emotionally.

9. Identify yourself. Provide valid reasons why you speak with knowledge or authority. Include your address and phone number.

10. If you prefer to remain anonymous should your letter be printed, give a sound reason for this request.

Editors encourage responses to the items, stories, and features they publish. "Letters to the Editor" columns are among the best-read sections of any publication. Opposing viewpoints, give-and-take, and often outright controversy are at the heart of the ongoing dialogue on important issues reported in the news. But editors insist on responses that are factual, specific, tightly written, and provocative.

Meet these requirements and speak your mind, and your chances of getting published will greatly improve. If your letter is not published, don't be discouraged from writing letters to the editor on other subjects or to different publications. An overwhelming response to an article or broadcast could prompt editors to assign a reporter with a new perspective. Your letters do count!

Understanding Proofreader's Marks

Proofreading is a basic editorial skill to use when correcting the writing of others or working on your own. In publishing, proofreading marks give instructions to the typesetter on how to amend text, but they can be used on any written piece to indicate changes.

Tips When Reading

✓ Pay close attention to the material; read every word.

✓ Look for common and careless mistakes such as spelling errors—these can be the hardest to detect.

✓ Refer to grammar guides, dictionaries, style manuals, atlases, thesauruses, and other reference materials for help.

✓ Don't rely solely on computer programs to check spelling and grammar. If you mistype pet as bet, a spell-checker won't correct it.

How to Use Proofreader's Marks

✓ Be precise. Sloppiness may cause new errors to be introduced.

✓ Marks come in pairs: one in the text and one in the margin of the line where the error appears. The mark in the text generally indicates only where the change should occur, while the mark in the margin tells specifically what the change should be.

✓ If more than one change occurs in a line, write the margin marks in their order of appearance in that line. Separate changes with slashes:/. You may use both right and left margins.

✓ Anything you write in the margin that you do not want to be incorporated into the text, such as instructions or notes, should be circled.

✓ Consult *The Chicago Manual of Style* for more information, or take a class at your local college. If you are writing for a specific publication or publisher, ask whether there is a house style writers should follow.

Common Proofreader's Marks

Change	Margin	In text	New text
align	‖	‖proofread	proofread
bold	bold or BF	proofread	**proofread**
italics	ital	proofread	*proofread*
close space	⌒	proof read	proofread
center	center or ctr	]proofread[	proofread
delete letter	ℰ	prooₑfread	proofread
delete word	ℰ	proofread it	proofread.
indent	□	proofread	proofread
insert apostrophe	⌄	Ill read	I'll read
insert bracket	[/]/	⋀read⋀	[read]
insert colon	⊙	Read this⋀	Read this:
insert ellipsis	.../	read⋀it	read...it
insert em dash	⅟ₘ	read⋀now	read—now
insert hyphen	=	pre⋀read	pre-read
insert parentheses	(/)/	⋀read⋀	(read)
insert period	⊙	proofread⋀	proofread.
insert question mark	?	proofread⋀	proofread?
insert quotation marks	⌄/⌄/	⋀read⋀	"read"
insert semicolon	;	read⋀mark	read; mark
insert space	#	read⋀this	read this
insert text	it⋁	read⋀now	read it now
leave as is	stet	proofread	proofread
ligature	⌒	æ	æ
lower case	l.c.	Ⓟroofread	proofread
move left	⊏	⊏proofread	proofread
move right	⊐	proofread ⊐	proofread
new paragraph	n.p.	proof.⌐Read	proof.
			Read
no new paragraph	run on	proof. Read.	proof. Read.
reduce space	less #	read ⎮ this	read this
roman type	rom	*proofread*	proofread
transpose	tr	this read	read this
upper case	u.c.	proofread	PROOFREAD
small caps	sc	Proofread	Proofread

Calligraphy

Calligraphy, the art of decorative writing, is thousands of years old and still flourishes today. Once used primarily for religious manuscripts, today calligraphy enhances formal documents such as diplomas and wedding invitations. Patience and practice are the real requirements for perfect technique.

Materials

Pen. Many types of calligraphy pens are available. While quills made from bird feathers and reeds made from plant stems are popular with advanced calligraphers, it's best to start with a pen that has a metal nib.

Paper. Choose a paper without a glazed surface. Very rough paper can be difficult to use, and porous paper tends to make ink bleed. Handmade paper or vellum is best, but for beginners any scrap paper will do.

Ink. Use dark black ink with a very fluid consistency. India ink is common.

Surface. The surface you write on should be hard, flat, smooth, and inclined like a drafting desk. Tilt the surface so that the pen is almost horizontal to the floor (pointing down slightly) when you are writing. A cutting board propped up on a table is an easy, inexpensive device to use while you are learning.

Other materials. You will also need a pencil and eraser for drawing and removing guidelines. Keep a clean cloth handy for wiping up blots or spills.

Setup

1. Lay one or two sheets of paper underneath the piece you will write on to blot any ink that might bleed through.

2. Lay the writing sheet on the calligraphy surface and fasten it in place with tape or clips. Angle the paper slightly if that makes writing easier.

3. Use a piece of paper above the writing sheet to protect the rest of the page from ink and your hands.

Form

Hold the pen securely with the thumb and first two fingers, as you would any pen, but not so rigidly as to inhibit your hand movement. Above all, be comfortable. Rest the heel of your hand lightly on the desk, and angle the pen slightly inward.

Calligraphy pens are generally held so the flat nib of the pen touches the paper at an angle. Commonly the angle between the pen nib and the horizontal writing line is 30 degrees, or perhaps 45 degrees. The larger the angle, the thinner the vertical strokes and the thicker the horizontal strokes (Figure 1).

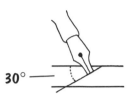

Figure 1. Pen angle   Figure 2. The main strokes

Drawing the Main Strokes

Draw light pencil lines on the paper to use as guides. With the pen at a 30-degree angle, practice the following strokes until you can draw them correctly and consistently (Figure 2).

✓ Circle: alternates thin and thick, symmetrical along the diagonal
✓ Horizontal: parallel to the writing line, thin
✓ Vertical: straight up and down, medium thick
✓ Diagonal: use full pen width
✓ Opposite diagonal: thin, but not hairline

Alphabets

Lower-case letters. For these letters to be well proportioned, they should be five nib widths high. Letters that extend above or below the lines should extend three pen widths (Figure 3). Once you feel comfortable with forming these letters, try adding serifs, or slightly curved endings on the letters.

Upper-case letters and numerals. To be well proportioned, capital letters and numbers should be seven pen widths high. In these diagrams, the serifs have already been added (Figure 4).

For specific alphabets and advanced lettering techniques, consult one of the many books available on calligraphy.

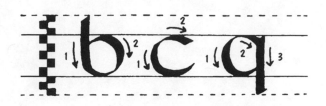

Figure 3. Lower-case letters

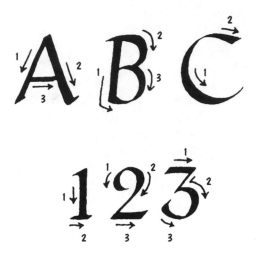

Figure 4. Upper-case letters and numerals

Edit Your Own Writing

All good professional writers understand the importance of the editorial eye. Learn to fine-tune your content and style with self-editing techniques that can help tighten and polish any piece of writing. Don't underestimate the benefits of a second look at your report, article, or story. The best writers always revise—often many times. Here's how to assess your own prose.

✓ Read the text on the page. Even if you write on a computer, it's best to edit and proofread on hard copy. You will see mistakes you might otherwise pass over on a screen, and you will be able to think in more than paragraph groupings. This is important for assessing transitions between ideas. Use a pen to mark changes on the text.

✓ Check spelling and grammar very closely yourself. Don't rely solely on spelling-, style-, and grammar-checker programs. Computer programs can be very useful for catching the mistakes you missed, but they should never replace your own editing. A spell-checker, for instance, will not differentiate between too and two if you use the words incorrectly. Style-checkers can be good at pointing out such things as passive language (which, though discouraged, is by no means unconditionally forbidden) but may not be helpful in solving problems of complex sentence construction.

✓ Use a dictionary, atlas, or thesaurus to check words and facts. Pay particular attention to proper names and nouns.

✓ Read the text more than once. Go over the writing until you have considered each part and its relationship to the whole work.

✓ Examine each word individually. Strive for precision of meaning. Look for repeated words and try to vary usage.

✓ Examine each sentence. Consider each sentence apart from the rest of the work. Determine whether the sentence is too wordy or vague, and whether it can be restructured more tightly to convey a concise, accurate meaning. Aim for clean, straightforward prose with active nouns and verbs to engage the reader.

✓ Examine each paragraph. Paragraphs convey a central meaning that moves the work along. Pay close attention to a paragraph's opening and closing; they should transition smoothly in a progression of ideas.

✓ Examine the entire piece. Read the writing as a whole. Think about how cohesively the argument or narrative flow develops. Make sure the text is consistent in tone, voice (first person, third person), and tense (past, present).

✓ Separate yourself from your writing. It's often best to do this a day later or even several days later. Read the work as if you hadn't written it. Ask yourself if the piece is interesting, lively, active, and thought-provoking. Play devil's advocate: Are ideas too narrowly presented? Are all bases covered? Try to anticipate your target audience's concerns and expectations. Have you made your point completely and effectively?

✓ Look for unnecessary bias. Edit out any unfortunate or improper uses of language that diminish anyone on the basis of gender, ethnicity, race, or religion. Be sensitive to pronoun usage, alternate he and she; try to use other words like co-worker or staff member instead. Know what your audience will find acceptable, and write with tact and respect.

See also "Write Without Bias" and "Understanding Proofreader's Marks."

Publish a Magazine Article

In considering articles for publication, editors take into account their own specialty or personal taste, the format and editorial focus of the magazine, subject, content, reader response, and authorship. Here are some pointers to get an editor's attention when you submit a query letter or article for possible publication.

1. *Develop a strong idea or premise.* Know your subject, whether it is local events, an area you study or work in, or a topic you have written about before. Do research to see whether other articles with a similar theme have already been published. Make your article as original as possible in viewpoint and presentation of content; make sure you have the resources to write a complete text.

2. *Target the right publication.* Hone your idea and match it with an appropriate magazine or journal. Consider magazines you are familiar with, and consult *Writer's Market* (in libraries and bookstores) to find publications potentially interested in your idea. Call to determine whether freelance writing is accepted and ask for a copy of any submission requirements. Find out specifications concerning the format of manuscripts or queries; ask if the magazine has an editorial calendar available that outlines upcoming special issues. If you are unfamiliar with a publication, find out about its readership demographics, circulation size, and editorial leanings. Get a recent copy and read it carefully. Consider the average length and complexity of articles in each magazine or journal. Is there an overriding editorial philosophy regarding content or choice of topic? What kind of audience does the magazine cater to: women? men? professionals? children? teens? fashion followers? Approach only the publications where your idea will fit—don't waste time and money on submissions to unlikely markets.

3. *Write a query letter.* Present yourself and your idea in a desirable way to the editor. Call to find out which editor you should send your letter to, and get the proper address. Fully explain your idea(s), your background and qualifications, and any other pertinent information (length of article, time needed to complete the article). You may want to send your resume and clips of any other published articles that may be persuasive. Don't overwrite. Editors receive thousands of query letters. The best are straightforward, concise, well researched, well written, and appropriate to the magazine or journal.

4. *Call to follow up.* Allow about three weeks for the editor to receive and read your query letter. The editor may call you during that time or send a response. If you have not received a response, call the editor to make sure your letter was received. Speak to the editor personally, if possible, to establish rapport.

5. *Acceptance.* If your article idea has been accepted, find out the article's due date, the desired length of the article, the pay, the reimbursable expenses (if any), and the research materials available to you. Contact the National Writers Union for their guidelines on contracts for journalists.

6. *Rejection.* Don't be discouraged; try another publication immediately. This may require you to modify your idea slightly to suit a different editorial style.

7. *No response.* After six weeks, it may be time to try another publication. Simultaneous submissions are allowable in this event. Never, however, agree to write the same article for more than one magazine.

8. *Sending manuscripts.* You may want to submit an article you've already composed on speculation. Instead of a query letter, send the article with an introductory letter explaining what it is about and why the magazine or journal should publish it. Include a self-addressed stamped envelope (SASE).

Hire a Book Agent

"If you want to get your book published, you really should have an agent."

The good news: this is sound advice. The bad news: authors—especially unpublished ones—often find it difficult to engage an agent. Agents make their income from commissions, shares (usually 15 percent) of advances, royalties, and other monies paid to the authors they represent for books, articles, film scripts, poetry, stories, and other works. Most agents earn commissions on the works they market, receiving payments directly from publishers and deducting their commissions and agreed-upon expenses before transmitting the balance to writers.

An agent generally will not choose to represent a writer until the agent is reasonably sure the writer's work is marketable. Some will work with new or unknown authors only by charging reading fees for manuscripts (the cost depending upon the length) and then evaluating the writer's talent and potential. Before making any payment for "a reading" or "advice," make sure you know not only what the payment will be but exactly what the agent will be doing on your behalf. Beware of any literary agency that demands excessive fees.

There is no doubt that an experienced, reliable agent can be a boon to a competent writer. According to the Association of Author's Representatives (AAR), "effective agents know where to sell marketable work, which rights to market, and how to negotiate contracts. They are constantly in touch with professionals, such as editors and subsidiary rights buyers, who an author alone would have to approach cold. Agents can also help writers collect payments due and keep accurate records."

How can you find an agent if you believe you have a novel, a nonfiction book, or some other work that is marketable? Reputable literary agents are listed in *Literary Market Place (LMP)*, the directory of the publishing industry, available at most libraries. Most of these agents belong to the Association of Authors' Representatives (AAR), which have strict standards for their members.

To contact an agent, write a brief letter to one or more who are in your area or who are listed as being experienced in your genre or subject field. Describe your work and list your prior published works (if any) and your qualifications. One or more recipients may suggest fellow agents if they feel you have potential but not in the areas of their own specialization. Do not submit manuscripts or other enclosures unless an agent asks you to do so.

If you are fortunate enough to receive an affirmative response, discuss the following stipulations before concluding any agreement: the commission (which may vary for different classes of works, as well as for domestic vs. foreign placements), the nature and scope of the agent's functions, the expenses for which the agent will be reimbursed, the list of publishers to which the agent has sold client's properties, and areas of specialization or limitation. Some agents also want exclusive rights to a writer's work, so make certain that you have a mutual understanding. This may seem unimportant for a beginning writer who is happy to have *any* agent—but suppose you become successful and do not feel that your agent is equal to the demands of your literary growth!

Many agents now require authors to sign contractual agreements before submitting work to publishers. Don't feel timid about negotiating terms. Consult the National Writers Union (NWU) for help in understanding these agreements and for feedback from other writers on their experiences with particular literary agents or agencies.

What can agents do for authors they represent? In addition to the services listed above, they may also

✓ Offer editorial guidance.
✓ Give advice about current publishing trends, editors, and publishing houses.
✓ Alert clients to changes in contracts, rights, and editorial practices.
✓ Provide legal assistance in writer/publisher disputes.
✓ License and monitor income potential from licensees and secondary markets, especially with the burgeoning use of material for CD-ROM and other electronic applications.

Write Without Bias

The words we choose every day—those we don't think twice about—often harbor unintended bias. Work to streamline your word choices away from bias toward gender, ethnic, age, religious, racial, or other stereotypes.

Avoid sentence constructions that choose the feminine or masculine pronouns "she" or "he," unless the sentence is about a specific individual. Substitute the pronoun with a concrete noun; for example, instead of "She did her homework," write "The student finished the homework."

Avoid linking professions or activities with gender stereotypes: nurse/she, football player/he.

Alternatives to "Man"

Masculine term	Change to
man, mankind	human, humankind
manpower	workforce, staffpower
man-made	artificial, created
policeman, fireman	police officer, fire fighter
chairman, spokesman	chair, chairperson, spokesperson, designated speaker
clergyman	minister, cleric
foreman	supervisor
salesmanship	selling talent or ability
master/mistress	administrator, head, owner, proprietor, host

Be sensitive to labels and use specific terms when referring to general groups of people. Avoid referring to groups of people in an objectified way: write "elderly people" instead of "the elderly." Call specific groups by the name they prefer: "African-American" instead of "black." Always be respectful and use language appropriate to your context and audience.

Use nonhandicapping language when referring to the disabled. In fact, the deaf community no longer views deafness as a disability at all. You wouldn't say that a member of the deaf community "suffered from deafness." Don't use language that equates a person with a physical or mental condition that may have negative overtones; for example, don't write "stroke victim." Instead of "confined to a wheelchair," write "uses a wheelchair."

Unless someone has indicated a preference for a form of address, always use the full name when writing and choose the generic identifier "Mr." or "Ms."

When referring to sexual orientation, be specific. Use "lesbian," "gay man," or "bisexual man/woman" over the generic "homosexual." Remember, sexual preference is not the same as sexual orientation—one implies choice, the other does not. Use these terms articulately.

Avoid the personification of objects or qualities. Be alert to hidden connotations. Adjectives can often connote a gender identification, for example, "virile" for "manly." Instead of "mothering," write "nurturing" or "caring."

As our cultural values change and mature, so does our language. By carefully considering the words we use, and how we use them, we can influence perceptions and ideas about our world and the people who live in it, emphasizing our rich global heritage and diversity.

Bibliography

Business

Attard, Janet. *The Home Office and Small Business Answer Book*. New York: Henry Holt & Co., 1993.

Blanchard, Kenneth, William Oncken, Jr., and Hal Burrows. *The One Minute Manager Meets the Monkey*. New York: William Morrow & Co., Inc., 1989.

Bykofsky, Sheree. *500 Terrific Ideas for Organizing Everything*. New York: Simon & Schuster, Inc., 1992.

Case, Samuel. *The First Book of Investing*. Rocklin, Calif.: Prima Publishing & Communications, 1994.

Crittenden, Alan, ed. *The Almanac of Investments*. Novato, Calif.: Crittenden Books, 1984.

Dunnan, Nancy. *Dun & Bradstreet Guide to Your Investments 1994*. New York: HarperCollins, 1994.

Gardiner, Robert M. *The Dean Witter Guide to Personal Investing*. New York: New American Library, 1988.

Kanarek, Lisa. *Organizing Your Home Office for Success: Expert Strategies That Can Work for You*. New York: Plume, 1993.

Post, Elizabeth. *Emily Post's Etiquette*. 15th ed. New York: HarperCollins, 1992.

Car

Biardo, John C. *The Safe Driving Handbook: A Guide to Driving Defensively*. Elmwood Park, Ill.: Elmwood Park Publishing Co., 1989.

Department of Transportation. *The Car Book*. Washington, D.C., 1981.

Drake, Gilbert N. *Survival Behind the Wheel*. New York: Phoenix Books Publishers, 1987.

Federal Trade Commission. *Facts For Consumers: New Car Buying Guide*. Washington, D.C., February 1988.

Maintenance Awareness Program. *How to Find Your Way Under the Hood and Around the Car*. Bethesda, Md: MAP.

Tire Industry Safety Council. *Consumer Tire Guide*. Washington, D.C.: TISC, 1990.

"Used Cars: Finding a Good Buy." *Consumer Reports*, April 1993.

Webster, Jay. *Automotive Fundamentals*. Encino, Calif.: Glencoe Publishing Co., 1986.

Do-It-Yourself

Alth, Max. *Do-It-Yourself Plumbing*. New York: Sterling Publishing Co., Inc, 1987.

Armpriester, K.E. *Do Your Own Plumbing*. New York: Sterling Publishing Co., Inc., 1991.

Bix, Cynthia Overbeck, ed. *Sunset Home Repair Handbook*. Menlo Park, Calif.: Sunset Books, 1992.

Carrier Corporation. *A Guide to Operating and Maintaining Your Residential Heat Pump Unit*. Syracuse, N.Y.: Carrier Corporation Consumer Products Division.

Cy DeCosse Inc. Staff. *Basic Wiring and Electrical Repairs*. Black & Decker Home Improvement Series. Minnetonka, Minn.: Cy DeCosse, Inc., 1990.

Cy DeCosse Inc. Staff. *Everyday Home Repairs*. Black & Decker Home Improvement Series. Minnetonka, Minn.: Cy DeCosse, Inc., 1988.

Cy DeCosse Inc. Staff. *Home Plumbing Projects and Repairs*. Black & Decker Home Improvement Series. Minnetonka, Minn.: Cy DeCosse, Inc., 1990.

Ehrlich, Jeffrey, and Marc Hannheimer. *The Carpenter's Manifesto*. New York: Henry Holt & Co., 1990.

Florman, Monte, and eds. of Consumer Reports Books. *How to Clean Practically Anything*. Mt. Vernon, N.Y.: Consumers Union, 1986.

Jackson, Albert, and David Day. *Popular Mechanics Home How-To*. New York: Hearst Books, 1989.

Johnson, Lorraine. *How to Restore, Repair, and Finish Almost Everything*. New York: Macmillan Publishing Co., 1977.

Kozloski, Arnold. *Do Your Own Drywall: An Illustrated Guide*. Blue Ridge Summit, Pa.: TAB Books Inc., 1985.

Moore, Alma Chesnut. *How to Clean Everything*. New York: Simon & Schuster Inc., 1977.

Reader's Digest Editors. *Complete Do-It-Yourself Manual*. Pleasantville, N.Y.: Reader's Digest Association Inc., 1973.

Reader's Digest Editors. *Fix-It-Yourself Manual*. Pleasantville, N.Y.: Reader's Digest Association Inc., 1977.

Sunset Books Editors. *Basic Plumbing Illustrated*. Menlo Park, Calif.: Lane Publishing Co., 1992.

Sunset Books Editors. *Basic Woodworking*. Menlo Park, Calif.: Lane Publishing Co., 1986.

Time-Life Books Editors. *Plumbing*. Alexandria, Va.: Time-Life Books, Inc., 1989.

Time-Life Staff. *Cleaning and Stain Removal*. Fix-It-Yourself Series. Alexandria, Va.: Time-Life Books, Inc., 1990.

Vila, Bob. *This Old House: Guide to Building and Remodeling Materials*. New York: Warner Books, Inc., 1986.

Weldon, John B. *Paint Your House Inside and Out*. Williamsburg, Va.: Shepherd Publishing, 1989.

Education

Butterworth, Rod R., and Mickey Flodin. *Signing Made Easy*. New York: Perigee Books, 1989.

Chelekis, George. *The Action Guide to Government Grants, Loans, and Giveaways*. New York: Perigee Books, 1993.

Costello, Elaine. *Signing: How to Speak with Your Hands*. New York: Bantam Books, 1983.

Gregg, John R., et al. *Gregg Shorthand*. 2nd ed. New York: McGraw-Hill, Inc., 1970.

Lefferts, Robert. *Getting a Grant in the 1990s: How to Write Successful Grant Proposals*. New York: Prentice Hall, 1991.

Ohio College Association. *Toward College in Ohio*. Vol. 53. Columbus, Ohio: OCA, 1993.

Talbot's Student Planning Book. Wellesley, Mass.: Dexter Publishing Co., 1993.

Electronics

Apple Computer, Inc. *Macintosh Reference*. Cupertino, Calif.: Apple Computer, Inc., 1990.

AT&T. *Answering System 1317 Owner's Manual*. New York: AT&T.

Dvorak, John C., Peter Harrison, and Steven Frankel. *PC Crash Course and Survival Guide*. Rockville, Md: Scandinavian PC Systems, Inc., 1989.

Electronic Industries Association. *Consumers Should Know: How to Buy a Personal Computer*. Washington, D.C.: EIA, 1986.

Engle, Mary E., et al. *Internet Connections*. Chicago, Ill.: CITA/American Library Association, 1993.

Gookin, Dan, and Andy Rathbone. *PCs For Dummies*. San Mateo, Calif.: IDG Books Worldwide, Inc., 1992.

Kobler, Ronald D., ed. "Buying a Computer." *PC Novice*. Premium Issue P7 (1994): 24–25.

Kobler, Ronald D., ed. "Setting Up a Multimedia PC: Not an Impossible Mission." *PC Novice*. Premium Issue P7 (1994): 38–41.

Lien, David A. *MS-DOS: The Basic Course*. El Cajon, Calif.: CompuSoft Publishing, 1989.

Murray, Katherine. *Introduction to Personal Computers*. Carmel, Calif.: Que Corporation, 1990.

The New York Public Library Desk Reference. 2nd ed. New York: Prentice Hall General Reference, 1993.

Nintendo of America. *Control Deck Instruction Manual*. Redmond, Wash.: Nintendo of America, 1994.

NYNEX White Pages. New York: NYNEX Information Resources Company, 1994.

Rathbone, Andy. *Windows 3.1 For Dummies*. 2nd ed. San Mateo, Calif.: IDG Books Worldwide, Inc., 1994.

Sears, Roebuck and Co. *Video Cassette Recorder Operation*. Series LXI Owner's Manual. Chicago, Ill.: Sears, Roebuck and Co., 1993.

Food, Kitchen, and Entertaining

Baldridge, Letitia. *Letitia Baldridge's Complete Guide to the New Manners for the 90s*. New York: Macmillan Publishing Co., 1990.

Gervas, Charles, ed. *Rodale's Basic Natural Foods Cookbook*. Emmaus, Pa.: Rodale Press Inc., 1984.

Harlech, Pamela. *Pamela Harlech's Practical Guide to Cooking, Entertaining, & Household Management*. New York: Atheneum Publishers, 1981.

Hazard, Edith, and Wallace Pinfold. *Rising to the Occasion*. Chapel Hill, N.C.: Algonquin Books, 1993.

Kozer, Jean E., ed. *Betty Crocker's Microwave Cookbook*. New York: Prentice Hall, 1990.

Mager, N. H., and S. K. *The Household Encyclopedia*. New York: Washington Square Press, 1964.

Microwave Times, eds. *Microwave Cooking Lite*. Chicago, Ill: Contemporary Books Inc., 1985.

The New York Public Library Desk Reference. 2nd ed. New York: Prentice Hall General Reference, 1993.

Post, Elizabeth. *Emily Post's Etiquette*. 15th ed. New York: HarperCollins, 1992.

Robards, Terry. *The New York Times Book of Wine*. New York: Avon Books, 1977.

Simon, André L. *Champagne*. London, Eng.: Constable & Company, Ltd., 1934.

Health and Exercise

Balaskas, Arthur. *Bodylife*. New York: Grosset & Dunlap, 1977.

Bottom Line Personal Editors and Experts. *Book of Inside Information*. New York: Boardroom Classics, 1989.

Dehejia, Marsha V. *The Allergy Book*. New York: Van Nostrand Reinhold Co., 1981.

Family Health and Medical Library. London, Eng.: Bay Books, 1984.

Fanning, Tony, and Robbie Fanning. *Keep Running*. New York: Simon & Schuster Inc., 1978.

Fonda, Jane. *Jane Fonda's Workout Book*. New York: Simon & Schuster Inc., 1984.

Franck, Irene, and David Brownstone. *The Parent's Desk Reference*. New York: Prentice Hall, 1991.

Marshall Cavendish Encyclopedia of Family Health. New York: Marshall Cavendish Corp., 1991.

Mumby, Dr. Keith. *The Allergy Handbook*. New York: Thorsons Publishing Group, 1988.

Murray, Michael, and Joseph Pizzorno. *Encyclopedia of Natural Medicine*. Rocklin, Calif.: Prima Publishing & Communications, 1991.

The New York Public Library Desk Reference. 2nd ed. New York: Prentice Hall General Reference, 1993.

Subak-Sharpe, Genell, ed. *Columbia University College of Physicians and Surgeons' Complete Home Medical Guide*. Rev. ed. New York: Crown Publishers Inc., 1989.

Tapley, Donald F., et al., eds. *Columbia University College of Physicians and Surgeons' Complete Home Medical Guide to Pregnancy*. New York: Crown Publishers Inc., 1988.

Theiss, Barbara, and Peter Theiss. *The Family Herbal*. Rochester, Vt.: Healing Arts Press, 1993.

Holidays

Hazard, Edith, and Wallace Pinfold. *Rising to the Occasion*. New York: Algonquin Books, 1993.

Mager, N. H., and S. K. *The Household Encyclopedia*. New York: Washington Square Press, 1964.

Home

American Electric Power. *Smart Choices in Heating and Cooling*. Columbus, Ohio: AEP, 1993.

American Electric Power. *Smart Energy Saving Tips*. Columbus, Ohio: AEP, 1992.

Aslett, Don. *Stainbuster's Bible*. New York: Penguin USA, 1990.

Bortz, Paul. *Getting More Heat From Your Fireplace*. Pownal, Vt.: Garden Way Publishing, 1982.

Bottom Line Personal Editors and Experts. *Book of Inside Information*. New York: Boardroom Classics, 1989.

Deutch, Yvonne. *Popular Houseplants*. New York: Gallery Books, 1987.

Falcone, Joseph D. *How to Design and Build Efficient Fireplaces and Chimneys*. New York: TAB Books, Inc., 1981.

James, Theodore, Jr. Photography by Harry Haralambou. *The Cut-Flower Garden*. New York: Macmillan Publishing Co., 1993.

Kamen, Rima. *The Complete Guide to Decorating Your Home*. White Hall, Va.: Betterway Publications, Inc., 1989.

March, Ken. *Houseplants for Free*. New York: Chartwell Books Inc., 1988.

Reader's Digest Editors. *Guide to Household Emergencies*. Pleasantville, N.Y.: Reader's Digest Association Inc., 1989.

Simons, Violet. *Very Basic Book of Sewing: Altering and Mending*. New York: Sterling Publishing Co., Inc., 1976.

Taylor, Jean. *Plants & Flowers for Lasting Decoration*. New York: Larousse and Co., Inc., 1981.

Just For the Fun Of It

Baker, Dusty, et al. *You Can Teach Hitting*. Carmel, Ind.: Bittinger Books, 1993.

Battershill, Norman, et al. *Drawing for Pleasure*. Cincinnati, Ohio: North Light Publishers, 1992.

Betti, Claudia, and Teel Sale. *Drawing: A Contemporary Approach*. 3rd ed. Fort Worth, Tex.: Harcourt Brace Jovanovich, 1991.

Bosman, Dick, et al. *How to Pitch*. New York: Grossett & Dunlap, 1966.

Dow, Allen. *Ballroom Dancing*. Northbrook, Ill.: Domus Books, 1980.

Edwards, Betty. *Drawing on the Right Side of the Brain*. Los Angeles, Calif.: Jeremy P. Tarcher, Inc., 1979.

Encyclopedia Americana. Deluxe Library Edition. New York: Grolier Inc., 1991.

Gibson, Walter B. *Hoyle's Simplified Guide to Popular Card Games*. New York: Doubleday, 1971.

Graham, David. *Your Way to Winning Golf*. New York: Golf Digest/Simon & Schuster Inc., 1985.

Hazard, Edith, and Wallace Pinfold. *Rising to the Occasion*. New York: Algonquin Books, 1993.

Hunt, Leslie. *25 Kites That Fly*. New York: Dover Publications Inc., 1971.

Kirkham, Gene (consultant). *Bowling*. N. Palm Beach, Fla.: The Athletic Institute, 1971.

Martin, Ray, and Rosser Reeves. *The 99 Critical Shots in Pool*. New York: Times Books, 1977

Peck, Abe, ed. *Dancing Madness*. New York: Anchor Press, 1976.

Poynter, Margaret. *Frisbee Fun*. New York: Simon & Schuster Inc., 1977.

Schlossberg, Dan. *Pitching*. New York: Simon & Schuster Inc., 1977.

Seaver, Tom, and Steve Jacobson. *Pitching with Tom Seaver*. New York: Prentice Hall, 1973.

Stanbury, Dean, and Frank DeSantis. *Touch Football*. New York: Sterling Publishing Co., Inc., 1961.

White, Betty. *Betty White's Teen-Age Dance Book*. New York: McKay Publishers, 1952.

Wilson, Mark. *Mark Wilson's Complete Course in Magic*. Philadelphia, Pa.: Ottenheimer Publishers Inc., 1988.

World Book Encyclopedia. Chicago, Ill.: World Book Inc., 1991.

Legal

Barrett, E. Thorpe. *Writing Your Own Business Contracts*. Oregon: Oasis Press, 1991.

Clifford, Denis. *Plan Your Estate*. Berkeley, Calif.: Nolo Press, 1989.

Daly, Eugene. *Thy Will Be Done*. Buffalo, N.Y.: Prometheus Books, 1990.

Fishman, Stephen. *The Copyright Handbook*. Berkeley, Calif.: Nolo Press, 1992.

Joseph, Joel D., and Jeffrey Hiller. *Legal Agreements in Plain English*. Chicago, Ill.: Contemporary Books Inc., 1982.

Kemp, Thomas J. *Vital Records Handbook*. Baltimore, Md.: Genealogical Publishing Co., Inc., 1988.

Levy, Richard C. *Inventing and Patenting Sourcebook*. New York: Gale Research Inc., 1992.

Pressman, David. *Patent It Yourself*. Berkeley, Calif.: Nolo Press, 1988.

Rudy, Theresa Meehan. *Small Claims Court*. New York: Random House Inc., 1990.

The Mind

Kopolow, Louis E. *Plain Talk About Handling Stress*. Washington, D.C.: U.S. Dept. of Health and Human Services.

Marshall Cavendish Encyclopedia of Family Health. New York: Marshall Cavendish Corp., 1991.

Subak-Sharpe, Genell, ed. *Columbia University College of Physicians and Surgeons' Complete Home Medical Guide*. Rev. ed. New York: Crown Publishers Inc., 1989.

Money, Math, and Finance

Abromovitz, Les. *Family Insurance Handbook*. New York: Liberty Hall Press/TAB Books Inc., 1990.

American Association of Retired Persons. *Your Credit: A Complete Guide*. Washington, D.C.: AARP, 1993.

Baxter, Ralph C. *The Arthur Young Preretirement Planning Book*. New York: John Wiley & Sons Inc., 1985.

Bottom Line Personal Editors and Experts. *Book of Inside Information*. New York: Boardroom Classics, 1989.

Brod, I. Jack, and Tad Tuleja. *Consumer's Guide to Buying and Selling Gold, Silver and Diamonds*. New York: Doubleday & Co. Inc., 1985.

Bundy, Darcie, and Stuart Day. *Total Coverage*. New York: Harper & Row, 1987.

Crittenden, Alan, ed. *The Almanac of Investments*. Novato, Calif.: Crittenden Books, 1984.

Cross, Wilbur. *The Henry Holt Retirement Sourcebook*. New York: Henry Holt & Co., 1992.

Daily, Fred. *Stand Up to the IRS*. Berkeley, Calif.: Nolo Press, 1992.

Dunnan, Nancy. *Dun & Bradstreet Guide to Your Investments 1994*. New York: HarperCollins, 1994.

Federal Reserve System. *A Consumer's Guide to Mortgage Refinancing*. Washington, D.C.: FRS, 1992.

Federal Trade Commission. *Facts for Consumers: Choosing and Using Credit Cards*. Washington, D.C.: FTC, February 1993.

Federal Trade Commission. *The Mortgage Money Guide*. Washington, D.C.: FTC, 1989.

Federal Trade Commission. *Using Plastic: A Young Adult's Guide to Credit Cards*. Washington, D.C.: FTC, January 1989.

Gardiner, Robert M. *The Dean Witter Guide to Personal Investing*. New York: New American Library, 1988.

Information Please Almanac. New York: Houghton Mifflin Co., 1994.

Kaplan, Lawrence J. *Retiring Right*. New York: Avery Publishing Group Inc., 1990.

Kovel, Ralph, and Terry Kovel. *Kovel's Guide to Selling Your Antiques and Collectibles*. New York: Crown Publishers Inc., 1987.

The New York Public Library Desk Reference. 2nd ed. New York: Prentice Hall General Reference, 1993.

Newman, Renee. *The Diamond Ring Buying Guide*. Los Angeles, Calif.: International Jewelry Publications, 1991.

Raby, William L., and Victor H. Tidwell. *Introduction to Federal Taxation*. New York: Prentice Hall, 1987.

Scott, Robert. *Office At Home*. New York: Charles Scribner's Sons, 1985.

Taylor, Barbara. *How to Get Your Money's Worth in Home and Auto Insurance*. New York: McGraw-Hill Inc., 1991.

Outdoors

Coombes, Allen J. *Trees*. New York: Dorling Kindersley Inc., 1992.

Cronin, Edward W., Jr. *Getting Started in Bird Watching*. New York: Houghton Mifflin Co., 1986.

Dorn, Edward G. *Surviving Family Camp Outs*. Palatine, Ill.: CEL Publications, 1992.

Edlin, Herbert. *The Illustrated Encyclopedia of Trees*. New York: Harmony Books, 1978.

Heintzelman, Donald S. *The Birdwatcher's Activity Book*. Harrisburg, Pa.: Stackpole Books, 1983.

MacFarlan, Allan. *The Boy's Book of Backyard Camping*. Harrisburg, Pa.: Stackpole Books, 1968.

Parenting

Franck, Irene, and David Brownstone. *The Parent's Desk Reference*. New York: Prentice Hall, 1991.

Samuels, Mike, M.D., and Nancy Samuels. *The Well Baby Book*. New York: Simon & Schuster Inc., 1979.

Personal

Crandall, Ralph. *Shaking Your Family Tree*. Vermont: Yankee Publishing Inc., 1986.

Feldon, Leah. *Dress Like A Million*. New York: Villard Books, 1993.

Gibbings, Sarah. *The Tie: Trends and Traditions*. New York: Barron's, 1990.

Greenwood, Val D. *The Researcher's Guide to American Genealogy*. Baltimore, Md.: Genealogical Publishing Co., Inc., 1990.

Hammerslough, Jane. *Everything You Need to Know About Skin Care*. New York: The Rosen Publishing Group Inc., 1994.

Heloise. *Heloise's Beauty Book*. New York: Arbor House Publishing Co., 1985.

LaCroix, Nitya. *Learn Massage in a Weekend*. New York: Alfred A. Knopf Inc., 1992.

Lidell, Lucinda. *The Book of Massage*. New York: Simon & Schuster Inc., 1984.

Ray, Tony, and Angela Hynes. *The Silver/Gray Beauty Book*. New York: Rawson Associates, 1987.

Pets

Aslett, Don. *Pet Clean-Up Made Easy*. Cincinnati, Ohio: Writer's Digest Books, 1988.

Barrie, Anmarie. *A Step By Step Book About Our First Aquarium*. Neptune City, N.J.: T.F.H. Publications, 1987.

Boy Scouts of America. *Dog Care*. New Brunswick, N.J.: BSA, 1952.

Eckstein, Warren, and Fay Eckstein. *How to Get Your Cat to Do What You Want*. New York: Fawcett Books, 1990.

Kaplan, Elizabeth, and Michael A. Kaplan. *Good Cats*. New York: The Putnam Publishing Group, 1985.

Keppler, Sarah Fell. *School of Fish*. South Hamilton, Mass.: PetsPubs Press, 1990.

Mills, Dick. *You and Your Aquarium*. New York: Alfred A. Knopf Inc., 1986.

Monks of New Skete. *How to Be Your Dog's Best Friend*. Boston, Mass.: Little, Brown & Co., Inc., 1978.

Urcia, Ingeborg, PhD. *For the Love of Cats*. New York: Howell Book House Inc., 1985.

Safety and Emergencies

American Automobile Association. *Get a Grip! Wet Weather Driving Techniques*. Heathrow, Fla.: AAA, 1993.

Barthol, Robert G. *Protect Yourself*. New York: Prentice Hall, 1979.

Dorn, Edward G. *Surviving Family Camp Outs*. Palatine, Ill.: CEL Publications, 1992.

Information Please Almanac. New York: Houghton Mifflin Co., 1994.

The New York Public Library Desk Reference. 2nd ed. New York: Prentice Hall General Reference, 1993.

Ohio Department of Public Safety. *Digest of Ohio Motor Vehicle Laws*. Columbus, Ohio: ODPS, 1993.

The World Almanac 1994. New York: Funk & Wagnall's Inc., 1994.

Travel

Delta Airlines. *Frequent Flyer Newsletter*. Atlanta: Delta Airlines.

Fodor's '94: France. New York: Fodor's Travel Publications Inc., 1993.

Hazard, Edith, and Wallace Pinfold. *Rising to the Occasion*. Chapel Hill, N.C.: Algonquin Books, 1993.

Hoffman, Mark S., ed. *The World Almanac and Book of Facts, 1994*. Mahwah, N.J.: Funk & Wagnall's Inc., 1994.

Hughes, Charles A. *Grosset's Italian Phrase Book and Dictionary for Travelers*. New York: Grosset & Dunlap, 1971.

Information Please Almanac. New York: Houghton Mifflin Co., 1994.

The New York Public Library Desk Reference. 2nd ed. New York: Prentice Hall General Reference, 1993.

Writing

Haines, Susanne. *The Calligrapher's Project Book*. New York: HarperCollins, 1987.

Information Please Almanac. New York: Houghton Mifflin Co., 1994.

Judd, Karen. *Copyediting: A Practical Guide*. New York: Crisp Publications Inc., 1988.

Kissling, Mark, ed. *1993 Writers Market*. Cincinnati, Ohio: Writer's Digest Books, 1992.

Lynskey, Marie. *Creative Calligraphy*. New York: Sterling Publishing Co., Inc., 1988.

Mahmoud, Shah. *Research and Writing*. White Hall, Va.: Betterway Publications Inc., 1992.

Stoughton, Mary. *Substance and Style*. Alexandria, Va.: Editorial Experts, 1989.

Index